A DIFFERENT LIGHT

A PLURALIST ANTHOLOGY

THE BIG BOOK OF HANUKKAH

Pluralistic Perspectives on the Festival of Lights:
A broad-ranging anthology of short essays by thinkers,
historians, and scientists on Hanukkah themes

Profiles in Modern Jewish Courage:
A collection of dramatic stories about contemporary Jewish heroes —
great and small — and their inner search for courage

BY NOAM SACHS ZION
AND BARBARA SPECTRE

חנוכה
HANUKKAH

ישראל
ISRAEL اسرائيل

חנה סמוטריץ   התשנ"ו 1996

A companion to
A Different Light:
The Hanukkah Book of Celebration

**The David and Rae Finegood Institute for Diaspora Education and
the Charles and Valerie Diker Family Resource Center for Jewish Continuity
at the
Shalom Hartman Institute in Jerusalem**

Language Editors and Consultants — Marcelle Zion and Jeni Friedman

Graphic Design — Joe Buchwald Gelles

Published by **Devora Publishing**
40 East 78th Street Suite 16 D
New York, NY 10021
Tel: 1-800-232-2931
Fax: 212-472-6253
pop@netvision.net.il
ISBN hb 1-930143-34-6, pb 1-930143-37-0
Printed in Hong Kong

The Shalom Hartman Institute
P.O.B. 8029, Jerusalem, Israel 93113
Tel: 972-2-5675320
Fax: 972-2-5611913
zionsacs@netvision.net.il
© 2000 by Noam Zion
www.hartmaninstitute.com
LC 99-76450

זִכְרוֹנָם לִבְרָכָה

This volume is dedicated to the memory of all those Dutch Jews who were sent to Westerbork transit camp and from there to extermination camps. In particular we remember the Zion and Meijer families of Eibergen and Borculo, the Netherlands.

Dutch-Jewish children light the Hanukkah menorah in the Nazi transit camp Westerbork, the Netherlands, December 28, 1943. Later Anne Frank would pass through this camp on her way to extermination.

(Nederlands Instituut voor Oorlogsdocumentatie, courtesy of United States Holocaust Memorial Museum,)

DEDICATIONS   חֲנוּכַּת הַסֵּפֶר

The many people who worked on this Hanukkah project as writers, editors, consultants
and sponsors would like to dedicate this book to several very special people:

**In honor of my 25th wedding anniversary
to my wonderful wife Marcelle
and our children — Tanya, Mishael, Heftziba, Eden, and Yedidya —
who share our creative celebration of all the Jewish holidays**

from Noam Sachs Zion

**In honor of my husband, Phil, our children, David, Michal and Guy,
Levi and Galia and our grandchildren, Omri and Tamar**

from Barbara Spectre

**In honor of Paul, Rachel and Laura Wiener
and the many joyous Hanukkahs we shared**

from David and Sheila Wiener, their parents

**In memory of Grandfather
Samuel Chazankin,
שמואל חזנקין ז״ל**

from Gloria זהבה and Mark משה מרדכי Bieler and family

**In honor of the 80th birthdays
of Harry and Marilyn Saltzberg**

from Marc מרדכי Saltzberg

Marc Chagall, 1946 (© ADAGP, Paris, 2000)

TABLE OF CONTENTS

V. Scientists' and Kabbalists' Thoughts on Light and Lamps
Physical Light, the Light of Creation, and the Menorah

VI. Profiles in Modern Jewish Courage

The second volume of *A Different Light* is entitled *The Big Book of Hanukkah*. It is a pluralist Hanukkah anthology in the spirit of the Shalom Hartman Institute in Jerusalem where it was created. At the Institute we encourage a dialogue of interpretations between Jewish scholars and educators representing different religious denominations, academic disciplines, and political perspectives. When we study the great debates throughout the ages, our goal is not to reach the one truth, whether historical or philosophic, but to illuminate the multiple faces of truth and the interests and ideals that lead us to read classical sources in alternative ways. Each of the following six chapters attempts to further that dialogue. Each invites you to browse and to sample what thoughtful people have written about Hanukkah themes.

Chapter I, *Multiple Jewish Identities, Multiple Versions of Hanukkah*, is a unique review of the competing interpretations of the common ritual of candle lighting. The shared narrative of the Maccabees is refracted through the prism of Jewish life: Hasidic rebbes, American Reconstructionist rabbis and Reform educators, Zionists of all brands, and even medieval Christian kings revere the same story but derive opposed lessons from its outcome.

Chapter II, *The Historians' Hanukkah*, presents two great contemporary historians' reconstruction of the civil war that underlay the Maccabean revolt. In our age of Jewish denominational polarization, it gives us pause to examine in greater depth the worst Jewish civil war in history, the one we "celebrate" so happily on Hanukkah.

Chapter III, *The Philosophers' Hanukkah: Where Hellenism and Judaism Differ*, describes the essential conflict of the ways of life manifested in the days of the Maccabees. Yet the thinkers also help us reflect on the possibility of a fruitful dialogue between the Jewish and the Greek elements that make up modern Western society.

Chapter IV, *The Rabbis' Hanukkah: Rabbinic Reflections on the Warrior, the Zealot, the Martyr and the Family Peacemaker*, summarizes some of the original research done in the Shalom Hartman Institute on the way the Rabbis radically transformed biblical values in the process of explicating texts. The values of peacemaking and the priority of life over the fanatical desire to die as a martyr or to kill as a zealot are some of the surprising perspectives presented by the Rabbis. The articles written by Noam Zion and David Dishon explicate basic insights learned from the oral teachings of their teacher, Rabbi David Hartman.

Chapter V, *The Scientists' and the Kabbalists' Thoughts on Lights and Lamps*, is a radical departure from earlier chapters in that it transcends the topic of Hanukkah itself in order to explore the possible analogies between the mystical Jewish and the modern scientific views of light. Albert Einstein's life and thought are discussed, as is the chemistry and physics of a burning candle and the light it produces. Then we move from light and the candle to the history of the *menorah*, whether it is used for a household lamp, a seven-branched Temple menorah or a nine-branched Hanukkiyah. The menorah became a central symbol of Jewish national independence in the Maccabean and the modern eras, along with the *Magen David*.

Last but not least, Chapter VI, *Modern Jewish Profiles in Courage*, allows us to explore in greater depth the resources of Jewish heroism that make rebellion, martyrdom and ethical protest possible, whether in the days of the Maccabees or in the last sixty years. We read the exciting and inspiring tales of *tzedakah* heroes, soldiers, social activists and righteous gentiles. The chapter opens with contrasting conceptions of the heroic in Rabbinic thought, in Greek tragedy and in psychological and sociological research. In this concluding chapter, as in the preceding ones, *The Big Book of Hanukkah* offers you *A Different Light* on so many important themes related to Hanukkah.

CHAPTER I

Multiple Jewish Identities, Multiple Versions of Hanukkah

A Pluralism of Interpretation

How different communities and denominations find
their particular identity symbolized in the light of the Menorah

Multiple Jewish Identities, Multiple Versions of Hanukkah
A Pluralism of Interpretation

Hanukkah Gelt for JNF.
A stamp of the Jewish National Fund depicting the Israeli Chalutz (Pioneer) with gun and plow in hand, with Judah the Maccabee and the Shield of David in the background. The stamp is entitled "Hanukkah Gelt" and its purchase involved a contribution to the JNF for re-forestation and land reclamation in Israel.
(Chicago, 1938 from the Gross Family collection, Beit Hatefutsoth Photo Archive, Tel Aviv)

Introduction

HOW DIFFERENT COMMUNITIES AND DENOMINATIONS OF JEWS FIND THEIR PARTICULAR IDENTITY SYMBOLIZED IN THE LIGHT OF THE MENORAH

As Rabbi David Hartman has argued, Judaism is a "community of interpretation" rather than a community of common dogmas. In celebrating foundational events of their communal history, Jews redescribe the past in light of their analysis of the present and their blueprint for the future. The Jews share the events, texts and rituals of their collective past, but each sub-community of Jews carves out its own particular interpretation of that past. Just as in families, each member experiences and remembers common events from his or her own unique perspective. In retelling the family autobiography s/he may argue and persuade the others to accept his/her version as the authentic, official account of what happened and therefore of what lessons must be learned.

As Jews worldwide light the same Hanukkah candles, a ritual shared by all denominations whether religious or secular,

whether North American or Israeli or Russian, we may be misled into a false sense of unanimity about what is being commemorated and to what values we are rededicating ourselves by lighting these candles. These candles are symbolic — they are meant to "proclaim the miracle" *(pirsum hanes)* to all those who pass by our Jewish windowsills. Yet in fact Hanukkah lacks an agreed common text as to what the candles symbolize. There is no *megillah* and no book of the Jewish Bible devoted to its story; there is no agreed interpretation of the symbols. For example, secular Israelis explicitly reject the "miracle" performed by God as they proclaim even in a children's song taught in every nonreligious nursery school in Israel.

Moreover, the history of the Maccabean period reveals a terrible cultural, class and religious civil war among Hellenist, Hasidic and moderate nationalist Jews. Each sub-community of Jewish society identifies itself with Mattathias and Judah the Maccabee and often condemns its contemporary Jewish rivals as self-hating Hellenists or as passive self-ghettoized martyrs. Each group claims the symbols and the heroes of Hanukkah as its own and villifies the darkness of war, of obscurantism, of false enlightenment and of assimilation represented by competing Jewish ways of life.

In our contemporary era of polemical polarization as well as pluralism, Hanukkah becomes a crucial test for the self-understanding of various groups of Jews. Precisely because Hanukkah lacks an agreed narrative, yet celebrates a Jewish ideological civil war, it becomes a kind of Rorschach test for the self-projection and self-creation of Jewish communities. Interestingly enough, Israeli Zionism, Lubavitch Hasidim and even North American Liberal Judaism have invested a great deal of creative energy to revive and reshape Hanukkah so it can carry their banners for Jewish renaissance. For each, Hanukkah is no minor holiday about ancient history.

In the essays below we have tried to epitomize radically different interpretations of Hanukkah, each reflecting a key to the self-interpretation of an entire community, rather than just the philosophic reflections of an individual religious thinker. You may very well disagree with some of these seemingly forced readings of the Festival of Lights presented by competing camps in the Jewish world. Yet you may also discover surprising and enlightening perspectives and implications on a holiday too often regarded as a simplistic children's festival promoting obvious and banal values.

Our collection of interpretations begins with **(1) the American Jewish Renewal Movement** with its psycho-spiritual understanding of darkness and light as symbols of personal despair and hope. Then come **(2) the Zionist debates** about the significance of the Maccabees for the building of a Jewish State from a left wing and a right wing, a secular and an ultra-Orthodox perspective. **(3) The Reconstructionist Movement** celebrates the ethical evolution of Jewish and American nationalism by drawing a parallel to the increasing number of candles lit each night of Hanukkah. **(4) The Reform holiday curriculum**, although it is not an official statement of the Reform rabbinate, reveals the struggle to accommodate the anti-war sentiments central to the Reform movement's social action platform in the 1970s with commemoration of the Maccabean victories. **(5) The Hasidic worldview** of Habad (Lubavitch) and Gur portrays the battle between Greek and Jew, between darkness and light, as an ongoing struggle fought both within the inner Temple of our souls and without in the public squares of Moscow, Washington and Jerusalem. Finally, we included **(6) the Christian Cult of the Maccabees**. In fact, the Church not only preserved the *Books of the Maccabees* but regarded the Maccabean heroes as saints and role models for themselves.

In conclusion, the multiple interpretations presented here are meant to challenge us to choose our own perspective. It is not enough to light the candle and say we recall the past. Each recollection is an interpretation, and we must reflect on the implications of these interpretations for the Jewish tasks that lie before us "in our days and at this time."

THE AMERICAN JEWISH RENEWAL MOVEMENT
THE PSYCHO-SPIRITUAL HOLIDAY OF REDEDICATION

The Jewish Renewal Movement grew out of the 1960s Jewish student activist organizations (like Arthur Waskow's Farbrengen in Washington, D.C.) and alternative Jewish religious communities (like the Havurah in Boston). In the 1990s it began to establish its own synagogues and a rabbinic smicha program (with a former Lubavitch Rabbi, Zalman Schachter-Salome). While preserving its progressivist politics (ecological, feminist and Israeli Peace Now leanings), it has developed a personalized mysticism drawing from Kabbalah and Hasidism

as well as from Yoga and meditation techniques.

Jewish Renewal is attuned to the parallel structures of the life cycle, the natural cycle of seasons, the psychological cycle and the mystical processes of the universe. Therefore it interprets Hanukkah in a way that transcends historical commemoration. We offer two selections:

__Arthur Waskow__, a Jewish political activist and a recently ordained Jewish Renewal rabbi, begins his reflections from the fact that the historical events of

Hanukkah are commemorated at the darkest time of the solar and lunar cycle. The darkness represents personal exile and despair, while the light represents hope and rejuvenation.

__Joel Ziff__, a psychotherapist, describes the partnership of both human and Divine initiatives necessary to gain victories in our personal battles between light and darkness. The historical narrative and the ritual lighting are allegories for the inner struggle for spiritual victory over the forces of despair.

JEWISH RENEWAL'S HANUKKAH:
DARK OF THE SUN, DARK OF THE MOON

by Arthur Waskow[1]

By the twenty-fifth of Kislev, we are ready to experience the moment of winter . . . By the twenty-fifth of every lunar month, **the moon has gone into exile**. The nights are dark, and getting darker. And late in Kislev, we are close to the moment of the winter solstice — when **the sun is also in exile**. The day is at its shortest and the night at its longest, before the sunlight begins to return. It is the darkest moment of the year, the moment when it is easiest to believe that the light will never return, the moment it is easiest to feel despair . . . .

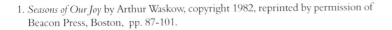

ישראל חנוכה 2.50
HANUKKAH ISRAEL

The Israeli-American Hanukkah Stamp. Flags on the first day issue envelope surround a cruse of oil.
(Hannah Smotrich, graphic artist. Used by permission of the Israeli Philatelic Service.)

At this dark moment, we celebrate Hanukkah — the Feast of Dedication — by lighting candles for eight nights. Night after night, the candle-light increases. And night after night, we make our way into, through, and out of the darkness of the sun and moon. **We experience and feel the turn toward light from the moment of darkness, the turn toward salvation from the moment of despair . . . .**

. . . The single bottle of oil symbolized the last irreducible minimum of spiritual light and creativity within the Jewish people — still there even in its worst moments of apathy and idolatry. The ability of that single jar of oil to stay lit for eight days symbolized how

---

1. *Seasons of Our Joy* by Arthur Waskow, copyright 1982, reprinted by permission of Beacon Press, Boston, pp. 87-101.

with God's help that tiny amount could unfold into an infinite supply of spiritual riches. Infinite, because the eighth day stood for infinity. Since the whole universe was created in seven days, **eight is a symbol of eternity and infinity** . . . .

There is a great deal of evidence that in much of the eastern Mediterranean and the Middle East, the winter solstice was a time for imploring the sunlight to return and celebrating its readiness to do so. In Rome, the twenty-fifth of December was the birthday of the Unconquerable Sun. In Persia at the winter solstice, the common people set great bonfires and their rulers sent birds aloft bearing torches of dried grass.

It is a short leap to surmising that the Syrian Greeks may have chosen the twenty-fifth of Kislev as a time to desecrate the Temple by making their own sacrifices there, precisely because it was a time of solar and lunar darkness, the time of the winter solstice and the waning of the moon. And it is a short

---

Hanukkah is treated in the Talmud in a very off-hand way, without the focused attention that is normal for deciding how to observe a holy day.

---

leap to surmise that the Maccabees, when they took the anniversary of that day as the day of rededication, were rededicating not only the Temple, but the day itself to Jewish holiness; they were capturing a pagan solstice festival that had won wide support among partially Hellenized Jews, in order to make it a day of God's victory over paganism. Even the lighting of candles for Hanukkah fits the context of the surrounding torchlight honors for the sun.

If we see Hanukkah as intentionally, not accidentally, placed at the moment of the darkest sun and darkest moon, then one aspect of the candles seems to be an assertion of our hope for renewed light . . . .

The Rabbis' Ambivalence about the Maccabees' Victory

But Jewish tradition about Hanukkah is not so simple. The *Books of the Maccabees* themselves became an issue. They seem to have been treated as holy books by the Greek-speaking Jews of Alexandria. But the Rabbis [of Eretz Yisrael] never regarded them as holy, never entered them among the books that made up the Jewish Bible. And it was the Rabbis who determined what became Jewish Tradition. Ironically enough, these books that celebrated the Maccabees' victory over Hellenism survived not in Hebrew but only in the Greek language. Greek became one of the common tongues of the eastern Mediterranean as Hellenism grew stronger over the next few centuries. And it was the most Hellenized Jews [in Egypt] who most honored these [written] memorials of resistance to Hellenism.

Indeed, the Maccabean books survived into modern times only because some of these Hellenized Jews became recruits to Christianity, and brought with them the assumption that these *Books of the Maccabees* were holy writings. The Christian Church then included *Maccabees I and II* among its version of what it called the "Old Testament." They were among the books, available in Greek rather than Hebrew, that the early Church father Jerome called "the Apocrypha." But they held no honored standing among those Jews who continued being Jewish.

For the classic Jewish view of the origins of Hanukkah, therefore, we must turn to the Talmud. Here we find Hanukkah in a most peculiar position. It is the only one of the traditional festivals that does not have a place in the *Mishnah* — the earlier level, or layer, of the Talmud. And in the later layer — the *Gemara* — it is treated in a very off-hand way, without the focused attention that is normal for deciding how to observe a holy day. The Rabbis are discussing what kinds of candles may be used for Shabbos when one of them asks, rather casually, whether the rules for Hanukkah candles are different. They

> The Rabbis were not happy with the Maccabean approach to Jewish life. They were writing in the period when similar revolts against Rome had been systematically and brutally smashed by the iron fist of Rome. Only the rabbinical kind of power — the power not of rock but water, fluid and soft from moment to moment and yet irresistible over the long run — had survived.

explore this for a bit, talk about how the candles are to be lit, and then one of them says, as if he cannot quite remember, "What is Hanukkah?" They answer him:

> Our Rabbis taught: On the twenty-fifth of Kislev [begin] the eight days of Hanukkah, on which lamentation for the dead and fasting are forbidden. For when the Greeks entered the Temple, they defiled all the oils in it, and when the Hasmonean dynasty prevailed over them and defeated them, they searched and found only one bottle of oil sealed by the High Priest. It contained only enough for one day's lighting. Yet a miracle was brought about with it, and they lit [with that oil] for eight days. The following year they were established as a festival, with *Hallel* and Thanksgiving.[2]

And at once the Rabbis go back to discussing the [Shabbat] candles. They have no more to say about the internal divisions of the Jews, the revolt against Antiochus, the victory of the Maccabees, or the rededication of the Temple. Why this cautious attitude toward Hanukkah?

The reason is that the Rabbis were not happy with the Maccabean approach to Jewish life. They were writing in the period when similar revolts against Rome, seeking to win the Jews political independence, to turn Judea into a rocky fortress, and to toughen the Jewish people, had been systematically and brutally smashed by the iron fist of Rome. Only the rabbinical kind of power — the power not of rock but water, fluid and soft from moment to moment and yet irresistible

over the long run — had survived. **Only the rabbinical kind of power had protected and preserved Jewish peoplehood . . . .**

All these Maccabean ways of exercising power seemed to the Rabbis a subtle surrendering to the habits of the Gentiles — ironically, [the Maccabean victory over the Greeks had led to] a form of assimilation — as distinct from pursuing a life-path that the Rabbis saw as authentically Jewish. So in retrospect the Rabbis were critical of the meaning and ultimate outcome of the Maccabean revolt. And so, without utterly rejecting the national liberation movement, they refocused attention away from it toward God's miracle — toward the spiritual meaning of the light that burned and for eight days was not consumed . . . .

The Zionist "Maccabees" and their Ambivalence about the Miracle of the Cruse of Oil

Through almost two millennia, Hanukkah remained a real but secondary festival of the Jewish people. Beginning late in the nineteenth century in central and eastern Europe, **Hanukkah had a second birth.** There were two major factors in this second birth, both of them stemming from the emancipation of the Jewish people and their increasing day-to-day contact with the Christian and secular world. One of these factors was that as secular, non-religious or rational religious ideas grew during the *Haskala* or Jewish Enlightenment in the nineteenth century, there was a special disdain for the notion of such a miracle as the eight days' light from one day's oil in the Temple.

---

2. *Babylonian Talmud, Shabbat* 21b

[Another factor was the increasing power of] secular notions of Jewish peoplehood — including the Zionist notion of the Jews as a nation needing political rehabilitation through politico-military action. In that atmosphere, the Maccabees began to seem less dangerous and more heroic than they had throughout the centuries of rabbinic tradition. Indeed, many Zionists [in the 19th and 20th centuries] identified the Rabbis' fear of militant action against oppressive governments as a major element of exile mentality to be transcended in rebuilding the Jewish people.

Thus the miracle of the lights declined and the Maccabees advanced in attention and popularity from about 1890 on. **Hanukkah became more and more important as a celebration of Jewish political courage and military prowess.** Meanwhile, the Christian Apocryphal *Books of the Maccabees* were becoming more accessible to Jews, as the barriers between the Jewish and Christian worlds crumbled . . . .

New Approaches:
The Struggle Between the Light of Hope and the Darkness of Despair

. . . The Rabbinic tradition was hostile to the Maccabees; and modern Zionism, identifying with the Maccabees, was often hostile to the Rabbis. Thus Hanukkah has been a kind of battlefield between **"Rabbi"** and **"Maccabee"** as models of Jewish life. Is there any way to integrate these conflicting orientations to Hanukkah?

From the standpoint of the **Rabbi**, Hanukkah celebrated God's saving Spirit: *"Not by might and not by power . . . ."* To the Rabbi, this spiritual enlightenment required a kind of inwardness and contemplation that was contradictory to insurgent politics.

From the standpoint of the **Maccabee**, Hanukkah celebrated human courage and doggedness, the human ability to make history bend and change. The need to organize, to act, to fight, to build might and use power, seemed in the aspect of the Maccabee to contradict study, prayer, and contemplation.

Can a new generation of Jews help to resolve this contradiction? If our forebearers repressed and ignored the sense of Hanukkah as a festival of the darkened moon and darkened sun, what could we contribute by opening up to that aspect of the festival? What could we add by seeing Hanukkah as part of the nature cycles of the year and month?

Seen this way, Hanukkah is the moment when light is born from darkness, hope from despair. Both the Maccabean and Rabbinic models fall into place. The Maccabean revolt came at the darkest moment of Jewish history — when not only was a foreign king imposing idolatry, but large numbers of Jews were choosing to obey. The miracle at the Temple came at a moment of spiritual darkness — when even military victory had proven useless because the Temple could not be rededicated in the absence of the sacred oil. At the moment of utter darkness in Modiin, Mattathias struck the spark of rebellion — and fanned it into a flame. At the moment of utter darkness in the Temple, when it would have been rational to wait for more oil to be pressed and consecrated, the Jews ignored all reasonable reasons, and lit the little oil they had . . . .

The real conflict is not between the Rabbi and the Maccabee, between spiritual and political, but between apathy and hope, between a blind surrendering to darkness and an acting to light up new pathways. Sometimes the arena will be in outward action, sometimes in inward meditation. But always the question is whether to recognize the darkness — and transcend it.

The necessity of recognizing the moment of darkness is what we learn from seeing Hanukkah in its context of the sun and moon. There is no use pretending that the sun is always bright; there is no use pretending that the moon is always full. **It is only by recognizing the season of darkness that we know it is time to light the candles, to sow a seed of light that can sprout and spring forth later in the year.**

> Nobody can do everything, but we can nearly all
> do more than we think we can.
>
> — ASHLEIGH BRILLIANT

Primacy of Human Initiative

In the battle with the Greeks, the Israelites take most of the initiative for the struggle. The Maccabees organized the Jews to fight the oppressors. In contrast to the conflict with the Egyptians when God brought plagues and split the sea, no dramatic miracles occur in this war. The Maccabees' initiative and responsibility reminds us that we need to take responsibility at this stage of our work to recognize old, dysfunctional responses to problems, interrupt the habitual mode of coping, and respond with our new, more effective way of being.

Divine Intervention

Although more human effort is required, God is also active and present. The Israelites are victorious even though they are fewer in number. In the same way as the tiny candle produces enough light to banish a great darkness, the Maccabees' effort produced results beyond what one might have expected from their military prowess. In addition, a dramatic miracle does occur when the oil lasts for an entire week instead of just one day. In this respect, the story of Hanukkah is the story of a collaboration between God and the Israelites; as we immerse ourselves in the story, we are reminded that God is with us in our struggles. **The old habits, developed and strengthened with years and years of repetition, seem much stronger than our fragile new experiments with change; nonetheless, our efforts to fight the old ways succeed out of proportion to what we might expect.**

Focus on Spiritual Victory

The political success of the Israelites was limited: 200 years later, the kingdom of Israel was destroyed [by the Roman Empire] and the Jews sent into exile, an exile that lasted 2,000 years. In spite of that limited success, we still celebrate eight days, reciting the full version of the traditional prayer of thanksgiving, the *Hallel*. Our focus is on the spiritual victory. We celebrate the miracle of the lights more than the material success of the Maccabees. In the same manner, efforts to change our way of being do not always produce immediate results in the world. Our work is difficult, our successes are fleeting, and the struggle is unending. In spite of our limits, we retain a sense of power, competence, and optimism. Even though the results of our efforts are not yet realized, we can celebrate the changes we have made, trusting they will eventually lead to success. Even though we live in darkness, we can light a candle illuminating our way.

The Candle as a Symbol

The candles' importance is not limited to their value as a reminder of the miracle from the time of the Maccabees. In the tradition, it is said that "God's candle is the human soul" — *"Ner Hashem, nishmat adam."*

As we light the candles each day, we are reminded that the process of transforming life-long patterns of response does not usually occur with one experience of inhibiting a particular, dysfunctional behavior and replacing it with a new response. We often need to re-experience over and over again the same dysfunctional impulse, stop ourselves from acting, and replace it with our new choice. Learning is not only step-by-step and cumulative. It requires a series of successive approximations; at each stage, a new more sophisticated and complete understanding replaces an earlier, more primitive, and incomplete understanding.

Although we have experienced a transformation, our old habits are still strong. We experience a battle between the new spirit within us and the old way of being, which mirrors, within ourselves, the battle of the Maccabees and the Greeks.

3. *Mirrors in Time*, by Joel Ziff, pp. 256-262, reprinted by permission of the publisher, Jason Aronson, Inc., Northvale, NJ, © 1996.

2.

THE ISRAELI POLITICS OF THE MACCABEAN HOLIDAY

SECULAR AND RELIGIOUS ZIONISTS VERSUS ULTRA-ORTHODOX ANTI-ZIONISTS

by Eliezer Don Yehiya and Ehud Luz

Zionism and the founding of the State of Israel have given rise not only to new interpretations of the Maccabees, but also to new forms of celebration of the revolt. While Hanukkah was celebrated in Rabbinic tradition as a minor home holiday focused on the miracle of the cruse of oil, the Secular Zionist movement, with Theodor Herzl in the lead, transformed this undramatic observance into an extensive public celebration of political

"The Maccabees will be resurrected!"

— THEODOR HERZL
(CONCLUDING SENTENCE OF HIS PROPHETIC BOOK, THE JEWISH STATE, **1897**)

liberation. The Religious Zionists followed suit, while the small Jewish Communist party in Palestine and the large community of Ultra-Orthodox Jews offered anti-Zionist interpretations of Hanukkah.

Even the name of the holiday was disputed. The Secular Zionists rejected the name "Hanukkah" (Dedication) that focuses on the renewal of worship in the Temple and the supernatural miracle of the

pure oil that burned for eight days. They wrote a song still sung in every Israeli secular nursery school and in the official torch lighting ceremony on Israeli Independence Day: **"No miracle happened here. No cruse of oil was found."** They called Hanukkah — "Hag HaMaccabim/The Holiday of the Maccabees or the Hasmoneans" whose battle for political independence relied on human energies. While the Books of the Maccabees *were rejected by the Rabbis (who did not make them a portion of the traditional Bible), these very books were made a part of the national school curriculum by the Zionists. Even the word "Maccabee" was spelled and explained to mean "Hammer" — referring to Judah's hammerlike military strength. That is the original significance of the "Maccabee" in the* Books of the Maccabees *where the Hasmonean history was written.*

The Rabbis for their part interpreted "M**a**CC**a**B**e**E *as an acronym for* "**M**i Chamocha **B**a-elim **E** (Adonai)" = "Who is like God among the gods?"[4] *God is the supernatural warrior both at the Red Sea in defeating Pharaoh's chariots and presumeably in Judea in the defeat of Antiochus IV.*

In the face of the success of the Israeli secular state, the Ultra-Orthodox have been reinforced in their view that the Zionists are continuing the work of ancient Hellenist Jews, not that of the Maccabees. In their view, the secular Israelis have desecrated the holy symbols of Judaism just as the Hellenists desecrated the Temple. The Israeli Shabbat is celebrated by driving through the Holy City on the Holy Day to the stadium to drink "Maccabee" beer and to watch Shabbat violators called

---

4. *Exodus* 15:11

"Maccabees" play Olympic-style sports. Not far from the stadium are the honored Greek institutions of the "Jewish" state — the Hebrew "University," the Israel "Museum," the secular Supreme Court and the Knesset, home of a Greek style "democracy." In short, the Israeli state is a form of collective assimilation that defiles the name of "Israel" and calls forth a zealous priestly rejection by the Ultra-Orthodox.

Even among the Zionists there were very different emphases in celebrating Hanukkah. Religious Zionists, left wing Labor Zionists and right wing Revisionists (later the Likud party) read the heroes and villains and the lessons to be learned in distinctively different ways.

In the articles below we have created a composite of two fine historical retrospectives on the changing significance of Hanukkah in Israel — one by **Ehud**

*Luz, whose father was the Labor Party's Speaker of the Knesset, and the other by **Eliezer Don-Yehiya**. Both have written extensively on the philosophy and sociology of Zionism. Included as well is an autobiographical story by **Theodor Herzl**, founder of the Zionist movement in 1897,* *who abandoned his custom of putting up a Christmas tree and found meaning in lighting a Hanukkah menorah. There is also a memoir about **Eliezer Ben Yehuda** (who revived the modern Hebrew language in the early 20th century). It reports a piquant anecdote about the* *clash of Zionist and Ultra-Orthodox interpretations of a famous statue of Mattathias erected in Jerusalem in 1908. The selections below display a wide variety of ideological interpretations of Hanukkah, the most important Zionist holiday.*

THE ISRAELI POLITICS OF OBSERVANCE: REMEMBERING THE MACCABEES IN A PARTISAN WAY

by Ehud Luz[5] and Eliezer Don-Yehiya[6]

Writing History is a Self-Projection on the Past

History is a mirror by which we can view ourselves. The motive for our interest in history is to interpret our life ideal and to prove that the ideal is achievable in reality in the future just as it once was a fact of history. This approach is especially relevant for Revivalist Movements that seek to shape the future in the image of the past. Revival is never a simple return to the past, but always a reflective trialogue in which the present seeks to shape the future in the image of a particular past which it has reconstructed in its own image. We turn to the past to derive a concrete model of our soul's dream and the faith that the dream is realizable. The past is an interpretation and a justification for our aspirations. In this sense, modern study of history functions like ancient myths. Myth gave meaning to one's private life by anchoring it in the eternal comprehensive lawfulness of life. What is ephemeral is really an example of the eternal; private life is a repetition and a revival of a holy event that belongs to eternity.

Therefore the myth of "revival" plays such a central role in the national awakening of historical peoples in the 19th-20th century.

Historical romanticism is the cradle of modern nationalism because the past is mythic and eternal and it grants the power of renewal to the present. [E.L.]

The Secularization of Hanukkah

Of all the historic symbols used by modern Zionism, none is as important as "the Maccabees." The rabbinic religious tradition — in so far as it recalled the Hasmoneans at all — emphasized the religious miracle in their battle against persecution of Judaism and the desecration of the Temple (see the traditional prayer *"Al HaNissim"*). However the Secular Zionists rejected the miracle and emphasized the earthly realism of Hasmonean heroism. Zionism made Hanukkah a nationalist holiday. The secularization and nationalization of religious celebrations focused on minor religious holidays and reprioritized their significance.

Lag BaOmer became a celebration of Bar Kochba's revolt against the Roman Empire (132-135 CE); Tu B'Shvat became a celebration of the redemption of Eretz Yisrael through reforestation. However, Hanukkah was the main site of national re-creation. The early religious Zionist Rabbi Shmuel Mohilever proposed that Hanukkah be the official holiday of the proto-Zionist organization in Russia — Hovevei Zion (1881). This minor holiday provided neutral ground for religious and secular Zionists to share their nationalist program. [E.L.]

5. Ehud Luz, "On the Myth of Revival of the Maccabees," *HaUmah*, Kislev 1978 vol. 1:56 p. 44 ff. by permission of the author [E.L.]
6. Eliezer Don-Yehiya, "Hanukkah and the Myth of the Maccabees in Zionist Ideology in Israeli Society," reprinted by permission of the author and the *Jewish Journal of Sociology* XXXIV:1 (June, 1992) 5ff. [E.D-Y.]

Israeli Youth movements gather for a torchlight parade for Hanukkah in downtown Jerusalem.

(December 1958, Central Zionist Archives, Jerusalem)

Hanukkah Displaces Pesach as the Holiday of Freedom

While traditionally Pesach has been the holiday of national liberation, its family observance and its exclusive emphasis on God's supernatural redemption could not serve the Zionist slogans of "auto emancipation" and *"if I do not do for myself, who will do for me?"* Yitzhak Ben Zvi, early pioneer and later second president of the State of Israel, wrote in 1911:

> The glory and the educational value of the Hasmoneans is that their example revived the nation to be its own redeemer and the determiner of its own future. [E.L.]

The Secular "Hanukkah" becomes the "Festival of the Hasmoneans"

The various new ways of interpreting and celebrating Hanukkah prompted some observers to claim that the traditional holy day had been in fact replaced by a new festival which differed from the older one in content and even in name. Thus, while the Hebrew word *"Hanukkah"* (which means "dedication") refers to the religious dedication of the Temple in the wake of its liberation from the control of the Hellenizers, the preferred name now was the "Festival of the Hasmoneans." The historian Joseph Klausner, who was one of the mentors of the Revisionist movement, stated:

> Hanukkah is an ancient festival, but a modest one. The "Festival of the Hasmoneans" is a new holy day, but full of high spirits and popular gaiety.
>
> **What *was* Hanukkah?** "A memorial for the Miracles," the lighting of the little candles at home, potato pancakes and playing cards for the adults, spinning tops for the toddlers.
>
> **And what *is* Hanukkah *now*?** — The Festival of the Hasmoneans, a holiday filled with cheering, a big national holiday which is celebrated by the Jewish people in all its dispersions with parties and speeches, songs and ballads, hikes and parades. This is our Festival of the Hasmoneans as it is today. Does any nation have a national holiday as great and as consecrated as this? [E. D-Y.]

Haredim (Ultra-Orthodox) Condemn the Zionists

The traditional concept of Hanukkah stressed the miraculous salvation from above, in contrast to the Zionist emphasis on the

Zionist Torch Bearers and the Original Olympic Races

There are enough irksome and troublesome things in life; aren't things just as bad at the Olympic festival? Aren't you scorched there by the fierce heat? Aren't you crushed in the crowd? Isn't it difficult to freshen yourself up? Doesn't the rain soak you to the skin? Aren't you bothered by the noise, the din and the other nuisances? But it seems to me that you are well able to bear and gladly endure all this, when you think of the gripping spectacles that you will see.

— EPICTETUS, 1ST-2ND CENTURY CE

The origin of the torch bearing runner in the modern Olympics and the Maccabia is the ancient opening event of the Olympics, the *"lampadedromia."* It was a relay race with a torch as a baton and the winner lit the sacrificial altar to Zeus. The most important ancient Olympic race was a footrace of 200 meters. There was no cross-country marathon, even though in 490 BCE the original "marathon runner," Pheidippedes, ran 26 miles from the battle at Marathon to Athens, bearing good tidings that the Greeks had repulsed the Persian invasion. In 1896 at the modern renewal of the Olympics in Greece, the marathon race was inaugurated.

The track races originally took place on an open stretch marked at its beginning with a scraped line in the earth. This gave rise to our phrase "starting from scratch." Their length was 600 Olympic feet which according to mythology was equilavent to Hercules' foot length.

Later, the *"Gymnasium"* was dedicated to outdoor footraces while the *"Palaistra"* was reserved for indoor training in combat, wrestling, boxing, and jumping events. The *"Palaistra"* also served as a private social club for aristocratic members where philosophic discussions were also frequent. It included a powder room and an oiling room as well as an *"ephebium,"* a common room for athletes. The *"hippodrome"* was for chariot and horse racing.

Olympic contestants began the games with a solemn oath not to sin against the fairness of the games. They swore upon slices of boar's flesh before a statue of Zeus carrying a thunderbolt in each hand. Physicians attended the contestants and the great Hippocrates (460-380 BCE) of the Hippocratic oath prescribed an "Olympic Victor's" brown ointment made of opium, aloe and zinc oxide, to relieve strains. He also discovered a kind of aspirin in the willow bark, which is a pain reliever.

Some trainers held that sexual activities were bad for athletes, but older men often sought male lovers among the younger athletes in the gymnasium and palaistra. Women were not usually present. The rule was, "any woman who is discovered at the Olympic games will be pitched headlong from a cliff."[7]

Since athletes always competed in the nude, they used olive oil to prevent sun burn. Those disturbed by insects prayed to Zeus for protection, and those by heatstroke, to Hercules.

---

7. Pausanias, 2nd century CE

theme of the self-liberation. This clash between the two approaches to the festival was apparent from the very beginning of modern Zionism. In 1903, a rabbi deplored the actions of the Zionists who, he claimed:

> magnified the festival of the Maccabees and augmented their strength and power, and this is truly a great mistake. For under natural conditions they were incapable of winning the war, and [they were victorious] only because they were completely righteous men and sought with selfless devotion to save our sacred religion.

The fiercest opponents of the Zionist version of Hanukkah were the Haredim, who also dismissed Zionism as a movement which ran counter to the spirit of religious tradition. They claimed that the manner of the Zionist celebrations of Hanukkah was closer to the outlook of the Hellenizers than it was to that of the Hasmoneans, although the Zionists were pretending to be praising the latter. They added that the Zionists expressed admiration for the values fostered by the Hellenizers under the influence of a foreign culture, such as the worship of physical strength. Yitzhak Breuer, a major Haredi leader, commented:

> The Hellenizers loved their people and their land in their own fashion. They loved the land, but loathed the Land of Torah, loved the people but despised the People of the Torah, loved the Greek

---

The fiercest opponents of the Zionist version of Hanukkah were the Haredim, who dismissed Zionism as a movement which ran counter to the spirit of religious tradition.

---

licentiousness but hated the burden of Torah. It is not for the Jewish State that the Hasmoneans fought but for the People of the Torah. They did battle against the kingdom of evil when it threatened the People of the Torah with destruction.

In the 1950s and 1960s Israel transformed the graves of the Maccabees near Modiin into a national shrine from which a torch-bearing relay race began annually before Hanukkah. Athletes of the Maccabee sports clubs ran from town to town, including up the steep archeological site of the Massada massacre, the last site of armed resistance before the fall of Judea in 73 CE. Imitating the Olympic runners, the "Marathon race" concluded with the lighting of the menorah atop the Knesset, symbol of modern Jewish sovereignty. The Maccabees were identified by the Zionists with Greek notions of the Olympics and of democracy.

They also fought against the wicked among their own people. This was a *kulturkampf* [a clash between two cultures] — Greek culture triumphed over the whole world, and only the Torah culture was able to withstand it. [E.D-Y.]

Not Martyrs, But Heroes

[In reading the *Book of Maccabees* there is praise for courageous religious martyrs like Hannah and her seven sons as well as for Judah the military hero. However the Zionists in their battle against the Ultra-Orthodox saw these as mutually exclusive ideals.]

The Zionist pioneer Zerubavel argued in 1911 that Jewish history is characterized by two different ideal types: (1) the passive religious martyrs who died for the sanctification of God's name were nurtured in the exile, and (2) the activist hero nurtured in Eretz Yisrael. The Zionist pioneers are inheritors of the later zealous Hasmoneans:

> Martyrs are evoked at a time of weakness,

Theodor Herzl's "The Menorah"
From Assimilation to Zionism, From a Christmas Tree to a Menorah　　BY ALEX BEIN[8]

The growth and evolution of Herzl's conception of the Jewish problem, since the day when he [as a journalist in Paris] looked on at the degradation of Dreyfus [falsely accused of being a traitor to the French army, court-martialled and sent to Devil's Island, 1895], can be measured almost with laboratory accuracy by a study of the articles which he wrote immediately after the first [Zionist] Congress. He himself was quite aware of the transformation. Two years before, in December 1895, he had been outraged by [Vienna's Chief Rabbi Moritz] Gudenmann's declaration that the use of a Christmas tree in Jewish homes — an accepted custom with Herzl's parents — was essentially un-Jewish. Herzl believed then that it was permissible to interpret the Christmas tree as a "**Hanukkah tree**"; or it might be looked upon as the celebration of the upward turn of the Menorah. [But in 1897, after the Zionist Congress, he published a short story entitled, "The Menorah,"] in which he told how he had returned to Judaism, how he regarded the celebration of Hanukkah, and how this festival affected him. The story begins like a fairy tale: *"Once upon a time there was a man who had discovered deep in his soul the need to be a Jew."* The man was an artist; he had made his peace with the surrounding world; he had long since ceased to concern himself with his Jewish origins and the faith of his fathers. But the ever-rising tide of anti-Jewish sentiment, the incessant attacks on the Jews, tore open something within him *"so that his soul became nothing more than an open and bleeding wound."* He came by degrees to "a deep inner love" of Judaism, and to the conclusion *"that there was only one way out of the Jewish tragedy, and that was a return of the Jews to their homeland."* Everyone believed that the man had gone mad. Everyone believed that "the way out" which he had chosen would result in a deepening and

> "A great light streamed out from the menorah. The eyes of the children flashed, but what our good friend saw was the kindling of the light of the nation."
>
> — THEODOR HERZL

intensification of the evil. *"But he was sure now that the moral catastrophe in Jewish life was all the sharper because the Jews had lost that inner compensation which had existed so strongly in their ancestors."*

Undistracted by the mockery and contempt which were directed at him, the man followed to its logical conclusion the consequences of his conviction. He realized that the first problem was that of the education of the young generation of Jews. He therefore decided to revive the festival of the Maccabees for his children, and to plant in their young souls a feeling of relationship to the past of their people. As he held aloft the nine-branched candlestick he suddenly recalled, in a strange rush of feeling, his own childhood, and the celebration of the festival in his father's house. He looked at the antique symbol, the prototype of which had so obviously been a tree, and asked himself *"whether it was possible to bring new life into its petrified menorah form, and to water its roots again as if it were really a tree."* Herzl wrote:

"The first candle was lit, and the story of the origin of the festival recited: the miraculous origin of the undying lamp, the saga of the return from Babylon, of the Second Temple and of the Maccabees. Our friend related to his children all that he knew. It was not much, but it was enough for them. When he lit the second candle, it was the children who recited the story to him, and as he heard it from their lips it seemed not only beautiful, but quite new. And from then on he looked forward joyfully to the coming of each evening, always brighter than the evening before. Candle stood by candle in the menorah, and by their light, father and children dreamed their dreams. In the end it all grew into something more than he had sought to tell them, for it had risen beyond their understanding . . . .

"Amid these meditations the week passed. The eighth day came, and now the *shamash*, the servant among the candles, which until then had been used

---

8. Alex Bein, *Biography of Theodor Herzl*, includes quotes from Herzl's "The Menorah" translated by Maurice Samuel, used by permission of the Jewish Publication Society.

only for the kindling of the others, burned together with them. A great light streamed out from the menorah. The eyes of the children flashed, but what our good friend saw was the kindling of the light of the nation. First one candle, and dimness all around it, so that the candle was sad and lonely. Then a companion was added to it. Then a third, and a fourth. The darkness is compelled to retreat.

The first candles are lit among the youth and the poor, and gradually they are joined by all those who love truth and beauty and justice and freedom. When all the candles burn there is admiration and rejoicing for the work that has been done. **And there is no office more beneficent and creative than that of a Servant of Light."**

Theodor Herzl with his children at home in Vienna, Austria.
(Circa 1900, Central Zionist Archives, Jerusalem)

heroes are emulated at a time of courage and action. That was why the pioneers of the national renaissance tended to identify with the Hasmoneans and with the other heroes of the Second Temple. The Hasmoneans did not make do with prayers. The Biryonim [the rebels against Rome in 66 CE] did not expect miracles. They shed their blood for the people's freedom.

In the Hasmoneans, the Zionist secularists saw the beginning of a revolt that was not only nationalist, but secularist in its reliance on human effort to redeem the nation. [E.L.]

Traditional practices in the celebration of the festival, such as the lighting of the candles in the menorah, were observed but they were reinterpreted. The candles were said not to be in memory of the miracle of the cruse of oil, but to betoken the light of national deliverance.

New Songs: "No Miracle Occurred"

The miracle of the cruse of oil was openly belittled since it was believed that it was a salient example of the passive approach, which characterized traditional Diaspora Jewry. Indeed, a popular song, widely heard during Hanukkah, states: **"No miracle befell us, no cruse of oil did we find."** The divine intervention of the Lord was replaced by reference to the heroic people who delivered the Jewish community by their own courage and strength. A children's song chanted on Hanukkah altered the Biblical verse: *"Who can utter the mighty acts of the Lord?"*[9] to *"Who can recount the exploits of Israel?"* The very name "Maccabees," traditionally considered to be an acronym for the verse, *"Who is like You, O Lord, among the gods?"*[10] was given a new rendition by a Zionist functionary: 'Who is like unto thee among the nations, Israel?'

Traditional practices in the celebration of the festival, such as the lighting of the candles in the menorah, were observed but they were

reinterpreted: the candles were said not to be in memory of the miracle of the cruse of oil, but to betoken the light of national deliverance. Furthermore, the ceremony of lighting the candles which traditionally took place in the home was now observed in the town square or other places of public assembly; and instead of the traditional blessings, there were speeches, declarations, and songs of a national-political character, and torches were lit and were carried through the streets in festive parades.

One elaborate event was a pilgrimage to Modiin where members of the youth movement, Maccabee, lit a torch and relayed it in a marathon to light Hanukkah candles along the way. On the first occasion of such a ceremony in Modiin, the audience was told that the torch which was being kindled there would be carried by runners who were the descendants of the Maccabees "not only to light the Hanukkah candles but to light up the hearts of Hebrew youth and to herald unity and national action." [Ironically] the Modiin Marathon [a Greek term and institution] became part of a series of sports events which were held during the Hanukkah period. [E.D-Y.]

Labor and Likud (Revisionists): Parties of the Left and Right Celebrate a Different Hanukkah

The vast majority of the Jewish community of pre-state Israel regarded Hanukkah as chiefly expressing the values associated with the struggle for national liberation. This perception was shared by the two rival movements which competed for hegemony in the Zionist movement and in the Jewish community of Palestine (the *Yishuv*): the Labor movement which was established in 1905 [and led by David Ben-Gurion] and the Revisionist movement which was founded in 1925 [and led by Zeev Jabotinsky and later Menachem Begin and his Likud-Herut Party]. However, the two movements differed in their approach and in their

---

9. *Psalms* 106:2   10. *Exodus* 15:11

The Maccabees and Muscular Judaism[11]   BY MAX NORDAU

In Europe and Palestine in the early 20th century newly created Jewish youth movements and student groups were named after heroes like "Maccabees" or "Bar Kochba" and devoted to physical education and sports. Max Nordau,[12] Herzl's second in command in the Zionist Congress and a famous writer who lamented the degeneration of Europe at the turn of the century wrote in the newspaper of the Bar Kochba Sports Club of Berlin:

Two years ago, during a committee meeting at the Congress in Basel [the Zionist Congress of 1898], I said: We must think of creating once again a Jewry of muscles. Once again! For history is our witness that such a Jewry had once existed. For too long, all too long have we been engaged in the mortification of our own flesh.

Or rather, to put it more precisely — others did the killing of our flesh for us. Their extraordinary success is measured by hundreds of thousands of Jewish corpses in the ghettos, in the churchyards, along the highways of medieval Europe. We ourselves would have gladly done without this "virtue" [i.e. the Christian virtue of corporeal mortification]. We would have preferred to develop our bodies rather than to kill them or to have them — figuratively and actually — killed by others. We know how to make rational use of our life and appreciate its value.

If, unlike most other peoples, we do not conceive of [physical] life as our highest possession, it is nevertheless very valuable to us and thus worthy of careful treatment. During long centuries we have not been able to give it such treatment. All the elements of Aristotelian physics — light, air, water and earth — were measured out to us very sparingly. In the narrow Jewish street, our poor limbs soon forgot their gay movements; in the dimness of sunless houses, our eyes began to blink shyly; the fear of constant persecution turned our powerful voices into frightened whispers, which rose in a crescendo only when our martyrs on the stakes cried out their dying prayers in the face of their executioners. But now, all coercion has become a memory of the past, and at least we are allowed space enough for our bodies to live again. **Let us take up our oldest traditions, let us once more become deep-chested, sturdy, sharp-eyed men.**

This desire of going back to a glorious past finds a strong expression in the name which the Jewish gymnastic club in Berlin has chosen for itself. "Bar Kochba" was a hero who refused to know defeat. When in the end victory eluded him, he knew how to die. Bar Kochba was the last embodiment in world history of a bellicose, militant Jewry. To evoke the name of Bar Kochba is an unmistakable sign of ambition. But ambition is well suited for gymnasts striving for perfection.

For no other people will gymnastics fulfill a more educational purpose than for us Jews. It shall straighten us in body and in character. It shall give us self-confidence, although our enemies maintain that we already have too much self-confidence as it is. But who knows better than we do that their imputations are wrong. We completely lack a sober confidence in our physical prowess.

Our new muscle-Jews *(Muskeljuden)* have not yet regained the heroism of our ancestors who in large numbers eagerly entered the sport arenas in order to take part in competition and to pit themselves against the highly trained Hellenistic athletes and the powerful Nordic barbarians. But morally, even now the new muscle-Jews surpass their ancestors, for the ancient Jewish circus fighters were ashamed of their Judaism and tried to conceal the sign of the Covenant by means of surgical operation, while the members of the "Bar Kochba" club loudly and proudly affirm their national loyalty.

May the Jewish gymnastic club flourish and thrive and become an example to be imitated in all the centers of Jewish life!

---

11. "Muskeljudentum," *Juedische Turnzeitung* (June 1903). Republished in Max Nordau, *Zionistische Schriften* (Cologne and Leipzig: Juedischer Verlag, 1909), pp. 379-81. Translation by J. Hessing reappears in Arthur Hertzberg's *The Zionist Idea.*

12. Max Nordau (1849-1923), physician, avant-garde literary critic, novelist, and one of Herzl's earliest supporters. At the Second Zionist Congress, Nordau proposed a program to promote the physical fitness of Jewish youth. In response, the Bar Kochba gymnastic club was founded in Berlin in 1898. Similar clubs were soon established throughout Europe under the name Maccabee. Today Israel's best sports teams are part of the Maccabee Sports Club.

Israel's first President Chaim Weizmann lights a Hanukkah menorah made from Israel's biggest export at the time, Jaffa oranges.
(*December 1948, Central Zionist Archives, Jerusalem*)

interpretations of Jewish historical myths.

Revisionists emphasized the theme of combatting rule without hesitation and without compromise, however dangerous the fight, and even if the [majority of their] own nation was not willing to rebel. The Revisionists glorified the Zealots who revolted against the Romans in 66-70 CE as well as Bar-Kokhba's fighters who also rebelled against the Romans in 132-135 CE. Bar-Kokhba's last stronghold was Beitar and this was also the name of the youth

A Biblical Psalm Becomes a Secular Song

PSALM 106

Hallelujah.

Praise the Lord for God is good;

God's steadfast love is eternal.

Who can retell the mighty acts of the Eternal,

proclaim all God's praises?

God saved [our ancestors], as befits God's name . . .

God delivered them from the foe,

Redeemed them from the enemy.

MI Y'MALEL — An Early Zionist Folksong

Who can retell the mighty acts of Israel,

Who can count them?

In every age a hero rises to save the nation.

Hark! In those days at this time,

a Maccabee overcame and redeemed.

And in our day the whole nation of Israel

will be united and rise to be redeemed.

Prime Minister Yitzchak Rabin lighting 13 candles at a Bar Mitzvah.
(Israeli Government Press Office)

movement of the Revisionists, while their most radical group was called Brit HaBiryonim, after the most militant of the Zealots.

Although other Zionist groups also admired the fighters against the Romans, they gave pride of place to the Hasmoneans who had waged war only after grave acts of provocation and of suppression by the Greek rulers. Such a reaction was more in tune with the "defensive ethos" of the **Labor movement** and of other moderate groups in the

Yishuv, while the revolts against Roman rule were more in line with the militant ethos of the **Revisionists**.

Many Zionist leaders, writers, and poets, who inspired the Revisionist movement, were admirers of the Hellenistic culture, which was anathema to the Hasmoneans. The Revisionists saw themselves as disciples of the renowned Zionist leader, Max Nordau. In an article published in 1900, Nordau urged the cultivation of a **"muscular Jewry,"** which he associated especially with Bar-Kokhba, whom he described as "a hero who never knew defeat" and who embodied "the Jewry that is steeled in war and is enamoured of weapons." Nordau also lauded, as representatives of "muscular Jewry," the young Hellenizing Jews who took part in wrestling competitions and who were among the bitter enemies of the Hasmoneans.

Many Zionist leaders, writers, and poets, who inspired the Revisionist movement, were admirers of the Hellenistic culture, which was anathema to the Hasmoneans.

One of the Zionist leaders who admired Hellenistic culture was the founder of the Revisionist movement, Ze'ev Jabotinsky, who in 1905 declared:

> Mankind will be eternally grateful to Hellenism, which was first to point to sports, as the best educational means for creating, by prolonged training and will power, a type imbued with spiritual beauty and courage. The Hellenes were the first to establish special gymnasia for this purpose.

The ideological differences between the Revisionists and Labor also became apparent in their differing concepts of the Hanukkah festival and of the Hasmonean revolt. The Revisionists saw the revolt as [a militant demand for national] independence, while their political rivals interpreted that revolt as a popular uprising of peace-loving peasants who had to defend themselves against their cruel oppressors.

Thus, in 1910, the Labor Zionist Yitzhak Ben-Zvi (who later became the second President of Israel) depicted the Hasmoneans as "simple peasants" who liberated their people from foreign rule, as well as from exploitation by Jewish priests and

The "Battle" over the Maccabees in the Streets of Jerusalem, 1881-1908

Eliezer Ben Yehuda, the reviver of Hebrew as a modern secular language, believed that the Talmudic Rabbis had intentionally downplayed the proto-Zionist military heroism of the Maccabees while upgrading the exilic holiday of Purim. Purim's story was included in the Bible and a full tractate dedicated to its observance in the Mishna and Talmud. Many mitzvot and customs fill the day of Purim (reading, costumes, eating and drinking), while the Rabbinic Hanukkah has no tractate and few observances and no mention of Judah the Maccabee at all. So Ben Yehuda wrote school plays for Hanukkah and in 1881 published in his Hebrew newspaper, issued in Jerusalem, an article calling metaphorically "to gather strength (military?) and proceed forward (eastward?) like Judah the Maccabee." The anti-Zionist Ultra-Orthodox informed on Ben Yehuda to the Turkish authorities ruling Palestine, accusing him of calling for armed revolt. Ben Yehuda was jailed until the Turks could be persuaded that he had no concrete plans for an uprising.

In the light of the harrassment by the Ultra-Orthodox, Eliezer Ben Yehuda sought to enlighten his Zionist colleagues about the dangers of the romanticization of the Maccabees. When the Secular Zionist artist Boris Shatz, founder of the Jerusalem Institute of Art, Bezalel, unveiled his famous statue of Mattathias the Zealot, Eliezer Ben Yehuda refused to make a speech in its honor at the Zionist Hanukkah party in 1908. (See a picture of this statue on page 151.)

Ben Yehuda[13] explained, "it is a mistake to think of the Hasmoneans as the middle way, the moderates combining foreign content with national form, bringing the beauty of the Greeks into the tents of Israel. The truth is that the Hasmoneans never succeeded in finding a middle way of compromise between Hellenist and Hasidic Jews because it was not really possible then nor is it possible in our day. When Professor Shatz asked me to speak in honor of his new statue of Mattathias holding a sword, I refused because I was afraid of the wrath of that image of Mattathias. I imagined that Mattathias' eyes were looking at our Hanukkah party with zealous anger. If his statue were to come to rise from his grave and find himself in this Temple of Art, (the Bezalel Institute of Art in Jerusalem), surrounded by statues and pictures, then he would surely stab me with his sword with the same holy zealous emotion that he stabs the Jew who agreed to sacrifice pig on the altar in his hometown of Modiin two thousand years ago. He would smash all the statues while screaming in a great voice: "Accursed Hellenists! Violators of the Covenant! Are you the inheritors of the Maccabees? Did we spill our blood so that you would come to our land, pollute it and put statues in the Temple?" [E.D-Y.]

---

13. Eliezer Ben Yehuda, *Hashkafah* newspaper, Year 9, vol. 24, 6th Tevet 1908

"capitalists," who enriched themselves "at the expense of people."

The Zionist scholar Joseph G. Klausner wrote:

> The great victory of Judah Maccabeus, whose memory is honored in every Jewish house and every Jewish heart during the eight days of Hanukkah, was **the triumph of the Jewish tiller of the soil**. It was not the city of Jerusalem nor the ranks of the wealthy and large landowners, but the obscure village of Modiin in Judah, with its peasants whose plot of land was their all, that produced Mattathias the Hasmonean and his sons, who saved Jewish culture and perhaps the whole Jewish race from destruction. We have here an historic

---

The Revisionists saw the revolt as a militant demand for national independence, while their political rivals interpreted that revolt as a popular uprising of peace-loving peasants who had to defend themselves against their cruel oppressors.

> fact which speaks more than all the theoretical arguments in the world for the importance of national land and agricultural workers who literally draw their bread from their soil by the labor of their hands, for the sake of the culture, the freedom, the life of the nation.

> Zionism knew how to raise the Feast of Hanukkah, that feast of small candles, which shed their eternal light from the past into the future, to the height of a new national symbol. Can one ever forget that fine sketch, "The Menorah," written by the founder of Zionism, Theodor Herzl? The picture of Herzl standing wrapped in troubled thought, in front of a menorah, is one of the most beautifully symbolic in the life of the leader. But it seems to me that **this festival has come to tell the people**, through its two thousand year old symbol, **of the principle of land

redemption, and the creation of a class of workers on the soil that shall serve as a basis for the future existence of the race.

The Jewish Communist Hanukkah

A peculiar attempt to use Hanukkah for **class-struggle propaganda** was made by the Palestinian Jewish Communists, who supported the anti-Zionism of the Arabs and who went so far as to portray the anti-Jewish riots of 1929 as a popular uprising of Arab peasants against Zionist efforts to dispossess them. In 1929, the Communist Youth League of Palestine published a pamphlet in which the leader of the Palestinian Arabs and self-confessed foe of Zionism — **the Jerusalem Mufti, Hadj Amin al-Husseini** [later a Nazi collaborator in Berlin during World War II] — was portrayed as the equivalent of Mattathias the Hasmonean, since both were spiritual leaders who encouraged the emergence of a national class-liberation movement:

> It may well be that the symbol in whose name the Hasmonean muftis fought was a fanatic-religious character, but the real cause for which the peasant masses rose up was that of a movement of liberation from foreign domination and cruel exploitation.

The Moderate Religious Zionist Compromise

As for the religious Zionists, they sought to reconcile the national myth of the Maccabees with the traditional elements of Hanukkah. They held that the struggle of the Hasmoneans was fueled by both religio-spiritual and national-political goals. Rabbi Yeshayahu Shapira, the Hapoel-Hamizrachi leader, considered the exploits of the Hasmoneans to be a shining example of the special obligation on the Orthodox community to rally to the cause of national redemption:

> In the days of the Hasmoneans the banner of the revolt was raised expressly by Torah

The establishment of the State of Israel led to a decline in the importance of Hanukkah in Israeli political culture. It is no longer a major national event.

followers, and they risked their lives for the liberation of the land and of the Jewish spirit. Today, we face a similar war, a war for the redemption of our land and a war for the liberation of the Jewish spirit from the alien cultures that we have absorbed.

The Decline of the Zionist Hanukkah

The establishment of the State of Israel apparently led to a decline in the importance of Hanukkah in Israeli political culture. It is no longer a major national event, with public assemblies, declarations and speeches, or with mass parades. One reason for this decline was that there was now a new annual national celebration — Independence Day.

The changes in the public perceptions of the festival are also reflected in the patterns of its celebration. Today, Hanukkah is celebrated mainly in the circle of family and friends, in the home or in parties. This whole process is linked in turn to the great decline in the status of secular ideologies, such as Socialist Zionism, or Ben-Gurion's version of *Mamlachtiut* (Statism). These ideologies were intended to replace traditional Jewish religion as a symbol-system, which would underpin the cohesiveness of Jewish society and be a source of inspiration for the achievement of national goals. With the decline of these ideologies, institutionalized and politicized structures of festivals and ceremonies were abandoned in favor of more traditional or more individual and spontaneous styles, which do not reflect clear and well-defined ideological commitments. A related development is the attenuation of political authority in Israeli society, as evidenced in the refusal of large sections of the Israeli public to accept the dictates of the establishment concerning the management of social and cultural affairs, including symbolic and ceremonial behavior.

Gush Emunim: The Messianist Religious Settlers Movement

The only exception to the current trends of divesting Hanukkah of its political and heroic overtones is to be found in the symbol-system of Gush Emunim. In that movement, which advocates a mixture of devoutly religious and national values, Hanukkah symbolizes the uncompromising struggle for both religious and national goals. In 1980 one of the spiritual leaders of Gush Emunim, Rabbi Shlomo Aviner [who heads a Yeshiva in the Moslem quarter of the Old City of Jerusalem] declared that the chief feature of the festival was a commemoration of the victory of the heroic Hasmoneans over their people's oppressors. But that victory, the rabbi added, was achieved because the Jewish fighters were divinely inspired with spiritual power, which proved miraculous just like the miracle of the cruse of oil. Here we have a conception which stresses the centrality of the heroism of the Hasmoneans in the struggle to liberate their people, but which asserts that the source of that heroism was divine inspiration.

The members of Gush Emunim consider themselves to be the successors of the Maccabees. Gush Emunim played a dominant role in "The Movement to Stop the Withdrawal from Sinai," which was engaged in 1982 in a struggle against the implementation of the Camp David agreements with Egypt. Members of that group described themselves as "the Hasmoneans of their generation, the few against the many, fired with the spirit of truth and faith." The case of the Hasmoneans was used by the [extreme] political radicals of Gush Emunim in their polemic against their rivals on the Israeli left.

Dan Be'eri was a member of the "Jewish

Underground" which was active in the West Bank occupied territories in the years 1980-84, and he received a prison sentence in 1985 for his part in the plot to blow up the Dome of the Rock — the Muslim shrine on the Temple Mount. At the trial of Be'eri and his comrades, one of the defense's arguments was that "this court would also have convicted Judah the Maccabee for removing the idols from the Temple." The same reaction was implicit in a comment by the father of one of the accused: "This court is situated on Salah al-Din Street [in East Jerusalem] and not on Judah the Maccabee Street: that's the whole problem in a nutshell."

In an article published on Hanukkah, 1987, Dan Be'eri commented caustically that Hanukkah celebrations hailing the heroism of the Maccabees were increasingly becoming "something both creaking and grating." [With tongue in cheek he presented the Maccabees through the eyes of Israeli liberals who view both Gush Emunim and hence "necessarily" the Maccabees as "dangerous religious fanatics"]:

The prevailing tendency now is to observe the festival in a manner which reflects a mild fusion of national and traditional elements and which to a large extent is characteristic of Israeli political culture in general.

"Just between ourselves, the Maccabees were at bottom pretty 'fascistic.' They were also terrorists and religious fanatics who thrust the nation into mortal danger. They operated out of irrational, Messianic motives, and fomented a civil war. They also spurned the nation's legitimate legal institutions, which enjoyed the solid support of a broad consensus, whereas they were a radical, violent minority. They despised progress and universal cultural values. So, is it the deeds of these people that we are instilling in Jewish youth, not to mention

the miracle of the cruse of oil? This must be stopped at once! It's all very well and fitting for Orthodox Jews. But it cannot be a Zionist holiday, glorious and positive, a source of inspiration for a progressive and humanistic society."

Gush Emunim made efforts to link Hanukkah to its settlement activities. On Hanukkah, 1976, it established its first settlement in the occupied territories at Sebastia, and on Hanukkah, 1981, it launched a countrywide campaign to stop the Sinai withdrawal, using the slogan, [taken from a famous popular song by Naomi Shemer], "Do not uproot what is planted." However, despite the importance which Gush Emunim has attached to Hanukkah, it has not been able to restore its standing as a central national event. One reason for this is that Hanukkah could not compete with new national festivals, such as Independence Day — and since the Six-Day War of 1967, also Jerusalem Day, which has acquired special importance and is indeed particularly celebrated by Gush Emunim. But the important factor is that while Gush Emunim can boast of its achievements in establishing Jewish settlements in the occupied territories, it can hardly boast of having made a deep impression on Israeli culture.

There has clearly been a great weakening in the link between Hanukkah celebrations in Israeli Jewish society and the national myth of the Maccabees. The prevailing tendency now is to observe the festival in a manner which reflects a mild fusion of national and traditional elements and which to a large extent is characteristic of Israeli political culture in general. [E.D-Y.]

THE AMERICAN RECONSTRUCTIONIST

HANUKKAH LIGHTS AND THE AMERICAN BICENTENNIAL (1976)

by Leo Trepp[14]

The Reconstructionist Movement was founded by Rabbi Mordecai Kaplan who was born into an Orthodox rabbinic family, but later became a leader of the Conservative Movement and eventually founded the Reconstructionist Movement. Some of Kaplan's key concepts are that: (1) Judaism is not merely a religion or a nation but a civilization. (2) Judaism is not an eternal essence but an evolving entity that must interact with the progressive voice of God's ongoing revelation. (3) America's democratic vision is congruent with Judaism and so an American Jewish civilization needs to be created to serve the needs of all of humankind. (4) Modern science teaches us that there are no supernatural miracles and no supernatural personal God, but modern history reminds us that there is a miraculous force for salvation working through humankind in history that should be identified with the Divine. (5) The notion of the chosenness of the Jewish people must be eliminated as undemocratic and unethical, for all nations are called to increase ethical holiness in the world.

Rabbi Leo Trepp summarizes the ideals of the Reconstructionist Movement in an imaginative way by recreating a discussion among Beit Hillel and Beit Shamai, two schools of Rabbinic thought 2000 years ago, who disagreed on whether the lights of Hanukkah should be lighted in an ascending way (Hillel) or a descending way (Shamai). The Talmudic source is Shabbat 21 but the debate has been recast in an American-style parliamentary discussion.

For Leo Trepp both Hillel and Shamai believe Hanukkah stands for the spread of ethical light to all humankind. However Hillel's method of candle lighting is closer to the spirit of American Judaism (i.e. Reconstructionism), for Hillel adds a new candle every night, just as American Judaism with its belief in moral progress has an ever-evolving message.

The Time: First Century of the Common Era — and beyond.

The Place: The Academy at Yavneh [in Eretz Yisrael, just after the destruction of Jerusalem in 70 CE].

Shamash (official of the Sanhedrin): Will the assembly please rise for the arrival of the Av Beit Din? *(Assembly rises, and sits down as the Av Beit Din, the head of the Supreme Court and legislature, takes his seat.)*

> **Av Beit Din (Head of the Sanhedrin):** We are concerned with the lighting of the Hanukkah lights. In our previous session, we determined that the lights are to be placed at the door or window, in order to be visible from the outside, in order "to broadcast the miracle." As the Prophet said, *"Israel is to be a light unto the nations."* We are called upon to remind humankind of the duty to grow in **ethical evolution**, based on an awareness of God's presence in the world and his universal command to advance ethics. Our task is to spearhead the movement toward this goal, to lead mankind in the spirit of *"maalin bakodesh"* ("we ascend in holiness, never regressing"). Hanukkah is therefore a universal holiday, testifying to the universality of Judaism. Let us move to the topic of today's discussion: *Are the lights to be kindled in an ascending order during the eight days, from one to eight, or in a descending order, from eight to one?* I call on the school of Hillel for its views.

Beit Hillel: We would like to yield to our brethren, the House of Shamai, and give them the honor of starting the debate.

Beit Shamai: The lights ought to be lit in **descending order**. This procedure is valuable from the psychological point of

---

14. I would like to thank Dr. Eric Caplan, McGill University in Montreal, Canada, who made available his collection of Reconstructionist writings on Hanukkah as well as Rabbi Richard Hirsch who gave us permission to reprint this article entitled "The Hanukkah Lights and the American Bicentennial" from *The Reconstructionist Magazine*, Dec., 1975, originally published by the Reconstructionist Rabbinical College.

An American Jew wearing a top hat lights Hanukkah candles with his family.
(Harper's Magazine, New York, 1890)

(Beit Hatefutsoth Photo Archive, Tel Aviv)

view: the Jew, lighting the candles, will be reminded every night that, after an initial effort, his task of promoting *kedushah* (holiness) in the world will be easier; the obstacles recede and the goal will be nearer. He will thus grow in his determination.

Beit Hillel: We hold the opposing view. The growth of *kedushah* must rest on an awareness of our historical past, on the lights we have kindled in the past. To this past we add the contribution of the present, thereby modifying the past, increasing illumination. The approach of our brethren of the House of Shamai may actually symbolize a relaxation of the spirit of the enlightenment, as time progresses. Therefore, in the spirit of an evolving Judaism, we hold that the lights be **increased** in number from day to day, in accordance with the days yet to follow.

Beit Shamai: We are agreed that the meaning of the Hanukkah lights is to inspire a growing dedication to *kedushah* (holiness) among Jews and humankind. May we therefore remind our brethren of a similar symbolic action in the Torah? When our

holy Temple still stood, may it be restored in our days, on the Feast of Sukkot, 70 sacrifices were offered in a *descending* order, beginning with 13 on the second day of the feast, followed by 12 the following day, etc. The Hanukkah lights express the same symbolism, hence a decreasing sequence is indicated, as we find it *"in the steers of sacrifice on the festival of Sukkot."*[15]

Beit Hillel: With all due respect to our brethren of the House of Shamai, we have to disagree for various reasons:

(1) Beit Shamai mechanically transposes the rite of Sukkot to the practice of Hanukkah, without considering its meaning.

The sacrifices are our expression of *prayer* for the nations. We realize that the complete unification of humankind under God will come to pass only "at the end of days," and we refer you to the prophecy of the Prophet Isaiah. We pray however that, from the very beginning, a large number of nations may cast off their power drives, to be followed by the others, until, at the end, only a few stragglers will be left, who will then find their way to true national ethics and that all will then follow the ideal of Israel, namely, **ethical nationhood**. Therefore we offer one sacrifice at the end of the feast, symbolizing Israel. The decreasing number of sacrifices thus reflects our prayer for a growth in holiness.

The Hanukkah lights express our task and the tasks of the nations: each is to add to the light of *kedushah*, until its light dispels all darkness. Therefore we must add lights to make *manifest* the need for growing world-wide *kedushah*.

(2) The task of promoting *kedushah* runs counter to the usual historical development. The nations usually start out with great ideals and high aims. In the course of their development they forget their past and their ideals. Their high goals are replaced by power drives and materialism; eventually, they go to war and the lights go

---

15. *Numbers 29*

out. Decreasing the Hanukkah lights would express what *is*; we must increase them, in order to demonstrate what *ought* to be: a growth of *kedushah*.

We need but remind our brethren of the historical events in our country since the days of the victory over the Syrians. The Maccabees saw their victory as a spiritual victory. Finding the menorah destroyed, they fashioned a temporary one out of their spears, a marvelous symbol of their purpose, reminding us again of Isaiah's words: *"They shall beat their swords into plowshares."* The subsequent events under the House of the Hasmoneans, descendants of the Maccabees, are too well known and

---

Nations usually start out with great ideals and high aims. In the course of their development they forget their past and their ideals . . . Decreasing the Hanukkah lights would express what *is*; we must increase them, in order to demonstrate what *ought* to be: a growth of *kedushah*.

---

painful to relate. *Kedushah* decayed and with it the nation; we lost our freedom, our sovereignty. We must teach that every generation has to add to the lights of *kedushah*; it must buck the trend of history.

Av Beit Din: I recognize a hand in the rear of the hall. Please identify yourself and state your point.

First American Jew: We are Jews of a distant land and distant time. We live in America, in the year 5736 [1976]. America contains the largest Jewish community in our world. Though far removed, we are your disciples.

Second American Jew: America has been good to us. We are fully equal and fully integrated. We live in two civilizations, the Jewish and the American; at least, we should live in two, as we have the opportunity. America is an idealistic democracy based on human rights. We have a popular hymn, including the words: "God mend

thine every flaw, and crown thy good with brotherhood." It is a nation "under God" striving for *kedushah*. We mention this by way of introduction, as we now wish to support the idea of Beit Hillel.

First American Jew: In America, too, ideals yielded to expediency, and in the course of the years, the lights kindled by the Founding Fathers were extinguished — to our sorrow. American Jewry has followed this decline in spirit; it decreased its spiritual lights, when it should have added to them.

Second American Jew: Our nation attained its independence exactly 200 years ago, in the year 5536 [1776]. I would like to outline its development by citing its spirit at various anniversaries.

(1) Similar to the Maccabees, the Founding Fathers regarded independence as a spiritual act. They fought a war against Britain and won it. They fought this war because they saw in Britain nothing but materialistic imperialism; its morals were low, its church, a state institution, was domineering and tried to pervert the people from their simple and true devotion to God to an alien, idolatrous worship. The Revolution was seen by the Americans as an act of **redemption**. A simple, God-fearing, ethical nation was to arise, a nation of brothers, dedicated to reason. All men were to be equal. **Ethical nationhood** was the ideal.

(2) Fifty years later, the nation had embarked on a great industrial expansion, the industrialists were to be granted privileges; the lawyer had become leader, and the loopholes of the law permitted the circumvention of ethics. It was all in the early stages of development, but it was obvious that the light of idealism was diminishing.

(3) One hundred years later, in the year 5636, a great exhibition at the City of Philadelphia was held to celebrate the 100th anniversary of the founding of the Republic.

Its centerpiece was a gigantic steam engine. The material progress was celebrated. Strong racial feelings were in evidence, destroying brotherhood. The Day of Independence came to be seen by "The Daughters of the American Revolution" as a White

Our Zealous Modern Hellenists — A Historical Analogy (December, 1943)   BY RABBI MORDECAI KAPLAN

The observance of Hanukkah assumes for us a deeper meaning than ever, now that not only the Jewish people but all the democratic forces of the world are engaged in a struggle for survival and freedom. The historic similarity between the Maccabean war of liberation and the present conflict is deeper than would appear at first sight.

The fundamental likeness of the two wars is that both are clashes not only between antagonistic political and military powers, but between antagonistic civilizations. The foes against whom the Maccabees, for example, had to contend, were not merely the Greco-Syrian armies but the Jewish Hellenists. These were the men who, deeply impressed by the brilliance of Greek civilization and the success of its eastward march, felt that they were riding "the wave of the future" when they identified themselves with the cause of Hellenism. Some of them were undoubtedly venal scoundrels eager to curry favor with any who had favor to dispense. But others were probably sincerely convinced that Greek civilization was inherently superior and that it was sheer obstinacy and obstructionism for Jews to insist on loyalty to the Torah. They no doubt considered the Jews who persisted in their ancestral ways as narrow-minded, and regarded every protest of theirs against Hellenistic encroachment as intolerance.

Among our people too, we still have the modern equivalent of the Hellenists. **A Jewish congregation in Houston, Texas, for example, excludes from its membership, and by implication from the fellowship of Israel, all who adhere to the rules of kashrut or espouse Zionism.** What a vile insult to the martyrs who gave up their lives rather than eat forbidden food at the behest of the Syrian tyrant, and of the warriors who perished for the freedom of Judea from the Syrian yoke! If it is a principle with these Texas Jews that they must eat *trefot* (unkosher meat), nobody will deny them the right to do so. But this does not give them the right to deny equality of status in Israel to those who see in kashrut an expression of Jewish loyalty.

And what justification have they for their sabotage of Zionist effort? The strangest thing about these modern Jewish Hellenists is their effrontery in waging their fight against Zionism in the name of Jewish religion. They identify Zionism with secularism, and secularism with irreligion. Why are they so furious against Zionism? The reason, but thinly concealed behind their absurd rationalizations, is that they are embarrassed by being identified with a people which the tremendous forces of tyranny and oppression would like to destroy or suppress. Like their prototypes in the days of the Maccabees, they have no faith in the value of Jewish life and would like to see Jews give up all those aspects of Judaism which seem to stand in the way of the social acceptance of Jews by non-Jews. We do not challenge their right to refrain from participating in the establishment of a Jewish Commonwealth in Palestine, if it means nothing to them, any more than we challenge their right to disregard kashrut. But we do deny their right to interfere with the effort to establish a Jewish Commonwealth on the part of other Jews who find its establishment necessary to their security or to their self-fulfilment as Jews.

How ironical it is that these Jewish Hellenists celebrate Hanukkah! They no doubt rationalize their doing so on the ground that Hanukkah stands for freedom of religion.

We Reconstructionists, because we have resented the effort of the American Council for Judaism[16] to frustrate Zionism, have been charged with intolerance. Well, Zionism is part of our religion. If combatting efforts to interfere with our freedom of religion is intolerance, we admit the charge with pride. We do not think that the Maccabees were any more tolerant of the Jewish Hellenists in their day.

---

16. The American Council for Judaism was a group of anti-Zionist Jews, many of them wealthy Reform Jews, who opposed Zionism in the name of Americanism.

Anglo-Saxon Protestant (WASP) festival, to be denied to the immigrants. The unity was gone; lights had gone out.

(4) The 150th anniversary saw America submerged in a "business spirit;" morality had decayed, gangsterism reigned, and the WASP spirit had grown. The bonds with humanity had been severed by an isolationist America. The fighters and the ideal of the Revolution were forgotten.

(5) As we set about to observe the Bicentennial year, we are all confused, not knowing how to celebrate it. It must be added that American Jews, sucked in by the spirit of the country, followed the same line; Jewish knowledge and observances declined, the family fell apart, marriages out of the faith multiplied, the wealthy, rather than the dedicated, emerged as leaders. Lights have gone out. Jews should have increased the light, as Hillel suggests.

First American Jew: As we set about to celebrate the Bicentennial, new forces are stirring: minorities have gained many of the rights due them being "men, created equal," women have progressed, social legislation has expanded, labor is no longer exploited, youth is stirring in search for new answers, based on justice and love, America is supporting Israel. It is all not perfect, many lights have yet to be kindled, but many lights have been kindled. Unlike the progress of the Hanukkah lights, fully determined step by step, we do not see as yet the steps next to

be taken and the rate of progression.

I may add that the non-Jewish American is better acquainted with Hanukkah than any other holiday of Jews. There are extraneous reasons for that, but perhaps, the spirit of the *increase* in light has caught the imagination of the American people, so closely fashioned, in principle, on lines of Jewish ethics.

Second American Jew: We have outlined the fact that **the *decrease* in light means decay**, and **the *increase* in light means spiritual growth**. We believe that the American example speaks for the opinion of the House of Hillel, and would respectfully submit that this opinion be given preferred consideration in the shaping of *Halakhah* [Jewish law].

Av Beit Din: Your view is of importance to us. It reflects the living spirit of the Jewish people. It is the voice of the people. We conclude that Beit Hillel expresses the Jewish people in its historical growth.

Hillel has always placed emphasis upon this voice, calling the people "if not prophets, then sons of prophets." The voice of the people is essential. The Romans have a saying: *"Vox populi, vox dei;"* **the voice of the people is "*Bat Kol*," the daughter of God's voice, and Bat Kol pronounces in favor of Hillel.**

I want to stress that Beit Shamai and Beit Hillel are in agreement on the principle — the purpose of the Hanukkah light is *"maalin bakodesh,"* ascending holiness. This agreement reinforces our conviction that the opinions are indeed "the words of the living God;" discussants must be taken seriously. Nevertheless, Beit Hillel has shown the greater practical insight. Closer to the people, Beit Hillel has truly articulated how the ideal can be best symbolized and taught.

The *Halakhah* is according to the House of Hillel: the Hanukkah lights are to be kindled in increasing number from the first to the eight day. The meeting is adjourned.

A Reconstructed Version of *Maoz Tzur*

The editors of the Reconstructionist prayerbook of 1945 were appalled by the sentiments of the traditional verse in *Maoz Tzur* — *"When You prepare the slaughter of the enemy dogs."* Its vengeful dehumanization of Israel's foes led them to substitute a Hebrew phrase meaning literally, *"When You put an end to all slaughter."* They translated the new verse into rhyming English:

"When the force of hate is demolished,
And war at last abolished,
We then will greet with joy complete
Thine altar's consecration."

4

AN AMERICAN REFORM HOLIDAY CURRICULUM
THE ANTI-WAR CELEBRATION OF THE MACCABEES (1971)
by Harry Gersh[17]

Hanukkah Among Reform Jews

Hanukkah may be difficult for some Reform Jews to embrace because of its emphasis on the Temple, on political independence of the Jewish nation, on the negative image of Western culture (Hellenism) as a coercive source of assimilation, and on the military heroism of the Maccabees. In contrast, freedom of conscience, faith in God and ethics have been central Reform values.

Thus it should not be surprising that Isaac M. Wise, who introduced Reform Judaism in the United States, suggested in 1865 the elimination of the Hanukkah lights. However, six years later the Augsburg Synod, with delegates mostly from German Reform congregations, introduced a resolution urging the appropriate commemoration of Hanukkah, which had been neglected in many Reform Jewish congregations. The rationale for this resolution was to counteract the celebration of Christmas by many Jewish families "in direct opposition to Jewish consciousness."[18]

A hundred and thirty years later, American Jews continue to give great significance to Hanukkah as a counter-weight to Christmas. Consistent with the Reform movement's essential values, the curricular efforts of 1971 and 1993 sought to retool the meaning of the holiday to emphasize peace, not war, and religious freedom, not traditional religious rituals. Read carefully these familiar retellings of the story for children and try to discover the educational message of the authors.

Freedom of Worship

Jewish holidays have to do with nature and God, with the growth of crops and the growth of the Jewish people. **Only one Jewish holiday — Hanukkah — centers on a war.** Even that one does not celebrate victory but cleaning the Temple and dedicating it once again.

Jews never take up the sword willingly. No one can take joy in the death of another human being. But sometimes we have no choice. We must stop and fight those who would deny us the freedom to be Jews. If we do not, we are, in effect, agreeing to become slaves.

That's why Mattathias, the priest of Modiin, is the real hero of Hanukkah. He had the courage to stand up to the Syrians. **Mattathias did not want war. When many people shouted for war, Mattathias ran away from Jerusalem hoping to avoid war.** But when he found that meant he would have to give up his Judaism he knew what he had to do. If war and death were the price the Jews had to pay for the right to be Jews, then war and death it would be.

Two thousand years before Abraham Lincoln said that "a nation cannot endure half slave and half free," Mattathias, the priest of Modiin, sent his five sons into war against the Syrians because he knew that the Jews could not exist half slave and half free.

When Antiochus' soldiers came to the village of Modiin, Mattathias stood firm. The *Book of Maccabees* (in the Apocrypha) tells what he said:

Even if all the nations within the king's empire listen to him and give up, each its own faith, yet will I and my sons and my brothers follow the Covenant of our fathers. God forbid that we give up the Torah and the Commandments. We will

---

17. While the title is the editor's, the text is from *When a Jew Celebrates* by Harry Gersh with Eugene Borowitz and Hyman Chanover, 1971, (pp. 171-181). Reprinted by permission of the publisher, Behrman House.
18. Based on *The Hanukkah Anthology* by Phillip Goodman

not listen to the king's words, to leave our faith. Let all who will obey the Torah and keep the Commandments follow me.

Mattathias and his sons fought with the Syrian soldiers and drove them from Modiin. And the war began. Mattathias' son Judah gathered together groups of Jews and created an army in the hills of Judea. For three years they fought and beat the Syrians. As winter came in 165 BCE, Judah's soldiers entered Jerusalem and then Judah's army came to the Temple. The great stone altar stood there,

with a great statue of Zeus — or was it Antiochus?

Cleansing the Temple

The soldiers threw down their arms and began to clean the Temple. The idols were thrown out and everything cleaned. Priests and Levites came forward from among the soldiers, and animals for sacrifices were brought. All was ready for the beginning of services — except for the great menorah. One legend says that then the soldiers found eight iron rods stuck in the walls. They put them together in the shape of a menorah and lit candles in them.

And on the twenty-fifth day of Kislev, exactly three years to the day from the day the Temple was taken over by the Syrians, the Temple services were held. **Each soldier waved a palm branch instead of a sword.** For many years after the end of that war of independence the Jews celebrated Hanukkah. But it was a kind of old soldiers' holiday, when those who fought the war got together and recounted their battles and victories. As these soldiers died, the holiday became less important.

The sons and grandsons of Mattathias died, and new kings ruled the Jews. Like so many kings, they became tyrants. The Jew in the street cursed the Hasmonean tyrants and would not celebrate the holiday of the victory of the Hasmoneans.

The Legend of the Oil

Then the Hasmonean kings were pushed off the throne by the Romans. Foreigners ruled the Jews and they were cruel. The Jews hated them and wanted to rebel. Now the people began to remember their last fight for freedom, from Antiochus. And they remembered Hanukkah. New stories and legends began to grow up around this great victory. That may be when the story about the oil was born. It explained why Hanukkah is eight days and not just a week. The spears and torches legend is another. We don't know

---

Another Reform Curriculum for Hanukkah (1993): Assimilating yet Drawing the Line — "No compromises on our inner faith!"
BY ADAM FISHER[19]

Many Jews also followed Greek ways. But there was one thing the Jews would not do. They would not worship the Greek gods. No matter what the Jews looked like on the outside, on the inside they remained faithful to God.

— *STUDENT BOOK*

Introducing the Lesson

Begin by explaining that it is usually a good idea to follow rules and accept regulations that are imposed upon us by parents, school officials, government, and so on. But there are exceptions when we know that a rule or regulation is wrong. At those times we need to speak out against it, rather than just to continue doing the wrong thing.

Come to class prepared to relate an experience you had when you felt compelled to speak out against something you felt was wrong. Try to make it something on the students' level so that they will be able to appreciate it fully.

Many Jews also followed Greek ways. What were some Greek things that Jews began to do? (Speak and read Greek, study Greek art and music, play Greek games, learn Greek math.) Do we do some Christian things because we live near many Christians? In what ways is this good? In what ways is this not a good thing? (Try to steer the discussion toward expressing that we can learn from others and absorb new things as long as we don't compromise ourselves and our beliefs.) You can also express that it is important for others to learn from us.

— *TEACHERS' GUIDE*

---

19. *My Jewish Year*, Behrman House, 1993, p. 61. Used by permission.

which one is exactly true. But it doesn't much matter. Sometimes there's more real truth in the legends than in the bare facts of history.

The Right to Worship

Today some people try to use Hanukkah to show that the Jews were a warrior people. They were not. **Most Jews in all ages thought war was stupid.** The great men of the Jews were not warriors. They were men of learning, lawgivers, wise men. In a period of about 1,500 years there were only four great generals among the Jews. Two of them are not thought of as generals, Joshua and David. Only Judah Maccabee and Bar Kokhba are remembered as warriors, and they are more important to us today, because our times are so troubled, than they were to the Jewish tradition.

Some people try to change the meaning of Hanukkah so that it celebrates a war for

---

Some people try to change the meaning of Hanukkah so that it celebrates a war for independence. It wasn't. The Jews would rather have had their own government and king, but they did not go to war over politics.

---

independence. It wasn't. The Jews would rather have had their own government and king, but they did not go to war over politics. As a matter of fact, they accepted Antiochus; they accepted his taxes, even when he taxed the Temple. But they would not accept his interference with their worship, their belief, their religion.

Freedom to Serve God

So this war was the first for the right of a people within a country to believe as they wish — so long as they followed the king's law in worldly matters. For thousands of years, Jews have lived under kings, princes, dukes, caliphs, governors, presidents. And they have always been loyal to these rulers — so long as they were permitted to practice their own religion. **This idea of religious freedom is followed in all free nations today. It was first given to the world by the Jews.**

One thing more: Antiochus offered the Jews complete equality with all the rest of his subjects — so long as they would agree to *be* like all his other subjects. He said: If you Jews become like all my other people, you can enjoy all the rights my other subjects have. So the Jews fought, not for equality, but for the right to be different.

For Jews life is very, very important. But it is not the most important thing. Jews will *not* do *anything* to survive. For some things one must stand up and not give in. The Maccabeees risked their lives for freedom to serve God.

That's why the festival of Hanukkah does not take place on the day of a great battle. It does not take place on the day the Jews reconquered Jerusalem. It takes place during the week that the Temple was cleansed and a new fire lighted in the menorah. Such a day is so important that it must be celebrated.

This is the meaning of Hanukkah. Hanukkah is a Festival of Dedication. It reminds us of the value of freedom of worship. It recalls our dedication to God.

5

THE HASIDIC HANUKKAH OF LUBAVITCH (HABAD) AND GUR

THE INWARD AND THE OUTWARD LIGHT OF OUR SOULS

Hasidism has long sought the spiritual meaning of Jewish rituals and events, interpreting them both literally and allegorically, as referring to psychological and spiritual processes within the cosmos, history and the individual. Generally Hasidim have been spiritual activists who believe that by the proper channelling of spiritual intentions (kavanot) they can transform themselves and the cosmos in a redemptive way.

We have selected two Hasidic interpretations of the lighting of the menorah — one from the Hasidism of Lubavitch and one from Gur. Although the reader will see a familiar story retold, the special value emphasis of each Hasidic school will become apparent.

__Lubavitch__ is the town in Lithuania where the Habad movement developed. In recent years Lubavitch Hasidism has been involved in a redemptive and sometimes messianic campaign to redeem every assimilated Jew, every Divine spark in the world and thereby the cosmos.

Lubavitch is well-known for its missionary activity to Jews seeking to bring them to observe at least one mitzvah. The lighting of a giant menorah in the public square has become a central event, even though it is not a halachic act since the menorah is meant to be lit at home. Habad promotes public candle lighting ceremonies at the White House, on highways and on satellite television as an analogue for their own mission to publicize God's hidden miracles and help each Jew to discover the Divine spark hidden within.

__The Gerer Rebbe__, from the village of Gora (or Gur or Ger) outside Warsaw, founded one of the largest and most intellectual dynasties of Polish Hasidism. His son Yehudah Leib Alter (rabbi from 1871 to 1905) collected his very popular weekly spiritual meditations on the Torah reading and the holidays into a book called Sefat Emet: The Language of Truth. *The selection on Hanukkah can be juxtaposed to Habad. While Habad emphasizes the light of one's soul used to illuminate the darkness of the Western world and to rekindle the darkened sparks of assimilated Jews, the Gerer Rebbe focuses on the need to shine a light into our inner darkness and to purify our inner Temple. It is not to publicize the miracle to others, but "to find the hidden light within all our own chambers." Although Habad is also concerned with inner illumination, its emphasis lies with lighting the souls (candles) of others. The lighting of the menorah is a fulfillment of the Divine purpose of creation — "Let there be light," "for a world without the light of Torah is mired in darkness."*

Contemplating a Candle: "The Last Prayer" by Samuel Hirschenberg, 1897

WHAT IS A LUBAVITCH HASID? A LAMP LIGHTER

by Menachem Mendel Schneerson[20]

My father-in-law reported this conversation with his own father Rebbe Sholom Dov-Ber, then the Lubavitcher Rebbe:

The Hasid asked: Rebbe, what is a Hasid?

The Rebbe answered: A Hasid is a streetlamp lighter.

In olden days, there was a person in every town who would light the gas streetlamps with a light he carried at the end of a long pole. On the street corners, the lamps were there in readiness, waiting to be lit. A streetlamp lighter has a pole with fire. He knows that the fire is not his own, and he goes around lighting all lamps on his route."

Today, the lamps are there, but they need to be lit. It is written, *"The soul of man is a lamp of God,"*[21] and it is also written, *"A mitzvah is a lamp and the Torah is light."*[22] A Hasid is one who puts personal affairs aside and goes around lighting up the souls of Jews with the light of Torah and mitzvot. Jewish souls are in readiness to be lit. Sometimes they are around the corner. Sometimes they are in a wilderness or at sea. But there must be someone who disregards personal comforts and conveniences and goes out to ignite these lamps with his or her flame. That is the function of a true Hasid.

Hasidism in general demands that one disseminate Torah and Yiddishkeit all over and seek to benefit fellow Jews. In the words of Rebbe Sholom Dov-Ber: "A Hasid is he who surrenders his self to seeking the welfare of another." Over and beyond that, Habad demands *pnimiyut* (inwardness): one should not act superficially, as a mere act of faith, but with inner conviction, with the soul-faculties of **HaBaD** (**H**ochma — conceptual wisdom; **B**ina — comprehensive understanding; and **D**a'at — penetrating analytic knowledge).

The message is obvious. This function is not really limited to Hasidim, but is the function of every Jew. Divine Providence brings Jews to the most unexpected, remote places, in order that they carry out this purpose of lighting up the world.

May God grant that each and every one of us be a dedicated "lamp lighter," and fulfill his or her duty with joy and gladness of heart.

CANDLE LIGHTING BY SATELLITE (1992)

An Address by Menachem Schneerson, the Lubavitcher Rebbe

Recently we can "proclaim and propagate the miracle" world over using a satellite or other scientific inventions to honor God, because as the Rabbis said *"everything God created in the world was for his honor."*[23]

In fact the ability to see visually by satellite how one person, even a child, can light a candle seen round the world instantaneously teaches us that it is within the power of each one of us to light up the whole world. By satellite we can unite Jews all over the world no matter how dispersed; thus Hanukkah teaches the oneness of Israel, of God and of Torah.

The satellite connection teaches the Jews that what happens in one place can have an

---

20. The Lubavitcher Rebbe from 1950 to 1994. Based on *Sichot HaRebbe* (Talks) from the years 5701, 5700, 5722.
21. *Proverbs* 20:27   22. *Proverbs* 6:23   23. *Pirkei Avot* 6

effect in any other place, what happens in heaven (satellite) can have an effect on what happens on earth. If it is a mitzvah "to place the candle on the outside of one's doorway to proclaim the miracle," then even more so is it a mitzvah to place it "outside" in a central public space for even greater "proclamation of the miracle" — including for the nations of the world, for they too are commanded to observe Torah, the laws of Noah. Of course one's house should also be a source of light for one's environment — a house filled with

inner spiritual light of Torah, prayer and loving kindness.

The Hanukkah candles we light are comprised of two aspects: (a) illuminating the world during the time of exile, and thereby (b) preparing the world for the coming redemption.

Kindling Hanukkah Lights Today, Illuminating the Exile

The Hanukkah candles are lit for eight days. This does not mean that the same mitzvah is repeated eight times in succession. Just as in a physical sense new candles are lit each night, so it is in a spiritual sense, every night a new mitzvah is fulfilled with new fire. Also, each night we add another candle, indicating how we must constantly increase our efforts to spread light. The Hanukkah lights reflect the fire within the Jewish soul, as it is written, *"The soul of man is the lamp of God."* Each person possesses this light within his body. Hanukkah teaches how this light must be ignited and shine forth and how it must be renewed and increased each day.

The Hanukkah candles are to be placed "at the outside of the entrance to one's home." This indicates how the light of a person's soul should shine not only within the confines of his own being, but must also be projected outward, thereby illuminating his environment and filling it with light.

The kindling of each person's individual menorah, the fire of his soul, leads also to the kindling of the collective menorah, the Jewish people. The light they produce is not self-contained, but rather shines "outside" and illuminates the world at large, spreading light in the totality of the darkness of exile.

Projecting light to the world at large is the underlying intent of all the mitzvos, as it is written, *"A mitzvah is a lamp and the Torah is light."* However, to a greater degree than in other mitzvos, this intent is reflected in the Hanukkah candles, for they produce visible light and they spread that light throughout their surroundings.

A Lubavitch Children's Story: The Young Hasmonean   BY R. ZAMIR

When little Yisrael returned from *Heder* (Hebrew school) on Hanukkah evening, the whole family was ready to light the candles. "How much I desire to be one of the Hasmoneans, to join Judah the Maccabee in fighting the evil Greek Empire that tried to separate Israel from its Holy Torah," thought Yisrael. An inner desire to be one with the Hasmoneans took control of the young mind.

His sparkling eyes fastened on the candle that began to flicker and almost to go out. The flame rose and then fell again and again as if the candle were saying: I want to live, to light up the world . . . Yisrael's blue eyes closed for a moment and it seemed as if the candle was speaking to him before it departed and went out:

My dear son! I understand your desire to be a heroic Hasmonean, willing to sacrifice your life for the Holy Torah. Therefore I have come to assure you that you have the inner strength to be a Hasmonean. What the Maccabees did *"in those days,"* you can do *"in these days."*

How? Let me tell you: Not far from your house are hundreds and thousands of Jews. Though inside them they have a holy Jewish soul like yours, it is hidden. They have no idea what a great and holy day Hanukkah is and what the candles symbolize — all those miracles. They know nothing. Listen, my dear son! You have a wonderful opportunity to be a Maccabee, to fight the Greek spirit that distances them from the Hasmonean spirit. Go and talk to them. Tell them all the wonderous stories you have heard. Perhaps you can influence them so that they too will go with you to *Heder* (Hebrew school). Before I leave you, (said the candle), I promise that if you really want it, you can be a Maccabee just like Judah the Maccabee.

Our Children,
the Lights within the Exile

The darkness of exile is in fact being illuminated. Proof of this is that the majority of the participants in this gathering are children. Children perpetuate the golden chain of our people's bond with the Torah and its mitzvos. The fact that our children accept their responsibilities as *Tzivos HaShem* ("God's army") demonstrates how "the lamp of mitzvah" and "the light of Torah" are spreading throughout the world.

This special quality of children is also reflected in the very name of the festival, for Hanukkah is also related to the word *Hinuch*, meaning "education." It is written, *"Educate a child according to his way [so that] even when he grows older he will not depart from it."* This points to the unique role of childhood in, and the effect it has on all stages of one's life. It is the experience and training during one's childhood which affects the entire life of the person. Therefore, when we see the excitement of children participating in this gathering, we are certain that this will be carried into all different stages of their lives.

Bringing the Redemption Near,
Through Tzedakah

The preparation of the world for the era of redemption is enhanced by the mitzvah of *Tzedakah* (charity). In particular, this is accomplished by children, for we find a unique quality in the Tzedakah given by a child, which is not found in the Tzedakah given by an adult.

Adults work to earn their livelihood, and thus can perhaps replace the money that they have given away. In contrast, children do not earn their own money and have only what they have been given by their parents. Nevertheless, we see that a child gives generously.

24. Merkos L'Inyonei Chinuch, 770 E. Pkwy, Brooklyn, NY. *"And There Was Light"* (1987): A Photographic Chronicle of the Public Chanukkah Menorah Celebrations sponsored by Habad. (Permission requested.)

The White House
Washington
January 22, 1987

Dear Rabbi,

I was delighted to accept the handsome menorah from you and your fellow rabbis when you came to the White House for the third consecutive year. Thank you very much for this spiritual gift — and for the copy of <u>Let There Be Light</u>[24] which you also presented to me. I am particularly pleased to have these special remembrances in observance of Hanukkah — and your organization's steadfast support and friendship mean more than I can say.

Please convey my kindest regards to the Lubavitcher Rebbe, Rabbi Schneerson. You and all the American Friends of Lubavitch have my best wishes.

Sincerely,

Ronald Reagan

Furthermore, in keeping with the Hanukkah lesson of increasing light, a child does not remain satisfied with giving once, but continues to give many times. And most importantly, the child gives with joy, happy at the opportunity to fulfill God's will. Indeed, a child's eagerness and joy in the performance of this mitzvah should serve as lessons for his or her parents, inducing them to emulate these qualities in their observance of the mitzvos.

At the conclusion of this gathering, each child will be given three coins as Hanukkah gelt. Our Sages associate the number three with a *chazakah*, a sequence that firmly establishes a lasting practice. This word also signifies strength and is reflected in the Jewish people's growing stronger from day to day in their observance of the Torah and its mitzvos. A fourth coin will also be given to you, for you to give to Tzedakah, preferably together with additional money of your own. When the number four is doubled, the sum is eight, a number also associated with the future redemption.

The Menorah Around the World Lights the Path for the Menorah in the *Beis HaMikdash*

Through telecommunication, we have just witnessed how the Jewish people, dispersed as they are throughout the entire world, have gathered together to kindle the Hanukkah menorah, joining the individual lights of their souls together into the larger torch. The fusion of all these lights reflects the kindling of the worldwide menorah, the Jewish people. Its fusion shines *"at the outside of the entrance to one's home,"* kindling the fire in the hearts of other people, inspiring them to light their own menorahs, and illuminating the world at large.

May the merit of these achievements and the resolve to increase efforts to reach out, even to those who may not of yet been reached, cause God to grant our prayer and bring the coming Redemption so that *"at this time,"* now in our days, we will *"kindle the lights in Your holy courtyard,"* in the courtyard of the Third *Beis HaMikdash*.

Al HaNissim: "The impure were handed over to the pure, the evil to the righteous . . . ." BY THE REBBE, MENACHEM SCHNEERSON

The "impure" refer not to the Greeks as such, who as non-Jews have no basis for purity or impurity, but to the Hellenist Jews who have the potential to be pure. The miracle is even greater since the enemies of the Jews who were pure, righteous and students of Torah, were the majority of Jews who willingly and by force became Hellenized. Yet the minority of Jews — pure, righteous students of Torah — defeated the many.

This is a source of encouragement for our generation in which the true and complete observers of Torah and mitzvos are a tiny minority among the Jews. Contemplating this fact can lead one, God forbid, to despair, since redemption requires all the Jews to repent. But the model of Hanukkah shows that a minority of Torah-true Jews can, with God's help, win over the majority who are like "children who were captured" by others and never learned about Judaism. The minority is small in quantity, not in quality; because of their holiness they not only defeat the others but the others are "handed over" to the pure and become "pure, righteous, students of Torah."

This battle of majority impure and minority pure Jews is repeated inside each Jew. The minority, i.e. one's inner holiness and spirituality, can transform the majority, i.e. one's physicality. Thus we can be encouraged to repent and to build our own inner sanctum by purifying ourselves and then lighting within us our candle, for *"God's candle is the human soul."*

THE LIGHT OF LUBAVITCH:
THE INNER LIGHT OF JUDAISM AGAINST THE OUTER DARKNESS OF THE WEST[25]

The Messianic Menorah and the Mission of the Jew

There are two basic differences between the Hanukkah candles we light today at home and the Temple menorah lit in the days of the Temple. First, the Temple menorah is lit inside, while the Hanukkah menorah is lit in order to shine outside. Second, the Temple menorah is lit while still daylight, while the Hanukkah menorah is lit when it is dark, after sunset.

> Remember that the "light" symbolizes the holy Torah and its commandments. The "darkness" is the absence of Torah. The "inside" is the inner spirituality of Torah, while the "outside" is the material world.
>
> The message of Hanukkah is our obligation to propagate the "light of the Torah" into the "outside" which is still without Torah. Torah and the Jewish way of life are not meant to be confined "inside" on holy days or holy places but rather to fill every moment and every

---

25. R. Zamir, *Hagei Yisrael for Youth*, Center for Education, 770 Eastern Parkway, Brooklyn, 1984 pp. 315-323. Permission requested.   26. *Psalms* 139

A Month of Mitzvot: The Month of Kislev

Hanukkah is a particularly appropriate occasion for the 'kindling of lamps' — in the metaphorical sense of stirring the soul, as well in the literal sense. If the Hasidim of Habad-Lubavitch are "lamplighters" all year round, during the Hanukkah season their "wattage" is increased many times over.

The weeks immediately preceding and following Hanukkah also bear special significance. The tenth and the nineteenth of Kislev are important dates in the history of Habad-Lubavitch; they are Hasidic "festivals of liberation." In the early days of the Hasidic movement in Czarist Russia, the founder of Habad-Lubavitch, Rabbi Schneur Zalman was imprisoned on trumped-up charges of high treason spread by anti-Hasidic Jews. On the nineteenth of Kislev, 5559 (1798), he was released. Twenty-eight years later, Rabbi Dov-Ber, his son and successor, was similarly accused and was freed on the tenth of Kislev. These dates mark not just the personal liberation of these two great Jewish leaders, but the vindication of their teachings and the movement they established. As such, the commemoration of these festivals provides inspiration and impetus to Jews everywhere.

place whether at home, at school or in the market place. It is our mission to shine our inner light into the material world, even in public spaces.

Just as an added candle is lit on every night of Hanukkah, so each one of us must add to the light of Torah in the world. If each of us does his duty then we can confidently expect the Fulfillment of Divine promise that "night will be as light as day."[26] Then the end of our dark exile is near and the light of our Messiah will shine over the darkness of the nations, then the Third Temple will be built, the Temple menorah will be lit and never again be extinguished.

The Error of Greek Ways

Some people think that Hanukkah is chiefly about a military victory. However while the military victory was essential, it was a means to the final purpose of purifying the Temple, spiritual survival. In short, the point is to remove Greek pagan influence and to spread the light of holiness.

Greek culture has two faces. Outwardly, it is brilliant and attractive. Inwardly, it is rotten and corrupt. It is the culture of sports, circuses and theater. Nevertheless, even in Eretz Yisrael there were Jews who wanted to assimilate, "to live it up" as Hellenists.

However, the lesson of Hanukkah is "not to be impressed by the majority" and not to be swept up. **An observant Jew can survive as the only Jew in the city. He must see himself as the little candle, the single cruse of oil, lighting up the great darkness.** The nature of a candle is that one can light more and more candles (souls) from it — endlessly.

The Greeks made a gross error when they persecuted the Jews. They didn't know that when one "presses" a Jew to abandon the faith of his/her ancestors, then precisely at that moment the *"pintele Yid"* — the Jewish inner point is revealed and the Jew resists energetically and offers his whole self. That is the nature of the Divine soul, of the *"stiff necked people, Israel."*

THE HASIDIC HANUKKAH OF THE REBBE OF GUR: FINDING THE HIDDEN LIGHT WITHIN

by Yehuda Leib Alter of Ger[27]

t is written: *"A lamp [candle] of the Lord is the soul of man, seeking out all the belly's chambers."*[28] The Gemara (Talmud) notes that searching requires a candle. *"I will seek out Jerusalem with candles."*[29]

Sanctuary and Temple are found in every one of Israel, as the Torah says: *"I will dwell within them."*[30] These are present insofar as a person makes it clear to himself that all of life-energy comes from the soul. Thus we say each day in the prayerbook: *"The soul You have placed within me is pure . . . ."* This means that there is a certain pure place within each Jew, but it is indeed deeply hidden.

When the Temple was standing, it was clear that all life-energy came from God. This is the meaning of the phrase: *the indwelling of Shekhinah [in the Temple] was witness that God dwells in Israel.* But even now, after that dwelling-place has been hidden, it can be found by searching with candles. The candles are the mitzvot; we need to seek within our hearts and souls in order to fulfill a mitzvah with all our strength. The word *NeR* (candle) stands for *Nefesh Ruah* ("soul" and "spirit"). To fulfill a mitzvah in this way we also make use of all our 248 limbs. These, combined with love and fear, together add up to the equivalent of the word *NeR* (248 + 2 = 250/*Ner*). Then we are ready to find the sanctuary, to come to that hidden point within.

Especially at this season, when lights were miraculously lit for Israel, there remains light even now to help us, with the aid of these Hanukkah candles, to find that hidden inner light. By the power of the mitzvot that you do with all your strength, you can arouse the inner life-energy, which is the pure point. Of this, the Bible says: *"Seeking out all the belly's chambers."* By the power of inwardness we can find the hidden light within all our own inner chambers.

This is the meaning of the statement: "A person must always measure himself as though a holy being dwelt within his innards." Of a person who conducts himself in this way it is written: *"Let them make Me a sanctuary and I will dwell within them."*[31] Truly within them![32]

Arthur Green comments: *The Hanukkah candles are here reinterpreted as a spiritual symbol. They are the light of the mitzvot by which we search out our inner selves. We are looking for the hidden divine light within ourselves; the mitzvot are light-seeking candles, instruments given to us to aid us in that search.*

Hanukkah is the time of rededication, making the Temple once again pure enough to be a dwelling-place for God. Our inner Temple, too, needs to be dedicated anew, to become again the place where God can dwell "within them."

My grandfather and teacher quoted the Gemara that says: "Wicks and oils that the Rabbis said not to use to light Sabbath lamps may be used for the light of Hanukkah." This, he explained, refers to the impure souls within Israel. The word *NeFeSh* (soul) stands for *Ner/Petilah/Shemen* (lamp/wick/oil). Those that cannot rise up on the Sabbath — because "the light skips in them and [the wicks] are not drawn up" — can be brought up on Hanukkah.

These holidays of Hanukkah and Purim belong to the oral Torah. The three festivals which God gave us, [Pesach, Shavuot and Sukkot], are commanded expressly in the written Torah. God gave us those holy times, sanctified since Creation, for all was created through the Torah. They bear witness that the blessed Holy One has chosen Israel and is close to them, giving them his holy testimony. The word *mo'ed*, used for these festivals, is related to *edut* (testimony).

But Hanukkah and Purim are special times that Israel merited by their own deeds. These are called oral Torah; they are witness that Israel chose the blessed Holy One. Israel are

27. *Sefat Emet: The Language of Truth* is translated and interpreted by Arthur Green, 1998, p. 377 ff., published by the Jewish Publication Society. Used by permission.
28. *Proverbs* 20:27   29. *Zephania* 1:12
30. *Exodus* 25:6   31. *Exodus* 25:8
32. *Sefat Emet* 1:198

joined to God and their deeds arouse God, for here they are capable of creating new sacred times by their deeds. And because these holidays were brought about by Israel's own deeds, every Jewish soul can be restored through them. Every single Jew can find a way of belonging and attachment.[33]

> Arthur Green: *Every Jewish soul is kosher enough to be a candle in God's menorah! This is our holiday, one that became sanctified only because of our actions, not by original divine intent. For this sort of holiday no one needs to feel inadequate or insufficiently holy to participate.*

Because Hanukkah and Purim were brought about by Israel's own deeds, every Jewish soul can be restored through them.

> *It is interesting to note that such "Hanukkah and Purim" Jews existed already in Warsaw of the 1870s, when this teaching was given. Jews who were not "holy" when it came to observing the Sabbath every week still showed up at the rebbe's for the lighting of Hanukkah candles and were given a chance to warm their souls by the light of his teachings.*

The word Hanukkah can be divided and read as *hanu koh*, meaning "Thus did they camp." The essential miracle of Hanukkah was the victory in battle over the wicked Hellenistic kingdom. The Rabbis, wanting to show that the true joy of liberation from human bondage is that we are enabled to become servants of God, gave it this name.

We are taught that although there was sufficient oil to burn for only one day, it lasted eight days. This does not have to be seen only in temporal terms. "Eight" represents wholeness [completing the Sabbath cycle and beginning again]. Under the yoke of Hellenistic decrees, the power of holiness in the Jews was weakened, until only a tiny bit of it remained within them. After the terrible struggles and battles against the Greek

kingdom, they had no strength left to attain wholeness. Here God helped them, and the tiny point of holiness within them miraculously led them in an instant back to wholeness. They called this *Hanu-kah*, "thus did they camp," because here they attained true rest. Wholeness is the peace and rest of coming back to one's root.

All this shows that were it not for the evil forces and the wicked who cover over the power of holiness, Israel would be ready to ascend to the highest rung, to cleave to the Root above. But *"darkness covers the earth."*[34] As soon as they overpowered the Hellenists, they were blessed in a single moment and enabled to cleave to that Root above.

This should console our generations as well. Even though we see how lowly we are, how we sink lower and lower in each generation, we retain our hope that in a single moment, when the time of redemption comes, we may, with God's help, be carried all the way back to wholeness.[35]

> Arthur Green: *Here the miracle of the Hanukkah lights is interpreted symbolically, as it properly should be. The bit of oil that remained, miraculously lasting eight days, stands for the bit of strength that was present in the Jews, allowing them to last out the struggle with a much stronger enemy. In this Hasidic version it is the bit of holiness still within them, despite the violations of Judaism imposed by the Greeks, that blossomed forth into true wholeness as soon as the oppression was improved.*

---

33. *Sefat Emet* 1:207   34. *Isaiah* 60:2
35. *Sefat Emet* 1:211

6.

THE CHRISTIAN CULT OF THE MACCABEES
JUDAS MACCABEUS AND JUDITH AS SAINTS

*Crusader knight,
14th century Florence*

The Christians sanctified the Books of the Maccabees and of Judith contained in Egyptian Jewry's Greek Bible, the Septuagint.

Although Martin Luther, the founder of the Protestant Reformation, later relegated the Maccabees to the Apocrypha, the supplement to the Old Testament, both Catholics and Protestants revere the Maccabees, the religious martyrs like Hannah and warriors like Judah and Judith. Hanukkah is even mentioned in the New Testament. "It was the Feast of Dedication of the Temple at Jerusalem; it was winter."[36]

The Church Fathers (100-400 CE) fortified their congregants during the era of Roman persecution of Christian martyrs by praising the Maccabean martyrs — Hannah and Elazar. Gregory of Nazianzus identified Hannah's grief over her martyred seven sons with Mother Mary's grief over the crucified Jesus. St. Augustine designated August 1 as the spiritual birthday of the Maccabean saints (Commemoratio Sanctorum Macchabaeeorum Martyrorum). In Antioch, Syria, a church was built to house their relics, the bones of the Maccabees, and in the 6th century the bones of Hannah and her seven sons were reinterred in Rome on orders of

the pope. They are now located in the same church, San Pietro in Vincoli, in Rome, as is Michaelangelo's statue, "Moses."

In the Middle Ages the Christian warrior kings and knights identified with Judas Maccabeus and Judith. Below we have brought two selections from historian Barbara Tuchman's The Bible and the Sword, *about the 10th century English King Alfred and his Abbot Aelfric and about the Crusader King Richard the Lion-Heart, leader of the Third Crusade.*

In the modern era "Judith" was the subject of many European plays and "Judas Maccabeus" became one of Handel's great English oratoria (1746).

JUDAS AND JUDITH,
HEROES FOR KING ALFRED AND ABBOT AELFRIC

by Barbara Tuchman[37]

As the annual terror of the Norsemen [the Viking invaders from Norway who conquered and pillaged northern Britain in the 9th-10th century] lengthened into territorial conquests, and as the hope of ridding the country of its enemies all but flickered out, last-ditch fighters like King Alfred and religious leaders like the Abbot Aelfric (died 1020) tried to inspire a sense of national resistance among the people. To spread religious education, but also to foster a fighting patriotism among his people, Aelfric turned to the example of the ancient Hebrews. In addition to translating the Pentateuch he epitomized most of the Old Testament in a running narrative about

Esther, "who delivered her nation," Judith, and Judas Maccabaeus. He explains his choice of the last by "the great valor of that family who prevailed so much in fighting against the heathen forces encroaching upon them and seeking to destroy and root them from the land which God had given them, and they got the victory through the true God in whom they trusted according to Moses' law. I have turned them also into English so read them you may for your instruction."

Judas Maccabeus, whose history Aelfric included in his *Lives of the Saints*, was, he says, "as holy in the Old Testament as God's elect ones in the Gospel-preaching because he ever contended for the will of the Almighty. He was God's thane [vassal, warrior, baron, knight] that most often fought against their conquerors in defense of their people."

---

36. *John* 10:22
37. Barbara Tuchman, *The Bible and the Sword* (p. 89-91). Permission was requested from the publishers.

An illuminated medieval Christian manuscript depicts the martyrdom of Hannah and her seven sons. Hannah and her children are shown being boiled to death in a pot while Antiochus, holding his sceptre, looks on. In the background, another female martyr is being crucified and stoned. Inset at the top of the illustration shows the crucifixion of Jesus which, according to Christian interpretation, was foreshadowed by the death of the Maccabean martyrs, 200 years earlier. This illustration accompanies the translation of IV Maccabees by Erasmus of Rotterdam, 1517, and all the scenes are portrayed as foreshadowing the persecution and death of Jesus.

(Courtesy of the Library of the Jewish Theological Seminary of America)

Judas then girt himself with his shining breast plate
Even as an immense giant and completely armed
   himself
And guarded his host against the foes with his sword.
He became then like a lion in his strifes and deeds.

Likewise the story of Judith, Aelfric explains, "is also arranged in English in our manner as an example to you men that you should defend your land against the hostile host." Aelfric's homily on Judith's heroic tyrannicide was inspired by the most stirring of all the Anglo-Saxon Bible poems, *Judith*, which is supposed to have been composed in honor of Alfred's stepmother, the young Queen Judith (856 CE).

In the fragment that survives we read how Holofernes, drunk as a typical Saxon thane:

Laughed and shouted and raged so that all his folk
Heard far away how the stark-minded stormed and
   yelled,
Full of fierce mirth and mad with mead [alcoholic ale].

Judith enters the tent where the Assyrian king is sleeping off his drunken stupor; down flashes her glittering sword, beheading the tyrant. Triumphantly she holds aloft the black-bearded, blood-dripping head to the people assembled at the city's walls, exhorting them to revolt.

Proud the Hebrews hew a path with swords
Through the press thirsting for the onset of the spear.

Judas Maccabeus and Richard the Lion-Heart: The Maccabees, the Jews and the Bloody Crusaders

by Barbara Tuchman[38]

The Warrior Patriots: Richard and Judas Maccabeus

In some way men of the Middle Ages were able utterly to dissociate in their minds the contemporary Jews from the ancient Hebrews. The archetype of **warrior patriot** to whom both Richard the Lion-Heart and Robert Bruce were compared by their admirers was Judas Maccabaeus. In fact, it was the great captains and kings among the Hebrews, not their prophets, who particularly appealed to the mailed mentality of the age of "chivalry." Among the "Nine Worthies" of history, "three pagans, three Jews and three Christian men" whose figures so often appear carved over church doors or embroidered in tapestry, the three Jews were represented by Joshua (not Moses), David, and Judas Maccabaeus.

Richard the Lion-Heart's seal

Richard may have been a Maccabee in valor, strength, and strategy, but not in motive. He fought for fun, nor for liberty; that is, in Palestine. The fable agreed upon as regards Richard — a towering red-head — is of a sort of second King Arthur, which he was anything but. However, he provided England with a legend and with a feeling for the Holy Land as the locus of his legend, so that for his time and the hundred years that followed many an Englishman could have said: *"When I am dead and opened, ye shall find Palestine lying in my heart."*

His legend tells of the glorious tale of his prowess in Palestine as he hacked and slashed his way through the Saracen (Moslem Turk) ranks with sword in one hand and battle ax in the other. It was in Palestine that he became Richard the Lion-Heart and in Palestine that he was transformed from the quarrelsome, valorous, conscienceless man into England's first hero king since Alfred.

The Crusaders and Income Tax

At the outset the Crusades were set in motion by a thirst for gain, for glory, and for revenge upon the infidel [the Moslem conquerors of Jerusalem] in the name of religion. Exulting in bloodshed, ruthless in cruelty, innocent of geography, strategy, or supply, the first Crusaders in 1096 plunged headlong eastward with no other plan of campaign than to fall upon Jerusalem and wrest it from the Turks. This in some mad fashion they accomplished only because the enemy was divided against himself. Thereafter mutual dissension defeated them too; even the most elementary loyalty among allies that ought to have been dictated by a sense of self-preservation was lacking. For the next two hundred years the trail of their forked pennons [flags] across the heart of the Middle Ages was but a series of vain endeavors to recapture the victories of the first expedition.

The immediate cause of the Third Crusade was Saladin's capture of Jerusalem from the Franks in 1187. So great was the response that kings, nobles, and knights were taking the vow right and left until, says de Vinsauf, "it was no longer a question of who would take the Cross but who had not yet taken it." He reports, too, that it became the custom to send a distaff [an implement for spinning] and wool, token of a woman's role, to prod reluctant warriors.

Initially the Crusades were supported by placing alms boxes in all the churches for contributions in aid of the Templars, and a levy *ad sustentationem Hierosolymae terrae* [to sustain the Christians in Jerusalem] amounting to twopence in the pound for the first year . . . Later, one outcome of the fate of far-off Jerusalem was **England's first income tax**, devised by Henry II to meet the cost of the expedition. Crusaders were exempt, but everyone else had to pay a tenth of all rents and movables.

Henry died in July 1189. The rampaging Richard was king. He had taken the Cross two years earlier, within a fortnight of the news of Jerusalem's fall, and now he could be held back no longer. Unlike his father, he was unconcerned with the responsibilities of kingship or with England as a kingdom,

38. Barbara Tuchman, *The Bible and the Sword*, p. 50ff.

except as it gave him the opportunity to indulge in grand style his ruling passion for battle, adventure, and glory. The Crusade offered all these with chivalry's greatest gage [challenge], a renowned and valiant enemy, and salvation for his soul.

"The Sword of the Maccabees" and the Pogroms

Though armed with the "sword of the Maccabees," in the words of Pope Urban, the Crusaders struck their first blows at the people of the Maccabees before they ever left Europe. Every Jewish community on their path was put to the sword by the Christian warriors, who could not wait for the end of the journey to bathe their hands in blood. In part these massacres were an anticipatory lunge at the infidel in the person of the Jews who were the most convenient victims, the more so as it was rumored that they had devilishly inspired the Turkish persecution of Christians in the Holy Land. Partly also, the pogroms were an opportunity for loot, always a powerful motive among the Crusaders.

Popular hatred of the Jews was not a particularly active sentiment until inflamed by the Holy Wars. Medieval man's almost superstitious dread and detestation of the "heretic," the person outside the church, was one component. Another was the common feeling against the person to whom money is owed. Usury, the lending of money at interest, was practiced by the Jews in the Middle Ages because the guild system excluded them from other forms of livelihood, because their own law, while forbidding usury among themselves, permitted it toward non-Jews, and because usury, although Christian law forbade it among Christians, was necessary to the community. Ultimately, when the rise of capitalism and a money economy made it even more necessary, Christian scruples relaxed sufficiently to permit the practice of usury by themselves. But during the Middle Ages it was largely confined to the Jews, and through them it provided the Crown with a lucrative source of revenue.

The more the sovereign encouraged Jewish usury, the more the people hated the Jews. During the crusading era they learned that violence practiced under the banner of the Cross was a simple way to wipe out debt and to seize Jewish gold with impunity. By the time of the Second Crusade in 1146 its preachers were inveighing against the Jewish race in general, and the first recorded accusation of ritual murder [in which Jews supposedly used Christian blood for making matza] was brought in 1144 against the Jews of Oxford. By the time of the Third Crusade in 1190 the association of **Crusade and pogrom** was automatic, and the killings began immediately on Richard's coronation, though not at his order. Once started, they spread in waves from London to all the cities in which Jews lived, until the final ghastly climax at York, where the only Jews to escape slaughter by the mob were those who slew their wives and children and then died by their own hand.

"Jerusalem is Lost" and *Maoz Tzur*

[The red haired Richard the Lion-Heart of England (1157-1199) arrived in Eretz Yisrael in 1191 and valiantly recaptured the city of Acre from Salah-a-Din, brilliant commander of the Turkish Moslems. But Richard's ally, the red-haired Frederick Barbarossa of Germany (1123-1190), drowned on his march through Turkey. Due to bickering and disorganization, Richard never succeeded in recapturing Jerusalem. But his crusades kept him far from England where his corrupt brother John exploited his subjects. The legendary stories of Robin Hood focus on this period.]

Palestine was a lost cause. Exactly one hundred years after Richard the Lion-Heart broke the walls of Acre two hundred thousand Mamelukes marched against the Crusaders' last city. In 1291 Acre fell; the same year that Edward expelled the Jews from England the last Christians were driven from Palestine.

From the Crusaders' throats there first rang the sinister "Hep, hep!" *(Hierosolyma Est*

Perdita) (Jerusalem is lost!) that became the signal for Jewish pogroms from their day through Hitler's, or such is the Jewish tradition.

[Medieval German Jews wrote the last verse of the Hanukkah song, *Maoz Tzur*, with an explicit reference to red haired Frederick Barbarossa co-leader of the ill-fated Third Crusade. They prayed "Strike down the red haired son of Esau, the Roman Christian enemy of the Jews."

(below) Judas Maccabeus portrayed as a medieval Christian knight.

(16th century unknown French artist)

Judas Maccabeus — Oratorio by George Frideric Handel (1746) and Judith — the Play by Friedrich Hebbel (1840)[39]

When Handel began to work on the oratoiro *Judas Maccabeus*, he was caught up in the patriotic struggle of his patron the Hanoverian king of England who was threatened by an invasion led by his rival Prince Charles Edwards. In 1745-1746 the loyalists battled the invaders in Scotland, emerging victorious under the Duke of Cumberland to whom the oratorio *Judas Maccabeus* was dedicated. (At the same time the still-contemporary English national anthem was written.)

This oratorio reflects the popular nationalism of the day that saw in Judas the courageous defender against the Greek Syrian invaders.

Judas Maccabeus Act I reads, "Chorus of Israelites, Men and Women, lamenting the death of Mattathias, father of Judas Maccabeus." They pray for a new leader. Simon feels "the Deity within" and points to his brother Judas as the future liberator. Judas recalls God's traditional aid and his father's dying injunction to resolve on liberty or death. Disclaiming personal ambition, he leads the people to battle. In Act II the Jews celebrate at considerable length their victory. (The Jews of London were particularly enthusiastic supporters of this enormously popular oratorio, proud that Judas Maccabeus, rather than Judas Iscariot who betrayed Jesus, was the main character presented).

Handel continued the tradition of identifying Judith's and Judas' enemies with contemporary enemies. Hans Sachs (1551) wrote a play, "Judith," in which the enemy are the Turks then threatening the gates of Christian Europe. J. Greff (1564) identified the enemy as the Catholics besieging the Protestants. But the most sophisticated treatment of Judith is by the playwright Friedrich Hebbel (1840):

Hebbel himself remarks that he could not model his heroine on the Judith of the Bible, who deceives Holofernes and triumphs vociferously after she has murdered him in his sleep; for hers is a vile deed. In Hebbel's drama, Judith is still a virgin. She wants to save her people by a bold feat, but is enraptured by Holofernes and hates herself for it. Holofernes is a Near Eastern despot who envies Nebuchadnezzar for having first thought of making his people worship him as a god. He is given to pontificating about religion and morality. He violates Judith. After she has cut off his head, she realizes that she (like Schiller's *William Tell*) has not acted as representative of her people, but in order to avenge her virginity — that she committed the right deed for the wrong reason. She is plagued by doubts about whether her compatriots even deserved her sacrifice. In the last scene she addressed her people bitterly: "Yes, I have killed the first and last man on earth, so that you may let your sheep graze in peace, that you may plant your cabbage, and that you may pursue your trade and beget children who will be like you." As a reward she demands to be killed if she bears Holofernes' child: "Pray to God that my womb be barren. Maybe he will show mercy to me."

39. Joe Kirchberger, *Great Women of the Bible in Art and Literature*, p. 216, William Eerdmans Publishing Co., 1994. Used by permission.

Gallery:
A Children's Festival of Light

Menorah Shadows

The menorah casts its own shadow, and that of the little boy who lit it, onto the wall of his home.
(Kibbutz Tzora, December 1958, Central Zionist Archives, Jerusalem)

Kindergarten Celebration

A kindergarten in an immigrant transit camp celebrates Hanukkah with a homemade menorah, made out of Israeli oranges, displayed under a picture of Israel's first president Chaim Weizmann. A pile of simple gifts, donated to the immigrants, waits at their feet.

(December 1959, Central Zionist Archives, Jerusalem)

Hanukkah Toys for New Immigrants

A Child's Delight

Two new immigrant children in their transit camps enjoy their new Hanukkah gifts.

At left, a Yemenite boy rides his tricycle next to his tent (November 1950).
At right, a little girl proudly holds her new doll (December 1953).
The toys for new immigrants are collected annually in a drive organized by the Jerusalem Post.

(Central Zionist Archives, Jerusalem)

A Yemenite grandfather recites blessings on the second night of Hanukkah with his granddaughter in their new home in Israel.
(November 1950, Central Zionist Archives, Jerusalem)

50

From Generation to Generation

A Bukharan mother and her daughter from southern Russia celebrate their first Hanukkah in Israel, using a menorah made from glasses with oil and wicks.

(December 1949, Central Zionist Archives, Jerusalem)

A little kibbutznik stares up at the light created by his menorah.

(Kibbutz Tzora, November 1959, Central Zionist Archives, Jerusalem)

**Judas Maccabeus as a
medieval Christian knight**

(16th century, unknown French artist)

CHAPTER II

The Historians' Hanukkah:
Recalling the Worst Jewish Civil War

by Elias Bickerman and Victor Tcherikover

A medieval engraving of the battle of Judah the Maccabee in full medieval armor and plumed helmet.
(Courtesy of the Library of the Jewish Theological Seminary of America)

The Historians' Hanukkah:
Recalling the Worst Jewish Civil War

INTRODUCTION

THE JEWISH CIVIL WAR AT THE HEART OF HANUKKAH

FOR LOVERS OF HISTORICAL TALES

In this chapter we will present the history of the Maccabean period from a new and disturbing angle — from the perspective of an internal Jewish civil, economic and religious war. In the companion volume, *A Different Light: The Hanukkah Book of Celebration*, we presented readings from the *Maccabees' Megillah* (page 15). The dramatic moments in the Maccabean Revolt were retold using an abbreviated version of the original *Books of the Maccabees*. But now we will hear from the great **historians of the twentieth century** as they place these events into the broad context of the confrontation of Hellenism and Judaism. This should appeal to readers interested in history and politics.

The ***Historians' Hanukkah***[1] weaves together selections from the most creative historians of the Greek-Jewish encounter — Elias Bickerman and his chief scholarly adversary, Victor Tcherikover. Both are Russian-born academics who studied in Germany during the rise of antisemitism and emigrated — Bickerman to the United States and Tcherikover to Israel. While both of them are concerned with ancient internal Jewish conflicts, they offer opposed readings of the events. Just as we have presented a pluralism of religious views of Hanukkah, so too with varied historical perspectives. These historical selections are organized to follow the chronology of events from Alexander the Great to Antiochus and beyond Judah's initial victory and the rededication of the Temple (164 BCE) to encompass the founding of the Hasmonean Dynasty on the model of the Hellenist kingdoms (134-63 BCE).

Most of the historical narrative in this chapter is taken from Elias Bickerman

because his style is so clear and engaging. On a personal note, I recall the "aha experience" as a college student when I first read Bickerman's book, *From Ezra to the Maccabees*. Suddenly childish legends were enlightened by broad historical patterns. Bickerman's strongly argued case revolutionized my understanding of the Maccabees.

THE WORST CIVIL WAR IN JEWISH HISTORY

Most of us grew up on the prayerbook version of Hanukkah — the battle of the few against the many, the righteous believers against the wicked idol worshippers, the Jewish freedom fighters against the Greek conquerors. Historians, however, make the story more ambiguous and more interesting, and therefore more relevant to our world. According to them, the Jewish admirers of Alexander the Great's enormously successful empire, of the prosperous court of Antiochus, and of the excitement of the Greek Olympics, took the initiative in importing Hellenism into Jerusalem. These Hellenist Jews were the wealthiest, best educated, urbanized elites of the priesthood. Elias Bickerman argues that Antiochus never would have persecuted any Jew for his religious beliefs, if the High Priests in Jerusalem hadn't invited him to do so in support of their own Hellenist reforms. **Jews are persecuted first and foremost by other Jews, priests by other priests.**

In our contemporary era of increased Jewish ideological conflict between Orthodox and liberal Jews — Conservative, Reconstructionist, Reform and secular — we need to re-read the Hanukkah story as a civil war and learn its lessons. Its old heroes may no longer

---

1. Quotes are derived from Victor Tcherikover, *Hellenistic Civilization and the Jews*, copyright 1959, published by the Jewish Publication Society and used by permission and from Elias Bickerman, *From Ezra to the Maccabees*, © 1947, 1962, by Schocken Books and 1949 by Louis Finkelstein, reprinted by permission of Schocken Books, distributed by Pantheon Books, a division of Random House.

arouse such easy identification, but they may be appreciated even more when understood in a more sophisticated way.

In the following sections we will try to raise controversial issues in the historical tale, which have resonance for our contemporary situation, even though we will not directly address the present. For example, in reading what Bickerman has to say about **Mattathias the priestly rebel**, we may, on one hand, be reminded of contemporary religious fanatics and terrorists. Or, on the other, we may come to see him as a moderate religious reformer who helped lead the Rabbis to accommodate Jewish law to the historical need for survival. In reviewing the career of **Judah** and his brothers, we will see the military tactics of a freedom fighter but also the power of religious inspiration in a battle against a world empire. In studying Judah's brothers, we will discover the relative value of diplomacy that may have been even more important than actual military prowess in gaining independence from the Greek Syrians.

Victor Tcherikover offers a particularly penetrating analysis of the Maccabean revolt as a complex civil war with its ethnic, legal and class aspects, all of which are reminiscent of the way we see political struggles today. Both Bickerman and Tcherikover conclude their histories by relating to the ancient and yet contemporary question — *Did this Jewish state that arose after the Maccabean victory constitute just a new form of assimilation to Western forms, in effect, a capitulation to Antiochus; or did a Judaism with its own independent state create a truly Jewish state?* That is a matter of intense debate between Bickerman and Tcherikover because even today we are arguing to what extent Judaism and Western values are compatible. When our past is read in dramatic detail, it offers us analogies to our world, which will hopefully lead us to moderate internal Jewish conflict and develop a more pluralistic understanding of our people.

TIMELINE OF THE MACCABEES[1]

EARLY HISTORY

1700 BCE

722 —
Northern Kingdom of Israel is conquered by **Assyria** and ten tribes are exiled.

586 —
David's Dynasty falls when Jerusalem is destroyed with its Temple and the Jews of Judea are exiled to **Babylonia**.

circa 1700 —
Abraham arrives from Babylonia.

circa 1200 —
Exodus from Egypt

circa 1000 —
King David and King Solomon make **Jerusalem** capital of the United Kingdom of Israel and Judea, and erect the **Temple**.

539 —
Persian Emperor Cyrus allows Jews to return to Judea (539) to rebuild the Temple (516) and to establish Torah as the Constitution of Judea (Ezra, 450).

---

1. The chronology is based roughly on Elias Bickerman's timeline with variations in the light of other scholars' opinions. Sometimes articles in this book will use different dates than those in this timeline depending on the author being quoted.

1.

ALEXANDER THE GREAT (334-323 BCE) AND HIS JEWISH ADMIRERS (174-167 BCE)

In the days before the Maccabean Revolt there arose a great cultural alliance between Hellenist universalism and Jewish religious reform which foreshadowed some of the attempts of modern Jews to accommodate Judaism to Western civilization. Alexander the Great created the idea of a universal civilization based on Greek ideas, which came to be known as Hellenism. Every nation he conquered had to decide what its stand would be toward assimilation into his cosmopolitan religious culture. Many "progressive" Jews chose to abandon Judaism altogether. Others sought to reform Judaism in the Hellenist spirit. Below is the story of their motives and their issues in creating this reform version of Judaism, and why it engendered such resistance that it backfired and caused the Maccabees to revolt and defeat it.

ALEXANDER'S GREATNESS: HELLENIST INTERNATIONAL CULTURE

by Victor Tcherikover[2]

In spring 334 BCE Alexander of Macedonia crossed the narrow sea that divides Europe from Asia, and went to war with the King of Persia. In a few years he had successfully dealt the Persian army its deathblow and had put an end to the rule of the royal house of Persia. On the ruins of the mighty kingdom, which he had destroyed, Alexander established his own realm. Those eleven years (334-323 BCE) began a new chapter in the history of the ancient world, the so-called Hellenistic Period, chronologically set

2. *Hellenistic Civilization and the Jews*, p. 1,7

HELLENIST PERIOD

32 BCE

200 —
Antiochus III, the Greek Seleucid Dynasty of Greater Syria captures Judea.

174-172 or 171 —
High Priest **Jason** obtains the right to transform Jerusalem into a Greek polis (with a gymnasium) which is renamed "Antioch." Thereby he replaces the Torah as the constitution of Judea.

172 or 171-163 —
High Priest **Menelaus** bribes Antiochus IV to replace Jason and to completely Hellenize Judea.

167 December —
The Temple is rededicated to Zeus Olympius, the walls of Jerusalem are razed and the religious persecution of Jews begins. (**Book of Daniel** written).

332 —
Alexander the Great of Macedonia conquers the Persian Empire including Egypt and Syria.

3rd Century —
Greek Dynasty of Egypt — **Ptolemy** — rules Judea.

175-164 —
Antiochus Epiphanes IV replaces Onias the High Priest and governor of Judea with Jason in exchange for a bribe.

169 —
Jason recaptures Jerusalem from Menelaus apparently after hearing a false rumor that Antiochus IV was killed in war. In response, Antiochus IV puts down the revolt, robs the Temple of its golden Menorah, and builds a garrison fortress (Acra) in Jerusalem for Greek-Syrian soldier-settlers.

between Alexander the Great and the coming of the Romans to the countries of the East.

In order to bring the Macedonians nearer to the Persians, Alexander held a **great wedding** at Susa [Shushan in Persia where the story of Esther is set], in which at his command eighty eminent Macedonians married noble women of Persia. It is worth noting that the ceremony was according to Persian custom. Ten thousand Macedonian troops who wedded foreign wives received gifts from the king. His desire to merge the peoples affected even the Macedonian holy of holies — the organization of the army. Before the very eyes of the Macedonians, and despite them, he appointed generals from among the Persians, made Persians his bodyguards and even bestowed upon some of them the honorary title of "kinsmen of the king." The Macedonians tried to oppose him, but at last saw that they were incapable of breaking the king's will and gave in. Alexander, to celebrate peace and concord, held a splendid banquet in which Persians and Macedonians alike took part, while priests of Greece and Persian Magi poured libations and prayed for the welfare of those gathered. Thus did Alexander display at various opportunities his determination to efface the difference between victors and vanquished and to fuse westerners and easterners into a single nation.

Alexander died suddenly at Babylon, in the summer of 323 BCE, before he had lived to be thirty-three. What he would have done in the world had he continued to live is an idle question; but the work which he had succeeded in carrying out was sufficient to give the course of history a new direction. By destroying the Persian kingdom, Alexander had abolished the frontier between the East and the West and opened the countries of the Orient to the Greeks from the Mediterranean Sea to the frontiers of India. He had also shown to future generations the direction in which he desired the historical process to develop — **the merging of the East and**

164 or 163 —
Death of Antiochus in battle

160-142 —
Jonathan, Judah's brother, conducts guerrilla warfare, then allies himself to competing heirs to the Seleucid throne until Jonathan is officially appointed High Priest in 152, acknowledged by the Seleucid empire.

167 or 166 —
Mattathias the Priest refuses to sacrifice pigs to Zeus and declares a revolt which his son **Judah the Maccabee** leads.

160 —
Death of Judah: The defeat of Maccabees by Greek Syrians reinstates High Priest Alcimus, but does not renew forced Hellenization.

JUDEA INDEPENDENT

167 BCE

142 BCE

164 Kislev (December) —
The First Hanukkah celebrated on 25th of Kislev. After defeating one Greek Syrian army, Judah recaptures Jerusalem and rededicates the Temple.

163-161 —
After the **death of Antiochus IV** and a series of unsuccessful Greek Syrian campaigns against the Maccabees, the Greek Syrians cancel the persecution, reinstate the Torah as the constitution, kill the Hellenized High Priest Menelaus and appoint a traditional High Priest Alcimus. But Judah fights on defeating General Nicanor and then he signs a treaty with the rising Roman Republic for the political independence of Judea.

142-140 —
After Jonathan is assassinated, his brother **Simon** is appointed High Priest by the Greek Syrians, confirmed by the Judean assembly as Prince (*nasi*) and recognized as head of an independent state by the Greek Syrians and the Romans. The Greek Syrian garrison-citadel in Jerusalem, the Acra, is captured and dismantled, and the Jews begin to mint their own coins.

The Seleucid Empire and its Rivals

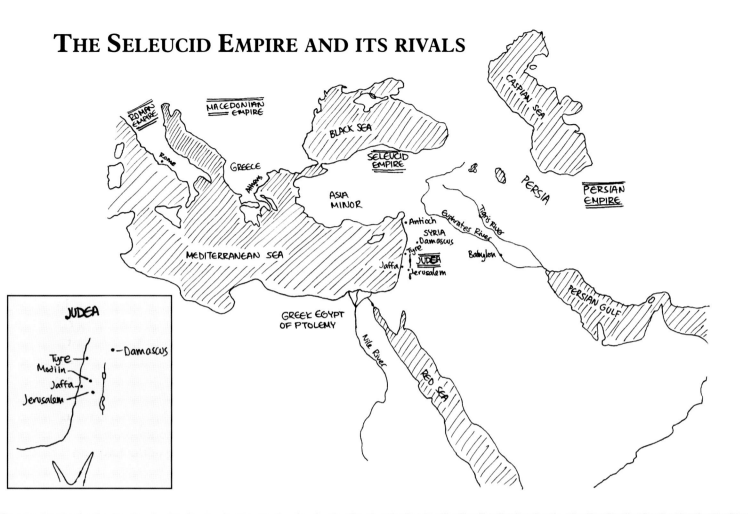

Roman Rule

63 BCE

37 BCE - 5 CE —
King Herod replaces the Hasmonean Dynasty in Judea but marries Hasmonean Marianne. Then he expands and renovates the Temple Mount. This is the era of Hillel and Shamai as rabbinic leaders.

5-66 CE —
Roman procurators rule Judea directly: Pontius Pilate orders the execution of Jesus.

134-63 —
Hasmonean Dynasty: King/High Priest John Hyrcanus (134-104 BCE)
(The *First Book of the Maccabees* is written).

Alexander Yannai (103-76 BCE)

Salome Alexandra (76-67 BCE)

Aristobulus II (67-63 BCE)

63 —
Roman Conquest: General Pompey invades Judea and appoints as governor, the Hasmonean subject-king Hyrcanus II (63-43 BCE) and later Rome appoints Antigonus Mattathias (40-37 BCE) who mints coins with the menorah imprinted on them.

66-70 CE —
The **Jewish Revolt** against Rome and then the destruction of the Second Temple and of all Jerusalem concludes with the fall of the Zealots on Massada (73 CE).

the West into one cultural body. History, indeed, confirmed the great king's dream. The fusion of peoples and cultures became a fact, although it was not realized at the pace that Alexander had hoped for, nor exactly in the form he had dreamed. The penetration of Greek culture to the Orient and the Orient's influence on the Greeks are the basic themes of the history of the centuries between Alexander's death and the conquest of the eastern lands by Rome.

THE UNPRECEDENTED GREEK THREAT TO JEWISH SURVIVAL

by Elias Bickerman

Until the time of Alexander the Great each **Oriental** people constituted a disparate unit, clearly differentiated from the others. There was no common supranational civilization; a Jew remained a Jew as an Egyptian remained an Egyptian. With the **Greek conquest of the East** (330 BCE), however, the situation changed. From its beginnings Greek culture was supranational, because the Greeks never constituted a unified state. In the East, Greek colonists lost their tribal peculiarities so quickly that the innumerable Greek papyri of the period, discovered in Egypt, show no variations of dialect. The new states in the East were the creation of the Greek race of Macedonia, as Alexander himself was a Macedonian. But their culture was Panhellenic, and was the same on the Nile as on the Euphrates.

The **Oriental** civilizations, on the other hand, were always based upon concepts of folk and religion. A man was born an Egyptian or a Jew, or became such when he forsook his own gods and served new gods. *"Your people shall be my people, and your God my God,"*[3] says the Moabitess Ruth to her Israelite mother-in-law Naomi, when Ruth resolves to follow Naomi back to Israel.

But **Greek culture**, like modern European culture, was based upon **education**. A man became a "Hellene" without at the same time forsaking his gods and his people, but merely by adopting Hellenic culture. A disciple of Aristotle presents his master conversing with a pious Jew whom he calls "a Greek man not only in language but in spirit." A century

later the great geographer Eratosthenes declared that men are not to be distinguished as Greek or barbarian, but rather according to their virtues or their vices ["for in the one the sense of right and community, of education and eloquence prevails, and in the other the contrary"]. Thus the Hellenistic epoch produced a new picture of man and the key concept in it was *paideia* (education). As the Greek Isoscrates put it:

> The designation "Hellene" seems no longer to be a matter of descent but of disposition and those who share in our education have more right to be called Hellenes than those who have a common descent with us.

Alexander's victorious expedition gave new possibilities to the idea of "Greeks by *paideia*." The Graeco-Macedonian soldiers, officials and merchants planted their customary institutions of education, the Greek school — the gymnasium. School and gymnasium together gave the Greek minority support against the threat of assimilation to the "barbarian" environment; they were "the basis on which Greek culture was built up." Here generation upon generation of the foreign ruling class received its traditional Greek education and life-style, which bound together all Greeks far beyond the boundaries of the world-empires.

During the three centuries which we call **Hellenistic** — that is, the period between Alexander the Great and Emperor Augustus (330 to 30 BCE) — the notion of the "Hellene," like the modern notion of the "European," grew into a concept independent of descent. In Hellenistic Egypt the whole population was officially divided into two classes: the natives, called the "Egyptians," and the immigrants, called the "Hellenes," regardless of their origin. In point of fact, the immigrants were Hellenized with singular rapidity. (As early as the third century BCE synagogues in Egypt were dedicated in honor of Greek kings and the Scriptures were translated into Greek. What could be more Hellenic and more alien to the Orientals than

---

3. *Ruth* 1

physical culture? But about 220 BCE we find in a Samaritan settlement in Egypt a gymnasium endowed by a Cilician, whose heir was a Macedonian.)

Whether or not to accept this culture was a question of life and death for every people.

In its tendency and in its claim, therefore, Hellenistic culture was **universal**. To it belonged the mighty of the world and the world's dominion. It was vested with the superiority that the judgement of war constantly reaffirmed. It was open to all. Whether or not to accept this culture was therefore a question of life and death for every people. **The nations of the ancient world were confronted by the same problem that confronts the Oriental peoples in the modern world from Tokyo to Cairo, whether to adopt the supranational and therefore superior European culture or else accept an inferior status.**

In antiquity the problem was actually solved by only two peoples, the Romans and the Jews. Other peoples shut themselves off from Hellenism and its effects upon them were therefore only negative. The native cultures were disintegrated and enfeebled. They lost their upper class, whose connection with the people had been ruptured by the process of Hellenization. (The Egyptians, for example, deprived of their upper class, their intellectual elite, for centuries lagged behind the inexorable march of history and so suffered the fate of enslavement to foreign conquerors).

Strategies of Jewish Survival: Separatism or Accommodation?

For **Judaism**, then, the *question of its historical existence or disappearance depended upon its ability to accommodate itself to Western culture*. But in the days of the Maccabees, the **law**

interposed a wall between Jews and non-Jews. Nothing brings people closer together than a common table. But dietary laws forbade the Jew to taste the food of the non-Jewish neighbor. There is no closer tie than the bond of matrimony. But the Jews told with approval the story of a father who abandoned his own daughter in order to free his brother from a passing attachment to a pagan dancing girl. [To a man of the Hellenistic age this "separation from the nations" could be regarded as nothing else than the expression of a Jewish "hatred of mankind."] No one outside Jewry itself has ever recognized positive merit in the separation. When the Jew declined to associate with pagan slave women, such an attitude seemed an invidious distinction even to a friend of the Jews, who posed the question: "Are they not human beings like yourself?" [The ritual separation of the Jews became one of the chief causes of ancient antisemitism. According to Eratosthenes (275-194 BCE), '*xenophobia*' was a typical characteristic of the barbarians: The ideal of the educated was not segregation in a national religion with separatist customs, but **world citizenship**].

To **"advanced"** Jews, therefore, it seemed imperative to let these bars fall. *"In those days,"* we read in First Maccabees, *"there emerged in Israel lawless men who persuaded many, saying, 'Let us go and make a covenant with the nations that are around us; for since we separated ourselves from them, many evils have come upon us.'"* [As in the traditional Jewish view, these "lawless men," these Hellenist Jewish reformers, present disaster in history as a punishment for the wrong conduct of the people. But its content is turned upside down: the catastrophe of past history has been caused, they claim, not by imitation of the Gentiles and their idolatry, but by separation.] *"In those days"* denotes the reign of the Syrian King Antiochus IV, surnamed Epiphanes (176-163 BCE). The new King entrusted the position of High Priest at the Temple in Jerusalem — and hence the rule over Judea — to men of that same "advanced" party, first to a man who called himself by the Greek name of Jason (about

175-171 BCE), then to Menelaus (171-162 BCE). These **Jewish "Hellenists"** promptly received royal approval for establishing a Greek community in Jerusalem, and with it permission to erect a gymnasium.

Jerusalem becomes Antioch

In 169 BCE, then, a regular **Greek city** surrounded by walls and fortified by towers, was founded upon one of the hills of Jerusalem, opposite the Temple Mount. The name of this city is unknown; in our tradition it is referred to simply as **Acra**, that is to say, the Citadel. Henceforward the Sanctuary was dependent upon this Greek city. This was only natural. The Hellenistic culture, understandably enough, had first affected the upper classes, the Jerusalemites and the priesthood. When the signal went up for the exercises upon the athletic field to begin, it was the priests who hastened to the contests and surrendered their priestly linens for the nakedness of Greek sports. Greek marks of distinction were prized above old-fashioned, native honors. **People strove to appear wholly Greek** — externally, by removing the marks of circumcision through a painful operation; inwardly, by participating in the games in honor of the foreign gods and even by contributing money for sacrifices to these gods.

But the leaders of the party understood perfectly well that all this must remain merely a diversion of the upper classes as long as the Sanctuary remained

A drawing of a Greek soldier found on a ceramic vase in ancient Greece.

inviolate and as long as the Law enjoining misanthropic [humanity-hating] separation continued in force. Like the **Emancipation** of the nineteenth century, that of the second century BCE must have necessarily led to **religious "reform."**

All of ancient life was carried on within the framework of cult acts whose execution did not entail complete belief. No gymnasium could be without the images of such patron gods of athletics as Heracles and without honorific statues of the kings. Every public act was invariably accompanied by sacrifice and invariably involved prayer. To accept Western culture fully, therefore, there appeared no other alternatives than **either** to renounce the ancestral religion, to which any participation in the cult of the gods was an abomination, **or** to transform the ancient law. Many Jews of antiquity chose the first course. (Among them, for example, was Tiberius Julius Alexander, nephew of the Jewish philosopher, Philo, of Alexandria. Tiberius pursued a military and administrative career that raised him to the highest stations. Among other things, he was chief of staff to Titus at the conquest of Jerusalem in 70 CE).

The First "Reform Jews" in History

Jason and Menelaus, in the reign of Antiochus Epiphanes, wished to follow the other course; they desired to accommodate traditional Judaism to the times. Their intention was to preserve those characteristics of the **Jewish religion which suited Greek taste** — the imageless God, for example — but to remove everything which smacked of **separation** of the "ghetto:" Sabbath observance, beards, circumcision and that namelessness of God which was otherwise to be met with only among the most primitive peoples.

Henceforth the Lord on Zion must bear a name, which could be communicated to Greek friends who might inquire what manner of God it was that the people of Jerusalem worshipped. In Greek that name was **Zeus Olympius**. For some time the Jews had been

> Henceforth the Lord on Zion must bear a name, which could be communicated to Greek friends who might inquire what manner of God it was that the people of Jerusalem worshipped. In Greek that name was Zeus Olympius.

in the habit of calling their God "Lord of Heaven," or even simply "Heaven," as is the regular practice in the First Book of Maccabees. But for the Greeks the Lord of Heaven was Zeus Olympius. In Aramaic the expression was probably *Baal Shemin*, under which title all the peoples of Syria worshipped the ruler of heaven. In this manner the "God of the Jews" was now accepted into the general pantheon. Now He was no longer worshipped in the dim light of the Holy of Holies, but under the open sky, in an enclosure, as was the practice in the most highly revered sanctuaries of Syria and in keeping with the Greek ideal. Even after its transformation, the cult naturally remained aniconic [without images] — educated Greeks had long ridiculed the notion that the gods had a human form. But the presence of the Almighty was now symbolized by a "sacred stone" upon the sacrificial altar in the middle of the forecourt of the Temple. All the requirements of the law concerning the sacrificial ritual were rescinded. The pig was now approved as a sacrificial animal: prohibition of its use for sacrifice or food had seemed the most striking mark of Jewish separatism.

[The ancient Greek historian Diodorus justifies Antiochus Epiphanes' persecutions in 167 BCE based on the Jews' presumed hatred of humankind (misanthropy). He reports that when Antiochus had entered the Holy of Holies, he had discovered an image, which he supposed to be that of Moses who had created the misanthropic customs of the Jews:

> And since Epiphanes was shocked by such hatred directed against all humankind, he set himself to break down their traditional practices. Accordingly, he

sacrificed before the image of their founder (Moses) and the open-air altar of their god a great sow and poured its blood over them. Then having prepared its flesh, he ordered that their holy books, containing the xenophobic (anti-foreigner) laws, should be sprinkled with the broth of the meat. The **lamp**, which they called undying [the *ner tamid*] and which burnt continually in the Temple, **should be extinguished**, and the high priest and the rest of the Jews should be compelled to partake of the meat.][4]

After **December of 167 BCE** sacrifices on Mount Zion were carried out according to the new ritual. Offerings were made to the same God and on the same spot as formerly, but the manner was new and in direct opposition to the old. Moreover, the God of Abraham, Isaac and Jacob was no longer sole ruler in Jerusalem. Adaptation to the religious customs of the Greeks was impossible without the surrender of monotheism. And so the festivals of Dionysus were celebrated in Jerusalem, and perhaps Athene, too, figured among the new divinities; certainly the deified kings of the ruling dynasty were included.

At the same time the High Priest Menelaus procured a decree from the King prohibiting the Mosaic law and ordering the introduction of pagan customs. Such a measure was in complete accord with the thought of the **Greek social reformers**, who, since Plato, had always regarded the lawgiver as the creator of social life. According to the historical principles basic to Greek thought, Jewish law was the invention of Moses, enjoined by him upon his followers. If Menelaus now wished to impose his own law upon the people, his conduct could not be regarded as improper. It was these measures that passed into the consciousness of contemporaries and posterity as the "persecutions of Epiphanes." With them the history of the Maccabees begins.

---

4. Diodorus XXXIV/ V.1

THE STRANGE ALLIANCE OF IMPERIALISM AND DEMOCRACY

by Victor Tcherikover[5]

How could Greek democracy be used to oppress the majority of Jews and other Oriental peoples to whom Alexander brought the enlightenment of Hellenism?

I used to be confused when I heard about Greek culture, to which I have a positive attitude, and then about Antiochus, the Greek tyrant. When I think of the Greek polis (city-state) I think of democratic politics, yet the transformation of Jerusalem into a polis (174 BCE) called Antioch dedicated to a tyrant and an imperial king named Antiochus Epiphanes (the deified one) provoked the Maccabean revolt for freedom from Greek "democracy." The following piece elucidates the relationship between imperial politics and "democratic" cities. The Hellenist empire used the Greek city-state model to create allies in its subjugation of the Oriental lands. Democracy for citizens of the polis was extended only to Orientals who would become thoroughly Hellenistic in religion, name and culture. [Editor]

The Independence of the Greek City

The most prominent feature of the Greek cities of the classical period was their independence. The Greeks took it for granted that no city (*polis*) could exist except under conditions of liberty. Two terms were the constant watchword of the cities in all their struggles against one another: "**autonomy**" — the right to conduct the city's affairs according to its own laws, and "**liberty**" — non-subjection to any power whatever outside the city. The original Greek *polis* was not a city in our sense of the term, but a petty state. Questions of war and peace, the making of alliances with other cities, monetary arrangements, the drafting of laws and statutes, the internal authority — all these were conducted by the members of the city with complete freedom and without coercion from outside.

In those cities which were conducted according to the rules of democracy (such as Athens), the whole people (the *demos*) participated in the exercise of power and everyone had the right to express his opinion in the general assembly of the city. The citizens elected a city council, which decided all questions on the agenda. This right to self-government constituted the outstanding superiority of the town over the village. Yet from the economic point of view the city itself was a sort of large village; not only merchants and craftsmen but also landowners and working farmers dwelt there as citizens and most of the lands about it were the private property of its members. Thus, in the economic sense, the town did not cease outside its own gates, but extended over a wide area round about, so that its borders touched the borders of the next city.

Every Greek city was surrounded by a **wall** and this fortification symbolized its independence. The greatest catastrophe and disgrace that could befall it was to be deprived of its rights, as a sequel to an unsuccessful war or an internal revolution. In such case the town was humiliated and deposed from its political eminence, its walls were dismantled, and it became a village. Such occurrences the Greeks called "the destruction of the city."

The Hellenistic Empire and its Cities in the East

Alexander was the first of the Hellenistic kings to build Greek cities in the eastern countries. He founded Alexandria of Egypt with the intention of creating an important commercial city which would serve as a bridge between Greece and the land of the Pharaohs. In the countries of central Asia and in western India, he built a large number of "Alexandrias" in order to fortify the frontier of his empire.

[The Macedonian generals who succeeded Alexander] introduced new political principles into the life of the ancient world making the main motivating factor the **unrestricted strength of a forceful personality aspiring to power**. The Macedonian people produced within a brief space a large number of aggressive characters, who used the confusion of the period to make themselves absolute rulers. Two men — Ptolemy and Seleucus — at length emerged victors from the hurly-burly of the period of the Diadochi.

---

5. *Hellenistic Civilization and the Jews*, p. 8-9,16,21-24,27-29,31-34

Seleucus obtained the largest portion of Alexander's empire; all the countries of Asia from the frontiers of India to the Mediterranean were under his rule. Seleucus I and his son Antiochus I founded a large number of Greek cities in Asia Minor, Syria, Mesopotamia, Persia, Media and Afghanistan. Every new city needed a name, and its endowment with such was in the Hellenistic period an act

The Hellenistic Age and the Contemporary Global Village

"Hellenistic," of course, must not be confused with "Hellenic." **Hellenic** refers to Greek culture in the period before Alexander (323 BCE), the classical period of Athens, while **Hellenistic** refers to the fusion of Greek and Oriental culture in the period after Alexander, when most of the urban populations of the Alexandrian Empire were as much at home in the Greek *lingua franca*, the *koine*, as most urbanized people are today with English. In fact, our contemporary global village reminds us of the Hellenistic age.

As in our day of the United Nations and the international court in the Hague, Alexander, encouraged by the philosophers, was inspired by the idea of a world civilization. "Ecumenical," today a Protestant term for interfaith dialogue, is derived from the Greek word *oikoumene*, which means "inhabited land" and assumed in Hellenistic thought the connotation of something like "one world" or "the brotherhood of man." His successors established scores of Greek city-states throughout Egypt, Palestine, Phoenicia, Syria, Asia Minor, Mesopotamia and Iran. These new foundations, or refoundations, of older Oriental cities became centers of Greek political institutions, science and art in western Asia and North Africa.

The political thinking of most educated men tended toward individualism and world citizenship, or cosmopolitanism, all of which were a creation of Stoic philosophy, itself a product of the Hellenistic period. Along with the idea of world community there flourished, first in Greek philosophy and later in Roman law, the idea of a "law of nations." As in our generation, national differences were being dissolved and individuals were eclectic in choosing their spiritual world. How could the powerless Jewish minority and its provincial Judaism survive this political, economic and religious steamroller? Isn't that our contemporary challenge as Jews today?

(Based on Ralph Marcus, "The Hellenistic Age" in *Great Ages and Ideas of the Jewish People*, edited by Leo Schwartz, Random House).

of importance to which political value also might attach. The vast majority of the names belonging to Greek cities were dynastic in origin and proclaimed their founders, who named them either after themselves or after their forebearers. Side by side with the "Alexandrias" there arose flourishing "Antiochs" and "Seleuceias," extensive and important cities.

[Theoretically the Greek cities were regarded as "**allies**" of the king; their relation to him was not that of subjects to their lord, but of two political powers possessing equal rights. The defense of city rights, of their "freedom" and "autonomy," was a matter of honor in the eyes of the kings and an attribute of civilized political behavior. Hence the kings accorded license to the ancient cities "to live according to their ancestral laws," that is, they confirmed the traditional constitutions of the cities. They also permitted new ones to conduct their internal affairs freely, to elect a council and officials, to strike coins, to hold athletic contests, and so on. Each city possessed laws of its own, according to which its officials conducted its public life].

Democracy for the Elite

Let us now turn to the inner life of the Greek town in the East. The urban population was divided juridically into two parts: citizens and mere inhabitants. [In Athens it is estimated that 80% were slaves and foreigners. All the natives living around the city in the agricultural hinterland as well as low-born persons born and bred within the city were subject to the rule of the minority of Greek citizens of the *polis*]. Only the [male] citizens enjoyed all civic rights, while the residents were regarded as foreign-born natives, although they might have been born in the city and have grown up there.

The citizen educated his sons in the municipal educational institutions — the *gymnasium* (for ages 17-20) and the *ephebeion* (for ages 14-16), which were the very embodiment of the spirit of Hellenism. Here the young citizens received their Hellenic education, developed their strength and agility by physical exercise, and learned poetry and music. [Literary instruction concentrated on one language — Greek, and on one book — Homer's epic tale of war, *The Iliad*. There was no test or report card because the public contests in all fields generated their own intrinsic motivation. The very idea of **constant competition**, the *agonistic* ideal of life, basically goes back to Homer. Its overall object was to fashion the ideal of Greek gentlemen. Because of its slant towards sport and its spiritual foundation in the chivalrous ideals of the Homeric world, Hellenism acquired an expressly aristocratic character. After hesitation at some unusual manifestations like the competition of naked youths in the *palaestra* had been overcome, it could also exercise a stronger attraction over the youths of subject peoples than the educational ideal of the oriental scribe, which was predominantly directed towards religious attitudes and traditional "wisdom"].

The oriental peoples were ignorant of this gymnastic education, and physical culture was

---

These athletic assemblies were for the Greeks not simply amusements, but affairs of the greatest gravity and moment, not only culturally but also politically.

---

generally alien to their outlook; hence the *gymnasium* became the symbol of Hellenism.

An inner connection existed, moreover, between the gymnasia and the **athletic contests**, which were held in the large cities every four years. The large crowds, which attended the contests, imparted to them the character of immense demonstrations in honor of Hellenism. These athletic assemblies were for the Greeks not simply amusements, but affairs of the greatest gravity and moment, not only culturally but also politically. During the festivals the Greeks were sensible of the living bond between themselves and all

their fellow Greeks scattered over the world, a bond that bound them to ancient Greek tradition and to their mother-country.

Religion occupied an important place in the life of the Greek city; it is possible to state without exaggeration that its entire public life revolved within the framework of Greek religion. Every *polis* had its particular god who was its guardian and whose cult was the focus of the religious life of the citizen body. [Moreover, the gymnasium possessed its own guardian deities: Hermes, Heracles and the muses. Young people at school played an important role in the feasts that honored the gods of the city. In the Hellenist monarchies the ruler cult gained overwhelming significance in the gymnasia in particular; this tendency to revere human heroes and benefactors as gods began at an early stage in the gymnasium].

To obtain the privileges of a *polis* was very beneficial to the economic development of a city. It received the right to strike bronze coins for the local market and to take part in international Hellenist undertakings (such as the athletic contests) which constituted a convenient means of creating political and economic connections with other countries. The city could further anticipate that the favor of the sovereign founder whose name, or alternatively whose father's or mother's name, it had received, would not be withheld in an hour of need.

The wealthy bourgeoisie of the Orient and the upper strata of the landed aristocracy and of the priesthood were interested in the conversion of their towns to a *polis*. They were prepared to purchase the valued privileges even at the price of some concessions in their traditional regimes, since every conversion of an oriental town into a Greek *polis* was bound up with the Hellenization of its social life. The king, for his part, was interested in the Hellenization of the eastern cities, since in this way he gained loyal friends among the local population. Thus an alliance was formed between the wealthy bourgeoisie of the ancient oriental towns and the Hellenistic kings, an alliance whose external mark was the exchange of the city's traditional constitution for the new constitution of a Greek *polis*. A "Greek city" means a city organized in the form of a Greek *polis*, not a city whose inhabitants were racial Greeks.

[When Jerusalem became a *polis* named *Antioch*, it ceased to be a Temple-centered *ethnos* (an ethnic province with its own recognized cultural traditions). It became a *democracy* for the elite only, wealthy Hellenized urbanites who could afford the education of their children. **Thus democracy and Westernization became tools for the oppression of the vast majority of Jews in the imperial state inspired by Alexander the Great.**]

Antiochus on his royal horse directs the massacre of Jews in Jerusalem, disregarding their pleas for mercy expressed by their clasped hands.

(Jean Fouquet's illustrated manuscript of Josephus' Antiquities)

2.

KING ANTIOCHUS THE "MADMAN" VERSUS HANNAH AND HER SEVEN SONS

THE CONFRONTATION BETWEEN AN EMPIRE AND THE INDIVIDUAL, BETWEEN RELIGIOUS PERSECUTION AND THE FIRST MARTYRS IN HISTORY (167 BCE)

by Elias Bickerman

At the end of the year 167 BCE, approximately in December, by order of Antiochus IV Epiphanes, King of Syria and so ruler of the Jews, the Temple on Zion was desecrated and given over to the uses of idolatry. At the same time the law of Moses was rescinded by a decree of the King. Observance of the commandments of the Torah, such as circumcision and the sanctification of Sabbath and New Moon, was made a capital offense. In addition, the Jews were required to worship the gods of the Gentiles. Altars were erected to these gods in every locality and the populace was commanded to offer sacrifice to the new deities. It was the **pig**, precisely the animal regarded by the Jews as unclean, that was the most acceptable offering to these gods. Pigs were offered even upon the altar of the Sanctuary at Jerusalem, upon which each day, in early morning and at the approach of evening, offerings had been made to the God of Israel. The "abomination of desolation" (probably an idol of Zeus) hovered over the Sanctuary and the wrath of God over the people. Never before and never thereafter was the spiritual existence of Israel so imperiled. Was this not the last trial, that "Day of the Lord" so often proclaimed and threatened by the prophets?

The Book of Daniel (167 BCE)

A book has come down to us from this period of persecution, the biblical **Book of Daniel**. In the midst of these afflictions a seer perceived the significance of the ancient prophecies concerning the world empires, their wars, and the tribulations of the holy people. To Daniel, these prophecies seemed to speak of his own time, and thus he interpreted them for his contemporaries,

---

Daniel felt that the end of time was approaching, and he could see no salvation for the people other than through the direct intervention of God.

---

suiting them to the events during the persecutions of Epiphanes. He felt that the end of time was approaching, and he could see no salvation for the people other than through the direct intervention of God. He knew well enough that the Romans had just driven Antiochus Epiphanes from Egypt, and that the King was then waging a campaign in the East. Yet he refused to think of the possibility, frequently suggested by the prophets, that another earthly power might, in fulfillment of the divine plan, crush the persecutor to earth. Rather would Epiphanes yet conquer Egypt, he foretold: *"There shall be a time of trouble as never before"* — until *"there will arrive with the clouds of heaven one like a son of man"* to rule over the world forever. The reader of this book knew that supplication

and fast — but never a human act — might alter the course of events and shorten the period of tribulation.

Assimilation or Martyrdom in Jerusalem

Daniel's resignation was no accident. Judaism's cause seemed desperate precisely because the Jews showed no zeal in its defense. (Two centuries later, when the Roman governor Pontius Pilate had his standards bearing the image of the emperor set up in the Temple area, the people went to his headquarters at Caesarea and for five days and five nights besought him to remove the human likenesses from the Holy City. And when Pilate's soldiers surrounded the crowd with swords drawn, the Jews bared their necks. They preferred death to acquiescence — and Pilate yielded). But in 166 BCE Jerusalem was filled with monuments of the pagan cult, and the princes of Jerusalem together with the men of Judea obediently heeded the will of the earthly ruler. Altars were built before the doors of the houses and sacrifices were offered upon them, to make a public display of zeal for the new paganism.

Only a few proved unyielding and openly transgressed the commandment of the King for the sake of the commandment of the living God. They were seized, scourged, martyred, and slain. More numerous were those who sought to evade the order of the King. Without standing forth openly as Jews, they still avoided any participation in the idolatrous rites. In order to lay hold of these, officers of the King journeyed from city to city, coercing the people into open apostasy. They would cause an altar to be erected in the market place, summon the populace, and require them to worship the gods and taste the flesh of the offerings. Many refused, and suffered **martyrdom**. *"They shall stumble by sword and by flame,"* says Daniel of them, *"by captivity and by spoil, many days."*

PORTRAIT OF A MAD MISSIONARY:
ANTIOCHUS "EPIPHANES" BECOMES "EPIMANES"

by Victor Tcherikover[6]

The persecution of the Jewish religion known as "the evil decrees of Antiochus" has puzzled the scholars of our time. *What caused the Greek king, a man who had been reared and educated in the atmosphere of religious tolerance so characteristic of Graeco-Roman culture, to attack the Mosaic Law by force of arms*, to substitute the cult of the Olympian Zeus for that of the monotheistic cult of Jerusalem, and to prohibit circumcision, the observance of the Sabbath and the other Jewish practices, as if they were the customs of a nation both criminal and corrupt?

[Historians have made] many attempts to explain the reasons and motives of the decree:

(1) FIRST, LET US DWELL UPON THE METHOD WHICH LINKS THE ANTIOCHAN DECREES WITH THE **CHARACTER OF THE KING**. The classical historian Polybius has strange things to tell of him. He lacked political tact and did not understand how to behave as befitted a king. Sometimes he would leave his palace and wander through the streets of his capital with two or three of his courtiers, enter shops and the craftsmen's places of work and converse at length with these insignificant people. Once, during one of his habitual visits to the public baths he poured a jar full of perfumed ointment over the heads of the bathers and enjoyed the sight of the people rolling on the slippery floor, unable to rise or to keep their balance, himself among them. Particularly fond of taking part in the carousings of common folk, he was more than once seen in the shady company of aliens of unknown origin and identity. If he heard of some drinking party that was being held by young people, he would appear suddenly among the guests accompanied by an orchestra, making so strange an impression on the participants that fear fell upon them and many would make their escape. Sometimes he walked the streets of Antioch splendidly garbed and crowned with roses, showering upon those he met now rings of gold, now simple stones.

Like Nero two hundred years after him, he liked to participate personally in theater performances. Once during a magnificent festival, which he was holding at Antioch, he appeared on the stage before the audience as an actor, and began to dance with the other players. The Greeks had never seen their king in such a role, and many left the banqueting hall in shame. His behavior toward other people was full of contradictions and sudden surprises, for he was silent in the company of his best friends and talkative with strangers. To some he gave precious gifts such as silver and gold, and to others, without clear reason, worthless objects such as dates and dice. Irritable and nervous, full of profound inner contradictions, ever striving to do something extraordinary and to astound the world — this was the figure cut by King Antiochus in the eyes of his Greek contemporaries. Hence it is not to be wondered at that humorists mocked him and called him in jest *Epimanes* ("mad" — instead of *Epiphanes*," the god manifest").

(2) THE VIEW WHICH PREVAILED IN THE NINETEENTH CENTURY, AND STILL FINDS ITS DISCIPLES TODAY, HOLDS THAT THE MAIN MOTIVE FOR ANTIOCHUS' POLICY WAS HIS GREAT DEVOTION TO **THE HELLENISTIC SPIRIT AND CULTURE**. Many scholars see in Antiochus, the Hellenizer *par excellence*, who was determined to spread Hellenic culture among all his subjects in order to make it an instrument for uniting all the inhabitants of his huge empire into a single body. In contrast to all the rest of the population, who accepted Hellenization, however, the Jews alone resisted it. In Palestine Antiochus' Hellenistic tradition encountered another tradition, deeply rooted in the soil, and scholars offer differing evaluations of the fierce clash between Greek culture and Jewish monotheism — each scholar according to his general views on Hellenism and Judaism respectively.

If we turn to the sources, we shall find in them many facts, which appear to support this manner of thinking. Antiochus was

6. *Hellenistic Civilization and the Jews* (p. 175-181)

renowned in the ancient world as an enthusiastic Hellenist. The leaders of the Greek people explicitly emphasized that he was the first and only Seleucid king to bestow benefactions upon the Greek people and to concern himself with their many needs.[7] His

---

The king's ultimate aim was to introduce into his realm the worship of himself in the form of Zeus Olympius.

---

generosity to the Greeks knew no bounds. The novel character of Antiochus' activity was [his design not to build new Greek cities, but to intensify the Hellenism of those that

Maccabees IV: Elazar the Martyr's Death as a Prototype for Jesus

Philosophical Reflections on Rational Martyrs and Vicarious Sacrifice

*The Book of Maccabees IV (written by an author different than Maccabees I, II or III) is a reflection on the virtues of the Maccabean martyrs like the elderly Elazar who refused to eat ritually impure food and like Hannah and her seven sons who refused to bow down to Zeus and Antiochus. Their courage is attributed to the supremacy of reason — the highest Greek ideal — not to enthusiastic zealotry and blind faith. Early Christianity, which produced its own martyrs under Roman Imperial persecution, was deeply influenced by this notion of vicarious sacrifice and the saving efficacy of the death of the martyred righteous. Perhaps this notion of the **death of the pure as a "ransom for the sinful"** directly influenced the idea of Jesus' death as atonement for the sins of humankind. [See the "Cult of the Maccabees in Christianity" on page 42 and the article by Eugene Wiener on "The Sociological Analysis of the Martyr" on page 176]. Maccabees IV quotes Elazar's prayer:*

> "Be merciful to your people and let our punishment [as martyrs by the Greek Syrians] be a satisfaction on their behalf. Make my blood their purification and take my life as a ransom for theirs." That prayer was answered. "The tyrant was punished and our land purified, since they became a ransom for the sin of our nation. Through the blood of these righteous ones and through the atonement of their death, the Divine Providence rescued Israel."[8]

already existed. He turned the ancient oriental towns, which had not yet been Hellenized into Greek *poleis*, by granting them special political privileges]. Some eighteen cities were linked by name to that of the philhellenic king, [a king who loves and promotes Hellenism].

The great political importance of the Hellenization of these oriental towns is not to be denied. This policy created friends for Antiochus among the wealthy bourgeoisie of those communities and so considerably strengthened the entire state. It has already been observed that Antioch-at-Jerusalem also was intended as a link in the long chain of strongholds of the new Hellenism in the Seleucid Empire. *Second Maccabees* relates that at the beginning of the persecutions an order was published by the king to extend the persecution to the Jewish population of the Greek cities of Syria. In it the king ordered the execution of those Jews "who do not wish to go over to Greek ways of life."

(3) THIS [PREVIOUS] VIEW WHICH IS TO ALL APPEARANCES SUPPORTED BY SUCH CONVINCING PROOFS CANNOT IN FACT STAND UP TO CRITICISM, for the following reasons. The Seleucids were never "bearers of culture" and never intended to Hellenize the populations of the Orient on profound spiritual matters. Hellenization expressed itself in a purely external political form, that of the transformation of oriental towns into Greek *poleis*. There are no grounds for supposing that the "philhellenism" of Antiochus was expressed in any other form. Antiochus saw in **Hellenism a *political* means** of strengthening his state; but it never occurred to him to abolish local culture and to substitute for it the Greek. [Rather Antiochus sought political unification by adding a level of worship of himself as "*epiphanes*" — god-manifest.]

The **doctrine of "unification"** holds that Antiochus sought to strengthen his crumbling kingdom by political centralization and

---

8. *IV Maccabees* 17:21-23, written in the first century BCE in Greek

7. Polybius XXIX, 9,13

Persecution under Antiochus IV: Elazar the Scribe, compelled to eat pork, prefers to die.

cultural unification. The establishment of one religion for all the people of the state was part of his plan of reform [but it did not necessarily require prohibiting other forms of local worship]. This explanation too finds authority in the sources. *First Maccabees* 4:1 relates: *"And the king wrote to all his kingdom that all should be one people and that each people should abandon its customs; and all the peoples did as the king commanded."*

This interpretation has found unexpected support in numismatics. Coins afford evidence that under Antiochus Epiphanes the cult of Zeus Olympius took root in his dominions, being especially fostered by the king and replacing the traditional cult of Apollo, the divine guardian of the Seleucid dynasty. Specialists further point to coins of Antiochus on which the image of Zeus resembles the king's features. From this they conclude that **the king's ultimate aim was to introduce into his realm the worship of himself in the form of Zeus Olympius, and that this also was the cult which was to prevail on the Temple hill at Jerusalem.** This doctrine looks much better founded than the preceding. [Antiochus created a syncretic cult, mixing Greek and Oriental elements.] Zeus Olympius was actually an original Greek deity, but could easily be identified with any "chief" god of the oriental pantheon, and particularly with the Syrian "Baal Shamin." The God of Israel could also (in Antiochus' view, at least) be readily identified with Zeus, [so Antiochus did not expect that suppressing the Jewish religion would need to be part of his program].

Hellenist sources present the tortures used regularly by the Graeco Roman authorities. They seek both to titillate their readers who loved melodrama and bodily gore (like the gladiators) and to impress Jew and Greek alike with the physical and spiritual heroism of the "martyrs" who bear witness by bearing their suffering stoically. Interestingly enough, a woman — the mother Hannah — is portrayed in Second Maccabees 7 as the most ideologically steadfast. [Compare this version to the medieval midrash about Hannah in the companion volume, A Different Light: The Hanukkah Celebration, *page 42]:*

It happened that **seven brothers** were also arrested with their mother, and were tortured with whips and thongs by the King, to force them to taste of the unlawful swine's meat. One of them made himself their advocate and said, "What do you expect to ask and learn from us? For we are ready to die, rather than transgress the laws of our ancestors."

Hannah and her seven sons defy King Antiochus: "Indeed, who would not be astonished at the courage of this woman, who was worthy to be a proverb for many nations."
(II Maccabees 7:22)
(Julius Schnorr, 19th century Germany)

The King was infuriated and gave orders that pans and cauldrons should be heated. And when they were immediately heated, he commanded that the tongue of the one who had been their advocate should be cut out, and that they should scalp him and cut off his extremities, while his brothers and mother looked on. And when he was utterly crippled, the King ordered them to bring him to the fire and fry him. And as the vapor from the pan spread quickly, they and their mother encouraged one another to die nobly, saying, "The Lord God is looking on . . . ."

But when he was at his last gasp, he said, "You wretch, you release us from this present life, but the King of the world will raise us up, because we have died for His laws, to an everlasting renewal of life."

But their mother was surpassingly wonderful, and deserves a blessed memory, for though she saw her seven sons perish within a single day, she bore it with good courage, because of her hope in the Lord. And she encouraged each of them in the language of their ancestors, for she was filled with a noble spirit and stirred **her woman's heart with manly courage**.

When the youngest son paid no attention to him, the King called the mother to him and urged her to advise the boy to save himself. After he had labored with her a long time, she undertook to persuade her son. She bent over him, and mocking the cruel tyrant, she spoke thus, in the language of her ancestors:

"My son, have pity on me, who carried you nine months in the womb, and nursed you for three years, and brought you up and brought you to your present age, and supported you. I beseech you, my child, to look up at the heaven and the earth, and see all that is in them, and perceive that God did not make them out of the things that existed, and in that way the human race came into existence. **Do not be afraid of this butcher, but show yourself worthy of your brothers, and accept death**, so that by God's mercy I may get you back again with your brothers."

Before she could finish, the young man said, "What are you waiting for? I will not obey the command of the King, but I obey the command of the Law that was given to our ancestors through Moses . . . . I, like my brothers, give up body and soul for the laws of my ancestors, calling upon God speedily to show mercy to our nation, and to lead you to confess, in trials and plagues, that he alone is God, and to stay through me and my brothers the wrath of the Almighty, which has justly fallen on our whole nation."

But the King was infuriated and treated him worse than the others, being embittered at his mockery. So the boy passed away unpolluted, trusting firmly in the Lord. Last of all, the mother met her end, after her sons.

So much then for the eating of sacrifices and **excessive barbarities**.[9]

---

9. *II Maccabees* 7:1-6, 9, 20-21, 25-42

3.

MATTATHIAS — THE REBEL PRIEST

RELIGIOUS ZEALOT OR MODERATE REFORMER?

by Elias Bickerman[10]

In the course of the winter of 166 BCE the agents of apostasy [abandonment of one's religion] made their appearance in the town of Modiin, situated upon a hill near Lydda, on the road from Jerusalem to Jaffa. When the first Jew of Modiin stepped up to the pagan altar to sacrifice according to the King's will, Mattathias, a priest whose family resided in Modiin, sprang out from the circle of bystanders. He struck the man down so that his body was stretched out upon the altar, slew the agent of the government, and then pulled down the altar.

In the age of the European religious wars, in the sixteenth and seventeenth centuries, the legitimacy of Mattathias' conduct was vigorously debated. His hallowed precedent was held to justify subjects who oppose the authorities in questions of faith. This conception of his deed, which is not without significance even today, would have seemed strange and perhaps dangerous to Mattathias himself. In the speech, which *First Maccabees*[11] puts into his mouth, Mattathias does not dispute the right of the ruler to alter the laws of peoples subject to him. He does oppose an order of the King, which is at variance with the revealed commandment of God. The struggle is not one of an individual conscience for freedom of belief, it is rather **a conflict between earthly power and the law of the state of God**. Mattathias championed the Torah as once the Biblical Pinchas had done, when he slew Zimri, who dared worship the Baal of the Midianites.[12] But looked at through the eyes of worldly power, Mattathias' deed was **an act of political terrorism**. Mattathias and his five sons, John (Yohanan), Simon, Judah, Elazar and Jonathan, fled from its punishment into the mountains of Judea.

In those days many in Israel sought out the **wilderness**. In order not to desecrate the holy covenant they went into the desert with "their sons, and their wives, and their cattle." Such **passive resistance by flight was common in antiquity**. If an Egyptian peasant was oppressed by taxes, a debtor harried by his creditor, or later, a Christian persecuted for his faith, they took this means of eluding the reach of the state, whose organization was not yet so perfected as to lay hold of them. They forsook house and land and lived as wretched vagabonds, as is said of the Maccabees, "after the manner of wild beasts in the mountains." But the state suffered a falling off in revenues as a result, and yielded more and more in the course of time, until finally an amnesty was proclaimed.

In the meanwhile, however, agents of the government sought to lay hands upon the fugitives. In 166 BCE a search was instituted in Judea for those who had disregarded the King's command and had hidden themselves away in the wilderness. In this case the task of the police was rendered easy by a Jewish practice which seemed to the pagans the height of superstitious unreason. The Jews, lest they desecrate the day of rest, offered an attacker no resistance on the Sabbath. Thus in 312 BCE Ptolemy of Egypt had been able to take possession of Jerusalem on the Sabbath, without a blow. Now, too, the fugitives made no attempt to defend themselves on the day of rest. They neither threw stones at the enemy nor walled up the caves in which they had sought safety, but preferred to die in order conscientiously to fulfill the law of God for which they had forsaken their homes.

---

10. Elias Bickerman, *From Ezra to the Maccabees*, p. 96-101.
11. *I Maccabees*, 125 BCE   12. *Numbers 25*

Mattathias realized the situation: *"If we all do as our brothers have done, and do not fight against the pagans for our lives and our laws, they will soon destroy us from off the earth."* Mattathias and his people therefore resolved, not indeed to attack, but at least to defend themselves on the Sabbath day. This rule continued in force even in the great uprising against the Romans (66-70 CE).

Mattathias and his people therefore resolved, not indeed to attack, but at least to defend themselves on the Sabbath day.

Even more significant is the fact that **Mattathias ventured to interpret the law upon his own authority**. In his day this privilege was vested in the High Priest and his council, who governed Jerusalem and Judea. It was the High Priest to whom God had given *"authority over statute and judgment, that he might teach His people statutes, and judgments unto*

Mattathias Leads the Flight from the Oppressors: "And Mattathias cried throughout the city with a loud voice, saying, 'Whoever is zealous for the law, and maintains the covenant, follow me.'" (I Maccabees 2:27-28)

(Julius Schnorr, 19th century Germany)

the children of Israel." Mattathias, a man previously unknown, one priest among ten thousand, resolved to interpret the traditional law and to impose his interpretation upon the people and thus to infringe upon the prerogatives of the High Priest. He raised himself, perhaps without intending to do so, to the position of an **opposition government**. Hence his resolve constituted a turning point in Jewish history. His measure immediately gave him the authority of a leader. The "community of the pious" [the early Hasidim], a fraternity zealous for the law of God, joined him and his following was filled with those who fled the evil. Those who had abandoned their homes in order not to depart from the law "either to the right hand or to the left" were united by that very measure [suspending the observance of Shabbat for purposes of self defense] which infringed the Torah for the Torah's sake.

Strengthened by these additions, Mattathias determined upon another deed, which was pregnant with consequences. Hitherto, like the other fugitives, he had evaded the royal decrees in order to seek a refuge in the desert where he might fulfill the commandments. But now the Maccabees determined to replace passive resistance by **active struggle**. They made a stealthy and roundabout entrance into the villages and summoned together those eager to fight. The force moved from place to place destroying the idolatrous altars where they found them, compelling the observance of the Torah by force. For example, they circumcised newborn infants, and killed apostate violators of the law. Thus, as their historian relates, they liberated the Torah from the hand of the heathen.

As is clear from this account, the wrath of the Maccabees was poured over the Jews and not the heathen. The company of the Maccabees was an active minority that sought to restore its law to the people. This law was in no sense an innovation, but the revelation of Moses.

Greek General Bacchides' Calvary attacking Jerusalem.

(An illuminated manuscript made by the Crusaders in Acre, circa 12th Century)

4.

JUDAH THE MACCABEE

A GUERRILLA WARRIOR FOR RELIGIOUS FREEDOM (166-162 BCE)

by Elias Bickerman[13]

*The brilliant military strategist of the Maccabean Revolt was Judah, nicknamed in Greek, the "hammer." His **guerrilla tactics** and his power to inspire **religious enthusiasm** enabled him to do the impossible — to defeat army after army of the mighty Greek Syrian empire with a group of ragtag Jewish irregulars. Step by step he forced the Greek Syrians to retract their policy of persecution of Jewish practice, the paganization of the Temple and the repeal of the Torah as Judea's constitution. However in his own lifetime during which he liberated the Temple (164 BCE) just three years after the revolt began, he never achieved political independence. Only a long 25 years later, after more warfare and much more diplomacy, did Judah's brothers finally achieve that goal. Then they were recognized as the legitimate high priests and political leaders of an independent Judea (140 BCE). The political miracle took much more effort and perseverance than the eight-day burning of a vessel of oil.*

STAGE 1:

Guerrilla Warfare against the Jewish Hellenist Reformers

When, during 166 BCE (or at the beginning of 165), Mattathias died, leadership devolved, we do not know why, upon the third of his living sons, Judah, surnamed the *Maccabee*. For two years **Judah waged guerrilla war** like his father, making surprise descents upon the Jewish apostates without venturing to attack any walled cities or the tyrant's stronghold in Jerusalem.

At first, the central government paid no attention whatsoever to the Maccabean uprising. It must be remembered that the Seleucid empire extended from Egypt to the Persian Gulf, and that disturbances of this nature flared up constantly at one point or another. The handful of Maccabees could only be regarded as another robber band on the highways. But in the meanwhile Judah was steeling his company in guerrilla warfare. He also gave it a regular organization by appointing "captains of thousands, and captains of hundreds, and captains of fifties, and captains of tens." It would appear that his force amounted to something more than three thousand men.

It was important for the future course of events that the **Hellenist reform party** made no attempt at mustering its strength to put an end, once and for all, to the activity of the marauders. Their failure is easy to understand if we reflect that they belonged to the upper strata of the people, being city dwellers and Jerusalemites, and did not particularly relish chasing after the Maccabees through gorges and over stony hills. The mass of the peasantry, on the other hand, remained secretly devoted to the old faith.

---

13. *From Ezra to the Maccabees*, p. 112-126.

Judah ruthlessly extirpated the few in the countryside who followed the reform party, but at the same time he restored freedom of faith to the majority.

Before a battle Judah's company fasted, clothed themselves in sackcloth, rent their garments, and prayed devoutly to the Lord of Hosts: *"Behold, the pagans are gathered together against us to destroy us. How shall we be able to stand before them unless You help us?"*

STAGE 2:

The Guerrillas fight the Empire

The new pagans of Jerusalem, the "sons of Acra" [the Greek citadel recently built in Jerusalem], sought protection against Judah from the King's officers, whom they assisted moreover with auxiliaries, guides acquainted with the terrain, and the like. Judah defeated the troops that were sent against him, one after the other. When the Syrians were making a slow and laborious ascent to the pass of Bet Horon along the mountain path that led from the coastal plain to Jerusalem, they were suddenly attacked by swarms of Maccabees, routed, and pursued the length of the slope into the lowland. Schooled by this defeat in the hills, another Syrian army took up a position in the plain near Emmaus. This afforded a convenient post for controlling the roads to Jerusalem. During the night, under

> The success of Judah can be more readily understood, if we reflect upon the difficulties that guerrilla warfare in a hill country presents even to modern regular troops.

cover of the rough terrain, Judah led his company to a point south of Emmaus. The Syrian general planned to overwhelm the Maccabees by a surprise night attack. But, while the King's troops were looking for Judah's forces in the hills, Judah made an attack at dawn upon the Syrian encampment. Later in the day, when the Syrian troops approached Emmaus, they saw their camp in flames and fled to the Philistine country.

The success of Judah can be more readily understood, if we reflect upon the difficulties that **guerrilla warfare** in a hill country presents even to modern regular troops. The Seleucid armies were composed largely of contingents of [poorly paid] auxiliaries from various cities and peoples. The professional soldiery [of the Seleucid army] was employed only for more important enterprises.

It was now, in the fall of 165 BCE, that Judah's successes began to disturb the central government. He appears to have controlled the road from Jaffa to Jerusalem, and thus to have cut off the royal party in Acra from direct communication with the sea and thus with the government. It is significant that this time the Syrian troops, under the leadership of the governor-general Lysias, took the southerly route, by way of Idumea. They encamped at Bet Zur, a fortress about thirty kilometers south of Jerusalem that was the key to Judea from the south. Judah was forced to quit his hiding place in the hills and hurry southward. Still he defeated Lysias.

STAGE 3:

Antiochus Rescinds Religious Persecution

And so Antiochus Epiphanes resolved to call a halt to the persecutions. In a proclamation to the Sanhedrin and the Jewish nation, he declared that he had been informed by the High Priest Menelaus that the Jews who had fled from their homes, those loyal to the ancient faith, amongst whom were the Maccabees, desired to return to their legal abodes. Exemption from punishment was guaranteed all who returned by March 29, 164 BCE and in addition, the assurance was given that the Jews would be permitted "to use their own food and to observe their own laws as of yore." The persecution was thus ended.

The edict makes no mention of the Maccabees, by as much as a syllable. It is represented as an act of royal grace instigated by Menelaus. But such an interpretation

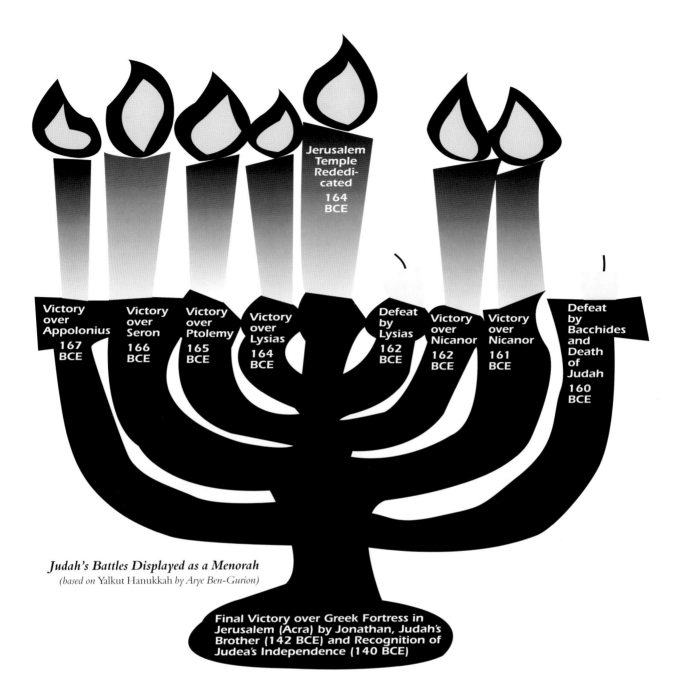

Victory over Appolonius 167 BCE

Victory over Seron 166 BCE

Victory over Ptolemy 165 BCE

Victory over Lysias 164 BCE

Jerusalem Temple Rededicated 164 BCE

Defeat by Lysias 162 BCE

Victory over Nicanor 162 BCE

Victory over Nicanor 161 BCE

Defeat by Bacchides and Death of Judah 160 BCE

Judah's Battles Displayed as a Menorah
(based on Yalkut Hanukkah by Arye Ben-Gurion)

Final Victory over Greek Fortress in Jerusalem (Acra) by Jonathan, Judah's Brother (142 BCE) and Recognition of Judea's Independence (140 BCE)

could not conceal the true state of affairs. The cessation of the persecutions signified the defeat of Menelaus, who had been their instigator, and the victory of the Maccabees, something that must have seemed unbelievable to contemporaries. David had again overcome Goliath. Only a year before, the prophet Daniel [whose Biblical book was written in part in this period] could see no help except through a miraculous intervention of God. And yet Judah had won his victory with casual irregulars who were often lacking in such essential arms as sword and shield. How could the issue be interpreted as other than explicit confirmation of the leadership which the Maccabees had assumed?

From the beginning Judah comported himself as the lawful leader of his people. He put into force **the law**[14] according to which a man who had just built a house or betrothed a wife or planted a vineyard or was fainthearted, was released from service. His people conscientiously separated first fruits and tithes, but these could only be offered in the Sanctuary, and the Sanctuary was still in the hands of the reform party.

14. *Deuteronomy* 20:5-8

The Guerrillas Capture Jerusalem

Antiochus Epiphanes' restoration of freedom of conscience had only brought an end to the persecutions, but not an end to the rule of Menelaus the High Priest and his friends. It was not to be expected that they would voluntarily surrender their position. Judah therefore determined to wrest their rule from them by force.

At the end of 164 BCE, about the beginning of December, Judah made a sudden descent upon Jerusalem. To understand that such a surprise attack could promise success, it must be remembered that in 168 BCE the central government had pulled down Jerusalem's city walls. The intention was to make the city completely dependent upon the citadel of Acra. It was this that made it possible for Judah, only four years later, to take possession of Jerusalem so easily.

The first act of the conqueror was the

By instituting this festival, Judah and his people declared themselves the true Israel. Never had a festival been instituted in Israel by human hand.

---

purification of the Holy City of all traces of idolatry and the restoration of the service of God in the Temple. According to the Jewish calendar, it was Kislev 25, precisely three years after the reform party had offered the first pagan sacrifice upon the altar, that Judah again carried out, in early morning, the prescribed sacrifice in the ancient usage. *"And all the people fell upon their faces, and worshipped, and gave praise unto heaven, to the God who had given them success."* For eight days the rededication of the purified altar was celebrated. Then *"Judah and his brethren and the whole congregation of Israel ordained, that the days of the dedication of the altar should be kept in their seasons year by year for eight days, from the twenty-fifth day of the month Kislev, with gladness and joy."* This celebration, which is the model for the annual festivals of dedication in all churches, is Hanukkah,

a word that literally signifies "dedication." But this name can be documented only from the first century CE. Originally the festival was called "Tabernacles *(Sukkot)* of the month of Kislev," as in an official communication from the Palestinian to the Egyptian Jews, dated 124 BCE.

By instituting this festival, Judah and his people declared themselves the true Israel. Their act was one of far-reaching significance, for all previous festivals were prescribed in Scripture. Never had a festival been instituted in Israel by human hand. Even the restoration of the Temple after the Babylonian Exile had not been solemnized by the establishment of a day of commemoration. Judah's measure was therefore an innovation without precedent. On the other hand, it was in complete accord with the usage of the Gentiles. Among the **Greeks** it was usual for a generation, when it regarded an event in its own history as important, to believe it should be commemorated for all time. Thus Judah imitated the practice of his enemies, but at the same time incorporated it into Judaism. This was the first step along the path, which was to constitute **the historic mission of the Hasmoneans — the introduction of Hellenic usages into Judaism without making a sacrifice of Judaism**.

Thus, at the beginning of 163 BCE, Judah was master of Judea; only the Acra in Jerusalem remained as refuge and citadel for those loyal to the King. Apparently the garrison in Acra was too weak to act independently and the central government was, as usual, little concerned with the affairs of Judea. Moreover, at this time Antiochus Epiphanes suffered a serious reverse in Persia when he attempted to plunder an Oriental sanctuary in the hill country, and was lying sick in Persia.

Judah Saved by a Miracle

At the end of the winter of 163 BCE Antiochus Epiphanes died in Persia. About the same time Judah began the siege of Acra, already employing in this operation the best equipment of the great armies of that period, siege towers and battering rams of various types. An unknown fugitive four years before, Judah was now, though without office or title, ruler over the Jewish nation. From Acra urgent dispatches went out to the central government. The reform party complained, with perfect justice, that the government was again leaving them, the group loyal to the King, in the lurch. "We were willing to serve your father," the messengers said to the new king, Antiochus V Eupator, "and to walk after his words, and to follow his commandments. For this cause the children of our people besieged the citadel, and were alienated from us, and many of us were killed, and our property pillaged."

At the head of the new government there stood as regent the same Lysias with whom Judah had negotiated a year previously and who had promised the Jews his good will if they would continue to be loyal. But, in the meanwhile, Judah had broken the peace and had taken advantage of the amnesty granted him to make himself master of Judea. The court at Antioch in Syria determined to dispose of the Maccabees once and for all.

In the summer of 163 BCE Lysias himself marched at the head of an army of professional soldiers through Idumea to Jerusalem in order to raise the siege of Acra. His way was barred by the citadel of Bet Zur, which Judah had in the meanwhile occupied. Lysias directed the siege of this fortress, and Judah, obliged to hasten to the assistance of his outposts, was forced to interrupt the siege of Acra. This was Lysias' first success. Near Bet Zechariah, halfway between Jerusalem and Bet Zur, where the hills merge into a plateau that permits the deployment of larger battle formations, Judah one morning came upon Lysias' superior army, which included cavalry, and even thirty-two elephants, arms that were wholly wanting to the Maccabees. The rising sun was reflected in the gilt and brazen shields of the Syrian heavy infantry, so that "the mountains shone and blazed like torches of fire." Judah's brother, Elazar, vainly immolating himself in an effort to save his people, rushed into the ranks of the enemy and attacked the largest of the elephants, upon which he naively supposed the young king to be riding. The beast, transfixed, fell, crushing the hero. Judah's army was defeated and Bet Zur capitulated.

Modern Israel's Wars and Peace Treaties

1948	War of Independence against 7 Arab nations	**1979**	Peace Treaty with Egypt
1956	Suez War: Sinai Campaign with France and England against Egypt	**1982**	Lebanon War against Palestinians in Lebanon
1967	Six Day War against Egypt, Syria and Jordan	**1991**	Gulf War when attacked by Iraqi missiles during Operation Desert Storm
1968-69	War of Attrition on the Suez Canal	**1995**	Peace Treaty with Jordan and Interim Agreements with the Palestinians
1973	Yom Kippur War against Egypt and Syria	**2000**	Peace Talks with Syria

The royal army now reached Jerusalem unhindered and laid **siege** to the fortified Mount Zion, where Judah and his people had taken refuge. In ancient times, before the use of explosives, every wall and every tower was an obstacle to the attacker. The besiegers therefore preferred to starve out rather than storm a besieged fortress. It was the summer of a Sabbatical year, in which, according to biblical law, nothing had been planted. Hence there were no considerable supplies in Zion. Judah's troops dispersed, each man to his own home. Only a small company of the most faithful remained shut up in Zion under Judah's leadership. Judah's life was in any case forfeit. Moreover, we may surmise, he was firmly convinced that the God of Abraham, Isaac, and Jacob would not forsake him. In his desperate situation, therefore, Judah awaited a miracle, and the **miracle** came about. Expressed in untheological language, Judah's tenacity made it possible to expect a favorable turn in the situation, which, in the unforeseeable complications of life, might at any time take place.

The deliverance of the besieged Maccabees on Mount Zion came about as result of Antiochus Epiphanes' last act on his deathbed in Persia. When the King marched to the east he had left the guardianship of his son and successor, a minor, to Lysias, who after the death of the King assumed the regency. But on his deathbed Epiphanes had appointed another general, named Philip, as regent of his realm. And so it came about, approximately in February of 162 BCE, that while Lysias was occupied with the siege of Zion, he received word that Philip was approaching Antioch at the head of the army of the east to secure the overlordship for himself. Lysias found it necessary to withdraw in great haste, and so quickly made a peace with the beleaguered Judah.

Elazar, Judah's brother, tries to bring down the war elephant of the Greek general.
(Gustav Dore, 19th century France)

STAGE 6:

The Empire Acknowledges Judean Religious Autonomy

Formally considered, the "peace" amounts on the one hand to a capitulation on the part of Judah, and on the other, to a remission on the part of the King. In actuality, its basis was an understanding between Lysias and Judah, which was tantamount to a restoration of the conditions that had obtained in Judea prior to Antiochus Epiphanes. The King's remission was addressed to Lysias, and solemnly proclaimed renunciation of the policy of forced Hellenization. *"As for our Jewish subjects,"* the new King wrote, *"we understand that they object to our father's project of bringing them over to Hellenism, preferring their own ways of life and asking permission to follow their own customs."* The king resolved *"that the subjects of the realm should live undisturbed and attend to their own concerns."* He agreed *"to give them back their Temple and to permit them to live according to the laws of their ancestors."*

A year earlier the government had consented to tolerate the Jewish religion; now the dominion of the Torah was fully restored. According to the decree of 163 BCE, those Jews who wished to do so might give obedience to the Jewish law. The new decree of 162 BCE again obliged the entire people to observe this law. This marked the consummation of the victory of "Orthodox" **Judaism**. For centuries thereafter the Jews celebrated the recurrence of this day (Shevat 28) "upon which King Antiochus withdrew from Jerusalem."

5

The Maccabean Brothers — Judah, Elazar, John, Jonathan, and Simon (163-140 BCE)

Beyond Religious Freedom toward National Liberation

by Elias Bickerman[14]

The consequences of the peace of 162 BCE were twofold. For one thing, it marked the end of the reform party. Its chief, the former High Priest Menelaus, was executed upon the King's orders, "for he was the cause of all the evil in that he persuaded Epiphanes to abolish the ancestral constitution of the Jews." This was the ground on which the verdict was based. The remaining partisans of reform, who continued to find refuge in the Acra, had in the meanwhile lost all touch with Judaism. The reformers had now become apostates.

On the other hand, the task of the Maccabees also seemed to have been completed. The government had deserted the reform party, traditional Judaism had been recognized as alone valid, and the conditions which had obtained before the promulgation of Epiphanes' measures were thus restored. The rebellion of the Jews now seemed pointless and at an end. "Now therefore let us give the right hand to these men, and make peace with them, and with all their nation; and let us settle with them that they be permitted to walk after their own laws, as aforetime; for because of their laws which we abolished were they angered, and did all these things." This opinion of the young King's counselors proved correct; **Judah** was deserted by his partisans. The government appointed a new High Priest, a member of the previous high-priestly family called Jakim, who then Hellenized his name into Alcimus. The government even caused an assembly of legal scholars to be convoked so that it might confirm, after exhaustive investigation, that Alcimus was in fact the legitimate prince. The **Hasidim**, the "Pious," a group known for the strictness of its faith and who had been the first to join Mattathias, these very Hasidim were now the first to recognize Alcimus. From this time forward, supported by a royal guard, Alcimus ruled over Judea, and his power was so secure that he could without misgivings cause the execution of sixty of the "Pious" who had shown themselves rebellious. Once again the burnt offering for the reigning king was daily offered upon Mount Zion.

At first Judah again retired into the mountains. But when a new palace revolution took place in Antioch — Antiochus V was overthrown by his cousin, Demetrius I — Judah took advantage of the occasion to reappear in Jerusalem. He took possession of the Sanctuary and even prevented Alcimus from approaching the altar. Judah's supporters maintained that Alcimus had "voluntarily polluted himself" in the time of Epiphanes; that is, without being compelled to do so, he had participated in pagan festivals and sacrifices. Was such a man now eligible to perform the service of God? The question was one of conscience, fought out by zealots and moderates, similar to the question, which later arose among the early Christians during the time of persecutions: Can there be forgiveness for apostasy? We know that the various answers to this question led to numerous schisms within the Church and to reciprocal excommunications. It is therefore not surprising that Judah and his followers refused to recognize Alcimus, even after an assembly of legal scholars convoked by the government had pronounced in favor of Alcimus' legitimacy.

---

14. *From Ezra to the Maccabees* p. 127-139.

Jewish Civil War Renewed and the Invasion by General Nicanor

This time the **cleavage** in the Jewish people was quite different from that in the days of Epiphanes. The struggle no longer concerned the validity of the Torah but whether or not Alcimus was justified in functioning as High Priest. **Civil strife** began anew. Judah again marched forth. He swept through all the territory of Judea, taking vengeance upon his enemies and punishing the "apostates" who were worse than pagans in his eyes.

Afterword: The Forgotten Judah[15]

Israel quickly forgot Judah. In the Talmud he is nowhere mentioned. In Megillat Antiochus, a post-Talmudic (and quite spiritless) account that was read at the Hanukkah festival in the Middle Ages, Mattathias and his grandson, John Hyrcanus — but not Judah — are the principal figures. It was only during the Middle Ages, thanks to the Hebrew compilation called Josippon, composed on the basis of the writings of Josephus, that Judah again became a hero for the Jews. The Christian world, which had taken the *Books of Maccabees* into their Holy Scripture, meanwhile honored Judah as a paragon of knighthood. Even today the statue of Judah may be seen in the principal market place of Nuremberg, Germany. His figure, along with those of eight other heroes (three pagans, three Jews, three Christians), decorates the Schone Brunnen (1385), a masterpiece of the age of chivalry.

Putting Down Judah: A Passing Victory

The Christian historian Emil Schurer dismisses Judah's importance:

The downfall of Judah offered final proof of the futility of any opposition by the nationalists to Syrian power. However brilliant the earlier achievements of Judah had been, he owed them primarily to the rashness and conceit of his opponents. Lasting military success was unthinkable so long as Syrian power remained to some degree united. In the following years there was not even a passing victory of the kind won by Judah. What the Maccabees finally achieved, they won through the voluntary concessions of the rival pretenders to the Syrian throne, and as a result of the internal disorganization of the Syrian Empire.

Twice Alcimus went to the royal court to request the government's help against the Maccabees, "who are keeping up the feud and stirring sedition; they will not let the kingdom settle down in peace." But King Demetrius was entirely taken up with other difficulties, especially with the uprising, which with Roman support, had wrested Mesopotamia from the King. Finally the King sent out one of his generals, **Nicanor**, with orders to take the Maccabees captive. Nicanor first sought to lay hands on Judah by cunning; but when the attempt miscarried, he marched his troops out of Jerusalem into the neighborhood of Beth Horon, where he was joined by troops from Syria. He himself led a levy of Jews loyal to the King out of Jerusalem. Because his troops were Jewish, he was constrained, much against his will, to abandon his intention of attacking Judah on the Sabbath. This was approximately in the month of March, 161 BCE.

The political situation had rapidly changed. It was only four years before that the government had punished the observance of the day of rest with death, and those wishing to hallow the Sabbath had sought help and refuge with Judah. Now they marched side by side with pagan soldiers in the attempt to capture Judah and send him to his death. An hour and a half north of Jerusalem, where the road narrows as it passes through the hills, the opposing forces encountered one another. Judah's troops again proved far superior to the city levies. Nicanor fell on the field of battle and his army fled. Judah besieged Jerusalem and the Sanctuary a second time, and again had the day of his victory (Adar 13) entered in the calendar of festivals. This amounted to a demonstration that Judah and his followers represented the true Israel. **For the first time in the history of Jacob a day in a war between brothers was declared a joyous festival.** The victory over Nicanor in March 161 BCE made Judah master of the country once again.

---

15. Emil Schurer, *The History of the Jews in the Age of Jesus*, p. 173.

The "Alliance" with Rome

What did Judah know of Rome?

The *First Book of Maccabees* represents him as having heard of the great reputation of the Roman people, *"that they were valiant men, and that they were friendly, disposed towards all who attached themselves to them, and that they offered friendship to as many as came unto them."* That

Judah's death in battle.
(circa 12th Century, Latin Bible located in the Winchester Cathedral, England)

was enough for him. An exact knowledge of the details of a situation is often unnecessary, frequently even a hindrance, to resolute action. Judah knew that a Roman embassy had once before helped him (164 BCE); he knew too that *"whomever they will to make kings, become kings; and that whomever they will, do they depose."* He therefore sent **emissaries to Rome**. They were well received and the Senate, anxious to cause Demetrius I all possible difficulty, approved the treaty that was concluded, not, to be sure, with Judah and his brothers, but with the "nation of the Jews." "When the Jews rebelled against Demetrius I," an ancient historian writes, "and sought the friendship of Rome, they were the first of all Oriental peoples to receive a grant of freedom. The Romans were generous in disbursing what was not theirs." **In any case, for the first time since the Exile the Jews were recognized as an independent power, and by the very people that ruled the world.**

Christian theologians have often wondered at the fact that Judah, who was so zealous in the service of the Lord, made a treaty with and sought security through a pagan power, despite all the admonitions of the prophets. It must be said that there is ground for such wonder. The Maccabees had again taken a step that brought them nearer to the pagan world; they had again accommodated devout Judaism to the ways of the nations.

Judah's Death in Battle

It may be argued that the Roman alliance, which was Judah's greatest success, became the immediate cause of his downfall. The Seleucid government could look on calmly at the occasional successes of a guerrilla chief, in expectation of a favorable moment for delivering a blow. But when Judah became a protege of Rome, it seemed essential to act at once. Judah's emissaries returned to Jerusalem towards the end of the summer of 161 BCE. In the first month of the following spring, as soon as the rainy season was ended, the King's general Bacchides, accompanied by Alcimus and at the head of a regular army, moved through Galilee towards Jerusalem. As always, the professional soldiers were qualitatively far superior to the Maccabean irregulars. When the Syrians approached, the greater part of the Maccabean levy, which amounted to three thousand men, fled. Only eight hundred remained with Judah, and "he

The Mallet-Headed Hero

"Maccabeus" may refer to Judah's mallet shaped head. In the Mishnah[16] there is a list of defects that disqualify priests from serving in the Temple. "These blemishes, whether permanent or temporary, disqualify priests from Temple service. Among them are a wedge-shaped head, a turnip-shaped head, or a mallet-shaped head (*Maccaban*)."

16. *Bechorot* 7:1

was very troubled in heart." Friends advised him to avoid the battle, and their counsel was undoubtedly strategically sound. But he preferred death in battle, and fell fighting. *"All Israel lamented for him and mourned many days, and said: 'How is the mighty one fallen, the savior of Israel!'"*

ON THE ROAD TO INDEPENDENCE: JONATHAN AND SIMON, THE DIPLOMATS

by Elias Bickerman[16]

Judah fell in April 160 BCE. After his death "the lawless put forth their heads in all the borders of Israel, and all those who had sinned [the Hellenists] rose up." The partisans of Judah were tracked down everywhere and large numbers were executed.

Jonathan, Judah's brother and successor, again became the simple chief of a band, and sought refuge in Trans-Jordan. Eight years elapsed after the death of Judah before the Maccabees again entered history. It was the Syrians who aroused Jonathan from his slumbers. In 152 BCE, a pretender called Alexander Balas arose against the reigning king, Demetrius I, the conqueror of Judah. There was only one man who commanded sufficient authority among the Jews to muster an army for Demetrius I, — Jonathan, Judah's brother and heir. Demetrius gave Jonathan full power to collect troops.

Jonathan naturally used the opportunity first to secure his own position. He occupied Jerusalem. Naturally, too, Alexander Balas now sought to draw the Jewish leader over to his side. Jonathan demanded his price, and it was given him. At the Feast of Tabernacles in 152 BCE Jonathan clothed himself, by the authority of Alexander Balas, in the sacred vestments of the High Priest.

Jonathan's fantastic rise in the few months of the autumn of 152 BCE from petty chieftain to High Priest of the Temple in Jerusalem and Prince in Israel ushers in a chapter in the history of the Maccabees which, except for the identity of the family,

has little in common with the previous course of their destiny. **Judah's lifework had been to prevent the threatening Hellenization of Judaism and the surrender of the Torah. He succeeded, and gave his life to his success. Jonathan and his successors, his brother Simon and Simon's descendants, now seek to accommodate Hellenism to Judaism. Under them Judea becomes a Hellenistic principality.**

Jonathan's first task was to maintain himself. This required that he watch the political currents and keep in touch with the pagan princes, but it also meant that he had to sacrifice the blood of Jews for the cause of one or the other of the pretenders. He became a Seleucid official, a *strategos* and governor of a province; he received a court title and wore the purple reserved for the *"friends of the king."*

Their political success consisted in the emancipation of the Jews from the rule of the Seleucids. In May 142 BCE Simon obtained Israel's complete freedom from tribute. *"Therefore the yoke of the pagan was taken away from Israel."* Public documents began to be dated according to the years of Simon. A year later the Hellenistic city and the citadel in Jerusalem, Acra, was taken. In the year 139 BCE Simon received the royal privilege of striking (copper) **coins** in his own name. On Elul 18 (about September) of the preceding year (140 BCE) "in a great congregation of priests and people and princes of the nation, and of the elders of the country," it was determined that Simon should be "their leader and High Priest forever." Heretofore the legal basis for the power of the Maccabean princes had been royal appointment. Now the rule of Simon and of his successors rested upon the decision of the people itself; hence Simon assumed the new title, **"Prince of the People"** (Ethnarch).

These various successes the Jews owed not so much to their own strength as to the adroitness of their leaders, Jonathan the "Sly" (so is his nickname *Aphphus* probably to be interpreted) and his brother, the Ethnarch Simon.

---

16. *From Ezra to the Maccabees*, p. 136-144

THE HOUSE OF THE MACCABEES (HASMONEANS)
(167-29 BCE)

Black boxes indicate high priest or monarch; double lines indicate marriage.

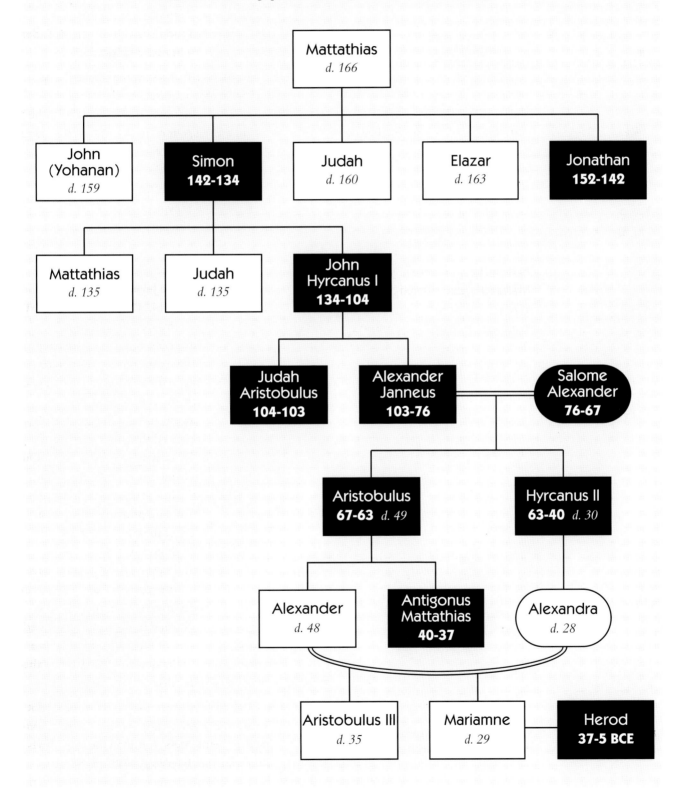

6

READING THE REVOLT FROM A DIFFERENT ANGLE
BY PROFESSOR VICTOR TCHERIKOVER,
WHO CHALLENGES PROFESSOR ELIAS BICKERMAN

INTRODUCTION

Professor Victor Tcherikover set out to challenge the views of Elias Bickerman regarding the underlying causes of the Maccabean Revolt. Tcherikover presents the Maccabean Revolt in a new light. It was not a religious war, but a political civil war between social climbing opportunists, between competing economic classes and ultimately between ethnic nations. Bickerman, a Diaspora Jew, saw the main conflict as a religious-cultural one between Hellenist and Jewish values instigated by Jewish religious reformers who tried to change Temple practice. Tcherikover, a secular Zionist, saw things in class and national terms.

*To present Tcherikover's views we will quote from his book, **Hellenistic Civilization and the Jews** (originally published in Hebrew in 1931). There will be some retelling of the Maccabean Revolt from the beginning though it was just described above by Bickerman. However the emphasis will be quite different. We will present three stages and three levels of the civil war as Tcherikover sees it:*

> *A. Social Climbing Opportunists — Jason and Menelaus, High Priests and Hellenist Jews*
>
> *B. Class War: Landowners and Financiers against Farmers and Urban Workers*
>
> *C. Ethnic Nations: The Jews of Palestine against the Greek Syrians of Palestine*

ELIAS BICKERMAN BLAMES THE RELIGIOUS REFORMERS

by Victor Tcherikover

Elias Bickerman seeks to account for the persecution of Antiochus in a new way. His book *Der Gott der Makkabaer* is an important study. But [it is] precisely the central idea of the book that evokes numerous doubts. Bickerman's basic assumption is that Antiochus, a king of Greek education and a pupil of the Epicureans, could not have been the initiator of the persecution, since it meant not simply an abolition of the existing law, but the imposition of a new religious law in a way which implies religious fanaticism. However **in the entire ancient world there is no example of religious fanaticism of this sort.** It would never have occurred to the king to order the burning of the Torah, to prohibit circumcision, compel people to eat pork, and the like.

But all this is comprehensible, according to Bickerman, if we assume that not Antiochus but the **Hellenistic reformers** of Jerusalem, the High Priest Menelaus and his group, were the real initiators of the decrees. Antiochus' function was merely the abolition of the rule of the Torah in Judea, and it was the Jewish Hellenizers who filled the formal abolition

with real content. What was their aim? They sought to abolish Jewish particularism and to come to terms with the peoples around them. In this they were influenced by Greek views, since in Greek eyes all exclusiveness was barbarism. The Jews therefore faced the alternative of being thought barbarians or of joining the Hellenistic way of life and worship.

Bickerman wrote, "It is sufficient to follow the trend of thought of these Jewish Hellenists (Philo and the other Alexandrian commentators), in order to understand an ideology of the sort held by Jason and Menelaus in Palestine. They desired to reform Judaism by abolishing the barbaric exclusiveness which had infected it with time, and to return to an original worship of God free of all distortion."

Bickerman, then, shifts the onus from Antiochus to the Hellenizing Jews. For this he finds authority in the sources which all ascribe the attempt to Hellenize the Jews not to Antiochus but to the Hellenizers among the Jews themselves. Bickerman's innovation is in seeing the Hellenizers, not only as the initiators of the reform, but also as the initiators of the persecution. [However, Bickerman underestimates the political motives of the period.]

THE SOCIAL CLIMBING OPPORTUNISTS — JASON VERSUS MENELAUS, HIGH PRIESTS FOR A PRICE

The civil war in Judea that ultimately led to the Maccabean Revolt five year later, began as an internal conflict among the upper class priestly land owners and financiers who were struggling for recognition by the Seleucid empire. These Hellenizing Jews wanted to be the official political, financial and (only secondarily) religious leaders of the province of Judea. They sought to turn Judea into the Greek polis of Antioch-in-Jerusalem. The traditionalist High Priest, Onias, was replaced by social climbing, aggressive individuals — first Jason (174-171 BCE) and then Menelaus (171-162 BCE). The transfer of power had everything to do with bribes to Antiochus IV, promises of political support to the Seleucids (or the Ptolemies) and opportunities for control over the treasury of Judea, that is, the Temple. The Hellenist upper classes sought the rights to levy taxes on the Judeans and only secondarily to impose policies of Hellenization on the city, the Temple and later on all of Judea itself.

Hellenism was not introduced into Israel by the forces outside. Part of the Jewish public itself developed an attachment to alien customs and became eager for Hellenistic modes of life to obtain a foothold in Jerusalem. What was the **motive** of those who inclined in this direction? The obvious and simple answer is that their aim was the spread of **Greek culture** and that for them Hellenization was based on their consciousness of the advantages of Hellenism over Judaism.

Hellenism, from its first appearance in Judea, was internally bound up with one particular social class — with **the wealthy families of the Jerusalem aristocracy**. The crafty and resourceful tax-collector, the powerful and unscrupulous businessman, were the spiritual fathers of the Jewish Hellenizing movement, and throughout the entire brief period of the flourishing of Hellenism in Jerusalem, lust for **profit** and pursuit of **power** were among the most pronounced marks of the new movement.

The Social Climbers: Jason the High Priest (174-171 BCE) versus Menelaus the High Priest

The Hellenistic period was a period of revolution, which all over the world broke up the fixed frameworks of tribe, *polis*, and family, and put in their place the **will of the strong individual**. A man's success in life frequently depended, not on the support he obtained from his relatives, but on his own personal talents and characteristics. In Jerusalem the priestly class was divided into families, among them rich and highly

Greeks sacrifice a pig to their gods. (Greek bowls, circa 500 BCE)

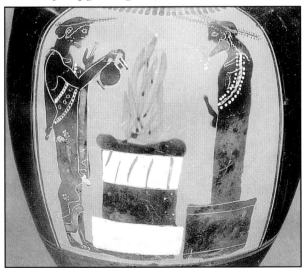

The Temple as the National Bank

The Temple was first and foremost the religious center of Judaism; but besides its religious value it had considerable economic importance. Among ancient peoples every temple served as a financial as well as a religious center; this was the case in Babylonia and Egypt, Greece and Rome. Every temple had a regular income, its treasuries were full of silver and gold, and the Jerusalem Temple was no exception. Great wealth accumulated in its store rooms; the half-shekel which the Jews paid each year to the cult probably covered most of the daily rites, and in the course of generations this income grew and amounted to a considerable sum. "It is no matter for wonder," says Josephus, "that great wealth was concentrated in our Temple, for all the Jews and God-fearers of the whole world, both Asia and Europe, had been sending their contributions ever since ancient times."[17] These treasures, besides their main duty of furnishing the needs of worship, also performed a practical function. "We have no public resources apart from the sacred funds," says Josephus.[18] The Temple treasury played the part of a state exchequer, which was otherwise lacking in Judea. This was the direct outcome of the fact that the government of Judaea was "theocratic" or "hierocratic," that is, the priests who stood at the head of the cult also held the secular power. In addition to the public moneys, the money of private individuals was also kept in the Temple treasury on deposit, since this was the safest place in Jerusalem and acted as a sort of bank in the modern sense.

17. Josephus, *Antiquities* XIV, 110   18. *ibid.*,113

connected families that controlled the Temple, the city and the whole country, while others had to be content with little. Among all these, that of the Oniads, who held the hereditary post of High Priest, was the noblest and the wealthiest. Hence in Judea we find a fratricidal struggle blazed up in the Oniad clan to replace the traditionalist High Priest Onias.

To seize the post, Jason had to depose Onias, and this was impossible without the king's permission; so Jason journeyed to see Antiochus. We do not know how he managed to discredit Onias — the latter's pro-Egyptian tendencies probably played a primary role — we only hear of the results. Jason promised the king, in addition to the 300 talents which were evidently the usual tribute, another 60, and a further 80 "of another revenue";[19] by this payment he purchased the High Priesthood from Antiochus. Antiochus was constantly in need of money, for from the day that his father had been defeated by the Romans (190 BCE), the Seleucid kingdom had become involved in a recurring financial crisis. The wealthy temples fulfilled the function of banks in ancient times, and Antiochus III, Epiphanes' father, had already coveted their treasures. This act of Jason introduced an important innovation in the character of the High Priest's function. Whereas till now the post had been hereditary and the king had been in the habit of only granting or withholding his ratification in respect of the new candidate, henceforth the candidate paid the king the price of the position. **So the High Priesthood became a normal official post and the High Priest a Seleucid royal official utterly dependent on the king's favor.**

[Once Jason had established this new mode of political advancement, the way was open for Menelaus (171 BCE) to offer a bigger bribe to the King and form a stronger military band of supporters in Jerusalem to replace Jason. The civil war begins between 171 BCE and 169 BCE as **upper class factional bloodshed** in the streets of Jerusalem between pro-Jason and pro-Menelaus forces, each one allied opportunistically either with the Seleucid Syrians or Ptolemaic Egyptians during the perennial Seleucid-Ptolemy wars. It is under Menelaus that Antiochus IV transforms the Temple into an out-and-out pagan temple and decrees the outlawing of traditional Jewish observance throughout Judea (167 BCE). The Seleucids execute Menelaus in 162 BCE when they abandon their policy of forced Hellenization and seek the compromise with the Maccabees by appointing a new traditionalist High Priest Alcimus.]

Most of the people supported Jason, while

19. *II Maccabees* 4:8

Menelaus had attained power against the will of the Jerusalem population and could only maintain himself by brute force. In the words of *The Second Book of Maccabees*[20] he was an unparalleled tyrant, "like a beast of prey in his wrath," which means that he was forced to conduct his rule by means of terror in order to protect himself and his party. His position was difficult, the people hated him, and he did not receive sufficient support from the king of Syria.

A People's Revolt in the Name of the Temple

While Menelaus was in Syria, his deputy, his brother Lysimachus, carried out the spoliation [plundering] from the Temple treasury of the vessels which Menelaus needed [in order to pay off the bribes he had promised to Antiochus]. This lawless deed aroused the ire of the population of Jerusalem; the Temple treasure, accumulated over generations, was the property of all Israel, and it was hard to tolerate the fact of a small group of people disposing of it as if it were their own.

The Temple, this national and religious center, was now in the hands of men who had cast off the restraints of religion and followed strange customs belonging to other peoples. **The plundering of the Temple plate [vessels] made good material for religious propaganda among the masses, and the people came out openly against the Hellenizers.** Lysimachus armed some 3000 men and a battle took place in the streets of Jerusalem. The people were victorious: Lysimachus' men gave way and he himself was killed near the Temple.[21]

Antiochus, seeing in the happenings at Jerusalem a **rebellion** against his royal authority, came to put it down with a strong hand. [In 169 BCE Antiochus Epiphanes himself robbed the Temple, taking its **golden menorah** as well as other holy vessels].

---

20. *II Maccabees* 4:25   21. *II Maccabees* 4:39-42

THE MACCABEAN CIVIL WAR AS A CLASS WAR

Tcherikover argues that the civil war within the opportunistic, capitalist priestly class gave way to a much deeper inter-class war between the priest-led urban ruling class and the scribe-led urban plebes. Each group rallied their allies, the large landowners on one hand and the village dwellers on the other. One group identified with and relied on the military and political support of the Seleucid Greek Syrians, while the others defended traditional Judaism and, more significantly, the traditional constitution of Judea since the days of Ezra (the priest-cum-scribe) — the Torah.

[Long before the revolt broke out in Judea] social antagonisms existed among the people and could not be ignored, in particular, **the contrast between zealots of the traditional faith and the freethinking Hellenizers.** The **Jerusalem theocracy** had gradually transformed the priests into an exclusive caste, superior to the people, sometimes oppressing it with a high hand. They constituted the Jewish aristocracy, the wealthy landed group, and quite naturally drew away from the poor and their troubles. The urban population sought other **intellectual leaders** who lived and thought in a manner more akin to themselves. Hence rose the class of scribes, the flesh and bone of the broad city populace, which took upon itself the task of interpreting the Torah neglected by the priests. Thus was created the Oral Law as a continuation, interpretation and supplementation of the Written Law.

Possibly the new scribal interpretations were delivered in the synagogues which had now for the first time risen and spread in Judea, and thus was created the important opposition between the **Temple** and the **Synagogue**. A special sect among the scribes, the sect of the **Hasidim**, constituted its external expression.

A Constitutional Revolution

Once Jason became the High Priest appointed directly by Antiochus IV in 174 BCE the class antagonisms led to radical political — not religious reforms.

Jason built a *gymnasium* and *ephebeion* [a school for 15-17 year olds] in Jerusalem and registered the wealthy people of Jerusalem as Antiochenes. The establishment of the *gymnasium* and *ephebeion* was also in harmony with the city's **aristocratic** character, for

---

The Law of Moses became the war cry of the masses, just as Greek culture was the watchword of the aristocracy.

---

education in the *ephebeion* was bound up with no small expense and therefore became in the Hellenistic period more or less the monopoly of the sons of the wealthy.

Jason's reform, as described in *Second Maccabees*, is not a superficial attempt to introduce a few changes into the customary political and religious constitution of Jerusalem, but a complete abolition of the existing constitution and its replacement by a new one. The former regime had been based on the Mosaic Law. Jason was the founder of the Greek city of **Antioch-at-Jerusalem**. The new city was identical with Jerusalem.

The theoretical founder, however, was not Jason but Antiochus, for the town was called after him. According to Hellenistic tradition, the city named after the sovereign was bound to him by an inner bond, for he was its "divine" guardian, was entitled to a special cult there in his capacity of *ktistes* (founder).

Did the conversion of the theocracy to a *polis* entail the abolition of the Jewish religion, or at least far-reaching modifications of the cult?

Modern history writing [in particular Elias Bickerman] has seen in this program of the reformists predominantly an aspiration to

religious reform, or at any rate a change in the traditional way of life. However, the Greek *politeia* ("way of government") was not a religious concept, but a **political one**. The conversion of Jerusalem into Antioch meant first of all the transfer of the Jewish state from one political category to another (from *ethnos* to *polis*). The changes in the spheres of religion and culture were not the reason for the reform, but its consequences.

By granting rights to these towns Antiochus deepened the gulf between the wealthy urban population and the backward oriental countryside; he anticipated that in the decisive struggle that was to break out between the Seleucid kingdom and the awakening Orient, the wealthy **bourgeoisie** would stand by him. The Hellenization of a city like Jerusalem, lying in the vicinity of the southern frontier of the realm, on the road to Egypt, was likely to be extremely advantageous to him, especially in the event of war with his Ptolemaic rival. Thus the interests of both sides met — the striving of the Jerusalem aristocracy for economic and political growth and the king's endeavor to acquire a friendly power in this part of his kingdom — and the outcome of the meeting of interests was Jason's Hellenistic reform.

The Hasidim were the **chief scribes** and authoritative interpreters of the regulations and commandments of the Torah. The attitude of the scribes in general and of the Hasidim in particular to the Hellenizers is quite plain. The abolition of the "ancestral laws" by Jason made their entire class superfluous; if the Law of Moses was no longer to be the prevailing law in Israel, what point would there be in interpreting it? Naturally, isolated individuals might go on resorting to the scribes with their queries, but the *polis* of Antioch took no account of them and had no need of them. Hence the struggle of the Hasidim against the Hellenizers was not merely an ideological struggle for the maintenance of the commandments of the Law, but also the struggle of an entire class for its existence. This class did not live in a social vacuum, but was supported by the broad sections of the urban population of Jerusalem, that is, by the mass of the people consisting of craftsmen, laborers, petty traders and kindred elements. **The Law of Moses, therefore, became the war cry of the masses, just as Greek culture was the watchword of the aristocracy.** When the urban *plebes* took up arms to oppose the Hellenizing government with force, it was natural that the Hasidim, meaning the scribes and their leaders, should be the popular directors and leaders of the insurrection.

The control of the city passed to the **opponents of the king** — the enemies of the Hellenizers. This means that a very significant thing had occurred in Jerusalem, namely, a **people's revolt** against Jason and the overthrow of the rule of the Hellenizers in the city. Antioch-at-Jerusalem was

liquidated and the people was preparing to return to its traditional form of government. Simultaneously, the rising was a demonstration of hostility toward Syria and of sympathy for Egypt, for only from Egypt could the rebels hope to receive support for the liberation movement. As a dissident movement arose also in other parts of Syria at this time, Antiochus perceived that his kingdom was in considerable danger and that he must put down the Jewish rising with a strong hand. According to *Second Maccabees*[22] the king, gripped by the fury of a wild animal, took the city by storm and gave his troops the order to put its inhabitants to the sword; some 40,000 people were slain and an equal number was sold into slavery. These figures are of course exaggerated, but it is clear that Antiochus now regarded Jerusalem as a hostile city and behaved toward it accordingly.

ETHNIC CIVIL WAR:
THE JEWS VERSUS THE GREEK SYRIANS OF PALESTINE

Tcherikover argues that only **after** (not before) the urban masses revolted against the Seleucid-appointed high priests, does Antiochus begin widespread intervention in the religious life of Judea. Only in reaction to rebellion does he transform the Temple into a pagan cultic center, forcibly convert the Jewish population and settle Jerusalem's main fortress, the Acra, with Greek Syrians. Now the war becomes a struggle of colonialist and colonializer where economics, politics and religion play a role as well as the ethnic struggle for control of Palestine between Hellenized Syrians and traditionalist Jews.

Tcherikover's point is that Antiochus' intervention is a move within a larger ethnic struggle over control of all Palestine. Since the great expulsion of 722 BCE by Assyria and 586 BCE by Babylonia, Judea, the area of Jewish autonomy, had been reduced to Jerusalem and its environs (not including any of the coastline, Hebron or Samaria). However, the Jews had increased and significant minorities of Jews filled the countryside and the Greek cities of Samaria, Idumea, the Trans-Jordan and the coast.

Parallel with the conflicts between Antiochus and the Judean traditionalists, there is bloodshed between Greek Syrians throughout Palestine and the Jewish minorities in their midst.

When the people threw out Jason and Menelaus, Antiochus declared Judea hostile and sent in Apollonius in 168 BCE to suppress the opponents of his royally appointed high priest and to introduce Greek Syrian soldier-settlers into Jerusalem itself.

According to *First Maccabees*, the king's commissioner Apollonius having captured the city and punished the rebels, fortified the "City of David" with a wall and towers. He converted it into a strong fortress, the Acra, which was occupied by the Jewish Hellenizers and so became the new center of the Greek polis. But not only Hellenizers settled in the Acra. *First Maccabees* says that Antiochus settled there "people of pollution, sons of Belial, who brought there spoils from

---

22. *II Maccabees* 5:11 *ff.*

the whole of Jerusalem and shed innocent blood about the Temple."[23] As a result, the inhabitants of Jerusalem abandoned the city, and it became an "abode of aliens."

It is quite clear what means were adopted by Apollonius to punish the rebellious city. He settled in it "a nation of a foreign god," that is, new settlers drawn from among the Gentiles, who were, of course, **soldiers** and local Syrians. It meant **confiscation of the agricultural property of the citizens**, the introduction of new settlers into their homes, deeds of violence and rape upon the former inhabitants, the imposition of taxes upon them and sometimes even their expulsion from the town.

These Syrian troops, who by the royal will had become settlers of the city of Antioch-at-Jerusalem, brought with them the cults of their native country. The importance of Bickerman's discovery of the oriental Syrian character of the divine cults on the Temple hill during the persecutions of Antiochus, may be understood and estimated in the light of these facts. It is his opinion that these were not the Greek gods, Olympian Zeus, Dionysus, or Athene, as they are called in the sources, but Syrian deities in Hellenistic garb. The "wanton women," moreover, whose presence in the Temple is referred to by the sources, were simply the **sacred prostitutes**

The idea of national and political revival was formulated clearly only under the Hasmoneans.

---

so characteristic of the cults of Syria, and so utterly foreign to any Greek cult.

The result could have been foreseen. A temple in which Syrians ruled and made their sacrifices to the God of Israel under the form of the Syrian Baal and to other Syrian gods as well — a temple in which Syrian prostitutes sported with Syrian soldiers — could not serve the needs of the Jewish religion. It was abandoned by the Jews, doubtless after

conflict and bloodshed, both grave and prolonged. Only the Hellenizers, who were now a mere worthless appendage to the Syrian troops, continued to serve in the shrine, and it is to be assumed that Menelaus still performed his function as official High Priest of the Jewish God. The Jewish masses neither acknowledged nor could possibly acknowledge what was being done in the Temple. The Temple of the Lord had been polluted by Gentiles and by a pagan rite. The people led by the Hasidim revolted against the desecration of the Temple and the imposition of a Greek Syrian fortress.

Our account has reached events at the end of the year 168 BCE; yet we have still heard absolutely nothing of a **religious persecution**. The order of Antiochus prohibiting the Jewish faith was promulgated about a year after Apollonius' political measures.

We are now in a position to understand the reasons for the decrees of Antiochus. If the revolt was led by the Hasidim, for whom the commandments of the Torah were of the utmost sanctity, and if devotion to the Mosaic Law was the watchword of the uprising, then that Law had to be extirpated if the rebellion was to be put down. This was the conclusion drawn by Antiochus from what was occurring in Judea.

The king sent an order to his emissaries at Jerusalem and in the towns of Judea prohibiting Sabbath observance, the festivals and the rite of circumcision. He further ordered the erection of high places and altars on which swine and other animals were to be sacrificed. Upon the altar of the Temple was set up the "abomination of desolation"; books of the Law were burnt and inspectors were appointed by the king to make sure that his order was being carried out in all the towns of Judaea.[24]

---

23. *I Maccabees* 1:35-36   24. *I Maccabees* 1:44 *ff.*

The War of Liberation against Local Greek Syrians

Of the beginning of the Hasmonean rebellion in 167 BCE we read in *First Maccabees*, that stirring account known to every Jew. It is the story of a company of Syrian troops that came to the village of Modiin to compel the inhabitants to bow down to the pagan gods. Then up rose old Mattathias, priest of the order of Joarib, and slew the Hellenizing Jew as he was about to obey the Syrian command. Then he slew the king's commissioner who had been appointed to carry out the royal decree, and fled with his sons to the hills, and so the uprising began.

What is not true is that this was the commencement of the rising. The movement of rebellion had been in progress for a year and was led by the **Hasidim**; but they had not been able to produce among themselves a leader of note who could give to the guerrilla struggle the character of a regular planned war.

Eventually Judah in 166 BCE took over the revolt and routed the Greeks. Judah the Maccabee, now master of the entire country of Judea, captured Jerusalem, with the exception of the fortress of the Acra, purified the Temple and restored the cult of the God of Israel.

*However, the successes against the imperial armies of Antiochus IV just expanded the ethnic civil war throughout Palestine. The **entire Greek population of Palestine** was taking part in its suppression and aiding the forces of the government to fight the Jews. Greek Syrians attacked Jewish minorities throughout Palestine. [Editor]*

The Greek army against which Judah the Maccabee was fighting was not therefore racially Graeco-Macedonian, but Syrian, and the troops recruited to suppress the rising were mostly volunteers native to the country. The Graeco-Syrian population of the Hellenized cities was quick to welcome the Greek commanders and joyfully anticipated a Jewish defeat. [Nicanor intended to sell cheaply the Jewish prisoners of war]. When Nicanor invited the citizens of the maritime towns (that is, the Hellenized cities) to meet him, with money in hand, for acquiring slaves, the wealthy were quick to throng to him from every place, bringing not only money but also fetters for the **slaves**. The Greek cities also took part in the persecution of the Jewish religion, in accordance with the invitation of the government to Hellenize the Jews residing in the Palestinian towns. There is no doubt that these persecutions swiftly created general hatred against the Jews and ruined them economically. The second period of the rising, opening with **Judah the Maccabee's attack on the Graeco-Syrian population in Palestine**, was a natural outcome.

The Jews were expanding over the entire land of Palestine and were bringing the Syrian population under their control. This too was no sudden phenomenon, but a continuation and conclusion of a prolonged process which had begun long before the Hasmoneans.

If the **idea of national and political revival** was formulated clearly only under the Hasmoneans, there can be no doubt that the national idea was secretly at work among the Jewish population of Palestine in an earlier period. The Jewish communities were sensible of a strong inner bond with the people's national center at Jerusalem and had no desire to assimilate among the Syrians or to give up an independent position. This independent stand no doubt irritated the Syrians, especially as the Jewish communities grew continually with the constant arrival of new immigrants from Judea. Thus hatred of the Jews increased among the Palestinian population and, the moment the government declared a persecution of Judaism, the Syrians willingly joined the army and helped it to fight against the Jews in order to exterminate them.

The gravest danger, which threatened the Jews, was the **confiscation** of lands in favor of new immigrants whom the Syrian government was proposing to send to Judea. This threat — the dispatch of Greek inhabitants to Judaea and Jerusalem and the reallotment of the land — is twice mentioned in the sources.

The Class War
Against the Hellenistic Jews

Besides the Graeco-Syrians, Judah the Maccabee had other enemies, namely, the Hellenizing Jews. Our sources term them "criminals" and "transgressors," and praise Judah the Maccabee fulsomely for his ruthless fight against them. The sources relate Judah's frequent attacks on towns and villages and the extermination of their Hellenizing inhabitants,[25] and from these brief reports it emerges clearly that the **civil war** which had begun in Jerusalem had now spread and embraced the whole of Judea. We know that these people whom Judah persecuted with such hatred were the high-born and wealthy, the rulers of the nation, people who saw in the Hellenization of the Jews an easy way of attaining prominence. They now stood defenseless before multitudes of insurgents filled with a spirit of religious fanaticism and detestation of their oppressors. Small wonder that the Hellenizers sought protection and shelter from the Syrians and became their loyal confederates. When Seron marched against Judah he was accompanied by a large **company of Hellenizers**,[26] and when Gorgias invaded the country of Judea to attack Judah the Maccabee, these ("the people of the Acra") acted as guides to the Seleucid army.[27]

A custom in the ancient world gave the victors the right to enrich themselves at the expense of the conquered. This was so in every political war, and much more in a social conflict. The Maccabees shared the spoil among themselves after their victory over the enemy, looting the estates of the Hellenizers.

The Constitutional
Counter-Revolution:
Reinstating the Law of the Torah

About six months later Judah the Maccabee appeared before the walls of Jerusalem and took the city. With this capture began a new chapter in the process of the war of liberation.

The capture of Jerusalem fundamentally altered the position of the rival parties. The Hellenizers, who had till now held the power, were compelled to yield their place to their opponents, to evacuate the town and to fortify themselves in the Acra. Part of them took refuge with the peoples in the vicinity of Judah, such as the Idumaeans.[28] Judah the Maccabee and his faction now controlled Jerusalem and the country. We do not know what his official title was — he was not at any rate High Priest — perhaps because Menelaus was still officially regarded as such. His first objective was to abolish Antiochus' decrees and to restore the **cult** of the God of Israel to its rightful place. On the 25th Kislev of the year 164 BCE, the Jews of Jerusalem celebrated the festival of the dedication of the Temple, after the shrine and the entire city had been purified from the remnants of the worship of the Greek deities.

Then came the **internal reform**. The Hellenizers had abolished the "ancestral laws" as the legal foundation of Jewish political and social life. It is clear that Judah's chief task was to procure **the restoration of the Torah** to its former place of primacy. According to *Megillat Ta'anit*, on the 24th of the month of Av the **Jewish courts** were set up afresh and "once again judged according to the laws of Israel." This reform is probably related to the information in *Second Maccabees*[29] on the gathering of the scrolls of the Torah by Judah the Maccabee. If we recall that the decree of Antiochus had condemned the Torah-scrolls to be burnt,[30] it will be easy to understand the Maccabees' decision to collect the surviving copies of the books of the Law.

The restoration of the Torah to its former position doubtless also restored its interpreters to their previous duties. Although there is no allusion to this in the sources, [it seems that] the Hasidim, Judah

---

25. *I Maccabees* 3:8; *II Maccabees* 8:6
26. *I Maccabees* 3:15   27. *I Maccabees* 4:2
28. *II Maccabees* 10:15   29. *II Maccabees* 2:14
30. *I Maccabees* 1:56

the Maccabee's loyal allies, now obtained full satisfaction and once again took over the monopoly of interpreting the commandments of the Torah and of building a national "ancestral code" as they understood it. As to the service in the Temple, Judah the Maccabee selected priests devoted to the Law of Judaism.[31]

Judah the Maccabee's victory over the Hellenizers was the victory of the small peasants and the "urban *plebes*" over a small group of high-born and wealthy people. This victory caused an important **democratization** of the public life of Jerusalem and perhaps also deprived the wealthy of part of the economic basis on which their lives had been built.

Judah the Maccabee's victory over the Hellenizers was the victory of the small peasants and the "urban *plebes*" over a small group of high-born and wealthy people. This victory caused an important democratization of the public life of Jerusalem.

For the first time after an interval of hundreds of years there had appeared among the Jews an **organized military force**, a fact which had its repercussions both on the Jewish world and on other peoples. Till now Judah the Maccabee had been only a leader of the rebels. With the capture of Jerusalem, he became a national leader, and the peasant force which had accompanied him at the beginning of the rising now assumed the form of a real army, which could be used not only for attacks on villages but also for organized warfare against strong enemies. Judah's army was never, of course, a professional force; in periods of peace the soldiers returned to their villages and resumed the working of their land.

There is no doubt that the simple soldiers loved and worshiped their leader, seeing in him a hero and trusting him implicitly. The admiration communicated itself from Judah's camp to the broad sections of the people, and to this day we feel, as we read the *Books of the Maccabees*, the tremendous impression made by **Judah the Maccabee** on his contemporaries.

Continued Ethnic Strife all across Palestine

Judah the Maccabee became leader of the nation, and the nation immediately had reason to know it. From every corner of Palestine — from Idumaea, Ammon, Gilead and Galilee, as well as from the maritime cities — messengers sped to Jerusalem bringing the evil tidings, that the **Syrians and the Greeks** were attacking the Jews and plundering their property. This was a sudden outburst of the forces of hatred, which had been accumulating for generations among the Syrian population. The Jews sought the protection of Judah the Maccabee, who naturally did not reject their appeal, but countered the Syrians.

Judah and his brothers regarded the Syro-Greeks not simply as enemies, but as "the worshippers of heathen gods." During the persecution of Antiochus, the Syrians had sought to convert the Jews by force, and now Judah took vengeance not only on the Syrians but also on their deities. He burnt the temple of the Syrian goddess Atargatis (Ashtoreth) over the heads of those who had taken refuge in it[32] and destroyed the high places and statues of the gods at Ashdod.[33] Thus did Judah's campaigns against the Syrians assume the character of **religious wars**. They were not merely campaigns in defense of Judaism, they were offensives against the local cults.

It is not surprising to hear that in some localities, Judah's assaults on the Syrian population were accompanied by the total extermination of all the male inhabitants. This ruthlessness was no doubt justified in the eyes of the fighters for freedom, for they were fighting for their religion and for the

---

31. *I Maccabees* 4:42
32. *I Maccabees* 5:44; *II Maccabees* 12:26
33. *I Maccabees* 5:68

sanctities of Judaism against pagans; hence, the conduct of the war was accompanied by religious ceremonies and religious slogans. This was the role of the Hasidim — to foster the religious zeal of Judah's warriors.

Conclusion

Let us now examine the rebellion itself. Scholars like Elias Bickerman have pointed to one phenomenon in the progress of the movement which has struck them as very important. The rising, which at its beginning was **entirely religious**, aiming to defend freedom of worship, became in course of time a **political movement**, in other words, a **struggle for power** on the part of Judah and his brothers. Scholars emphasize this new direction especially from the year 162 BCE onwards. In 162 BCE, Antiochus V Eupator rescinded the decrees of his father Antiochus Epiphanes and restored to the Jews the right to live "according to their own laws." The movement now had no further religious or cultural *raison d'etre*; yet despite this it did not come to an end, but made great progress. Why?

Antiochus' decrees were only the trigger, which set off the explosion of forces, the push needed to release the avalanche, but not the sole nor even the basic reason for the Hasmonean movement. If this is the case, there are no grounds for describing the movement as purely religious in its inception, or as purely political at a later stage. In all the doings of Judah the Maccabee and his brothers, the **political and religious** aspects were equally involved, and any distinction between them can only be artificial.

The Maccabean revolt was from a broader point of view only one link in a long series of uprisings on the part of the Oriental countries against their western rulers. These uprisings manifested the deep **social antagonism** between the towns, which supported the central power and compromised with Hellenism, and the countryside, which upheld ancestral tradition and fought the foreign power and the local aristocracy simultaneously. The Hasmonean movement, insofar as it was both **religious** and **political**, was also **social** [and **economic**].

Another Hanukkah Miracle: The Ferocious Angel

Lysias, the guardian and relative of the king, who was in charge of the government, was greatly annoyed [at the success of the Maccabean Revolt in rededicating the Temple]. He mustered about eighty thousand men and all his cavalry, and came to attack the Jews, with the intention of making a place for Greeks to dwell in, of imposing tribute on the Temple and of offering the high priesthood for sale every year. Taking no account at all of the power of God, he was made overconfident by his tens of thousands of infantry, his thousands of cavalry, and his eighty elephants. He invaded Judea, approached Jerusalem and besieged it.

When Judah Maccabeus and his men got news that Lysias was besieging the strongholds, they and the people prayed to the Lord to send some good angel to help save Israel. Judah Maccabeus himself was the first to take up arms and called on the others to risk their lives with him and go to the aid of their brothers. As they eagerly hurried off together, **a [mysterious] rider, clothed in white, appeared at the head [of their column] brandishing golden weapons**. They all blessed the merciful God together, their hearts were strengthened, and they felt equal to overcoming not only men but the fiercest animals and iron walls. So they advanced in good order with their heavenly ally, for the Lord had had mercy on them. Flying at the enemy like lions, they killed eleven thousand of them and sixteen hundred horsemen, and forced all the rest to flee. Lysias himself escaped only by a disgraceful flight.[34]

---

34. *II Maccabees* 11: 1-12

7

AFTERTHOUGHTS: THE HASMONEAN DYNASTY AND ITS LEGACY FOR TODAY

DID THE MACCABEES BETRAY THEIR MANDATE TO DEFEND JUDAISM FROM HELLENISM?

When we celebrate Hanukkah we usually concentrate on Judah's achievement of religious freedom and perhaps the later recognition of Judean independence. However, political statehood in a Hellenist world meant accommodations of Jewish society to Greek institutions. The descendants of the Maccabees became kings with the "appropriate" bloody internal feud. They too used foreign mercenaries, pursued expansionist conquest and even forcible conversion to Judaism of the conquered. The result was the alienation of the people and the early Rabbis from the splendor and tyranny of the new monarchy.

Yet Judaism in this period — by merging modern and traditional elements — survived, flourished and ultimately gave birth to Christianity, even though the Hasmonean state lost its independence early on (63 BCE). It is no surprise that the two leading historians of this period, **Bickerman and Tcherikover, come to diametrically opposed assessments of the question — did the Maccabean dynasty betray Judaism or ensure its success and growth?** Perhaps their historical views, first written in the 1930's, are somehow congruent with the values of the lands they chose to live in. Both were Russian Jewish scholars who later studied in Germany in the 1920's. However they chose different paths of emigration from Germany. Bickerman fled to France and then to the U.S.A. where he was involved in the Jewish Theological Seminary of the Conservative Movement. Tcherikover chose to make aliyah to Israel already in 1925. Perhaps Bickerman's decision to live in America goes with his more optimistic views about the nature of Judaism and its compatibility with the West. Perhaps Tcherikover's more nationalist reading of the Maccabean Revolt and his more pessimistic view of Judaism's compatibility with Hellenism fits his secular Zionist commitments.

The treatment by thinkers and historians of the Maccabean revolt has always been colored by their attitudes to coexistence of Western and Jewish culture. Elias Bickerman and Victor Tcherikover disagree radically about the possibility of a Jewish-Western synthesis as they disagree in their evaluation of the ultimate success of the Maccabean Revolt. For **Bickerman**, for example, the greatness and the survival of Judaism has always been its ability to borrow successfully and critically from its environment. The Greek-Jewish dialogue fertilized Judaism and helped promote Rabbinic culture as much as political survival. [See Bickerman's essay on "The Philosopher and the Rabbi" on page 133].

However **Tcherikover** is much more pessimistic. Judaism as a religion has always been at odds with Greek political forms. The Hasmonean Dynasty is a betrayal and a corruption of the Maccabean Revolt, but unfortunately that was inevitable. Jewish religion and the Western notion of state could never be reconciled. This debate over optimism/pessimism on cultural synthesis is still relevant to understanding the tensions between religion and democracy today.

THE SUCCESS OF THE MIDDLE WAY: MACCABEAN HELLENISM

by Elias Bickerman[35]

The Maccabees saved Israel from the Greek danger, but this danger was twofold. The Maccabees eradicated one kind of Hellenism — idolatry — only to facilitate the growth of another kind — a cultural synthesis of Judaism and Hellenism.

Hellenism was a supranational culture based upon reason and faith in reason. Hence its immediate effect upon all peoples whom it embraced was everywhere to disrupt tradition. **Contact with the "enlightened" and universal culture of Hellenism could only be salutary for one who, wrestling as Jacob did with the angel, did not allow himself to be overcome but extorted its blessing, not losing himself in Hellenism, but coming safely away with enhanced strength.** Only two peoples of antiquity succeeded in doing so, the Romans and the Jews. The Romans succeeded because they became the rulers even of the Hellenic world. To be sure, they lost much in the process, a good part of their national religion, whose gods Greek gods supplanted. The Jews succeeded because their knowledge of the oneness of God and of His world rule — in a word, the singular character of their faith — set up an inner barrier against surrender and separated them from the rest of the world.

But separation alone could by its nature only preserve past gains, it could not enrich the spirit and the inner life. Many other Oriental peoples, as for example the Egyptians, shut themselves off from Hellenism; but this led only to their becoming backward. Their leading classes, seduced by Hellenism, were lost to the nation.

Jerusalem had been threatened with a similar fate. The leading men of Jewry went over to a foreign culture. These were priestly reformers. The Maccabees protested. They defended the God of their fathers against the deity fabricated by the reformers. By their uprising they preserved the uniqueness and permanence of Judaism, and they preserved monotheism for the world.

But the question of a final settlement with Hellenism had not been resolved. Hellenism continued to be a universal spiritual power, like Western civilization in the modern world, and no people could isolate itself from it if it wished to live and assert itself. Above all, isolation would have involved a break with the already numerous communities of the Diaspora, which were scattered throughout the Greek world and hence were constrained to accept Hellenism.

With the Maccabees, the internal Jewish reconcilement with Hellenism begins. Ideas and concepts of the new age and the new culture were taken over without thereby surrendering native spiritual values. This was managed in two ways. **First**, the inner strengthening of the people achieved by the Maccabees made it possible to adopt unaltered ideas and institutions which had previously seemed to offer, or in fact did offer, a serious threat.

At the time of Antiochus Epiphanes the gymnasium in Jerusalem was enormously dangerous to Judaism. In the time of Philo the Jews of Alexandria thronged the games without sacrificing any part of Judaism; and the theater, amphitheater and hippodrome erected in Jerusalem by Herod were later visited even by Orthodox Jews.

There are several examples of the Maccabean process of Hellenization:

A first indication of "assimilation" is the accommodation of proper names to the taste of the surrounding world. The leaders of the reform party called themselves Jason instead of Jeshu, Menelaus instead of Onias and the real name of the High Priest Alcimus was Jakim. The Maccabees, on the other hand, bore purely Hebrew names. Mattathias, son of Yohanan, son of Simon, called his children Yohanan (John), Simon, Judah, Elazar, Jonathan.

But already Simon's son-in-law was called Ptolemaeus, and the sons of John Hyrcanus,

35. *From Ezra to the Maccabees*, p. 153-165, 173-182

Simon's grandson, had double names, Aristo-bulus-Judah, Alexander Jannaeus (*Yannay*, a short form of Jonathan). John Hyrcanus and Aristobulus struck their coins only in Hebrew; Jannaeus' coins are bilingual, bearing "King Jonathan" in Hebrew and "King Alexander" in Greek. The character and significance of Maccabean Hellenism is plainly revealed. The reform party wished to assimilate the Torah to Hellenism, the Maccabees wished to incorporate Hellenic culture in the Torah.

Let us consider, for example, the decree of 140 BCE, by which the people invested

---

The reform party wished to assimilate the Torah to Hellenism, the Maccabees wished to incorporate Hellenic culture in the Torah.

Simon with the rulership. The document is thoroughly Hellenistic in character. It must have been drafted in Greek. The very notion of drawing up a document to establish a constitution is purely Greek; the Bible provides no pattern for this.

Secondly, Hellenistic notions were appropriated only after their poison had been drawn. The recipe was very simple. The new

was fitted into the system of the Torah and was employed the better to serve the God of the fathers, not to elude Him the more adroitly.

In this way Maccabean Hellenism succeeded in parrying spiritual movements which might otherwise have destroyed traditional Judaism. For example, the Hellenistic world surrounding Judaism was caught up by a new revelation that solved the problem of evil on earth. Retribution would come after death, when the wicked would be punished and the righteous rewarded and awakened to new life. Such notions are alien to the Bible, indeed in contradiction to it, for the Torah promises reward and punishment in this life.

Thus Judaism was able to enrich itself with new and foreign ideas and to be saved from the mummification that overtook the religion of the Egyptians, for example, which shut itself off from Hellenism completely. If today the West and Islam believe in resurrection, the idea is one which Maccabean Judaism took over from Hellenism and then passed on to Christianity and Islam. **The Maccabees preserved the Judaism of the Greek period from both dissolution and ossification. It is through their deeds that the God of Abraham, Isaac, and Jacob could and did remain our God.**

BEYOND POLITICAL INDEPENDENCE TO HELLENIST MONARCHY: THE CORRUPTION OF THE MACCABEAN DREAM

by Victor Tcherikover[36]

The People Ratify Simon, Judah's Brother (140 BCE)

Complete political independence was obtained under Simon, when the High Priest ceased to be a Syrian official and became a free ruler of his people and his country. Three important changes occurred under **Simon**: the exemption of the Jews from the payment of taxes to the Syrian sovereign, the liquidation of the Syrian garrisons in the fortresses of Judea, and the laying of a legal foundation for the rule of the

new dynasty of the Hasmonean house.

By decision of the Assembly, Simon was elected High Priest, military leader and leader of the people. The people placed solely in his hands the traditional rule of the nation, previously in the hands of the Oniads, together with the political authority as head of the nation (ethnarch, *prostates*), whose function was to represent it before external powers. To these two forms of authority was added the military power which had grown up among the Jews as a result of the troubled

---

36. *Hellenistic Civilization and the Jews,* p. 232-233, 238-239, 250-253, 264

times, from the time of Judah the Maccabee on. Moreover, the Assembly granted the entire scope of this power to Simon in perpetuity,[37] a conception involving the right of the new ruler to bequeath his authority hereditarily to his son. Thus Simon gathered into his hands, powers of a genuinely **monarchical character**, and the new dynasty was established on a strong legal basis. As long as the Jews had not issued from the confines of the Judaean hills, they were of no importance in the world of politics. Now, after the Hasmonean state had been founded, it was inevitable that the new power should come into political and cultural contact with the wide world — with Rome, Egypt, Syria and the rest. That world was a Hellenistic world, hence the Hasmonean kingdom was destined to become a **Hellenistic state**.

The **reign of Simon** already reveals the lines of a new epoch. The coronation decree of Simon,[38] although it was a decision of "the Great Assembly," bears the stamp of a pronouncedly Hellenistic influence. [Note the external splendor bestowed upon the High Priest (*"he shall put on purple cloth and the clasp of gold"*), and the reckoning of the era by the year of his priesthood (*"and let all the bills of the country be registered in his name"*[39]).] Simon earned the praise of the Knesset because he "had spent much money of his own and had armed the warriors of his nation and given them fee" — the typical praise accorded to a Hellenistic king, who stands above the state and extends aid to his subjects out of his generosity and humanitarian feelings.

In the eyes of the outer world, too, Simon was an independent prince of Hellenistic type; Antiochus VII of Syria granted him permission to mint coins of his own,[40] a right given only to free Greek cities and to vassal princes of independent standing. Simon's great wealth, the gold and silver utensils which were appointed for use at his court, and the entire brilliance of his new state, amazed the envoy of Antiochus not a little and angered the king himself. It is clear then that the sons of the Hasmoneans had no sooner ceased to be leaders of the nation in rebellion, or officials of the Seleucids, than they appeared before their subjects crowned with **Hellenistic splendor**. They behaved just as did most of the petty monarchs who set up their kingdoms on the ruins of the disintegrating Seleucid Empire.

The Hasmoneans Become a Hellenist Dynasty

Simon's successor **John Hyrcanus** was the first to import **mercenaries** from abroad for his army.[41] This was characteristic of the epoch, and with the exception of Rome, all the states of those days utilized mercenary troops. The practice did not arise from lack of local forces. The Jewish population of Palestine, although it was small, could furnish Hyrcanus with some thousands of troops, and the wars of Judah the Maccabee showed conclusively that the peasants of Judea were not inferior in military prowess to the Syrians. The need of bringing mercenaries from abroad arose from the desire of the rulers to bind the army with strong and direct bonds to their own persons. This was the practice everywhere. In the Hellenistic world the ruler stood above the state, which he ruled, as a personal power independent of the population. This power was based mainly on formations of mercenaries who received permanent pay from the ruler and were alien to the local people and to the affairs of the state.

Josephus reports[42] that Hyrcanus obtained the money to pay his army in a strange way: by opening the tomb of King David and taking from it 3000 talents of silver. This manner of finding money was also typical of the period, for **Hellenistic rulers took money whenever they could, not always in lawful fashion**.

By these two acts — **the hiring of foreign**

37. *I Maccabees* 14:41   38. *I Maccabees* 13:27 *ff.*
39. *I Maccabees* 13:27 *ff.*   40. *I Maccabees* 15:6,32 *ff.*
41. Josephus, *Antiquities* XIII, 249   42. *Antiquities Ibid.*

troops and the plundering of David's tomb — Hyrcanus marked the beginning of the rift between himself and the people. The rule of Judah the Maccabee and his brothers had sprung directly from the national awakening which had swept the nation during the persecution of Antiochus and the government of the Hellenizers. The first Hasmoneans were national leaders and part of the people itself. Now the dynasty faced the people as an independent power, and the question was whether the two could find a common language.

The systematic and planned conquest of the country began only under John Hyrcanus. His war in the south was especially productive of results, for he overran the entire country of Idumaea with its Hellenistic towns and compelled the Idumaeans to convert to Judaism.[43]

The **life of the Maccabean court** was also fashioned on the model of the Hellenistic monarchies. In their private lives the Hasmoneans were very far from the austerity and stateliness befitting a Jewish High Priest. The Hasmoneans did the same as all the other monarchs of their time, having drinking parties, taking mistresses in addition to their lawful wives, and persecuting those of their relatives whom they suspected for personal or

---

Judaism and Hellenism were, as forces, each too peculiar to itself to be able to compromise within one country.

---

political reasons. Simon was killed by a member of his family during a banquet when he and his sons were drunk.[44] The Hasmonean rule was a **secular rule**, hence the life of the court was secular also, possessing no higher a level than that of the courts of Antioch or of the kings of Asia Minor.

Thus the Hasmoneans went the way of Hellenization and began to resemble the normal type of Hellenistic monarch; King

Herod (37 BCE) later trod the same road and trod it to the end. It may be assumed that the Hasmoneans too might have played down the nationalist side of their policy in favor of international Hellenism, had they been free to act as they chose, but they were not. From the time of John Hyrcanus they encountered strong opposition from the Pharisees (the early Rabbis), whose party fought obdurately against the secular monarchy of Alexander Jannaeus and finally under Queen Salome Alexandra, victoriously put an end to the Hellenistic aspirations of the Hasmoneans.

A Sad Conclusion

The Hasmonean aim was to build a Hellenistic state on a Jewish national foundation. This, however, was to prove impossible. **Judaism and Hellenism were, as forces, each too peculiar to itself to be able to compromise within one country.** A Hellenistic state could not be founded on the Jerusalem theocracy. A Jewish High Priest could not be a Hellenistic king, and the two conceptions had to be separated. This operation was carved out by Herod, who separated the **monarchy** from the **priesthood** and established a Hellenistic state. Yet this state did not rest on a national foundation. The Pharisees also wished to make a distinction between the secular power and religious life; from Herod's time began the great work of the scholars which aimed to set the people's religious life on a solid basis of Hebrew tradition.

In conclusion, the state created by the Maccabees was not a really a Jewish state according to Tcherikover and it could not survive half-priestly and half-Hellenist. However, for Bickerman, the synthesis of Judaism as a Western religion and the Greek modes of political thought was a great achievement of the Maccabees which has left us a useful legacy.

---

43. Josephus, *Antiquities* XIII, 257
44. *I Maccabees* 16:15

Many scholars and rabbis have argued, sometimes approvingly and sometimes angrily, that the Rabbis or the Pharisees (as they were known before the Second Temple destruction in 70 CE) did everything to repress the memory of the Maccabees. They have marshaled the following evidence:

(1) The historical book written in Hebrew by Maccabean scribes, *First Maccabees*, was never included in the Tanach or preserved in Hebrew in Eretz Yisrael.

(2) There is no Mishnaic tract on Hanukkah as there is for Purim and the other holidays.

(3) Neither Mattathias nor Judah are mentioned in Rabbinic literature.

(4) No megillah is read on Hanukkah.

(5) Only the miracle of the oil, not the amazing military victory, is commemorated in the Talmud.

Secular nationalists[45] of the 19th and 20th century condemned the Rabbis for denigrating military heroism and political activism and sought to reclaim the proto-Zionist image of the Maccabees. Non-Zionist rabbis on the left and on the right praised the original Rabbis for separating religion from politics and criticizing the secularist Hellenist dynasty of the Hasmoneans. Both groups referred to the sources (Josephus and Rabbinic literature) that describe the conflict between the Pharisees and the Hasmonean monarch, King Alexander Yannai (103-76 BCE).

> It is told: When King Yannai took sick, he had seventy elders of Israel seized, confined them in prison, and told the warden, "If I die, put these (Rabbinic) elders to death. Thus while the Jews rejoice at my death, they will at the same time be forced to grieve for their teachers." It is further told that King Yannai had a good wife whose name was Shalmonin. The instant her husband died, she removed a ring from his hand and sent it to the warden with the message: "As a result of a dream, your master has ordered the elders released." He released them, and they went back to their homes. It was only then that she announced, "King Yannai is dead." The day King Yannai died was declared a feast day [by the Rabbis].[46]

This view argued that the Rabbis rejected the Hasmoneans because as a priestly family they had usurped the messianic claims of David's descendants from the tribe of Judah. The Hasmoneans were too "modern," too Hellenized for the traditionalist Rabbis.

However the Israeli historian Gedalyahu Alon has argued that the so-called repression of the Maccabees is severely overstated:

(1) That *First Maccabees* was not canonized could be because of its late subject since the Tanach's last historical book is about Ezra (450 BCE).

(2) Although there is no Mishna on Hanukkah, the holiday is sanctioned in the earliest written document of the Rabbis — *Megillat Taanit* (1st-2nd CE) which recalls several Maccabean military victories and their annual commemorations (13th of Adar, the Victory over Nicanor by Judah the Maccabee).[47]

(3) Generally Rabbinic literature does not describe any political or military history, since its genre is legal and sermonic in character. While Judah the Maccabee is not praised, neither are the Maccabees ever criticized. In the Talmud God is praised for "raising up the Hasmonean (Mattathias) and his sons" to redeem Israel.[48] Only the Hasmonean monarchs appearing sixty to eighty years later are criticized in Rabbinic tradition.

(4) While there is no official reading of the Maccabean history on Hanukkah, there was an Aramaic version of *First Maccabees* written in Eretz Yisrael between 2nd and 8th centuries CE which was read aloud with traditional cantilation on Shabbat Hanukkah. It is called the *Megillah of Antiochus*.

(5) While the halachic literature focused on the miracle of the cruse of oil, the official synagogue prayer on Hanukkah (8th century CE), *Al Hanissim — "On the Miracles"* describes the battle of the few righteous and pure ones against the many wicked ones. The miracle is military; the heroes are Mattathias' family.

Whatever the historians may conclude, the lack of an official narrative for the commemoration of Hanukkah, invites each generation of Jews to fill that gap creatively and integrate their own new readings of the past along with new ideologies for the future.

45. Berl Katznelson, Avraham Yaari, Eliezer ben Yehuda, Simon Dubnov
46. *Megillat Taanit* 11   47. *T.B. Taanit* 18b   48. *T.B. Megillah* 11a

THE BIASES OF THE ANCIENT HISTORIANS

CONTRASTING THE BOOKS OF FIRST AND SECOND MACCABEES — THE COURT HISTORIAN AND THE DIASPORA HISTORIAN

When in 140 BCE the Jews gained political independence under a self-consciously national state with Simon the High Priest at its head, they turned self-reflective and began to generate and promote the writing of the new state's political and religious "autobiography" so to speak. This involved a return to the long neglected genre of Biblical history as well as its integration with Hellenist historiography. Following a bloody civil war, the revolutionary victory of a new high priesthood and the rise of a newly independent state after four hundred years of subjugation, the Jews needed to identify the villains and the heroes, to redefine their values and to clarify their theology. They needed to understand the new state that had arisen in terms of its place in Jewish tradition as well as to evaluate the Hellenism, which in some ways they rejected and yet in others had absorbed completely. Finally, they needed to praise God for their victory and define the nature of Divine intervention in the events that occurred.

The Hasmoneans, as the Maccabees were called, first collected all the old books and the documents into a national archive, which might be compared to the American Library of Congress, just as the Jews had done after the destruction of the First Temple:

> "Nehemia (450 BCE) founded a **library** and collected the books about kings and prophets, the works of David and the royal letters about sacred gifts. In like manner **Judah** also collected for us all the books that had been scattered because of the outbreak of war [and the explicit edicts of persecution that condemned the Torah scrolls to the flames] and they are in our hands."[49]

Then the Maccabees began to write new books. Four *Books of the Maccabees* survive into the twenty-first century, each written originally by different authors from different perspectives and sometimes in different countries and languages. In addition, a five-volume work by Jason of Cyrene is mentioned but now lost. We will focus chiefly on the *First* and *Second Book of Maccabees* which, unlike the First and Second volume of Samuel or Kings in the Bible, are not two volumes written by the same author in succession but two totally independent works covering partially overlapping periods of the Maccabean revolt. Let us summarize the perspective of each author.[50]

First Maccabees: **The Court Historian**

First Maccabees (written circa 134-104 BCE and describing the period of 166-135 BCE) is devoted to presenting the Maccabean dynasty, from Mattathias through his son, Judah, to Jonathan and Simon who became high priests and gained political independence. *First Maccabees* was written in Hebrew (though it is only preserved today in Greek) for a Judean audience in a Biblical style that emphasizes how God chose the Hasmonean family to save Israel. *First Maccabees* is in a way reminiscent of the book of Judges (The Maccabees are "those men into whose hand the salvation of Israel was given").[51] Many original prayers, speeches and poems embedded in *First Maccabees* reflect the strong religious feelings of the new rulers.

The book may have been designed to legitimate the Hasmonean dynasty in the face of two internal objections rooted in the worldview reported a generation before the revolt by Ben Sira:

> "Praise the God who planted the seed of the House of David!

---

49. *II Maccabees* 2:13-14
50. Daniel Schwartz, "Historiographic Sources for the Maccabean Revolt," in *Yimei Beit Hashmonai*, edited by David Amit and Chanan Eshel.
51. *I Maccabees* 5:62

Praise the God who chose the children of Zadok the priest."[52]

(1) Mattathias is not a direct descendant of the Zadok family of high priests chosen in the days of David, with whose descendants Jason and Alcimus were implicated in the Hellenist reforms in the Temple.

(2) The Hasmonean dynasty of priests cannot be the descendants of King David who came from the tribe of Judah.

However, the narrative of *First Maccabees* implicitly answers these objections:

(1) The author describes Mattathias' action and his rallying call, *"Let everyone who is zealous for the Law and who remains faithful to the Covenant, follow me."*[53] He uses terms directly analogous to Moses and the Levi tribe at the Golden Calf and Pinchas the zealous priest. They both attacked public desecraters of Jewish worship. In the Bible both the tribe of Levi and Pinchas himself are rewarded for their zealous action by being granted a special status in the Temple worship. Pinchas is even promised what most commentators understand as the high priesthood. Similarly, in Mattathias's case, **zealous action in face of desecration earns the volunteer the dynastic right to the priesthood for their children after them.**

(2) *Second Maccabees* legitimates the political claims of the Hasmonean dynasty by describing at length the people's assembly that ratified Simon's claim to the high priesthood and the governorship. The Greek Syrians acknowledge Simon's claim by granting him the "purple cloth and the gold clasp," while the Jewish people immortalize their agreement to Simon's rule by engraving the agreement on brass tablets set in pillars on Mount Zion. Yet Simon never claimed to displace David's house, therefore he never took the title "king" and left the agreement as a temporary one "until the true prophet will come."[54] *First Maccabees* also emphasizes the international recognition accorded the Hasmonean declaration of independence by quoting no less than nine royal documents from Greek Syria, Rome and Sparta. (This concern for legitimacy recalls the Zionist concern to obtain the Balfour Declaration, November 2, 1917, and the United Nations recognition on November 29, 1947.)

Interestingly enough, *First Maccabees* plays down the religious and political civil war that the Maccabees fought with the Zadokite priests and the Hellenizers. Rather it emphasizes the unity of the people around the inspiring religious figure of Judah the Maccabee who is described as a *heros* (military warrior) and *soter* (savior of his political community). The true villain is Antiochus IV, the Emperor who seeks to homogenize his empire's many ethnic and religious groups into one loyal Hellenistic kingdom. *("The king ordered all his kingdom to become one people."*[55])

Probably the author of *First Maccabees* was supported by the Hasmonean court and believed his book continued the Biblical tradition of Chronicles.

Second Maccabees:
The Diaspora Historian

In contrast to *First Maccabees*, the book of *Second Maccabees* is a summary of a history written originally in Greek for Diaspora Hellenistic Jews living in the Greek speaking area in Egypt. The Jews to whom the book was addressed were both loyal to their nation and its new Hasmonean state and yet faithful subjects of the kingdoms of the Greek dynasty of Ptolemies in Egypt. Jason of Cyrene wrote the original five-volume history of the Maccabees which was later summarized by an anonymous "epitomizer" in *Second Maccabees*. The original has not been preserved.

As we explained, the author of *First*

---

52. Ben Sira 51:28-29   53. *I Maccabees* 2:27
54. *I Maccabees* 14:41   55. *I Maccabees* 1: 44

Third Maccabees:
Ptolemy and the Elephants

Third Maccabees is really a Greek historical novel which has nothing to do with the Maccabees. It describes the Egyptian Hellenist king, Ptolemy IV, who lived two generations before the Maccabean revolt, when Judea was still ruled by the Ptolemies.

According to the story, Ptolemy IV resolves to visit Jerusalem. The scene moves swiftly to the Temple. Impressed by its magnificence, he insists, against the Torah and despite all the Jewish protests, on his right to enter the Temple. A mighty Jewish throng converges at once upon the Temple: *"The combined shouts of the crowd, ceaseless and vehement, caused an indescribable uproar. It seemed as if not only the people but the very walls and the whole pavement cried out. They all preferred death to the profanation of the Temple."*[56] Simon the high priest then offers a long prayer, rehearsing the mighty acts of God on behalf of his people Israel. God responds by imposing physical punishment upon Ptolemy who suffers a seizure. The description is a good example of the bombastic language of Third Maccabees: *"God scourged the one who was greatly exalted by his own insolence and effrontery tossing him to and fro like a leaf on the wind, until he fell impotent with his limbs paralyzed and unable to speak, completely overpowered by a righteous judgement."*[57]

We next find Ptolemy back in Egypt breathing vengeance against the Jews. He commands a census of all Jews in Alexandria in order that they might be reduced to slavery. Exemption is offered to those who agree to participate in the pagan mystery cult of Gnosis. Some Jews do accept the Greek religion, but the great majority gallantly hold on to their ancestral faith. The angry Ptolemy then decrees that all Jews in his kingdom be transported in chains and put to death. The account of their deportation[58] is a classic piece of "pathetic history," written in the most florid style. Once arrived on the outskirts of the city, the vast multitude is herded into the race track. Ptolemy plans their destruction with Hermon, the captain of his five hundred strong elephant brigade. Three times Hermon, and finally Ptolemy himself, set out on this nefarious exploit and three times this scheme is thwarted by God's miraculous interference on behalf of the Jews.[59] On the last occasion, by reason of the venerable Elazar's prayer, by an amazing reversal, the elephants, previously intoxicated by doses of frankincense and wine, turn back on the king's own troops and trample them to death. In a fit of remorse Ptolemy undergoes a complete change of heart towards the Jews, orders their release and he praises their God. The point of the narrative is to illustrate both the power of prayer and the absolute sovereignty of the Jewish God.

---

56. *III Maccabees* 1:28-29 was written in the 1st century BCE.
57. *III Maccabees* 2:21-22
58. *III Maccabees* 4:1-13
59. *III Maccabees* 5:1-22, 23-25; 5:46-6:21

Maccabees, who wrote for Judeans, sought to promote the legitimacy of the Hasmonean priesthood and its political rule. However *Second Maccabees* seeks to explain to Diaspora Jews and Greeks alike, that the Maccabean revolt was not the result of an inevitable clash of two cultures — Hellenism and Judaism — or of two peoples — Hellenes and Jews. The bloodshed was really unnecessarily caused by an unholy alliance between money-hungry so-called priests and irrational Greek leaders who caused the desecration of an ancient Temple and the persecution of a legally protected religion. The Jewish villains, Jason and Menelaus, threatened the peace of the city by undermining traditional Greek respect for native religious and legal practice. Greek readers, who always respected ancient traditions, were sure to condemn these Jewish innovators who wrought havoc.

In *Second Maccabees* there is a unique emphasis on religious martyrdom — Hannah and her seven sons and Elazar the elderly scribe — are presented as philosophers rationally defending the decision to die rather than to abandon their ancestral faith. Their deaths are seen not only as a way to sanctify God's name, but as a way to vicariously remove the sins of Israel and to evoke a supernatural intervention by God. This new phenomenon of religious martyrdom reflects the kind of religious loyalty valued in particular in the Diaspora. Their voluntary, tortured deaths assuage God's wrath over the desecration of the Temple by false high priests and explain **Judah's victories as God's salvation in response to the death of the Jewish martyrs** as well as God's appropriate punishment for Antiochus IV's insufferable arrogance.[60]

Supernatural intervention abounds in *Second Maccabees*, while religiously motivated military initiatives are emphasized in *First Maccabees*. (The miracle of the vessel of oil that burned for eight days is never mentioned in any of the *Books of the Maccabees* and appears only in later Rabbinic sources.)

The literary style chosen by Jason of Cyrene highlights the martyrdom. It is a melodramatic Greek style that describes graphically the death of innocent children, women and old men. It seeks to shock the audience with tear-jerking violence and to inspire the reader with heroic resolve to suffer horrendous torture rather than commit idolatry.

The summary of Jason of Cyrene was created by someone seeking to legitimize the celebration of Hanukkah in Ptolemaic Hellenistic Egypt. Therefore the anonymous "epitomizer" (summarizer) provides an abbreviated history with two letters written in 142 BCE by newly independent Judea to the Diaspora Jews in Egypt. The letters call upon their brothers to observe Hanukkah as the holiday of the rededication of the Temple.

---

60. *II Maccabees 9*

The Apocrypha

How were the Books of Maccabees preserved? In the Christian Bible. As we noted before, *First Maccabees* was written in Hebrew in Judea as a chronicle of the newly established Hasmonean Dynasty, probably 30-50 years after the Maccabean revolt. But it was never accepted by the Rabbis in Judea as a part of the canon. In fact, the Hebrew Bible contains no historical works after *Ezra* and *Nehemia* (450 BCE), which were written in the Persian period.

However, the Jews of Hellenist Egypt preserved two of the four *Books of the Maccabees*. *First Maccabees* was translated into Greek and the other three were written originally in Greek. *First* and *Second Maccabees* were incorporated into the Septuagint, the Greek translation of the Bible by Egyptian Jews which sometimes contains different versions of what we have in the Hebrew version as preserved. This Greek Jewish Bible, the Septuagint, was absorbed into the Christian Bible even before the New Testament was canonized. However,

when the Christians did begin to canonize or to categorize holy books, some church fathers like St. Jerome (4th century CE) distinguished the canonical "Old Testament" made up of the books found in the Hebrew Bible from the ecclesiastical works of a lesser status, like the *Maccabees* which is only in the Septuagint. Still the official bodies of Eastern and Western Christendom did regard all of the Septuagint, including all the books of the Maccabees, as sacred in some sense.

In 1534 the founder of the Protestant Reformation, Martin Luther, translated the Hebrew Bible into German leaving the *Books of the Maccabees* in his appendix under the title: "**Apocrypha**, that is, books which are not equated with Holy Scripture and yet which are useful and good to read." In response, the Catholic Church (Council of Trent in 1546) reaffirmed its status as a holy book just below the sanctity of the official Bible.

Gallery:
Elephants at War with the Jews

Suicide Mission

Elazar, Judah's brother, attacks the lead elephant of the Greek general. "And he crept under the elephant, and thrust in his spear from beneath and slew it." (I Maccabees 6:48) (Gustav Dore, 19th Century France)

Elephants on the March

Greek war elephants with their armor served as the tanks of the Hellenist period.

The Maccabees Face Off with the Elephants

The Greek war elephants of General Nicanor are massed for a charge against the Maccabees, while Judah the Maccabee rallies his troops. "So they cried unto the Lord with their voices, and they attacked the foe with their hands" (II Maccabees 15:34).

(Gustav Dore, 19th Century France)

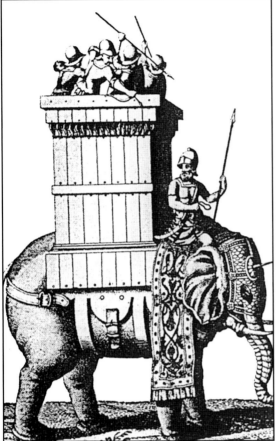

The Greeks attack Judah the Maccabee at Beit Zur
(illustrated German Bible 15th Century)

A Hellenist silver plate of a war elephant.

The Technology of Greek Warfare

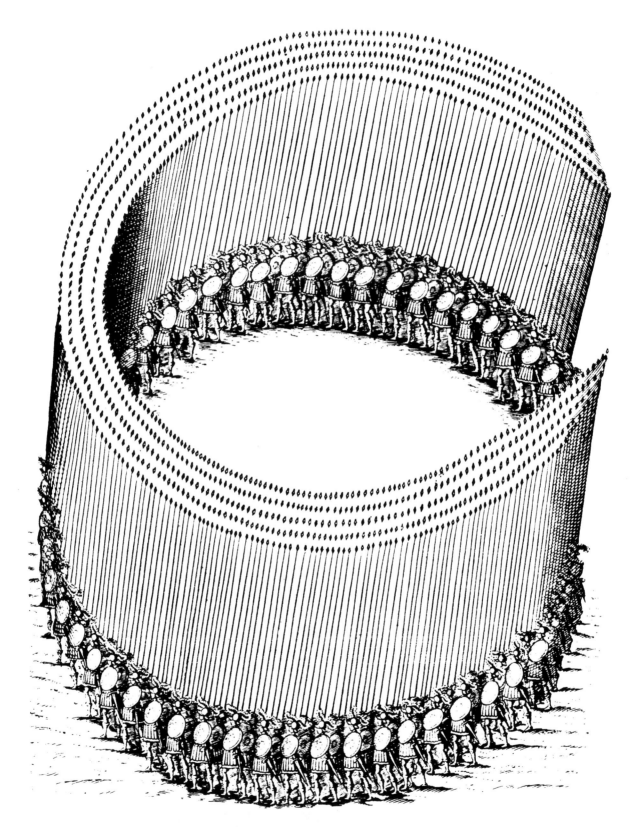

Macedonian soldiers in circular formation with long lances

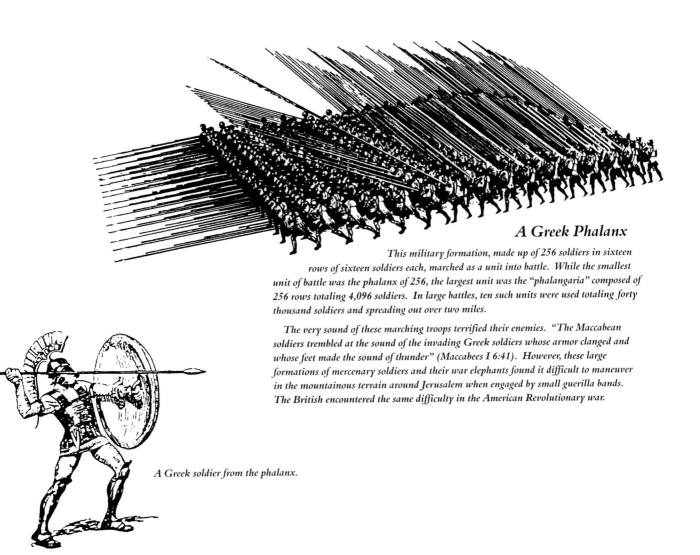

A Greek Phalanx

This military formation, made up of 256 soldiers in sixteen rows of sixteen soldiers each, marched as a unit into battle. While the smallest unit of battle was the phalanx of 256, the largest unit was the "phalangaria" composed of 256 rows totaling 4,096 soldiers. In large battles, ten such units were used totaling forty thousand soldiers and spreading out over two miles.

The very sound of these marching troops terrified their enemies. "The Maccabean soldiers trembled at the sound of the invading Greek soldiers whose armor clanged and whose feet made the sound of thunder" (Maccabees I 6:41). However, these large formations of mercenary soldiers and their war elephants found it difficult to maneuver in the mountainous terrain around Jerusalem when engaged by small guerilla bands. The British encountered the same difficulty in the American Revolutionary war.

A Greek soldier from the phalanx.

Armored Elephants in Hannibal's attack on the Roman Republic (217 BCE)

זה המערה ואהרן הטׄתׄ שׄמׄן בׄנׄירׄות

The Visionary Menorah by Joseph Hatzarfati

The High Priest rekindles the Temple menorah according to vision of the prophet Zechariah read on Shabbat Hanukkah. *(Cervera Bible, Spain, 1300)*

CHAPTER III

The Philosophers' Hanukkah:
Where Hellenism and Judaism Differ

Alexander the Great conquers the East. His head is crowned with a lion's head, symbol of Hercules, whose lineage he claimed.
(A Hellenistic sculpture from a sarcophagus)

The Philosophers' Hanukkah:
Where Hellenism and Judaism Differ

This chapter is devoted to understanding Western civilization as the ongoing conversation and/or confrontation of Jew and Greek.

"No other two races [but the Jews and the Greeks] have set such a mark upon the world. Each of them from angles so different, have left us with the inheritance of its genius and wisdom. No two cities have counted more with humankind than Athens and Jerusalem. Their messages in religion, philosophy and art have been the main guiding light in modern faith and culture. Personally, I have always been on the side of both."

— WINSTON CHURCHILL, PRIME MINISTER OF GREAT BRITAIN

INTRODUCTION

WHERE HELLENISM AND JUDAISM DIFFER

If Hanukkah is about the right to be different, then it is important that we understand what those deep differences are between Jewish and Greek culture. Many Jews today see no real difference between their worldview and that of their non-Jewish colleagues, or between modern Judaism and other ethical traditions. The more comfortable these Jews feel in a Judeo-Christian Western society, the less important it is to them to notice the distinctions between traditions. In fact, the culture we live in, both Jewish and non-Jewish, has already gone a long way toward synthesizing elements of the Jewish and the Hellenist cultures that first met in opposition in the era of the Maccabean revolt.

Let us add some historical perspective and philosophical depth to identify contrasting Greek and Jewish components of our cultures. Both are valuable to us, both have their strengths and weaknesses and hence the conversation between them and sometimes the ongoing disagreement between them is fruitful. As we search for renewed resources of spiritual growth we need to be attuned to the deeper elements beneath the homogenized synthesis of Jewish and Western tradition.

The scholars whose essays we have brought in this chapter have all studied Western tradition intensively and appreciatively yet have come to identify those features of Judaism which are still very different in emphasis.

Milton Steinberg, a learned, cultured Conservative rabbi, offers an appreciative survey of the greatness of Hellenist culture in the days of the Maccabees. Art, economics, philosophy, architecture and literature flourished in that era and justifiably attracted the provincial Jews of Judea. However, intuitively, many of those Jews also felt the deep lacunae in Greek thinking which still characterize Western society — the lack of a living spirituality and the overemphasis on competition to

the exclusion of compassion for the the stranger and the weak. Here Judaism has much to offer the Greeks and it is Steinberg's dream that the strengths of both traditions ultimately be combined.

David Hartman, an Orthodox Jewish philosopher and rabbi, focuses on two parallel differences between Greek philosophy and Judaism. The Greeks put too high a premium on **self-sufficiency**, on being a "self-made man," and at the same time they overemphasize the conquest of bodily desire by **abstract intellect**. Rabbinic Judaism, however, acknowledges our bodily needs and weaknesses and therefore is not ashamed to admit our dependence. Judaism promotes a **healthy interdependence** that counterbalances the exaggerated Greek desire for independence.

Mordechai Gafni, a young, contemporary Orthodox rabbi interested in spiritual renewal, uses the categories of Matthew Arnold, the 19th century English thinker, to contrast "Hebraism" and Hellenism. Gafni notes the strong attraction of young Jews to Eastern spirituality, which, like Western philosophy, puts a premium on detachment from everyday existence, on balance and emotional tranquility. Against that tendency Gafni counterposes the biblical God and the Jewish people who value a restless, passionate involvement with the world. That is the way of self-transformation and spiritual growth that Gafni recommends.

David Chidester, a cultural historian of religion is, unlike Steinberg, Hartman and Gafni, not a rabbi promoting an appreciation of where Judaism differed.

Yet he has much to teach us by contrasting the Jewish culture of the ear and the Greek culture of the eye. He points out that the differences between the two civilizations derive not only from their creeds and their philosophies, but from their preferred senses that "sensitize" them to divergent aspects of the world.

Elias Bickerman, the great Jewish historian of Hellenism, counterbalances all the other voices gathered in this chapter. For he shows that, beyond the polarity of Judaism and Hellenism, they share a passionate philosophic study of classical texts. In fact, our commemoration of the Maccabean rejection of Hellenism should not blind us to the greatest contribution of the Greeks to Rabbinic Judaism — the forms of study and centrality of text research for the achievement of truth and virtue. This is only one of the fruits of an open dialogue between cultures that Bickerman commends.

The Greek Culture of Competition.
In the struggle between two pankratiasts (on the ground), the man on the left tries to gouge out his opponent's eye, a foul for which the trainer is about to strike him with his cleft stick. Behind hang a bundle of boxing thongs and a discus in a bag, and on the left are two boxers.
From a Greek drinking-cup, c. 500-475 BCE.

1.

Judaism and Hellenism

by Milton Steinberg[1]

Western civilization is shaped by the input of Judaism, often mediated through Christianity, and Greek culture. For a Jew it is important to see how Judaism continues to differ from the Greeks, as well as how Judaism itself has been influenced by Hellenism, and in turn, influences Western society today.

According to a Jewish tradition which is transmitted both by Josephus and by Talmudic literature, Alexander the Great, on his way to Egypt (332 BCE), came face to face with the High Priest of the Temple at Jerusalem. The meeting between Alexander and the priest is probably a legend with no basis in fact. And yet, like so many myths, this one, if it does not possess literal accuracy, is nevertheless spiritually true. It symbolizes one of the most dramatic confrontations in the history of humanity. For, from the moment when Alexander touched the Orient until the hour when Christianity became the state religion of the Roman Empire, the culture of the Jew and the culture of the Greek were in continuous contact with each other. In the folk-picture of the conqueror and priest facing each other there is to be discerned a parable of the collision of two great civilizations.

For, as it happens, the two groups that wrestled with each other in Palestine in the 2nd century BCE represented more than artificial and meaningless national affiliations. They were the bearers and protagonists of

1. Milton Steinberg, "Judaism and Hellenism," from Philip Goodman, *The Hanukkah Anthology*, p. 5. Used by permission of the Jewish Publication Society.

distinct cultures, of different systems of living, each of which possessed virtues proper to it, but neither of which was complete without the other. Through the triumph of Jewish arms, then, there was preserved for mankind a cluster of religious and ethical values, which have been a vastly beneficent influence on subsequent generations. Of the larger implications of their actions the Maccabees themselves could have been only vaguely aware. As they saw it, they were fighting for freedom, for the faith and traditions of their fathers. Unwittingly, they fought also for certain concepts indispensable to adequate human living, which in the ancient world they alone possessed and which

The Cultural Legacy of Hellenism BY MILTON STEINBERG

Alexander the Great was more than a conqueror. He was, after all, a pupil of Aristotle. He felt that it was his function to civilize the lands he subdued. Into the Orient, then, he brought deliberately the whole wealth of that civilization which had grown up in Hellas. With him went the epics of Homer and Hesiod, the poetry of Alcaeus and Sappho, the drama of Aeschylus, Sophocles, Euripides and Aristophanes. The artistic standards which made the Acropolis, the philosophy of Plato and Aristotle, the deepest roots from which later sprang Stoicism, Epicureanism, Skepticism and neo-Platonism — all these were Alexander's gift to the East.

Within a short time the entire Orient was Hellenized. From India to the Hellespont, from Egypt to the Black Sea, peoples of diverse stocks learned to speak Greek, came to dress like Greeks, to worship like Greeks and to think like Greeks. For six hundred and fifty years thereafter the whole of the civilized world remained Hellenistic. From this fusion of the Orient and the Occident, from this syncretism of Hellenism and older cultures sprang as brilliant and as graceful a civilization, as human beings have ever known.

It was, in the first place, a world, which was infinitely rich in material things. At the wharves of Alexandria merchants bartered in all the products of all the lands of the world. Silks, spices and gems from the East were traded for furs and amber from the Baltic. In the banking houses of Rhodes, elaborate financial enterprises were planned and launched. In Alexandria and Antioch highly organized governments ruled over vast empires.

The cultural life of the Hellenic Orient was fully as brilliant as its economic activity. There was no field of human endeavor in which this age did not excel. The same architectural genius, which had created the unparalleled majesty of the Acropolis, now built the Pharos of Alexandria and the Colossus of Rhodes. The tradition of Phidias and Praxiteles lived again in those sculptors who carved out the Laocoon and the Dying Gaul. In scientific research also this world distinguished itself. It produced the Euclid who systematized geometry, the Ptolemy who charted the heavens, and the Aristoxenus who wrote on harmonics. The museum of Alexandria with its zoological and botanical gardens was no accident. It was a logical expression of the scientific interests of a civilization that had been born when the West met the East. And the library of Alexandria with its vast collection of books — that, too, was a symbol of this Oriental-Greek world. The poetry of Apollonius of Rhodes, and of Callimachus, the Idylls of Theocritus, the satires of Lucian, the biographies of Plutarch, the essays of Theophrastus, the history of Polybius, and the geography of Strabo and Pausanias — all these were fitting successors to the literature of classic Greece. Certainly, until the dawn of the modern era no other society has created literary masterpieces in such variety and profusion.

Closely akin to this literary activity ran a great philosophical tradition. The Stoicism of Zeno and Chrysippus, Epictetus and Marcus Aurelius, the Hedonism of Epicurus and Lucretius, the Skepticism of Carneades and Sextus Empiricus, and the neo-Platonic school which attained its climax in Plotinus — all these give vivid indication of the fact that the intellects of this age wrestled with the problem of truth, the riddle of the universe and the human's place in it.

Affluent in its possession of physical things, colorful in its art, glorious in its literature, and searching in its philosophy, this was indeed a magnificent world, a world startlingly like our own.

The All-out Struggle of the **Pankration.**
The victor aims a final blow, while the loser raises his left index finger in submission. The man on the right makes sure that the judge has noticed.

became the common possessions of mankind at large only through their heroic efforts.

The Jew's Objection to the Greek Way of Life

The Jew, to be sure, could not but be affected by this dazzling Hellenist culture [with its poetry, drama, sculpture, philosophy, sports, literature and material wealth]. The upper strata of Jewish society in Palestine were Hellenized as completely as the aristocracies of other lands. In Egypt, where Jews were fully exposed to Hellenism, Greek culture profoundly permeated Hebraic life. Books like those of Philo, the *Wisdom of Solomon*, and *Fourth Maccabees* show how deeply the Jewish community of Alexandria was influenced by the dominating civilization of its day. But as a whole, Palestinian Jewry stood unyielding in the face of all the seductions of Hellenism. And when Antiochus IV attempted to force the Greek way of life upon the Hebrews, the Maccabees rose in rebellion.

Considering the overflowing richness of the Hellenistic world, its elegance, and its culture, one is tempted to brand the

Maccabees and their followers as blind obscurantists, as benighted half barbarians who out of pure perversity resisted the transmission to themselves of elegance, beauty and truth.

And yet, the objection of the Jew to this Greek world, to its science, its art, its philosophy, and its amenities was not the blind, unreasoning hatred for intelligence of an uncultured group. It sprang from an intuitive but none the less profound and accurate judgment on the part of the Jews concerning Hellenism. There were in Greek life certain deep and fundamental voids, certain basic lacks, which the ancient Jew perceived. And there was in the Jewish tradition a body of religious and moral values for which the Maccabees fought justifiably. Almost by instinct, the Jew recognized that his culture possessed attitudes and ideals of which the Greeks were unaware but which were eternally necessary for human blessedness and salvation.

(1) In the first place, *the Greek world had no living religion*. The old pagan idolatry was dead. With the passing of the Olympian gods, philosophers took refuge in metaphysical abstractions. The masses, left without a satisfying faith, turned to a cynical skepticism, shot through with the blindest superstition. Humans believed in nothing and yet exhibited astonishing credulity in accepting any belief no matter how incredible. Organized religions have been accused of fostering superstition, and in instances, unfortunately numerous, the charge is justified. But it is equally true that when disciplined faiths disintegrate, men, far from being freed from faith and superstition alike, tend to take recourse to religious vagaries. The Hellenistic world is a classic case in point. The pagan, as Pliny testified, worshipped blind chance as the dominant power behind the world. But in a universe in which caprice rules, any ritual act, any charm or formula may possibly have efficacy. Whence it came to pass that magicians, astrologers and writers of amulets grew in

number, as organized religion decayed.

The ancient Greek, in addition, wanted, as humans always have, some faith to give meaning to their life. Unable to find it in their own world, they turned religious fadist, moving restlessly with tides of religious fashion from one cult to another. Now it was the Magna Mater, now it was Mithra, now Isis, now Serapis, now some fantastic meteoric stone worshiped as a god in some isolated Oriental hamlet. How desperately this world needed a religion can be seen from the eagerness with which it ultimately embraced Christianity.

"Three distinctive characteristics are to be found among Jews: they are merciful, they are chaste, and they are charitable." In this epigram are to be detected moral distinctions between Greek and Jewish society which the ancient Jew perceived.

The Jews considered this pagan world which had no faith and no assurance as to the universe, which maintained a system of state-endowed temples housing gods in whom no one really believed, which taught religions from which all vitality had fled. They viewed this society with its cults and fads, its blind superstitions and its religious stupidities. They concluded naturally that they possessed one thing which the pagans did not have — a reasonable and intelligible faith concerning the universe, a faith which told them that the universe was not a matter of blind chance, but the manifestation of a cosmic mind, that their life was not a meaningless accident, but an integral and infinitely significant part of a universal drama. They rejected the Greek world because it offered no adequate religion such as they found in their own tradition.

(2) Of equal weight in impelling the Jew's rejection of Hellenism was his awareness of *a profound difference in morals between the two worlds*. One of the ancient rabbis, contrasting Judaism and Hellenism, remarked, "Three

distinctive characteristics are to be found among Jews. They are **merciful**, they are **chaste**, and they are **charitable**." In this epigram are to be detected moral distinctions between Greek and Jewish society which the ancient Jew perceived.

The Jews, almost alone in the ancient world, had a sense of *the dignity of the life of every human being*. Their tradition taught them that humans were created through the infusion of the dust by the spirit of God, that each human being therefore was a divinity in miniature, and consequently of infinite moral significance. For that reason they were taught to detest all form of human exploitation, of the violent imposition by one human's will upon others. In their schools of law, these ideals were given practical application through a reluctance to inflict capital punishment, and through the attempt to mitigate human slavery by so protecting the rights of the bondsman as to make the possession of a slave economically unprofitable.

In contrast, the Greek world was entirely without a sense of reverence for the sanctity of life. *The Hellenistic social structure was built upon a brutal slavery*. From Plato and Aristotle to the last days of Roman paganism, only rarely were even the best spirits among the Greeks moved to protest against this extreme exploitation of men and women. To be sure, Hellenistic literature does contain discussion on the morality of human bondage. But these discussions, while they reveal an inner moral disquietude, tend to end either with a rationalization of the *status quo* or with the advice to the slaves to find their freedom in inner self-emancipation. In any event, the slave economy of the Graeco-Roman world was very little disturbed by moral protest. Observing the amphitheater where human beings were done to death for the amusement of blood-thirsty mobs, the Jew concluded, as Walter Pater did centuries later, that "what was needed was the heart that would make it impossible to witness all this; and the future would be with the forces that could beget a heart like that." One knew that the Greeks abused their slaves. One perceived that Greek society was founded upon violence, that in it the world belonged to the strong. One who had learned to reverence humans as an incarnation of God rejected the Greek world because, in addition to having no adequate faith, it had also no respect for life, no recognition of the inviolability of the human soul. It was not **merciful**.

Almost alone, too, the Jew had standards of

Bronze statuette of a girl runner, probably from Sparta, where women were expected to take part in athletics. Her appearance corresponds well with Pausanias' description of the girls who raced in the Heraia: "their hair hangs down, a tunic reaches to a little above the knee, and they bare the right shoulder as far as the breast."
(Description of Greece V 16.4)

chastity. Jewish society had developed a tradition of sexual continence that avoided sensual bestiality without being ascetic. The Greek world, on the other hand, by and large, vacillated between complete and abandoned self-indulgence and extreme, insane flight from the flesh. It exhibited, on the one side, the sensual excesses of the Gardens of Daphne, and, on the other, the rigid asceticism of the later neo-Platonists. This distinction in moral standards was reflected in a difference in the tone of family life and in the position of women. The normal Jewish world reverenced the marital state, and insisted on its spiritual significance and indispensability — in marked contrast to the Hellenistic family in which the wife served to breed children and from which the cultured Greek fled to find his social outlets in the companionship of cultivated courtesans, known as Hetaerae. In all that brilliant world with its science and its arts, the Jew then possessed an attitude toward sexual relationships which in its wholesomeness was distinctly superior to that of the society which surrounded him.

And, last of all, the Jew was unique in his recognition of the virtue of **charity**. From Plato through the Stoics, there is rarely to be discerned in Greek thought any vestige of compassion for the human underdog, for those who fail in life. Plato has no scruples of kindness in consigning the masses of men to bondage in his ideal state. Aristotle insists that some human beings are naturally slaves. The Stoics generally despise the great masses of humans as *typhloi* or blind fools. Only the Jew had a doctrine of charity and of sympathy for the oppressed. Only he had the feeling that the human being attains truest humanity in the giving of oneself to those who falter in the struggle for existence. In all the Greek world there was rarely heard a sentiment akin to that of the sages of Israel, "If you see a righteous person persecuting a righteous person, know that God is with the persecuted; a wicked person persecuting a wicked person, know that God is with the persecuted; a wicked person persecuting a righteous person, know that God is with the persecuted; and even when the righteous persecutes the wicked, by the very fact of persecution, God is with the persecuted."

This is not to say that the Jewish world was

The Greek world had wealth, science, art, and literature. They were not enough. It had no adequate faith and it had too little heart.

---

one of pure ethical light and the Hellenistic completely a realm of shadow. Not all Jews were saints and not all teachers of Judaism expounded an undiluted and ideal saintliness. Nor was Hellenism without mitigating religious and moral virtues. Indeed, among the Stoic legalists there appeared the axiom that all men are by nature equal — a proposition which, almost in the exact terminology in which these Stoics phrased it, appears in the American Declaration of Independence; it reflected an attitude which unfortunately was never competently applied by those who maintained it to the society of their day. There were currents of humaneness, movements of compassion, tides of a fuller religious life in the Hellenistic sea. But by and large and in essence the religious and moral distinctions which we have indicated above are unshakably valid. As a whole, each of these two traditions held virtual monopolies on attitudes and values of which the other possessed only fragmentary specimens.

It was because of this inherent difference in tone that the Jew rejected Hellenism. The Greek world had wealth, science, art, and literature. They were not enough. It had no adequate faith and it had too little heart. It

was inevitable that this world would fall into decay; that it would collapse into barbarism, that it would be conquered eventually by a religion born of Judaism, which supplied a rationale that made life significant and which conveyed standards of mercy, chastity, and compassion. In the very moment of its flowering, Hellenism was doomed, because *the intellect and the sense of the aesthetic are not sufficient for man.*

A Great Opportunity: When Judaism and Hellenism Met

The two worlds, as a matter of fact, did not exclude each other completely. On Palestinian Jewry, because of its rejection of the Greek-Oriental way, Hellenism had but little influence. On Jewry outside of Palestine, especially on that Egyptian Jewry which centered around Alexandria, the imprint of Hellenism was real and pronounced.

A great opportunity presented itself to mankind when Judaism and Hellenism met — an opportunity which unfortunately was not seized in its entirety. Had these two worlds interpenetrated each other peacefully, an ideal pattern for man's living might have been created. This would have preserved the intellectual alertness and aesthetic sensitivity of Hellenism in synthesis with the Hebraic religious outlook and ethical values. Such a fusion would have abstracted the virtues of both cultures and enabled them to supplement each other. Humankind still entertains the hope that the time may yet come when Hebraic faith and ethics will be harmoniously fused with Hellenistic science, philosophy, and art, into a pattern of living richer than either alone.

GREEK INTELLECT AND JEWISH BODY

A CONTRAST BETWEEN SELF-SUFFICIENCY AND BLESSED DEPENDENCE

by David Hartman[2]

A Tradition of Self-Sufficiency

For the sake of analysis and at the risk of oversimplification, one can divide what is generally referred to as Western thought into two distinct traditions. One tradition is characterized by the desire for **autonomy** and **self-sufficiency**. The highest perfection is intellectual excellence, which, ultimately, is an individual achievement. Though one may be seriously concerned with justice and with the needs of others, individuals aspire to overcome their need for others and to reach a perfection where they no longer feel dependent on anyone or anything. Perhaps it is more correct to describe this approach as choosing certain needs above other types of needs, i.e., intellectual above physical or social needs.

In Plato's *Phaedo*, for example, the metaphor used to describe the relationship of the body and the soul is that of a person locked in a prison. Platonic philosophy aims at liberating the human from the prison of the body. To anyone schooled in Western thought, the

Antiochus Epiphanes: "God Manifest" on a Coin of the Realm. The Greek ideal was to be self-sufficient, to be invulnerable, hence to be divine and to be worshipped as Antiochus IV wanted to be.

prisoner metaphor is most appropriate to the description of the relationship of the soul or mind and the body, and to the process of self-perfection. For Aristotle, although ethics and politics are the objects of serious attention and analysis, the essence of humanity, i.e. that activity which is distinctly human, is intellectual contemplation of eternal truths. Unlike practical deliberation, contemplation has no practical value. The highest human achievement lies in the privacy of one's thoughts; its content has no human utility; its subject, the philosopher, must be free of the claims of the body, which interfere with this activity.

A Tradition of Relationship

In contradistinction to this tradition is a tradition where relationship is an integral part of human perfection. The perfection aspired to is realized in relationship with others, and is associated with a pattern of life where the main focus is upon fulfilling normative demands within community and history.

The biblical tradition, which expresses the relationship of God and the people of Israel, is a paradigm case of this outlook. The God of the Bible, unlike the God of Aristotle, is described almost exclusively in terms of the Divine relationship with human beings. Indeed, many religious Jews consider that negating God's providential relationship to history and to humankind is tantamount to espousing atheism.

---

2. Rabbi David Hartman, "Moral Uncertainty in the Practice of Medicine" from *Joy and Responsibility* (Shalom Hartman Institute, 1978).

People are drawn to the Aristotelian God by virtue of the perfection they wish to contemplate. In this tradition, the "relationship" to God is like the "relationship" between a person and an object of one's curiosity or of one's aesthetic appreciation. It is no wonder that in the Middle Ages, a very serious distinction was drawn between belief in the eternity of the universe and belief in creation.

In the Greek tradition, with its ideal of intellectual perfection, it makes sense for humans to seek to be liberated from human relationships which demand intense emotional involvement.

The God of Aristotle was an object of intellectual contemplation. Only a God who could be conceived of as the Creator, as acting at a particular time, could give Law to humanity and could be conceived of in terms of a relationship.

On the inter-human level, the sentence epitomizing the biblical outlook is, *"It is not good for a human to be alone."*[3] As Soloveitchik explains in "The Lonely Man of Faith," the phrase *lo tov*, "[it is] not good," is not to be understood in the light of utilitarian or pragmatic considerations. The unqualified judgment that it is not good for the human to be alone has an existential basis. The biblical statement declares that humans are incomplete by themselves; biological, social, economic interests aside, it is not good that a person be alone. Humans must relate.

In the Greek tradition, with its ideal of intellectual perfection, it makes sense for humans to seek to be liberated from human relationships which demand intense emotional involvement. The **contemplative love** of the philosopher places the lover in a situation of control. **Interpersonal love**, however, places the lover in a context where one is vulnerable and dependent. The freedom of the beloved (an essential condition of mature

love) precludes the possibility of absolute control and self-sufficiency. In contrast, the relational perfection sought in the biblical tradition leads humans to accept dependency as a permanent, positive feature of the human condition.

Two Approaches to the Body: Our Prison or Our Spiritual Teacher?

The distinctive approaches of these two traditions extend to many more specific issues. Let us consider their differing attitudes to the body.

Common to the various expressions of the Greek tradition is the metaphor of "the prison of the body." The desire to escape the body and the glorification of the life of the "disembodied intellect" are psychologically tied to feelings of embarrassment at having a body with weaknesses and needs. In biblical thought, however, the body is not perceived as being in conflict with the soul. The distinction between body and soul is similar to a difference in organic functions; it does not reflect that radical dualism that is implicit in Plato's prison metaphor.

This difference may not be accidental. As suggested above, the God of the Torah-covenant differs from the god of Greek metaphysics in that He has a personal relationship with people. However scandalous it may sound to the ears of the metaphysical theologian, God, in the Bible, chooses inter-dependency with mankind. The God of history, who sends prophets, gives law, acts and reacts to what people do, is a God who, in some sense, "needs" humanity. The contemporary Jewish thinker A.J. Heschel's striking title *God in Search of Man* and his use of such notions as "divine pathos" penetrate to the heart of the biblical outlook. In choosing a covenantal relationship, God, in effect, chose inter-dependency.

In this framework, inter-dependency is an ultimate datum of reality. If to be fully human is to give up the quest for self-sufficiency, and if to be whole one must learn to love, to accept

---

3. *Genesis* 2:18

Greek Boxer. *(A Roman copy of a Greek sculpture)*

The body, and its functions, is dealt with in *Halakhah*. *Halakhic* man makes a blessing even after excretion:

> Blessed are You, Lord our God, King of the universe, who has formed the human in wisdom, and created within a system of veins and arteries. It is well known before Your glorious throne that if but one of these be opened, or if one of those be closed, it would be impossible to exist in your presence. Blessed are You, O Lord, who heals all creatures and does wonders.

It is significant that, in the normative sequence of prayers, this blessing is considered the antecedent of:

> My God, the soul which You placed within me is pure. You have created it; You have formed it. You have breathed it into me, and restore it to me in the afterlife. So long as the soul is within me, I offer thanks before You, Lord my God and God of my ancestors, Master of all creatures, Lord of all souls. Blessed are You, O Lord, who restores the souls to the dead.

Rather than ignore the body, *Halakhah* draws a person's attention to its complex functioning. The "body" heals human delusions of grandiosity. The body places one firmly in a world in which man cannot survive alone. In hunger and in need, in the interlinking of sexual desire, love and self-transcendence, in disease and in decay, the body is an important spiritual teacher. **To gain spiritual wholeness, the human soul must make contact with the body.**

---

4. *Numbers* 12:1

dependence, and to be able to say, honestly, "I need you," then spiritual liberation must consider the significance of the human body. The Greek tradition must be turned on its head. The human body can humanize us and dispel our delusions of self-sufficiency.

The source of human *hubris* can often be traced to the exaggerated emphasis on the intellect at the expense of recognizing the limitations of the body. The body gives persons a sense of humanity and dependency and, hence, teaches humility. And, in the Bible, humility is perhaps the most notable characteristic one can attribute to people of distinction. *"The man, Moses, was very humble, more than all the humans on the face of the earth."*[4] To the degree that people are alienated from the rhythms of their body, to that degree are they out of touch with the spiritual outlook of

Hebraism and Hellenism   BY MATTHEW ARNOLD[5]

One of the most politically and intellectually influential thinkers in the late 19th century in England was Matthew Arnold. He faced the crisis of industrialization and democratization in his land as a cultural crisis that might undermine educational standards. As he reflected on the culture he sought to preserve, Arnold conceived of Western civilization as a balance between the polarities of Hebraism, meaning Judaism and its offspring Christianity, and Hellenism and its offspring the Renaissance and modern science.

Hebraism and Hellenism — between these two points of influence moves our world. At one time it feels more powerfully the attraction of one of them, at another time of the other; and it ought to be, though it never is, evenly and happily balanced between them.

The final aim of both Hellenism and Hebraism, as of all great spiritual disciplines, is no doubt the same: human perfection or salvation. Still, they pursue this aim by very different courses. The uppermost idea with **Hellenism is to see things as they really are**; the uppermost idea with **Hebraism is conduct and obedience**. Nothing can do away with this ineffaceable difference; the Greek quarrel with the body and its desires is that they hinder right acting and thinking. The **Greek** notion of **felicity**, on the other hand, is when they think aright.

The **Hebrew** notion of **felicity** is *"He that keeps the law, happy is he;" "There is nothing sweeter than to heed the commandments of the Lord."* Pursued with passion and tenacity, this notion would not let the Hebrew rest till he had got out of the law a network of prescriptions to enwrap his whole life, to govern every moment of it, every impulse, every action.

The governing idea of **Hellenism** is **spontaneity of consciousness**, that of **Hebraism, strictness of conscience**. The difference, whether it is by doing or by knowing that we set most store, and the practical consequences which follow from this difference, leave their mark on all the history of our race and of its development.

To get rid of one's ignorance, to see things as they are, and by seeing them, as they are to see them in their beauty, is the simple and attractive ideal, which

Hellenism holds out before human nature. From the simplicity and charm of this ideal, human life in the hands of Hellenism is invested with a kind of aerial ease, clearness, and radiancy. They are full of what we call "sweetness and light." Difficulties are kept out of view, and the beauty and rationalness of the ideal have all our thoughts. "The best man is he who most tries to perfect himself, and the happiest man is he who most feels that he is perfecting himself."

Hebraism differs from Hellenism. [While the Greek thinkers sought restful contemplation of eternal truths], Hebraism has always been severely preoccupied with an awful sense of **the impossibility of being at ease in Zion**; of the difficulties which oppose themselves to the human pursuit or attainment of that perfection of which Socrates talks so hopefully, and so glibly. It is all very well to talk of getting rid of one's ignorance, of seeing things in their reality, seeing them in their beauty; but how is this to be done when there is something which thwarts and spoils all our efforts? This something is **sin**; and the space which sin fills in Hebraism [meaning Judaism and Christianity], as compared with Hellenism, is indeed prodigious. This obstacle to perfection fills the whole scene, and perfection appears remote and rising away from earth, in the background. Under the name of sin, the difficulties of knowing oneself and conquering oneself which impede man's passage to perfection, become, for Hebraism, a positive, active entity.

By alternations of Hellenism and Hebraism, of man's intellectual and moral impulses, of the effort to see things as they really are and the effort to win peace by self-conquest, the human spirit proceeds. Each of these two forces has its appointed hours of culmination and seasons of rule. As the great movement of **Christianity was a triumph of Hebraism** and man's moral impulses, so the great movement which goes by the name of the **Renaissance** was an uprising and re-instatement of human intellectual impulses and of **Hellenism**.

---

5. From *Culture and Anarchy*, c. 1870, England

3.

FROM ATHENS TO JERUSALEM

FROM BALANCED PERSONALITY
TO PASSIONATE RISK-TAKER

by Mordechai Gafni

Matthew Arnold, writing in his celebrated work *Culture and Anarchy*, suggests that Hebraism and Hellenism are the two essential philosophies of life between which civilized man must choose. Hanukkah is the tale of the clash between these two world visions. Thus, in the Jewish calendar, Hanukkah becomes the time of year when we try to relocate our spiritual direction on the road between Athens and Jerusalem.

Often, as Hanukkah approaches I wonder if I am becoming more of a Hellenist. Am I unconsciously sliding towards becoming a sort of "**inverted Marrano**," Jewish on the outside, Hellenistic on the inside. And so, as part of my own Hanukkah ritual, I try and look at some new dimension of that ancient conflict of ideas.

The Discus Thrower.
Myron

This year I'm thinking a lot about **balance and stability**. How many of us at some point in our lives thought of pursuing a new direction but held back for fear of being branded unstable? Balance and stability are certainly important values. However, it may not be irrelevant that their source in Western intellectual history is rooted in ancient Athens and not Jerusalem.

For the **Hellenist**, the **harmonious and balanced personality** is the ideal. However, Hellenistic harmony comes from a place of detachment. Plato's ideal is to "become a spectator to all time and existence." This is no Judaism. The basic **Hebraic** posture in the world is **passionate involvement** in the realness of life.

The Hellenist seeks eternity. He cannot find it in the world of particulars, which are here today and gone tomorrow. So he searches in the realm of essences, universals, and principles of logic. In their unchanging shadow, he feels the breath of eternity. For the Hellenist, theory is always more important than application, thinking is higher and more pure than doing.

For the Jew there is no greater sin than the sin of detachment. The ideal is the full embrace of the concreteness of being. God is in the details. God is in the ferment of our lives.

Jewish wisdom-masters rarely make sweeping universal statements about the nature of reality. They are relatively unconcerned with grand systems and elegant structures of logic. Their vision is almost always of the particular individual and his or her choices. For the Jew, eternity resides in the human encounter with the moment. God, the source of the eternal, is revealed in the infinite depths of the human personality no less than in the mathematical theorems of Pythagoras. The Hebraic worldview shapes the way we understand and live our lives in at least four important ways.

First, our vision of God differs from that of the Hellenist. The Jewish God is personal and cares deeply about all of His creatures. The Talmud describes God who is attendant and empathetic to the joy and pain of his creatures. **The Jew believes in a God who cares.** Our God knows our name. The mandate of Hebraic man is *imitatio dei*, to be like God. To be like God is about moral commitment to the betterment of our world and deep existential empathy with all who suffer. To be like God is to have a passionate social vision, which addresses all facets of humanity. It is to be concerned, engaged and attached.

Secondly, **for the Hellenist, God is a force in the universe, an unmoved mover.** The notion of a God who cries is blasphemous to the Hellenist. The notion of a god who doesn't cry is blasphemous to the Jew.

Thirdly, the Hellenist seeks to prove via rational demonstration that his God exists, while the Jew longs for **intimacy with God**.

Fourthly, as a function of this intimacy, the Jew on occasion even challenges God. Abraham becomes the first Jew by challenging the justice of God's intended destruction of Sodom and Gomorah. The Jew, writes Elie Wiesel, can be angry and even shout at God, but can never ignore God. Such is the nature of intimacy. The Hellenist however, must shape his God to be beyond taking any responsibility for the world. **For the Hellenist to contemplate is to embrace. For the Jew to struggle is to embrace.**

These ideas play themselves out in all sorts of very practical ways. One example: For the Jews there is always a legal obligation to rescue. That can apply to lost property or a friend drowning. Not to get involved is a violation of God. For the Hellenist and any of his Western descendants, "don't get involved for it may ruin your personal harmony" is the order of the day.

Now I am not arguing against balance and stability. However, for the Jew, balance and stability are values which are subservient to moral passion, reality, and empathy. They cannot become code words, which allow us to live blissfully in inherited truths unwilling to genuinely struggle with ourselves and the world.

For the Jew to realize the Divine within is to be always rising and becoming. And to become you have to risk falling, failing, and losing your place. Change by definition involves instability. **Balance needs to be disrupted when it fronts as an excuse for fear of growth and change.**

Let's give ourselves a Hanukkah present this year. Let's risk the new. We need to try and break the hold of the Hellenistic shadow on our psyche. There is something comfortable about the Hellenistic vision — all is harmony, life never really touches me and I don't have to pay the price of becoming. Perhaps it's time for commitment in places where we've been bravely maintaining our detachment because we were scared to death. Maybe we need to become unstuck from the tired idea that our life is what it is. Our life is what it could be.

Athens was a great city, but we are children of Jerusalem. Jewish eternity resides in the infinite value and holiness of our personal story and our potential for change. In the tradition of Hasidism, let us bless each other that this Hanukkah should be the year for us; a year in which the flame of the Hanukkah candle in our soul dispels the darkness of our fears — giving us courage to dare, to be, to care and love. Let the Maccabees be victorious.

The basic Hebraic posture in the world is passionate involvement in the realness of life.

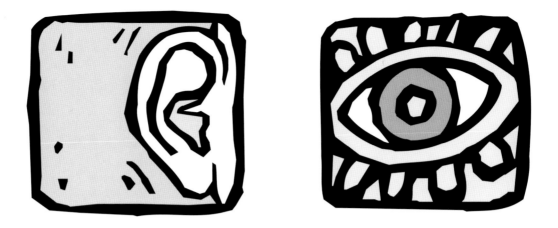

4.

THE WORD AND THE LIGHT, THE EAR AND THE EYE

CONTRASTING JEW AND GREEK

by David Chidester[6]

David Chidester has explored the way in which perceptual metaphors of seeing and hearing shape different cultural and religious understandings. He believes every culture uses both kinds of metaphors and often identifies its greatest insights with experiences that can only be described paradoxically using both of these two exclusive analogies simultaneously. For example, at Mount Sinai, "all the people saw the voices."[7]

However he summarizes an important strand of thought that holds that Greeks and thereafter Philo and many Christian theologians give priority to visual symbols: "God is light," ideas are visual forms, and gods can be represented pictorially.

In contrast, Biblical culture forbids making an image of God and emphasizes hearing God's voice. "The Lord spoke to you out of the fire; you heard the sound of the words but perceived no shape — nothing but a voice."[8] Nevertheless we must note that Jewish mystics and prophets in the Bible and beyond do use visual images, and over-generalization about whole cultures is always a danger.

Pagan and Jew

"The age-old battle between the eye and the ear is far from being decided one way or the other." Ambitious conclusions have been drawn about the perceptual orientations of entire cultures. **The visual orientation of ancient Greek culture and the auditory orientation of ancient Hebraic culture became a kind of cliche of cultural history.** This assumption that Hellenic culture was somehow fundamentally visual in its orientation, while Hebraic culture was fundamentally auditory, was clearly formulated in the nineteenth century by the historian Heinrich Graetz:

> To the pagan, the divine appears within nature as something observable to the eye. He becomes conscious of it as something seen. In contrast to the Jew who knows that the divine exists beyond, outside of, and prior to nature. God reveals Himself through a demonstration of His will, through the medium of the ear. The human subject becomes conscious of the

6. From David Chidester, *Word and Light: Seeing, Hearing and Religious Discourse,* © 1992, reprinted by permission of the Board of Trustees of the University of Illinois, University of Illinois Press.
7. *Exodus* 20:18   8. *Deuteronomy* 4:12

sight of the eyes, while the Jews, because they heard the divine word through the medium of the ear, located the sacred at a distance beyond the world. The visual mode, therefore, lends itself to a sensitivity to that which is immanent in the world; the verbal mode lends itself to the experience of a **transcendent** and invisible authority that speaks over against human beings and commands obedience.

divine through hearing and obeying. Paganism sees its god, Judaism hears Him; that is, it hears the commandments of His will.

Graetz suggested that, as a result of a characteristically visual orientation, the Greeks understood the sacred to be located in the world, **immanent** and accessible to the

Along the same lines, Thorlief Borman developed the difference between Greek and Hebraic thought: "Because the Greeks were organized in a predominantly visual way and

Seeing and Hearing in Greek Science   BY DAVID CHIDESTER

A phenomenology of perception must be sensitive to the ways in which the senses were understood to operate within specific historical and cultural contexts. The scientific explanation of vision was a major concern of those Greek philosophers known as the Atomists. Within that school of thought, visual perception was imagined to result from a direct contact between an object and the organ of vision. That contact was produced by images *(eidola)* or films *(simulacra)* that the Atomists thought were continuously being emitted from visible objects. In the act of seeing, those images or films entered through the pupil of the eye. In this "intromission theory" of vision, images from the object of vision were imagined to enter the eye to be simulated there as in a mirror. The visible object was duplicated in the eye.

A second theory of vision, the so-called "extramission theory" popularized by Plato and adopted by Augustine, explained seeing as the result of visual rays emitted by the eye. Beginning the analysis of vision with the organ rather than the object, **the eye was not a mirror but a lamp**. The eye was imagined to radiate visual rays that reached out and touched its objects of perception. This fire glows in the eyes. In the form of a visual ray, the fire extended from the eye to the object. Contacting the object, the visual ray then doubled back again to the eye.

What can be concluded from this all too brief sketch of ancient Greek optical theory? Certainly, the

dominant assumption about vision, from all perspectives, was that seeing resulted from a relationship between organ and object based on immediacy or continuity — the immediate presence of images in the mirror of the eye or the continuous bond between organ and object formed by the emanation of rays from the lamp of the eye. From ancient Greek speculations on vision, subsequent thinkers could derive certain basic associations that attended the process of seeing: continuity, connection, presence, similarity, immediacy, and even the union between seer and seen.

Hearing, however, was an entirely different matter. Unlike vision, hearing was not a process initiated by the organ of perception. Rather, auditory perception was always thought to be initiated by an external object. There was almost unanimous agreement that hearing resulted from a blow that struck the air, traveled over some distance, and impacted upon the ear. The discontinuity between perceiver and object was most clearly revealed in the temporal aspect of the process of hearing. Hearing required time.

In hearing, the object of perception was not immediately present to the perceiver as it was in vision. There was no presence, no connection, and no continuous bond between the subject and the object of perception. Because sound referred back to the agent that produced it, the auditory mode was referential rather than presentational.

Greek Symposium: Ancient Greeks reclining on couches, eating with their fingers, drinking from bowls and playing instruments.

(A Greek bowl, 5th century BCE)

the Hebrews were organized in a predominantly auditory way, each people's conception of truth was formed in increasingly different ways." Because hearing was most important to the Jews, Borman concluded that the decisive reality in their world was **the word**. For the Greeks, however, it was **the thing**. In both cases, an entire culture organized its conceptual life in terms of a predominant perceptual orientation toward either hearing or seeing.

Hearing is dependent on actions, events, and occurrences in the outer world, a world of becoming, while seeing has a constant and continuous access to the world's state of being.

The Phenomenology of Seeing and Hearing

There are definite contrasts between the ways in which the different sensory modes organize reality. Seeing defines a different orientation to the world than hearing. The most obvious difference has to do with the association of seeing with **space** and hearing with **time**. Vision is diffused in space, words move in time. Sight presents simultaneity and hearing presents sequence. The coherence of the visual mode is in simultaneous spatial presence. The sense of reality in hearing is a dynamic quality, a movement, a trajectory through time. Words move in time as "an indefinite series of discontinuous acts." Visual experience gives immediate disclosure of information, while the sequential nature of auditory experience involves a mediated [understanding. For example, the mind puts the individual words heard separately into a sequence that makes sense].

In vision the initiative for perception tends to begin with the subject [who decides to take a look, while the object creating the sound initiates the hearing in the recipient of sound]. Objects in the environment are by nature visible. They reflect light and are, therefore, immediately accessible to visual perception. They do not emit sounds simply by virtue of there being objects in the same way that they reflect light. Therefore, the perceiver cannot choose to hear something but must wait until something happens in the environment to cause sound. Hearing is dependent on actions, events, and occurrences in the outer world, a world of **becoming**, while seeing has a constant and continuous access to the world's state of **being**.

From these two perceptual orientations we might derive **active** and **contemplative** dispositions toward the world. Hearing evokes action, while seeing allows for a more neutral contemplation of the environment. Vision involves the discernment of patterns, configurations and spatial relationships — in other words, the recognition of order. Seeing permits a relatively neutral disengagement that contrasts with the dynamic interaction inherent in auditory experience. Sound informs the perceiver of an event, not merely the existence of things in a certain configuration. The hearer is compelled to respond to this independent change in the environment.

AFTERWORD BY THE EDITOR

In the light of David Chidester's contrasts it is easy to see how Biblical Judaism can be seen as more **oral** *and* **aural**. *God initiates contact with the Jews by calling them by name, then they must respond in action. As A. J. Heschel, the contemporary Jewish thinker, suggests, "God is in Search of Man" demanding action/mitzvah, unlike the Christian mystic who initiates the search for a vision of God. Not dogmas or revealed knowledge about God or the world, but moral action is central to Judaism. Not science i.e. a picture of a lawful pattern of nature, but history i.e. dynamic change over time is central to the Bible. God prefers "palaces in time" i.e. holy moments commemorated in holy days more than palaces in space, sacred sites. Of course Judaism has holy places, but their holiness is derivative from the holy events that occurred there. Telling and remembering orally are more important to Jewish self-understanding than seeing or imagining or making artistic representations. God acts through the word, through becoming, through history, more than through being and nature. As Mircea Eliade the historian of religion noted, the Bible added linear time to the pagan sense of cyclic time. As the literary scholar Robert Alter points out, the Bible offers the first example in human culture of prose narrative and of history writing, in contradistinction to the epic poetry that painted word pictures of pagan nature deities. Generally, though not without exception,* **Hebrew ears hear God's word, while Greek eyes see his light**.

When the Maccabees confronted the Hellenists, two radically different perceptions of the world met and conflicted. Since then, these two cultures have learned a great deal from one another and have become more balanced in their emphasis on the visual and on the aural perspectives.

5

THE PHILOSOPHER AND THE RABBI

THE GREEK CONTRIBUTION
TO THE RABBINIC IDEAL OF TORAH STUDY

summarized from Elias Bickerman[9]

All the previous selections on Hellenism and Judaism have been polemical, seeking an essential difference and sometimes a value polarity of these two competing cultures and identities. However, Elias Bickerman argues that Judaism — the Torah culture of the Second Temple Rabbis — is fundamentally altered and improved by the influence of Greek philosophic thought on traditional Biblical Torah study. He celebrates the way the Maccabees helped Judaism emerge as a self-confident, critical borrowing and adaptation of Greek ideals. Hellenism is the midwife by which Judaism evolves out of Biblical Hebraic religion.

"Hellenism is the epoch characterized by the union of Greece and the Orient. East and West were ripe for fusion, and cross-fertilization and metamorphosis quickly took place on both sides; newly-awakened popular life led to constantly new and further developments in Greece, invading the life of the world of the East and fertilizing it. Something fundamentally new arose in Hellenism — through the encounter of Greece with the Orient — which differed from the time of classical Greece, just as Judaism — underwent a gradual but deep-rooted change in the Hellenistic period through its encounter and conflict with the social, political and spiritual forces of this epoch. On this basis it differs in essential points from its earlier forms in the Old Testament.

"By and large, Judaism had its greatest influence on world history in the Hellenistic-Roman epoch. This included the reception and reworking of Greek thought side by side with self-assertion against alienation; the foundation of a national state after four hundred years of foreign rule, and the inner strength to withstand the new catastrophes which brought that state to an end and led to the final "dispersion." We may regard this as an expression of the incomparable vitality and dynamism of the Jewish people. Both its freedom fight against the Seleucids and its bitter struggle with Rome are probably unique in the ancient world. This dynamism developed most strongly in the religious sphere." — *Martin Hengel*[10]

The creation of the Rabbinic Torah culture that allowed Judaism to outlive the loss of its land, its Temple, its state and of the Graeco-Roman environment itself owes much to the Hellenism it fought so avidly under the Maccabees. Elias Bickerman identifies the Jerusalem scholar Ben Sira (190-180 BCE), just a generation before the Maccabean Revolt, as the key figure who adapts Greek philosophic ideals to Torah study.

Ben Sira's Revolution

Since the days of the Rabbis it has become axiomatic to identify universal male text study as a Jewish activity par excellence. However Elias Bickerman claims that this is a Greek innovation that can be dated to Ben Sira, the Jewish philosopher who lived in Jerusalem in the generation before the Maccabees. Previously, the Bible recommended that fathers teach their sons the basic laws by rote and retell the primary stories. Biblical law was part of public education only peripherally — once every seven years when portions were read aloud to the whole people. Only the priests like Ezra were intensively involved in Torah study.

---

9. This summary is based on but does not quote directly from Elias Bickerman, *The Jews in the Greek Age* (p. 166-174), published by Harvard University Press.
10. *Judaism and Hellenism*, p. 2-3, 309

However, Bickerman claims, Ben Sira absorbed the Greek ideal of learning for adult wisdom. Greek culture made it an ideal for the citizen's class to study a classical text as part of becoming a human being. The ideal of realizing one's humanity by education based on interpreting a classical text is the Greek notion of *paidea* — education. Homer was the text that educated Greece and with Alexander's conquest it became an ideal

---

Greek culture made it an ideal for the citizen's class to study a classical text as part of becoming a human being.

---

vehicle of Hellenization for upper class subjects of the Greek empires whatever their ethnic origin.

This Greek cultural practice was, says Bickerman, the direct model for Ben Sira. Ben Sira argued for the first time that Torah — both its ritual and ethical parts — should be the basic subject matter of Jewish education even if it was not tied to preparation for a profession as a priest or jurist. For Torah is understood as a wisdom literature that adds not only skills but virtues

and philosophic insight to human life and to the life of the individual scholar who devotes himself to study as a means to self-perfection. The Jewish term *chochma* (wisdom) became synonymous with *paidea* (education) and *sophia* (knowledge). The true disciple is out to learn the secret of a happy and successful life, not practical skills. But as Ben Sira emphasized, "fear of the Lord" is the beginning of this search for wisdom.

The study of the law by lay persons was, in short, a Hellenistic innovation imported into Jerusalem even before the Maccabean Revolt and continued unabated throughout and after the Maccabean struggle. While other great traditional religious cultures like the Egyptian and the Babylonian declined under Greek rule, Jewish culture flourished under the Rabbis even without political independence. The miracle of survival was simply that other traditional societies continued the monopoly of knowledge in the hands of the priesthood and continued to separate themselves off. However the Maccabees and their descendants, as ironic as it seems, imitated the Greek model of text study but gave it Jewish content. In fact Judaism went one step beyond Hellenism in opening up text study to the lower classes rather than restricting it to the leisure classes.

Talmud Torah:
To Study is to Become a Human Being, a **Mensch.**
(Hasidim, Eretz Yisrael, 1921, from a postcard photo by S. Narinsky)

Gallery:
Warrior Menorahs

Hanukkah on the Front, 1916

German-Jewish soldiers gather to light the Hanukkah menorah in the field on the Polish front, 1916.

(Zydowski Instytut Historyczny Instytut Naukowo-Badawczy,
courtesy of United States Holocaust Memorial Museum Photo Archives)

Greetings from the War

Lighting up the Darkness, 1973

Israeli Soldiers light Hanukkah candles on the Sinai Desert Front during the Yom Kippur War, 1973.

(photographed by Micha Bar-Am, Beit Hatefusoth Photo Archive, Tel Aviv)

An English, Hebrew and Chinese Hanukkah greeting card from the American-Jewish soldiers in Shanghai to Jewish refugee children, 1945. These soldiers, stationed in Shanghai, "adopted" Jewish refugee children from Europe who had spent the war in China. Each child received a card, along with an American dollar as Hanukkah gelt, inscribed with the greeting: "An American dollar for Chanuka gelt from your 'big brother' — An American Jewish soldier."

(photographed by Harry Fiedler, United States Holocaust Memorial Museum)

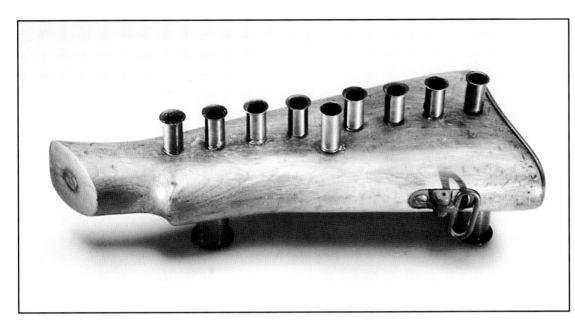

The Rifle Butt Menorah

During the War of Independence in Israel, a jeep driven by Leon Shalit, a British volunteer of the fledgling Israeli army, ran over a land mine near El-Arish. Years later, Shalit met an officer whose tank was sent to extricate his jeep. In commemoration of their common army experience, his comrade gave Shalit this Hanukkah lamp which he himself had made from a World War II English rifle butt.

(Leon Shalit, Jerusalem, Israel Museum)

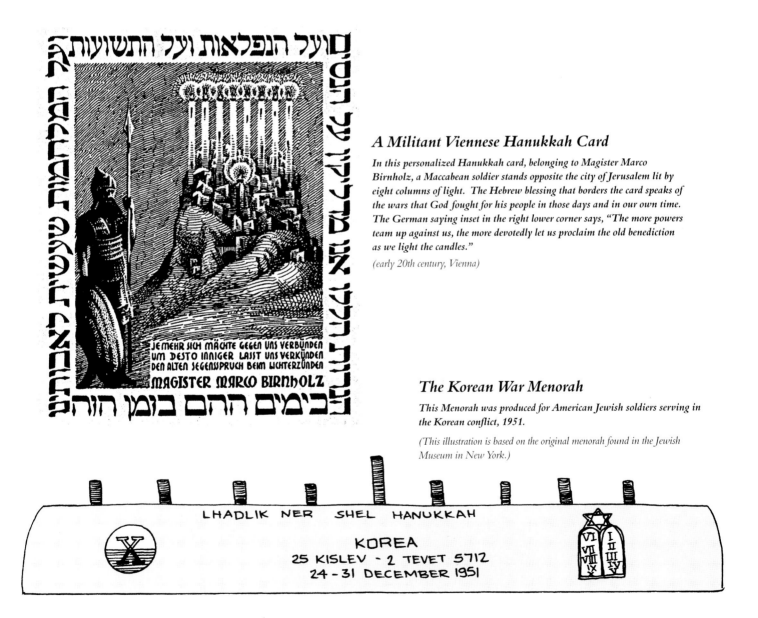

A Militant Viennese Hanukkah Card

In this personalized Hanukkah card, belonging to Magister Marco Birnholz, a Maccabean soldier stands opposite the city of Jerusalem lit by eight columns of light. The Hebrew blessing that borders the card speaks of the wars that God fought for his people in those days and in our own time. The German saying inset in the right lower corner says, "The more powers team up against us, the more devotedly let us proclaim the old benediction as we light the candles."

(early 20th century, Vienna)

The Korean War Menorah

This Menorah was produced for American Jewish soldiers serving in the Korean conflict, 1951.

(This illustration is based on the original menorah found in the Jewish Museum in New York.)

Recycled Menorahs

Hanukkah Lamps made of Soldiers' Hat Plates

Hanukkah lamps ornamented with the insignia plates from brass military hats are not uncommon from the period of the Seven Years' War (1756-1763) between Frederick II, "the Great," King of Prussia, and Maria Theresa, Empress of Austria and her allies. On the menorah can be seen military insignia such as a crown, an eagle, drums and bugles, with the motto "pro patria," "for the fatherland."

(Catalogue of Ritual Objects in Secondary Use, Israel Museum, Jerusalem)

Drawings of Prussian soldiers in their military hats
(Catalogue of Ritual Objects in Secondary Use, Israel Museum, Jerusalem)

The Buddhist Menorah

Although this is not a war menorah, like the menorahs made of rifle butts and military hats, it too is made from recycled materials. A Ukrainian menorah was placed on top of a model of a Buddhist Temple and presented to Sir Moses Montefiore in the 19th Century.

(Catalogue of Ritual Objects in Secondary Use, Israel Museum, Jerusalem)

The Judah Menorah

This brass menorah shows Judah going into battle, flanked by the Lions of Judah, which symbolize the tribe of Judah, even though Judah the Maccabee as a priest was from the tribe of Levi.

(Artist Fred J. Kormis, London, 1950. The Jewish Museum/Art Resource, New York)

The Un-Orthodox Menorah:
The Hulk Hogan Menorah

Joel Otterson, Cincinnati, OH, 1993.
(Jewish Museum/Art Resource)

This unorthodox menorah[1] features professional wrestling world champion Hulk Hogan as a symbol of heroism. While Hulk Hogan is not Jewish, his successor as world champion, Billy Goldberg, is undoubtedly Jewish. This six-foot-four, 285 pound wrestler often wears a Star of David, or a shirt saying "Goldberg: A Nice Jewish Boy." This son of a Harvard educated obstetrician and a concert violinist has added a new dimension to Jewish masculinity in America. After playing in the National Football League for three years, and tearing a stomach muscle, he became a professional wrestler in 1997. Goldberg, unlike many other American Jewish celebrities, chose to keep his surname. "The stupidest question I get is 'Is Goldberg your real name?'" he says. "I tell people, 'No, my real name is Killer, but I wanted a much more menacing name, so I picked Goldberg.'" "I had three intentions when I became a wrestler," he says. "One was to keep my integrity. Two was to give pro wrestling a more respectable image. And three was to be a role model to Jewish kids who may not have thought they could do what I do. I've got a lot of people I'm carrying on my back, but it's a light load because I take a lot of pride in who I am and where I came from."

(see Paul Farhi Goldberg: A David In Goliath's Shoes, Washington Post December 9, 1999)

---

1. Made of metal piping, cast bronze, glass and porcelain.

The Judith Menorah

In this Turkish menorah, the military heroism of Judith is portrayed as she beheads General Holofernes in his tent.

(Courtesy of Israel Museum)

CHAPTER IV

The Rabbis' Hanukkah:
Rabbinic Reflections on the Warrior, the Zealot, the Martyr, the Peacemaker, and the Believer in Miracles

The Menorah in the Modern Temple.
This modern German rabbi, dressed in clerical robes, is lighting the synagogue Hanukkah menorah.
(J. Tolmann, Frankfurt, 1899)

The Rabbis' Hanukkah:

Rabbinic Reflections on the Warrior, the Zealot, the Martyr, the Peacemaker, and the Believer in Miracles

INTRODUCTION

THE RABBIS' HANUKKAH: REFLECTIONS ON THE WARRIOR, THE MARTYR, THE ZEALOT, THE PEACEMAKER AND THE BELIEVER IN MIRACLES

The inspirational power of the Maccabean Revolt and of the miracle we celebrate on Hanukkah has been seriously undermined in the contemporary world. A shift in worldview in the West has made us very ambivalent about a series of concepts basic to Hanukkah. The **national** struggle for independence, requiring **military heroism** and **self-sacrifice,** is problematic in a post-nationalist era in the West where the praise of warlike qualities and collectivist identities seems outmoded and even dangerous. The belief that a **miracle** was involved in the victory appears unscientific and childish. The willingness to be a **martyr** for a religious cause is difficult for those with a pluralistic worldview because, for many, religious certainties have evaporated. Moreover, sacrifice of self is problematic in a society built on self-fulfillment and the pursuit of personal happiness as the ultimate purpose of human life. Finally, the **zealot** has become the incarnation of evil, since he has been identified with the fanatic who violently denies others individual freedom in the name of a totalitarian faith.

Though we cannot deal in depth with this massive attack on the traditional values associated with the Maccabees, we would like to explore the way the Rabbis themselves sought to qualify and bracket the problematic aspects of the national military hero, the zealot, the martyr and even the miracle. While still upholding these traditional values, they sought to counterbalance them with the ideal of the **family peacemaker**, the value of **preserving life** even when religious practice must be compromised and the precedence that **legal due process** takes over zealous vigilante activity.

This chapter's first essay, ***The Family Peacemaker***, begins with what seems like a halachic quibble over the lighting of a Shabbat lamp or a Hanukkah menorah when one has enough oil to light only one of them. This unlikely legal dispute is the vehicle for the Rabbis to promote the value of a self-effacing family peacemaker over the military effort to defend the dignity of one's holy sites and one's national honor.

In the second essay, on ***Mattathias the Priestly Zealot***, we examine the multiple ways the Talmudic tradition seeks to prevent anyone from emulating the fanatic behavior of Mattathias and his hero, the Biblical priest Pinchas.

In the third essay, ***How Hanukkah became a Home Holiday***, we speculate on the Rabbis' decision to make Hanukkah observance reinforce home values rather than to celebrate the political victory in the streets and the religious triumph in the Temple or synagogue.

In the fourth essay, ***To Be a Warrior or a Martyr?***, David Dishon shows the way in which the Maccabean martyr's willingness to die for the sanctity of Shabbat was qualified in two ways. First, Mattathias urged that Jews defend themselves if attacked on Shabbat rather than immediately choosing the role of martyrdom. Second, the Talmudic Rabbis insisted that *piku'ach nefesh*, saving a human life, was almost always to be preferred over the preservation of the sanctity of Shabbat.

In the fifth essay we transcend the Rabbinic world to bring a thoughtful sociological analysis of martyrdom in Eugene Wiener's ***The Martyr's Conviction: A Sociological Analysis***.

Finally, the sixth essay, ***Do I Really Believe in Miracles***, surveys different attitudes to miracles in order to clarify in what sense this central category of Hanukkah can still claim our faith.

THE RABBINIC IDEAL OF THE FAMILY PEACEMAKER

PREFERRING SHABBAT CANDLES OVER HANUKKAH CANDLES

by Noam Zion

Hanukkah not only commemorates past events, it celebrates the human virtues that shaped those events as well. Those are the martial traits of the priestly Hasmoneans led by Mattathias, the zealot, and by Judah Maccabeus, the warrior. Those values have their place in any society that seeks to defend its religious freedom, its national autonomy and its sacred places.

However, these uncompromising, combative virtues can be problematic in everyday life. Therefore the Rabbis —

though ambivalent — sought to temper this heroic stance appropriate for extreme situations, by constructing an alternative model more suitable to normal conflict resolution. On one hand, they still honored the memory of the impassioned priestly Mattathias (166 BCE), who like his ancestor Pinchas, the *priestly zealot*, stabbed to death a Jew collaborating with a non-Jew in a public desecration of holy values. On the other hand, the majority of Rabbis (from the school of Hillel) actively cultivated and emulated the model of Pinchas' peace-seeking grandfather, the High Priest Aaron, and his descendants who are idealized as the quintessential *pursuers of peace* within society. Opposite the "jealous/zealous God" of Mount Sinai who brooks no adulterous flirtation of his spouse Israel with idols like the golden calf, the Rabbis promoted an image of God as compromising the honor of his name in order to bring peace between earthly spouses. Most of the Rabbis preferred the Aaron model to the Pinchas / Mattathias model of Jewish leadership.

Oddly enough, the confrontation of the combative, national values of the Hasmonean heroes and the pacific values of family conflict-resolution is discussed in the Jewish legal discussion of what seems a purely ritual question: *When on Friday evening of Hanukkah one does not have enough oil (or money to buy sufficient oil) to light both the Shabbat candles and the Hanukkah candles, then what takes precedence?*

Lighting the Hanukkah Candles, by Marc Chagall, 1946

(copyright ADAGP, Paris, 2000)

Lighting the Shabbat Candles, an engraving from a Book of Jewish Ceremonies.
(Utrecht, the Netherlands, 1682)

Maimonides:
In Praise of Jewish Sovereignty

Maimonides[1] summarizes the laws of Hanukkah in a unique way in Rabbinic tradition. He alone — unlike the Talmud or the Shulchan Aruch — opens his laws of "how" to light Hanukkah candles by reviewing the military struggle that led to national independence. Yet paradoxically Maimonides alone concludes these laws with a panegyric of peace — *"Great is Shalom, for the whole Torah was given to make peace in the world."*

While the Shulchan Aruch[2] focuses on the miracle of the cruse of oil that burnt for eight days in the Temple rededication, Maimonides begins with the national emergency:

"In the Second Temple period [167 BCE] the Greek kings decreed evil decrees on Israel: they abolished their religion, prevented them from studying Torah and doing mitzvot, stretched out their hands to take their money and their daughters, entered the inner sanctum of the Temple, violated its restrictions and defiled its purities. Israel was terribly distressed because of them and the Greeks oppressed them greatly. Then the God of our ancestors felt mercy for all Israel, saved them from their hands and rescued them. The Hasmonean priests killed the Greeks and saved Israel from their hands and then established a monarchy led by their priestly descendants — [not by King David's tribe of Judah] — and restored sovereignty to Israel for over 200 years until the destruction of the Second Temple [70 CE].

"And when Israel overcame its enemies and wiped them out — it was the 25th of the month of Kislev [164 BCE], — then they entered the inner sanctum of the Temple. They were unable to find pure oil in the Temple except for one cruse of oil that could last only one day. They lit from it the Temple candles for eight days while in

Using insights I have learned from my teacher Rabbi David Hartman, let me explain how this shortage of oil becomes, in Maimonides' great work of Jewish law, the *Mishne Torah*, an occasion for praising the Maccabees for their uncompromising defense of Jewish sovereignty and self-respect, yet ultimately giving priority to family values of compromise.

Oddly enough, the confrontation of the combative, national values of the Hasmonean heroes and the pacific values of family conflict-resolution is discussed in the Jewish legal discussion of what seems a purely ritual question.

---

1. 12th century philosopher, physician, jurist and political leader of Egyptian Jewry
2. 16th century, Rabbi Joseph Caro's Code of Jewish Law.

the meantime they were pressing olives and extracting pure oil."[3]

Although Maimonides mentions secondarily the cruse of oil that burned for eight days, he speaks with pathos of the Greek kingdom's evil decrees against Israel — its religious laws, its Temple, its financial resources and its daughters. Then God has mercy on his people and "saves" them by allowing the Hasmonean priests to "save" them and by reestablishing Jewish autonomy in the form of a priestly royal dynasty.

Several points need to be highlighted in Maimonides' historical reconstruction:

(1) The "saving act" is God's intervention via human military and political action, thus both God and the Hasmoneans are "saviors."

(2) The persecution was aimed at Israel. Therefore God's and the Maccabees' battle was to save Israel from the Greeks, not to save God's Temple and God's honor from desecration. Unlike the *First Book of Maccabees* which portrays Mattathias as a zealot in the tradition of Pinchas who is defending God's jealously guarded dignity, Maimonides speaks in national religious terms about Israel's desire to protect its own religious laws as well as to achieve political autonomy. The loss of Torah is the first aspect of Jewish persecution, but "the Greeks' putting their hands on our money and our daughters" is equally grievous. The parallel of money and daughters, so strange to our ears, may refer to the indignity of adults who cannot prevent the invasion of their homes, their pockets, and their carefully protected daughters. It is similar to the "invasion of the inner sanctum of the Temple, the violation of its limits and the desecration of its purity." The Greeks threatened not only our religious freedom or God's sacred space, but our self-respect and autonomy as individuals, as families and as a nation. Therefore Maimonides — unlike any earlier or later rabbi — completes the narrative of redemption, not merely with the purification of the Temple, but with the return to national sovereignty "for two hundred years."[4]

Hanukkah Candles: Going Above and Beyond the Call of Duty

Maimonides' introduction with its

Trial by Ordeal: The Jealous Husband

In the Torah a "jealous/zealous husband" who suspects his wife of adulterous relations yet lacks conclusive proof may break off relations with her. She can establish her innocence by a trial by ordeal in which she goes to the sanctuary, takes an oath and drinks the bitter waters into which a parchment with God's name has been dissolved. Should she survive, then she has proven her innocence. The husband then must abandon his suspicions and be reunited with her. They are both granted a Divine promise that they will have children.[5]

In the Talmud, the Rabbis worked hard to minimize this trial by ordeal driven by male jealousies. For example, they insisted that there be prior warnings and then proof of the woman's repeated secret meetings with the suspected adulterer and that the husband not be suspected of his own extra-marital affairs. The ordeal was understood to be voluntary: only a woman who wanted to be reunited with her jealous husband would agree to this torturous way to reassure him that his suspicions were false.

However the Rabbis did derive one positive value from this strange ancient rite: God was willing to command that his Divine name be erased just to ease the irrational fears of a jealous, easily-threatened husband, and thereby to help his wife who wants to be reconciled with him. Though God is zealous in defending his name against traitorous idol worshipping Jews, God volunteers to have his name dissolved into the bitter waters, which will clear a woman's name and restore marital, domestic peace. Maimonides' rationale for preferring "domestic peace" over the national values of Hanukkah derives from God's commandment that "the Divine name be erased in order to bring peace between a husband and wife."

---

5. *Numbers* 5

3. *Mishne Torah, Book of Festivals*, Laws of Hanukkah Chapter 3:1-2
4. In fact, full Hasmonean sovereignty lasted only from 140-63 BCE, though Jewish kings like Agripas continue with limited power granted by the Roman Empire to 70 CE and beyond.

"Spit in My Eye" — Rabbi Meir's Marital Counseling

The Rabbinic preference for the value of compromise in family life is exemplified in the Talmudic story of Rabbi Meir whose popular lectures on Shabbat were frequented by, among others, a woman with a fiercely jealous husband.

Rabbi Meir used to give regular talks in the synagogue of Hamat [the hot springs in the Golan Heights] every Shabbat eve. A certain woman of that town made it a habit to listen to his weekly sermons. On one occasion when he extended his talk to a late hour, she waited and did not leave until he finished.

But when she came to her home, she found that the lamp was out. Her husband asked her, "Where have you been until now?" She told him, "I have been listening to a rabbi's talk." Now, the husband said to her, "I swear by such-and-such that you are not to enter my house again until you spit in your teacher's face."

She left her house and stayed away one week, a second, and a third. Finally the neighbors asked her, "Are you still angry with each other? Let us go with you to the Rabbi."

When Rabbi Meir saw them, he perceived the reason for their coming by means of the holy spirit. And so, pretending to be suffering from pain in the eyes, he asked, "Is there among you a woman skilled in whispering a charm for eye pain?"

Her neighbors said to her, "Go, whisper in his ear and spit lightly in his eyes, and you will be able to live with your husband again." So she came forward. However, when she sat down before Rabbi Meir, she was so overawed by his presence that she confessed, "My master, I do not know how to whisper a charm for eye pain."

But he said to her, "Nevertheless, spit in my face seven times, and I will be healed." She did so, whereupon he said, "Go and tell your husband, 'You asked me to do it only once but I spat seven times!'"

His disciples said to him, "Master! Is the Torah to be treated with such contempt? If you had only told us we would have brought that husband and

flogged him at the post until he consented to be reconciled with his wife."

Rabbi Meir replied, "The dignity of Meir ought not to be greater than that of his Maker. If the Torah enjoins that God's holy Name may be obliterated in water in order to bring about peace between a man and his wife [in the case of the suspected adulteress],[6] all the more so may Meir's dignity be disregarded."[7]

In the exemplary story of Rabbi Meir (whose name means to "give light") a great rabbi forgoes his personal honor and the honor of the Torah in order to relight the lamp of domestic life that has gone out between a pious woman and her difficult husband. The husband, in some sense, views the rabbi as his "adulterous competitor," a source of jealousy, and he seeks to keep his wife at home tending to his lamp and his needs especially on Friday night. The public study of Torah in the synagogue has become a threat to domestic tranquility on Shabbat evening, a prime time for conjugal intimacy.

While Rabbi Meir could have had the husband flogged until he recanted his jealous oath, he knew that legal and physical force would not lead to emotional reconciliation. Therefore he chose the pretext of spitting into his "eye" as a medicinal charm, to relight the lamp between husband and wife. He saves both the dignity of the wife and the husband and still fulfills the literal meaning of the husband's punitive oath. The woman is not forced to choose between public Torah and domestic Shabbat.

As Rabbi Meir explains to his students, the ordeal of *sotah* (the suspected adulteress) with its erasure of God's name is understood as a paradigm of ethical behavior placing the family peacemaker above the zealot. God's own honor, as well as the Torah's, is voluntarily compromised in order to promote *shalom bayit,* domestic tranquility.

6. *Numbers* 5:23-24

7. From *Sefer HaAggadah* edited by H.N. Bialik and V.H. Revnitzky, drawn from *Deuteronomy Rabbah* 5:15; *Leviticus Rabbah* 9:9; *Jerusalem Talmud Sotah* 1:4; *Numbers Rabbah* 9:20.

nationalist strains can be used as an interpretive key to understand the rationale of the ritual laws of how to light Hanukkah candles that he summarizes from the Talmud. The nationalist values are volunteerism, public display of one's collective symbols and self-sacrifice for the community. Perhaps some of the ritual requirements of candle lighting echo those values symbolically.

(a) For example, while one candle is legally sufficient for each night of Hanukkah, (not one per night but one candle alone along with the *shamash*), one who wishes to "expand and beautify the mitzvah" *(hiddur mitzvah)* is commended for lighting multiple candles each night — one for each night that has passed — and for multiplying the number of family members lighting their own set of candles.[8] Perhaps the **volunteerism** of the Hasmonean children is repeated in the voluntary act of every family member lighting multiple candles.

(b) The candle must be placed at the doorway or the window closest to the **"public space"** in order to be seen by passersby who are still outside returning from the market place. They should burn for up to half an hour after sunset.[9] Only in times of danger may the Hanukkah candle be placed inside the house on the table.[10] Perhaps the concern to propagate knowledge of the miracle of Hanukkah, from the family space to the public space, reflects the reversal of the process of persecution described above. The Greeks, who dominated the public space, our Temple, also sought to invade the private spaces of our homes, our pocketbooks, and our daughters. The Hasmoneans regained control of the public space in reestablishing the "kingdom of Israel." In the contemporary experience every North American Jew who leaves the Christian public space of the Christmas season and comes to Jerusalem for Hanukkah feels the national significance of a Jewish public space.

(c) The Hanukkah candle lighting — even though legally speaking it has no roots in the Torah — is still very important and enormously popular. Maimonides says people should be **willing to compromise their personal dignity** to promote this symbol of God's redemption of our national dignity.

"The mitzvah of lighting a Hanukkah candle/lamp is a very well-loved mitzvah and so one needs to be very careful to do it in order to proclaim the miracle and to add praise to God and gratitude for the miracles he did for us. Even if one has nothing to eat except from *tzedakah* (handouts), one should borrow money or sell one's coat in order to purchase oil and lamps to light."[11]

In Jewish tradition a poor person's coat is the last thing to part with. The Torah requires someone, who took a poor person's only coat as collateral against a loan, to return it every evening so the poor person has a garment to sleep in.[12] Yet to purchase oil in order to light a symbolic lamp in the window on Hanukkah is worth the indignity of selling your last coat or even going into debt. That level of self-sacrifice may be related to the Maccabean virtue of sacrificing their family's comfort to defend the nation's religious way of life.

Maimonides' praise for the Divine-human military rescue celebrated by the Hanukkah lights is expressed in the priority Hanukkah oil takes over Shabbat wine for *kiddush*. The Rabbis required a Jew to sanctify Shabbat on Friday evening by saying *kiddush* (the sanctification of the day concluding God's creation) and by joining this dedication ceremony of holy time to a toast over wine, a symbol of high culture. (Note that *kiddush* sanctifies the day, not the wine, and may be pronounced even without wine when necessary.)

If someone has only one coin and one is

---

8. *Laws of Hanukkah* 4:1-2
9. *Laws of Hanukkah* 4:7   10. 4:8   11. 4:12
12. *Exodus* 22:25-26

confronted with the [simultaneous mitzvot] to say *kiddush* over wine [on Shabbat] and to light the Hanukkah lamp, then one should give priority to buying oil for the Hanukkah lamp over wine for kiddush. Since both mitzvot derive from the Rabbinic legislation [and have equal status legally], it is better to prefer the Hanukkah lamp that contains the memory of the miracle.[17]

Aaron: The Pursuer of Peace

While Mattathias and Pinchas are priests who define their jobs as "being zealous/jealous for God's name" lest it be desecrated, the Hillel school of Rabbinic Judaism is famed for its preference for peace over truth and for pluralism over the monolithic truth of Shamai and his school of thought. It is no surprise that Hillel's school preached a view of Aaron as the father of family peacemakers.

Mishnah: **Hillel says, "Be among the followers of Aaron; for Aaron loved shalom and pursued shalom. He loved humanity and brought people close to Torah."**

Midrash: What does *"love shalom"* mean?

It means that we should bring harmony between each and every person in Israel, just as Aaron himself tried to bring harmony between each and every person. As it says, **"The Torah of truth was in his mouth and unkindness was not on his lips. In peace and righteousness he walked with Me; and he prevented many from doing wrong."** [13]

Rabbi Meir asked, What does *"He prevented many from doing wrong"* mean?

We could illustrate it as follows: Whenever Aaron encountered even someone of questionable reputation, he would stop and say *"shalom."* On the next day, that same person might want to do something wrong, but would stop and think to himself: "What would happen if I run into Aaron? How could I look him in the face? When he says *"shalom"* to me, I would be ashamed. Consequently, that man would restrain himself from wrong.

Another example: If two people were feuding, Aaron would walk up to one, sit down next to him and say, "My child, don't you see how much your friend is tearing his heart out and rending his clothes." The person would then say to him/ herself: "How can I lift up my head and look my friend in the face? I would be ashamed to see him; I really have been rotten." Aaron would remain at his/her side until s/he had overcome resentment *(kinnah)*.

Afterwards, Aaron would walk over to the other person, sit down next to him/her and say: "Don't you see how much your friend is eating his/her heart out and tearing his/her clothes." And so this person too would think to her/himself: "O, my God! How can I lift up my head and look my friend in the eye. I am too ashamed to see him/her." Aaron would sit with this person too until s/he had overcome resentment. And finally when these two friends met, they embraced and kissed each other. Therefore, it is said of Aaron's funeral, *"And they wept for Aaron thirty days, all the house of Israel."*[14,15]

How do we know that Aaron never made a man or a woman feel bad about him or herself?

Because it is written, *"and all the house of Israel wept for Aaron."* Moses, however, rebuked the people with harsh words. Therefore, of him it is written, *"and the children of Israel wept for Moses"* — some but not **all** of Israel. Moreover, just think of how many thousands in Israel are named after Aaron. Were it not for Aaron's domestic peacemaking, they would not have been brought into the world!

Moses was a judge and it is impossible for a judge to vindicate both litigants for he must exonerate the innocent and convict the guilty. Aaron, however, was not a judge but one who brought peace between human beings [and between God and Israel].[16]

13. *Malachi* 2:6
14. *Numbers* 20:20
15. *Avot d' Rabbi Natan "A,"* Chapter 12
16. *Avot d' Rabbi Natan"B,"* Chapter 25

God's historic redemption of Israel from Greek persecution is in some sense more important than the *kiddush* over wine which commemorates God's involvement in the creation of nature.

Giving Priority to Shabbat over Hanukkah

Maimonides, more than any other Jewish legal scholar, tried to promote the miraculous Divine-human military rescue of Israel celebrated on Hanukkah. Yet he concludes the Laws of Hanukkah and with it the whole Book of Festivals, with the "victory" of Shabbat candles over Hanukkah miracles.

> "If one is confronted with the [simultaneous mitzvah] to light one's household lamp [for Shabbat] and to light the Hanukkah lamp . . . then the [Shabbat] household lamp takes precedence because it contributes to *shalom bayit* (domestic peace and tranquility).

For Maimonides, the virtues of peace-seeking compromise must be preferred over the uncompromising idealism of the zealot.

> "After all, the Divine name is also to be erased [in the Biblical ritual of the wife suspected of adultery — *sotah*] in order to facilitate the making of peace between man and woman.

> "Great is *shalom* (peace)! For the whole Torah was given to make peace in the world as it says in the Bible: *'Its ways are ways of pleasantness and all its paths are peace.'*"[18,19]

The legal problem raised by Maimonides is as follows: On the one hand, **Shabbat candles** must be placed on the table for their light to accompany the whole Shabbat meal (approximately 4 hours) in the family space. Though there is no Biblical commandment to light Shabbat candles, the Rabbis enacted this mitzvah giving it three rationales:

(1) The candles are a way "to honor Shabbat *(Kibbud Shabbat)* because no important dinner is held without light;"[20]

(2) Candles add to the enjoyment of Shabbat *(Oneg Shabbat)* since "one who sees the food enjoys it much more than one who eats it in the dark;"[21]

(3) "A candle contributes to family tranquility *(Shalom Bayit)* — for in a place without a lamp there is no peace since in the dark people trip and fall."[22] At a Shabbat table without the light to see each other's faces there would be no social intercourse, no family integration.

On the other hand, **Hanukkah candles** may not be used for personal benefit, therefore making them the polar opposite of Shabbat candles, which must be used for the family's benefit. Given that the same candle may not serve for both Shabbat and Hanukkah, when there is a shortage of oil (or of money for oil), then halachic priorities must be determined. The issue is important not merely in those rare cases of poverty, but in establishing a value preference between what Hanukkah and Shabbat candles represent.

Maimonides chooses to conclude the Book of Festivals by declaring that Shabbat candles, which stand for domestic peace, take priority over Hanukkah candles that proclaim a Divine-human military victory. The private realm of the home takes precedence over the public realms of politics and religion. The virtues of peace-seeking compromise must be preferred over the uncompromising idealism of the zealot. The God of compromise who would forego his honor to encourage a husband to forego his jealous suspicions of his wife is prior to "the zealous/jealous God" who inspires zealous priests to execute idolatrous traitors.

---

17. Laws of Hanukkah 4:13
18. *Proverbs* 3:17   19. Laws of Hanukkah 4:14
20. Rashi, on *T.B. Shabbat* 25a
21. *T.B. Yoma* 74b   22. ibid.

MATTATHIAS THE PRIESTLY ZEALOT

A FREEDOM FIGHTER TO BE PRAISED OR A RELIGIOUS FANATIC TO BE CENSURED?

by Noam Zion

The Zionist Mattathias

(sculpture by Boris Shatz, director of the Bezalel art school, the flagship of the renaissance of Jewish art in Israel, early 20th century)

DEFINING MATTATHIAS' HEROISM

The essence of Hanukkah's heroism is epitomized in the phrase "the few against the many" used in the Rabbinic Hanukkah prayer *Al HaNissim*. Yet Judah, the brilliant and daring guerrilla warrior who led the Maccabees to military victories, the recapture of Jerusalem and the rededication of the Temple (164 BCE), was not mentioned in *Al HaNissim*. Rather the only one mentioned in this prayer is the priest Mattathias, Judah's elderly father who only lived during the first year of the revolt (167-166 BCE). The *First Book of the Maccabees* also gives pride of place to Mattathias over Judah.[23]

Mattathias holds the key to the revolt because he raised the cry to arms of a minor priestly family in a provincial town (Modiin) against the high priests of Jerusalem and the Greek Syrian empire. Mattathias is literally the father of the revolt in the sense that his five sons carried out his mandate over a 27 year struggle. After the death in battle of each son, he was replaced by the next in line — Elazar, Judah, Jonathan and finally Simon. Not only Mattathias' faithfulness to his ancestral religion but his ability to engender loyalty and courage in his descendants is the key to the family's heroism as an organic unit.

In focusing on Mattathias, Jewish tradition seeks to categorize him according to one or another model of a hero. For the Rabbinic prayer *Al HaNissim*, Mattathias is called a "High" Priest (though historically he was only a regular priest not from the familial

---

23. Unlike the *Second Book of Maccabees* whose historian-writer focuses on Judah as a warrior hero.

dynasty of high priests). He is identified with the pure and innocent few who overcame the Greek Syrians — impure and wicked. For the early secular Zionists, such as Boris Shatz, sculptor and founder of the new national art institute Bezalel in Jerusalem in the early 20th century, Mattathias was a national hero choosing loyalty to his ancestral identity over the antisemitic Western empire. Shatz sculpted him with sword raised calling for revolt and celebrated his sculpture at a big Zionist Hanukkah party. For the American Reform curriculum writers who wrote *"How a Jew Celebrates"* in 1971, he was the priest defending religious freedom, not national independence or priestly purity. For them, Mattathias never glorified war, as those Zionists who glorified Judah the Maccabee did.

However, the *First Book of Maccabees*, (our first and best historical source, written in 125 BCE) portrays Mattathias in the Biblical tradition of the religious Zealot purging deviant, idolatrous Jews. For the Books of the Maccabees, Mattathias was comparable to a series of Biblical zealots. He acted as did Moses and the tribe of Levi, who after the incident of the Golden Calf, massacred 3,000 idolatrous Israelites. Mattathias was also comparable to Pinchas, the grandson of the High Priest Aaron, who speared a tribal leader of Shimon and his Midianite royal consort to stop an epidemic of idolatry. He was also similar to Elijah the arch-zealot, who challenged the authority of King Ahab whose wife Jezebel introduced royal idolatry into northern Israel.

The historian of the *First Book of Maccabees*

describes Mattathias and reports (or constructs) the speech he made. The literary formulation resonates with echoes of Moses, Pinchas and Elijah at their most implacable, their most blood-thirsty and their most zealous:

> Then the king's officers who were forcing the people to give up their religion, came to the town of **Modiin**, to make them offer sacrifices. Many Jews, among them Mattathias and his sons, gathered together. Then the king's messengers answered and said to Mattathias:

> "You are a leading man, great and distinguished in this town, surrounded with sons and brothers; now be the first to come forward and carry out the king's command as all the heathen and the men of Judah and those who are left in Jerusalem have done, and you and your sons will be distinguished with presents of silver and gold and many royal commissions."

> Then Mattathias answered and said in a loud voice:

> "If all the pagans in the king's dominions listen to him, forsake each of them the religion of their ancestors and choose to follow his commands instead, yet I and my sons and my brothers will live in accordance with the covenant of our ancestors. God forbid that we should abandon the Torah and the ordinances. We will not listen to the message of the king, or depart from our religion to the right hand or to the left."

> As he finished these words, a Jew went up before the eyes of all of them to offer

PROVERBS ON ZEAL AND FANATICISM

Typical of modernity, almost all these proverbs, drawn from contemporary anthologies of quotations, are one-sidedly critical of zeal, usually identifying it with the psychologically imbalanced fanatic. Only a few of the sources still identify zeal with idealism and passion for a higher cause.

sacrifice as the king commanded, on the altar in Modiin. And Mattathias saw him and was filled with zeal, and his soul was stirred, and he was roused to **anger**, and ran up and slaughtered him upon the altar. Thus he showed his **zeal** for the Law, **just as [the biblical priest] Pinchas did to Zimri**. Then Mattathias cried out in a loud voice in the town and said, **"Let everybody who is zealous for the Law and stands by the covenant follow me."**

And he and his sons fled to the mountains and left all they possessed in the town.

Mattathias, like Moses at the worship of the Golden Calf, calls for zealous followers to execute idolatrous Jews. The words are almost identical.

And Mattathias and his friends went about and tore down the altars, and forcibly circumcised all the uncircumcised children that they found within the borders of Israel. And they drove the arrogant before them, and the work prospered in their hands. So they rescued the Torah from the hands of the pagan and their kings, and would not let the lawbreakers triumph.

When the time drew near for Mattathias to die, he said to his sons:

"Arrogance and reproach have now grown strong; it is a time of disaster and **hot anger**. Now, my children, you must be **zealous for the Law**, and give your

lives for the covenant of our ancestors. Remember the deeds of our ancestors.

Pinchas, our ancestor, was rewarded for his intense zeal with the promise of an everlasting priesthood. **Elijah** for his **intense zeal for the Law** was taken up into heaven. And you must gather about you all who observe the Law, and avenge the wrongs of your people. Pay back the pagan for what they have done, and give heed to what the Law commands."[24]

Many phrases of *First Maccabees* intentionally echo the Biblical zealots who in turn echo God who describes himself as a zealous/jealous God in relation to Israel worshipping idols.

"I, the Lord, am your God who brought you out of the land of Egypt, the house of bondage: You shall have no other gods besides Me.

"You shall not make for yourself a sculptured image, or any likeness of what is in the heavens above, or on the earth below, or in the waters under the earth. You shall not bow down to them or serve them. For I, the Lord your God, am a **jealous God**."[25]

Hence the era of "hot anger" mentioned by Mattathias refers to God's anger. "Anger" and "zeal" are twinned in *First Maccabees*. Mattathias, like Moses at the worship of the Golden Calf, calls for zealous followers to execute idolatrous Jews. The words are almost identical.

"As soon as Moses came near the camp and

---

24. *I Maccabees* 2:15-28, 45-51, 54, 58, 67-68
25. *Exodus* 20:2-5

WHAT IS ZEAL?

A certain nervous disorder afflicting the young and inexperienced.

— AMBROSE BIERCE, AMERICAN AUTHOR

Zeal without knowledge is the sister of folly.

— JOHN DAVIES, ENGLISH JURIST

Fire without light.

— ENGLISH PROVERB

What we do, which in a calmer condition we would not do.

— ROBERT ZWICKEY

Violent zeal for truth hath an hundred to one odds to be either petulancy, ambition or pride.

— JONATHAN SWIFT, AUTHOR OF GULLIVER'S TRAVELS

saw the calf and the dancing, he became **enraged**; and he hurled the tablets from his hands and shattered them at the foot of the mountain. He took the calf that they had made and burned it; he ground it to powder and strewed it upon the water and so made the children of Israel drink it.

"Moses saw that the people were out of control — since Aaron had let them get out of control — so that they were a menace to any who might oppose them. Moses stood up in the gate of the camp and said, **'Whoever is for the Lord, come here!'** And all the tribe of Levi rallied to him. He said to them, 'Thus says the Lord, the God of Israel: Each of you put sword on thigh, go back and forth from gate to gate throughout the camp, and slay brother, neighbor, and kin.' The tribe of Levi did as Moses had bidden; and some three thousand of the people fell that day. And Moses said, 'Dedicate yourselves to the Lord this day — for each of you has been against son and brother and let God bless you today.'"[26]

Why did *First Maccabees* choose the zealous hero model? Obviously the *First Book of Maccabees* has its own ideological axe to grind. Written most probably in Hebrew by court historians of the newly established Hasmonean dynasty,[27] *First Maccabees* seeks to frame Mattathias, the founding father of the revolt and the biological father of the remarkable Maccabean brothers, as a traditional leader who despite lacking the lineage of King David (the tribe of Judah) or the lineage of the High Priesthood (the family of Zadok = *Saduccees* appointed in the days of David) still has a claim to authority. The rebel who challenged not only Greek Syrian authority but the high priests of the line of Zadok who were ratified by the Seleucids (the family of Antiochus), must derive his legitimacy from another source.

In the Maccabean period Jews no longer believed their contemporaries could be true prophets of God, but they did experience genuine miracles. So the authority for the

Maccabean Revolt could be bolstered by supernaturally miraculous victories. For example, *Second Maccabees*[28] describes God's miraculous support of the Maccabees defense of the Temple from desecration by the pagan Heliodorus who had come to pillage the Temple.

"While the Jews called upon the Almighty Lord to protect the (golden vessels of the Temple) that had been entrusted to them, Heliodorus was carrying out what had been decided upon. But no sooner had he and his guards arrived before the treasury than the Sovereign of Spirits caused a great spectacle so that all were appalled at the power of God and fainted with terror. There appeared a **horse with a dreaded rider** adorned with magnificent trappings. Rushing swiftly at Heliodorus, it struck him with its forefeet. This horse's dreaded rider seemed clad in golden armor. Two young men also appeared to Heliodorus, remarkably strong, gloriously beautiful and splendidly dressed. They stood on each side of him and flogged him continually, inflicting many stripes on him.

"Heliodorus fell suddenly to the ground and was enveloped in deep darkness, and men picked him up and put him on a stretcher and carried him off. Thus the man who had just entered that treasury with a great retinue and his whole guard was now rendered helpless. The Greeks clearly recognized the sovereign power of God. So through **divine intervention** Heliodorus lay prostrate, bereft of all hope of deliverance, while the Jews blessed the Lord who had marvelously honored His own place. The Temple, which a little while before had been full of fear and commotion, was filled with joy and gladness."

---

26. *Exodus* 32:19-20, 25-29
27. Simon the High Priest, brother of Judah the Maccabee and son of Mattathias the Hasmonean priest, was installed by the Jewish people and recognized as the supreme political and religious leader by both the Roman and Greek Syrian Empires, in 140 BCE.
28. *II Maccabees* 3:22-30

> These zealots take the "law" into their own hands as violent vigilante volunteers confronting religious and political anarchy.

The *Second Book of Maccabees* describes supernatural miracles interspersed in the course of the Maccabean Revolt that in effect grant Divine legitimacy to the struggle. In contrast, the *First Book of Maccabees* attributes to Mattathias the rebel priest, a claim to authority derived from the tradition of zealots in the Bible who act without due process and without the support of the people and even without a direct command from God. These zealots take the "law" into their own hands as violent vigilante volunteers confronting religious and political anarchy. That is the tradition of the tribe of Levi. In relation to external enemies, Levi and Shimon kill the people of Shechem implicated in the rape of Dinah,[29] and Moses kills the Egyptian task master beating the Hebrew slave.[30]

Even more to the point, the tradition of Levi and especially of the priests within the tribe of Levi, involves protecting the mono-theistic religious faith of Israel from insidious traitors leading the people as a whole to apostasy. When Moses — on his own initiative — called out: *"Whoever is for God, join me!"* and the tribe of Levi proceeded to kill 3,000 offending Hebrews at the Golden Calf, the tribe of Levi earned its special sanctity, its mission and its office as the servants of God and thereafter the defenders of the *Mishkan* (the desert's portable sanctuary). When Pinchas, Aaron's grandson, son of the High Priest Elazar, on his own initiative — speared Zimri, a leader of the tribe of Shimon, and Kozbi, a daughter of a leader of the pagan enemy people Midian, he earned the right to inherit the High Priesthood for all his descendants. The precise crime of Zimri and Kozbi can be defined in many ways and thereby the title "Zealot" = *"Kanai,"* that Pinchas earned, will be characterized in correspondingly different ways. In any case, it is Pinchas who epitomizes the zealous priestly tradition whose mantle Mattathias dons, according to *First Maccabees*.

The Torah's Story of the Zealous Priest[31]

"While Israel was staying at Shittim, the people profaned themselves by whoring with the Moabite women, who invited the people to the sacrifices for their god. The people partook of them and worshiped that god. Thus Israel attached itself to Baal-peor, and the Lord was incensed with Israel. The Lord said to Moses, 'Take all the ringleaders and have them publicly impaled before the Lord, so that the **Lord's wrath** may turn away from Israel.' So Moses said to Israel's officials, 'Each of you slay those of his men who attached themselves to Baal-peor.'

---

29. *Genesis* 34   30. *Exodus* 2:11-12
31. *Numbers* 25:17

WHAT IS A FANATIC?

The gadflies that keep society from being too complacent.

— ABRAHAM FLEXNER,
AMERICAN EDUCATOR

The Devil's plaything.

— ARMENIAN PROVERB

One compelled to action by the need to find a strong meaning in life. The fanatic determines for himself what role he is to play in life, and his intense devotion to a cause is the means.

— EUGENE E. BRUSSELL

"Just then one of the Israelites came and brought a Midianite woman over to his companions, in the sight of Moses and of the whole Israelite community who were weeping at the entrance of the Tent of Meeting. When Pinchas, son of Elazar son of Aaron the priest, saw this, he left the assembly and, taking a spear in his hand, he followed the Israelite into the chamber and stabbed both of them, the Israelite and the woman, through the belly. Then the plague against the Israelites was checked. Those who died of the plague numbered twenty-four thousand.

"The Lord spoke to Moses, saying: Pinchas, son of Elazar son of Aaron the priest has turned back **My wrath** from the Israelites by displaying among them his **passion/zeal** for Me, so that I did not wipe out the Israelite people in My **passion/zeal**. Say, therefore, 'I grant him My Pact of Peace. It shall be for him and his descendants after him **a pact of priesthood for all time**, because he took impassioned/zealous action for his God, thus making expiation for the Israelites.'"

Despite the unequivocal Biblical praise for Pinchas' behavior, later Rabbinic texts reflect the Rabbis' profound ambivalence about the zealot. Should Pinchas be praised and emulated or censured and eschewed as an exception to the rule of law never to be imitated?

Let us explore the comparison of the Mattathias and Pinchas narratives and then examine briefly the Talmudic debate on the desirability of the zealot. Afterwards we will add some reflections on contemporary understandings of fanaticism and the policies of containment (or reinterpretation) necessary to handle such explosive "stuff" as Mattathias' or Pinchas' zealous acts.

Comparing Pinchas and Mattathias

The similarities of Pinchas and Mattathias lie in the way they kill an unholy pair — a Jew and the pagan tempter/temptress involved in this public act of desecration. The unholy act is also a form of political propaganda designed to undermine traditional religious authority and to speed even more the epidemic of pagan worship sweeping up the Jewish people. The pagan is involved in seducing the Jew, whether with sexual or financial gifts. No effective Jewish leadership is available — Moses and his assembly are in tears and the High Priest Jason and later Menelaus are collaborating with the state policy of Hellenization. The public nature of the vigilante violence of Pinchas and Mattathias is intended to call a stop to the paganization of the Jews. The vigilante is not an officially appointed leader in either case but he is a respected priest either because of his lineage — Pinchas is the son of Elazar, son of Aaron — or because of his elder status, as in the case of Mattathias. Both thereby earn the privilege of high priesthood for their descendants through taking the law into their own hands in an anarchic situation.

While Pinchas' single act ends the crisis, Mattathias' act incites a military revolt that is still far from victory. Pinchas acts in a situation where the women of Moab and

---

One who can't change his mind and won't change the subject.

— WINSTON S. CHURCHILL,
BRITISH PRIME MINISTER,
WORLD WAR II

One who does what he thinks the Lord would do if only He knew the facts of the case.

— ADAPTED FROM
FINLEY PETER DUNN,
AMERICAN HUMORIST

(One who) is perpetually incomplete and insecure. He cannot generate self-assurance out of his individual resources — out of his rejected self — but finds it only by clinging passionately to whatever support he happens to embrace.

— ERIC HOFFER, SOCIAL CRITIC

Midian are leading Jewish men astray by sexual allurement, however there is no direct threat of violent coercion against Jews who reject the attractions of paganism. Using prostitutes may be an unfair means but not a violent one. Mattathias, on the other hand, faces Greek Syrian soldiers who have already proven their willingness to use violence in Jerusalem and who constitute an implied physical threat in Modiin, even if they are offering honors and money to encourage resistant Jewish leaders.

Both zealots — Pinchas and Mattathias — are acting *extraordinarily* in their violence and in their unauthorized taking of the law into their own hands. In each case, their zealotry is legitimated only because of the crisis at hand.

In the context of a homogenizing superpower crushing religious freedom and national culture with the help of a coercive minority of wealthy Hellenist Jews, Mattathias could have been portrayed as a freedom fighter. However, the author of *First Maccabees* presents him as a zealot in the tradition of Pinchas, who became the guardian of God's honor from desecration and shame.

"In those days **Mattathias**, the son of John, the son of Simon, a priest of the descendants of Joariv, removed from Jerusalem, and settled in Modin. He saw the impious things that were going on in Judah and Jerusalem, and he said,

'Alas! Why was I born to witness the ruin of my people and the ruin of the holy city, and to sit by while it is being handed over to its enemies, and the sanctuary to aliens?

'Her Temple has come to be like a man disgraced,
Her glorious religious objects have been captured and carried off,
Her infant children have been killed in her streets,
Her young men with the enemy's sword . . .
Her adornment has all been taken away.
Instead of a free woman, she has become a slave.
Behold, our sanctuary and our beauty has been laid waste,
And the pagans have profaned her!
Why should we live any longer?'

And Mattathias and his sons tore their clothes and put on sackcloth and grieved bitterly."[32]

What is common to both Mattathias and Pinchas is this strongly felt concern for God's honor. However Pinchas' case is harder to defend to a Western democratic audience, because Zimri's sexual deviance is not portrayed as *coercing* other Jews to abandon their religion. In a liberal culture like ours that values the individual's freedom of self-determination, Zimri could be seen as asserting his freedom to intermarry against the atavist establishment — Moses and God — without denying other Jews' rights to remain traditional. Zimri could be crowned

---

32. *I Maccabees* 2:1-14

as the champion of religious and marital freedom and Pinchas and Mattathias could be saddled with the title of violent vigilante enforcers of religious orthodoxy.

In fact, however, a close reading of the narratives of Pinchas and Mattathias shows that neither is modeling a *"normal"* means of punishing religious deviants and denying them religious freedom. Both zealots are acting *extraordinarily* in their violence and in their unauthorized taking of the law into their own hands. Their zealotry is legitimated because of the *crisis* threatening the existence of the collective defined by its traditional identity. While thousands of Jewish soldiers fraternize with enemy women, probably sent by their Midian and Moab leaders, and thousands die of a plague brought by God, the interests of the individual are overridden by the zealot Pinchas acting in defense of his polity. The zealous Mattathias faces a similar crisis in which Jews are abandoning Judaism not only voluntarily but under extreme duress to the point of torture and martyrdom.

Both the Hellenist Jew, who volunteered to make a sacrifice in exchange for Greek honors, and Zimri, the leader of the tribe of Shimon who had intercourse with Kozbi the Midianite in public, are in effect leading a *political revolt* against the legally constituted society. Pinchas is defending the public order of Moses and the Ten Commandments mandated voluntarily at Sinai[33] by the whole people. Similarly, Mattathias is trying to protect the legal status quo in which the Judean ancestral religion ratified by all the previous conquerors of Judea — the Persians, Egyptian Greek Ptolemies and Antiochus III. The Torah is the internationally recognized and binding Judean constitution, long before Antiochus IV and the Hellenist Jews revoked it one-sidedly. The unique political-religious crises and the special circumstances in which both Pinchas and Mattathias operated render their zealous behavior a historical curiosity rather than a model for emulation for our generation, an exception which does not establish a general norm praising zealotry in everyday life.

Antiochus Persecutes the Israelites
(Julius Schnorr von Carolsfeld, Germany, mid-19th century)

33. *Exodus 24*

WHAT IS FANATICISM?

Zeal run wild.

— EUGENE E. BRUSSELL

False fire of an overheated mind.

— WILLIAM COWPER,
ENGLISH POET

That temperament which can only repose in fixed sanctities.

— HILAIRE BELLOC,
ENGLISH AUTHOR

There is only one step from fanaticism to barbarism.

— DENIS DIDEROT,
FRENCH ENCYCLOPAEDIST

RABBINIC STRATEGIES FOR DEFANGING A FANATIC

The story of Pinchas becomes an especially dangerous legal precedent for any zealot, when it is codified by the Rabbis. The Mishna Sanhedrin naturalizes and authorizes zealous vigilante murder of a Jew who violates sacred standards (especially if there is no legal remedy for this act of desecration through the courts). However, the Talmudic Rabbis, after debate, did much to "defang" or neutralize the problematic implications of the Pinchas story and the Mishna's ruling.

> *Mishna:* If one steals the *kiswah* (a holy vessel from the Temple), or curses God by enchantment, or cohabits with a pagan (literally, a Greek Syrian) woman, he is assaulted (executed) by **zealots**. If a priest performs the Temple service while unclean, his brother priests do not bother to bring charges against him in court, but the young priests take him out of the Temple court and simply split his skull with hatchets.[34]

It is unclear whether the Mishna is recommending vigilante action for all, permitting it for those who are so moved to defend Divine honor, or merely offering an amnesty *post facto* to those swept into violence by their impassioned identification with the defiled sacred objects. However, the Jerusalem Talmud brings an equally ancient source from the Mishnaic period that suggests "the Rabbis *(sic)* in Pinchas' era" wanted to censor him and excommunicate him for his dangerous behavior:

> "Pinchas acted without the approval of the Rabbis and Rabbi Yehuda ben Pazi says they sought to ex-communicate him, however the holy spirit intervened and declared: "Pinchas and his seed shall have an eternal covenant of priesthood."[35]

Some of the Talmudic Rabbis expanded this positive precedent-setting power of Pinchas' behavior. The Babylonian rabbi, Shmuel, explicitly commends Pinchas' disregard of due process and of hierarchical rabbinic authority. Pinchas was justified in stepping in — without waiting for Moses and the assembly to act or even to delegate their authority to him — because God's name was being actively defamed. Preemptive action in the midst of desecration should not be delayed out of deference to traditional legal authority.

> **Shmuel** said: *"Pinchas saw"*[36] that, "There is no wisdom nor understanding nor counsel against the Lord" which means whenever the Divine Name is being profaned, honor must not be paid to one's teacher [following due process by consulting with one's teacher, the higher authority, is not necessary or even desirable].[37]

However, the dominant Talmudic view that eventually determines recognized Jewish law follows the innovative policies of containment of Rabbi Yochanan[38] and Rav Hisda.[39]

> **Rav Hisda** said: If the zealot comes to take counsel [asking whether or not s/he should act as a vigilante to punish the transgressors enumerated in the Mishna], we do not instruct him/her to do so.

---

34. *Babylonian Talmud, Sanhedrin* 81b
35. *Jerusalem Talmud, Sanhedrin* Chap. 9; *Numbers* 25
36. *Numbers* 25:7   37. *T.B. Sanhedrin* 82a
38. Eretz Yisrael, 3rd century CE
39. Babylonia, 4th century CE

Fanaticism is only loyalty carried to convulsive extreme.

— WILLIAM JAMES,
PSYCHOLOGIST

Fanaticism is the effect of a false conscience, which makes religion subservient to the caprices of the imagination, and the excesses of the passions.

— VOLTAIRE,
FRENCH PHILOSOPHER

Fanaticism is religion caricatured.

— EDWIN P. WHIPPLE

Fanaticism is a fire which heats the mind but heats without purifying.
It stimulates and foments all the passions, but it rectifies none.

— ANONYMOUS

Rabbah son of Bar Hana said in **Rabbi Yochanan's** name: If the zealot comes to take counsel, we do not instruct him to do so. What is more, had Zimri ceased his forbidden intercourse with his foreign mistress and only then Pinchas had killed him, then Pinchas would have been [prosecuted by the courts as a murderer and] executed on Zimri's account. Had Zimri turned upon Pinchas [during the forbidden act] and killed Pinchas [in self-defense], then Zimri would not have been liable to trial and execution, since Pinchas

---

Even in the act of stopping desecration in progress, the zealot is considered to be acting outside the law. The desecrator therefore has every right to kill the zealot in self-defense. If Zimri had managed to kill Pinchas, then he would have been within his legal rights.

---

was a *pursuer* [an assailant seeking to take his life who did not have the authority of a law enforcement officer].

Maimonides[40] summarizes the *reductio ad absurdum* legal limits placed on zealots trying to imitate Pinchas. He shows that the law places so many restrictions on the zealot so that the law becomes intentionally absurd and inapplicable:

"In the case of an Israelite who has intercourse with an idol-worshipping woman in public, that is, in the presence of ten or more Israelites, whether by way of legal marriage or by way of harlotry, should zealots fall upon him and slay him, they are worthy of commendation for their zeal. This is a rule given to Moses from Sinai, as evidenced by the incident of Pinchas and Zimri.

"The zealot may assault the violator, however, only during the act of intercourse, as in the case of Zimri, as it is said, *and thrust both of them through, the man of Israel and the woman through the private parts.*[41]

Once the man has withdrawn from the woman, he may not be slain, and should the zealot slay him nevertheless, the zealot incurs the death penalty for it. Should the zealot come to request permission from the court to slay the violator, the zealot is to be given no instructions, even if the act is still in progress. And not only this, but should the zealot come forth with the intention of slaying the violator, and should the man elude him and kill him in order to save himself, the man may not be put to death on account of killing the zealot."[42]

In summary, the dominant halachic view, that of Rabbi Yochanan in Eretz Yisrael and Rav Hisda in Babylonia, restrict Pinchas' **window of legitimate zealotry** by establishing the following conditions:

(1) The zealot may act neither preemptively nor punitively. Neither before nor after the desecrator has completed his act of desecration may the zealot act. It is only in stopping the desecrator in the midst of the violation that the zealot may act. Thus Pinchas had to spear Zimri and Cozbi in the act of intercourse, otherwise due process and duly appointed authority are to be applied.

(2) Even in the act of stopping desecration in progress, the zealot is considered to be acting outside the law. The desecrator therefore has every right to kill the zealot in self-defense. If Zimri had managed to kill Pinchas, then he would be within his legal rights.

(3) The zealot must walk a tightrope to be legally exempt from the consequences of his religiously motivated murder. He *cannot* consult with Rabbinic authority. Once the zealot consults, the Rabbis do not teach him or authorize him to act even within the range of what is permitted. Only *after the fact* does the

---

40. the 12th century philosopher and jurist

41. *Numbers* 25:8

42. Maimonides, *Mishne Torah, Book of Holiness*, Laws of Forbidden Relations, Chapter 12:4-5.

Mishna serve to exempt zealous impassioned behavior from punishment.

(4) If the zealot accidentally oversteps the bounds — striking too early or too late — the zealot becomes culpable as a murderer to be prosecuted by the same religious law he claimed to be defending. Not only is the zealot *punishable* but he is also *guilty religiously* rather than lionized as a hero.

In short, Rabbi Yochanan, Rav Hisda and Maimonides reduce the possibility of emulating Pinchas *ad absurdum*, to zero. Only one confident of receiving the extraordinary protection of God, as Pinchas received (according to the midrash), dares act as a vigilante. These Rabbis clearly praise a **legal mind over a zealous one; due process over taking law into one's hands; weighing one's behavior rationally over impas-**

sioned anger to defend God's honor.

One modern rabbi[43] adds that zealots must be cautious in checking the purity of their motivation. That is why the Rabbis frowned on zealots since one could never be sure they were not moved by impure motives.

In summary, the Jewish narrative tradition still tells stories praising historic zealots like Pinchas and Mattathias, but the dominant Jewish legal tradition neutralizes these precedents, rendering them obsolete and illegitimate as ongoing models. While freedom fighters like the Maccabees remain heroes worth emulating today, insofar as they were also zealots coercing other Jews into observance, their model was problematic for the Talmudic rabbis as it is for many of us today.

---

43. Rabbi Baruch Halevi Epstein, author of the 19th century *Torah Temima*

OUR WESTERN AMBIVALENCE ABOUT FANATICS: THREE DEFINITIONS OF THE ZEALOT

In the Biblical and the Christian traditions, martyrs and zealots have often held places of honor. However, **the rationalist French Enlightenment** inaugurated a period of criticism of the impassioned zealot in the name of reason. Later the **democratic tradition** distanced itself from the zealot as one who threatens the religious liberty of others. As we have seen, the dominant **Jewish legal traditions** have also sought to constrain the zealot who takes the law into his/her own hands. Each critique understands the zealot in different terms. Clarifying these distinctions will allow us to understand Mattathias and his heroism in a nuanced way. Here are three different definitions:

1. The Proactive Fanatic

The French Enlightenment thinker Voltaire[44] invented the term *fanatic* as a pejorative term for anyone motivated by religious zeal who sought to use the state's power to coerce religious observance. The Catholic Church was the state church in France before the French Revolution. Adapting the Latin term *"fanum"* meaning sacred or priestly, Voltaire attributed irrational coercive passion to all religious belief and advocated an enlightened skepticism. The fanatics lack critical judgement due both to their emotional passions and their superstitious dogmas. They are **proactive** in their missionary desire to force their notion of salvation on others. (Interestingly enough, the word "fan" — as in sports fan — derives from this collective fanaticism.)

In Protestant England[45] the term for a fanatic was *"enthusiast,"* meaning literally one whom the divine (or the demon) has entered *(en-theos)*. Often this was accompanied with ecstatic behavior like shaking (as in the Shakers of Ohio) and speaking in tongues. "Enthusiasts," in this old fashioned religious

---

44. 18th century   45. 17th-18th century

sense of the word, like zealots in all periods, often feel themselves to be **instruments of** God rather than pursuers of self-interest or promoters of a merely human doctrine. Later, in the Romantic Era of the 19th century, when reason was less valued and passion became a commendable trait, the word "enthusiasm" began to take on a positive connotation rather than a fanatical one.

Today too, zealots and fanatics are often identified with irrational ideologies, but they see themselves as instruments of world-conquering movements of salvation. Often the zealot envisions a world-wide battle between the evil kingdom and the forces of good which will come to a head in the messianic or millennial end of time.

Today too, zealots and fanatics are often identified with irrational ideologies, but they see themselves as instruments of world-conquering movements of salvation. Often the zealot envisions a world-wide battle between the evil kingdom and the forces of good which will come to a head in the messianic or millennial end of time. At such a time of crisis there is no room for rational hesitation, nor for due process, nor for compromise.

In the 17th century in Europe, after the indecisive bloody religious wars between the zealous Catholics and Protestants or Anglicans and Puritans, a *modus vivendi* was established. The political realm was secularized, meaning politics was to be restricted to this-worldly pragmatic questions only, while postponing the other-worldly ultimate questions of religious salvation, to the end of time. Churches in their private function would deal with redemption, while states would avoid issues that arouse zealous, uncompromising religious feelings. However, whenever believers felt the millennium approaching by whatever computations, they often abandoned this division of functions and reverted to violence.

With the secularization of the state and the decline of religious belief (or its contraction into the private realm), thinkers in the West expected the end of public zealotry, which had always been associated exclusively with religious ideologies. However, early 20th century secular religions of redemption, like fascism and communism, offered a new field for zealous proactive coercive ideologues. No private space was respected, for the true believers sought to "indoctrinate" or to "liberate" individuals from false beliefs or "false consciousness." After the collapse of these grand secular ideologies there has been a resurgence of fundamentalist, often millennial religious groups along with fanatical nationalisms that reject all pluralism — whether ideological or ethnic.

2. The Hot-blooded Youth

Since "fanaticism" crops up in all kinds of ideologies and eras, psychologists and social scientists have suggested that the zealot is not a product of a certain kind of pathological belief, but of a particular kind of personality disorder or sociological disorder. This view goes back to Aristotle who identified zealous behavior with "hot blooded" young people whose emotions rule their minds. More generally, adolescents and others who are in transition or insecure, because they are in liminal (borderline) situations, seek absolutes of black-and-white, of homogeneous communities, of dogmatic certainties. The young idealists may seek purist causes to which they can dedicate or sacrifice their lives. Such personalities, age groups or social groups have a low tolerance for doubt and for pluralism since they need a high degree of psychological security. Of course, these psychological portraits of zealots are not ones that the zealots would agree to as the key to their self-understanding.

3. The Reactive Defender of the Sacred Community

The self-understanding of most zealots — especially Pinchas and Mattathias — is neither as proactive ideological missionaries nor as insecure psychological misfits. Rather they believe themselves to be **reactive** defenders of what is sacred to their community when the community and its *sancta* are being threatened and desecrated by unscrupulous forces. They are defending God's and the community's honor which has been affronted intentionally by aggressive missionary forces that violate the law and cause anarchy. Notice that the **zealot's enemy** is portrayed as the coercive missionary using extra-legal means to conquer what has been the traditional, taken-for-granted authority. However, the traditional leadership has collapsed and is no longer capable of meeting the enemy. Compromised by self-doubt or traditional rules or a fear of confrontation, the conservative leadership is unable to mount a counter-revolution to the insidious forces of revolution from within and without. The zealot is often most incensed by traitors-from-within, former spiritual brothers who are undermining society from within, spreading the heretical poisons introduced by foreign bodies turned into cancers.

The terms, *zealot (Greek)* and *kanai* קנאי *(Hebrew)*, reflect this reactive stance. *Zealous* and *jealous* share the same root both in Greek and Hebrew. God declares himself a "jealous God" in the Ten Commandments[46] in forbidding Israel to whore after other gods. The language is taken from the "jealous husband" law.[47] Therefore Pinchas is "zealous/jealous" for God, presenting Divine anger at the indignity of being jilted and betrayed by Israel, his covenantal spouse. Mattathias' zeal is explicitly compared to Pinchas', and it results from his identification with God's disgrace caused both by traitorous Jews and by foreign invasion of the Divine realm. The women of Moab and Midian in the Bible, like the Greek Syrian officers in the Maccabean period, have lured Israel into apostasy by appealing to their sexual or social climber instincts. The political leadership — Moses and his "weeping" assembly, and even worse, Menelaus the so-called high priest or Quisling (one who collaborates with the invader) — have been rendered impotent or worse, co-opted.

Only a zealous outsider, like a pure and traditional priest, can fulfill the priestly mission to guard God's *sancta* and save the day by going beyond the law. Public desecration that is designed to demoralize the Jewish public and its leadership must be met by a reactive counter desecration — spearing Zimri and Kozbi in a parody of their illicit prostitution, and sacrificing the Greek and the Jew in a parody of their idolatrous worship.

Three Strategies of Containment

These three definitions or characterizations of the zealot imply three different strategies of containment of this troubling phenomenon:

(1) The **proactive fanatic** needs to be countered with a dose of skepticism about belief in general, with a pluralism of truths and with the importance of the individual freedom to err while in pursuit of ultimate truth.

(2) The **hot-headed youth** in pursuit of absolutes might be restrained, if other sources of psychological and sociological security were provided — a caring support group for primary identification without extremist views.

(3) The **reactive defender of the sacred community** who sees the other as a threat, must be reassured that the traditional, sacred values s/he believes in will not necessarily be undermined by deviance. Pluralism must actively defend and reassure traditional minorities as well as liberal ones in order to make the zealot feel less threatened and decrease the urge to take the law into one's own hand in a crisis.

---

46. *Exodus 20*   47. *Numbers 5*

HOW HANUKKAH BECAME A HOME HOLIDAY

THE RABBIS TRANSFORM THE DAY OF THE DEDICATION OF THE TEMPLE INTO THE EVENING OF THE REDEDICATION OF THE HOME

by Noam Zion

THE ANCIENT AND THE MODERN INDEPENDENCE DAY PROCESSION

The original Hanukkah founded by the Hasmonean dynasty was probably not celebrated at home with the lighting of the family menorah. As described in the historical *Books of the Maccabees* (c. 125 BCE), the original festivities involved a victory march. "They celebrated for eight days . . . carrying palm branches."[48] (The palm branch is both a Jewish symbol of Sukkot and perhaps a Greek symbol of the goddess of victory, Nike, who later gave her name to sports shoes in the 20th century.)

Perhaps the festival was not fully formed in 164 BCE when the Temple was first recaptured and rededicated. Maybe only in 152 BCE when Judah's brother Jonathan became the High Priest or in 140 BCE when his other brother Simon became High Priest and dynastic prince of a recognized autonomous state, did this **ancient Israeli Independence Day** gain its ritual form as a public celebration of the founding of a new and renewed political-religious-national order.

The festival, which does not even have its own name in the *First Book of Maccabees*, seems to follow the Greek model of days that commemorate military victories, especially ones that founded a new political dynasty like the Maccabees. Elias Bickerman, the historian, notes that the Bible has no holidays established by political leaders and no commemoration of military events. Therefore Hanukkah itself is a Hellenist-style innovation.

If we search for a modern parallel to Hanukkah as a "State Holiday of Independence," the Zionist entity of the 20th century comes to mind immediately. It is no surprise that in the 1930s and 1940s the rising secular nationalist Zionist movement in Israel adopted Hanukkah as its central holiday.[49] Theodore Herzl concluded his book, *The Jewish State* (1896), with the visionary prophecy, "The Maccabees shall rise again," in the same spirit in which Greek and Italian 19th century nationalism envisioned a rise of their modern nation-state in the image of the ancient glory of Athens and Rome. (Note that modern Greece hosted the renewed Olympics in the same year, 1896.) In Eretz

---

48. *II Maccabees* 10:7

49. see Ehud Luz and Eliezer Don-Yehiya's article on page 10)

Lighting the Oil Menorah.
(French Book of Jewish Ceremonies, Amsterdam, 1713)

The Menorah in the Ancient Temple.
In this engraving, we have a peek into the inner sanctum of the Temple through a raised curtain revealing the twelve showbreads, the altar of the incense, and a giant seven-branched menorah.

(Illuminated Manuscript of Josephus, Amsterdam, 1704)

renewed settlement of Jews in Israel is the "Jewish National Home" (Balfour Declaration, 1917). To celebrate the emergence of Jewish consciousness from the home to the streets, from minority status to a claim to be an autonomous majority, the place of the menorah (later the national emblem of the State of Israel) was atop Jewish public buildings, *not only in private homes on the window sill.* The proper Zionist name for the holiday was **"The Festival of the Maccabees (or of the Hasmoneans),"** not **"Hanukkah"** which means "Rededication of the Temple."

Now let us return from the modern counterpart to the ancient context of the Maccabees and later, the Rabbis.

A Temple Rededication Ceremony

In addition to the victory parades of the ancient Maccabees that celebrated their political independence, the original holiday also took the form of a **Temple Rededication Ceremony**. In the *Second Book of the Maccabees*, which quotes from a letter sent circa 125 BCE from the Hasmoneans to the leaders of Egyptian Jewry, the holiday is called **"The Festival of Sukkot celebrated in the Month of Kislev (December),"** rather than Tishrei (September). Since the Jews were still in caves fighting as guerrillas on Tishrei, 164 BCE, they could not properly honor the eight day holiday of Sukkot (and Shemini Atzeret) which is a Temple holiday, hence it was postponed until after the recapture of Jerusalem and the purification of the Temple. This — not the Talmudic legend of the cruse of oil — explains the eight day form of Hanukkah. The use of candles may reflect the later reported tradition of *Simchat Beit HaShoeva*, the all-night dancing in the Temple

Yisrael in the 1920s-1930s the *form of celebration* for the new nationalist Hanukkah was public parades often by torchlight, youth movement pilgrimages to the graves of the Maccabees at Modiin and the creation of the Maccabia international sports competition. After the establishment of the state in 1948, the public Hanukkah candle lighting began at the graves of the Maccabees at Modiin with an Olympic-style runner carrying a lit torch to the Knesset with intermediate stops — including the Israeli President's home.

In the 1930's everyone was asked: what "bricks" have you contributed to rebuilding the "Temple," the Third Commonwealth, meaning metaphorically, the new Jewish political entity. Note that the Hebrew word for Temple is "sacred house," *Beit Hamikdash,* and that the British Mandate's term for the

---

To celebrate the emergence of Jewish consciousness from the home to the streets, from minority status to a claim to be an autonomous majority, the place of the menorah in modern Israel was atop Jewish public buildings, not only in private homes on the window sill.

---

on Sukkot which required tall outdoor lamps to flood light on the dance floor of the Temple courtyard.

> "They celebrated it for eight days with gladness like Sukkot and recalled how a little while before, during Sukkot they had been wandering in the mountains and caverns like wild animals. So carrying lulavs . . . they offered hymns of praise [perhaps, Hallel] to God who had brought to pass the purification of his own place."[50]

The connection between Sukkot and Hanukkah (as the Rabbis later called it) goes beyond the accident of a postponed Sukkot celebration. Sukkot is the holiday commemorating not only the wandering of the Jews in the desert in makeshift huts but the end of that trek with the dedication of the First Temple (i.e. the permanent *Bayit*/ Home of God in Jerusalem by King Solomon circa 1000 BCE).

> "King Solomon gathered every person of Israel in the month of Eitanim [Tishrei] on the holiday [Sukkot] in the seventh month . . . for God had said, 'I have built a House for my eternal residence.'"[51]

The medium is the message, and the new Rabbinic household ceremony offers us a new interpretation of Hanukkah, transforming it from the "Rededication of the Sacred House," the Temple, to the "Rededication of the Family Sanctuary."

Thus the Maccabean rededication celebration is appropriately set for eight days in the Temple.

The Rabbis' Home Hanukkah

After the brief review of the two rationales and two forms of celebration taken by the original unnamed Maccabean festivities of the 25th of Kislev, the Rabbis' decision to make Hanukkah a home holiday is all the more amazing. It would have been so much more appropriate to commemorate a national victory in the streets and a Temple purification in the Temple courtyard. After losing the Temple and political independence, the ceremonial lighting of the menorah would still have found its natural place in the synagogue. (Yet it is only in the Middle Ages that a new custom originates and it becomes customary to light a menorah in the synagogue on Hanukkah, even though the halacha is still that only home candles are an adequate fulfillment of the candle lighting obligation.) While no historical source (neither the *Books of the Maccabees*, Josephus nor Philo) mentions anything about home candle lighting in relationship to the original Hanukkah, the Talmudic Rabbis (2nd-5th century CE) assume that the only obligation is to light a lamp on one's doorstep (or window sill). One lamp must be kindled for each household just at dusk in order to publicize the miracle for the passersby on their way home from the market place.

Why then did the Rabbis make this Temple holiday into a home holiday? Was that the oral tradition since the days of the Maccabees or was it an innovation after the destruction of the Second Temple (70 CE)? Whatever the historical development of this custom, the home-based form of the holiday expresses a particular spiritual message. "The medium is the message," and the household ceremony offers us a new interpretation of Hanukkah, transforming it from the "Rededication of the Sacred House," the Temple, to the "Rededication of the Family Sanctuary." Let us suggest some possible rationales for this innovation, one we still observe, the family candle lighting at home.

First, the Rabbinic candle lighting is a liminal ceremony, meaning it occurs at the threshold (*"liminos"* in Greek) in two senses. **In space, the doorway is the border and the gate between home/street, private/public, family/national. In time, dusk is**

---

50. *II Maccabees* 10:6-7   51. *I Kings* 8:2,12

the border between day/night and light/ darkness with all their metaphoric significance. The Rabbis required that each household *"publicize the miracles of Hanukkah"* by sending a message from their home to the public sphere, the market place. It seems more than a coincidence that when the Greeks tried to force every Jewish family to renounce its Judaism and to proclaim its loyalty to Hellenist culture, religion and politics, that the doorstep was the location chosen.

> "At the doors of their houses and in the squares they burned incense[52] [to the pagan gods]."

In short, the Greek persecution was aimed not only at the Temple and not only at requiring notables like Mattathias to offer sacrifices on public altars, but struck at **family Judaism**. Circumcision, Shabbat and Kashrut (or at least eating ritually pure foods) were the target as well. Many rank and file Jews defended their family's Judaism even to the point of martyrdom. The martyrdom of the scribe Elazar and of Hannah and her seven sons is a personal "bearing witness" (***martyr*** in Greek means to bear witness) to the public persecutors that God, not Antiochus, is the final authority.

Therefore the Rabbinic "publicizing of the miracle," house by house is more than a clever advertising campaign to spread information. It is **a family bearing of witness to the public that we are a family loyal to Judaism.** When the Rabbis encouraged individuals to go beyond the minimum requirement of one lamp per house and to light one lamp per individual, they mandated individuals within each household to voluntarily reiterate their personal commitment to the family's public declaration of faith.

In ancient Hellenist and contemporary Western civilization the public realm usually overshadows the private, the street values invade the home in the name of "enlightenment." If you will, in contemporary terms the light of the TV spreads its messages within the home sanctuary. However it is the family of the Maccabees, one family, a father and five sons (parallel to Hannah and her seven sons), who rejected the external light and declared their loyalty to their ancestral "lights." The inside triumphed over the outside, the ancient over the so-called modern, the family values over the enforced fads of up-to-date society. Thus it makes sense for the Rabbis to sanctify Hanukkah as a home holiday.

Let us add a second note about the Rabbinic form of observance. The candles are lit one at a time in mid-winter at the darkest point of the cycle of the **moon** (the 25th of Kislev when the moon is just disappearing and then beginning as a new moon to reappear on the 1st of Tevet and then to wax slowly). This occurs also at the darkest phase of the **solar** cycle, the winter solstice (of the northern hemisphere). Unlike holidays of redemption like Sukkot, Purim and Pesach, which are celebrated at the full moon and at the fall and spring solstice, Hanukkah reflects the beginning of the redemptive process, not its completion. Historically the 164 BCE rededication of the Temple takes place only at the beginning of the 25 year struggle for political independence, when many "dark days" still lay ahead.

The Rabbis' Hanukkah celebration marks the miracle of a new beginning in the historical and natural cycle, so Hillel's form of adding one light each night reflects that process as it waxes gradually, as each person adds to the light of the previous day.[53] The Rabbinic Hanukkah which is celebrated in the home focuses on the power of family values to stave off the outside influences of the street, in this case Hellenism, and ultimately to transform the public space by the light that shines from within the house. This is a faith that begins, like the winter solstice, in darkness but has the power to generate unexpected illumination for the whole world.

---

52. *I Maccabees* 1:55

53. See David Hartman's "Courage to Begin," in the companion volume, *The Hanukkah Book of Celebration*, page 195.

4.

TO BE A WARRIOR OR A MARTYR?
SELF-DEFENSE AND WARFARE ON SHABBAT

THE CONFLICT BETWEEN THE SANCTITY OF LIFE AND THE SANCTITY OF SHABBAT

by David Dishon

Scene I

The Time: A Shabbat morning, sometime in the year 164 BCE.

The Place: A series of large caves in the Judean Desert, just east of Jerusalem.

The Situation: About 200 Jewish families, husbands, wives and children, have fled the Hellenist persecutions of Jewish practices in Jerusalem and have taken refuge in the desert caves. But they have been discovered. A cohort of Greek soldiers has surrounded the entrances to the cave. The Greek commander calls out to the Jews: "Enough! Come out and do as King Antiochus commands, and you will live, you and your children!" The Jews were well-armed. They had chosen the caves as a perfect refuge, easily defensible against a large force. But there was one problem. Today was the Shabbat, the holy day of rest. Any secular activity, let alone warfare, was totally anathema to the sanctity of the day. In Jerusalem their persecuted comrades had given themselves to torture and death rather than desecrate the Shabbat. Why should things be different here?

Confidently, the Greeks awaited a reply. They had cleverly chosen the Shabbat for the attack. They knew the insane religious scruples of the Jews — they wouldn't fight. They must surrender.

A reply was shouted out: "We will not come out nor do as the King commands and break the Shabbat!"

The Greek soldiers moved forward, climbing the steep cliff walls. Not a stone was thrown by the defenders; no effort was made to block up the hiding places. When the Greeks entered the caves they found mothers, fathers and children huddled together, praying. The Greek swords began to hack right and left. With their last breath the Jews called out: "Let us all die guiltless. We call heaven and earth to witness that you destroy us unlawfully." Then silence. A thousand people lay dead.[54]

---

54. Based on *I Maccabees* 2:29-38

Scene II

The Time: A few days later.

The Place: Camp of Mattathias and his guerrilla fighters, somewhere in the hills of Judea.

The Situation: Word had just arrived of the massacre in the caves. Weeping and cries of despair from the soldiers. Dozens of brave Jewish families destroyed without mercy! But beyond the grief lies a deeper fear — facing the dilemma of fighting on Shabbat can no longer be put off. A council is held chaired by the rebel priest Mattathias:

- "Our whole struggle is for the holiness of Torah. If we profane the Shabbat, our fight is meaningless!"

- "If we do as our brothers have done and refuse to fight, our entire people will be destroyed. There will be no one to keep the Shabbat!"

- "We must have faith in God. He will hear our cries and deliver us as He did in Egypt, and as in our exile He saved Daniel even in the lions' den!"

- "We cannot rely on miracles. We fight for God's cause and He will help us. God expects us to fight like Joshua, Gideon, and David. They didn't wait for miracles."

"On that day Mattathias and the government-in-exile reached this decision: If anyone attacks us on the Shabbat, let us fight against him and not die, as our brothers and sisters died in the hiding-places."[55]

---

55. *I Maccabees* 2:40-41

Judah goes into Battle. *(Woodcut illustration from Josephus, Amsterdam, 1743)*

JUDAISM AND MILITARY POWER:
THE PROBLEM OF RELIGIOUS ARROGANCE

The Maccabean Revolt is considered a turning point in Jewish history in many ways. Not the least were its implications — in its own day and for future times — for the use of military power in the service of God. The debate between the desert martyrs and the Maccabean rebels on their way to establish the Hasmonean dynasty (140-63 BCE) reflected the dialectic between two poles of the Biblical tradition: David and Gideon. David's battles are described in secular terms typical of his era involving the accumulation and use without restraint of military hardware to achieve imperial power. Gideon's battles — using the minimal force necessary and relying maximally on God's intervention (natural or supernatural) — reflect the desire not only to win but to demonstrate one's faith in the God of the few against the many. Gideon represents a complex of Biblical views of military power different than the standard of their day.

Let us review this unique tradition of **Biblical warfare** and then see how it may have influenced both the desert martyrs and the Maccabean warriors. Then we will see how their descendants, the Hasmonean dynasty and in their wake the later Rabbis opt for the Davidic tradition of "normal" warfare.

The Maccabean Revolt is a turning point in Jewish history — in its own day and for future times — for the use of military power in the service of God.

God appeared first to Israel as a "Man of War" at the Red Sea,[56] annihilating Egypt's war-chariots and cavalry. "God will fight for you, and you may be still," declared Moses to the frightened people, cowering at the approach of Pharaoh's army. In the desert the Jews took up arms to defend against Amalek, but only when Moses raised his arms were they victorious.[57] Addressing a people about to enter the land of Israel, the Book of Deuteronomy codified for all time the central Biblical religious concern about military power — the fear that its use could lead to a sense of self-sufficiency without God, to a feeling that *"my power and the strength of my hand have achieved all these mighty deeds."*[58] Deuteronomy's antidote is a series of laws: A priest addresses the army before battle, reminding them that God's aid is what secures the victory.[59] The army is deliberately kept small: those who are afraid are sent home along with those whose minds are on a newly built house, a newly planted vineyard or a newly betrothed bride. Special laws of sanctity attach to the army's camp as a reminder that *"The Lord your God walks in the midst of your camp, to deliver you, and to hand over your enemies before you."*[60] And the King, the commander-in-chief, is prohibited from maintaining a large-scale cavalry or a large financial war-chest and from marrying many wives, the key to military and diplomatic alliances in ancient times.[61] The Jewish army was to remain a popular militia sufficient for self-defense, but inadequate for empire-building.

The Biblical concern with the religious arrogance of military power is made explicit in the story of Gideon.[62] Gideon, appointed by God to fight the Midianite invaders and their huge army, gathers together a force of 32,000 volunteers. He is then told by God: *"The forces you have are too numerous for Me to give over Midian into their hands — lest Israel boast*

---

56. *Exodus* 15:3   57. *Exodus* 17:12
58. *Deuteronomy* 8:17   59. *Deuteronomy* 20
60. *Deuteronomy* 23:15   61. *Deuteronomy* 17
62. *Judges* 7

before Me saying, 'My own hands have rescued me!'" Gideon, at God's command, tells all who are afraid, to go home — and 22,000 leave! The remaining 10,000 is further culled to a mere 3,000 warriors, and with those Gideon defeats the enemy, his soldiers shouting *"The sword of God, and of Gideon!"*

But the people grew tired of spontaneous leadership and ad-hoc militias. They demanded a king and an organized army. Saul, the first king, took some initial steps, and then David, his successor, vigorously established an empire, conquering neighboring peoples, and professionalizing the army.

The policy of making military alliances came under withering critique by the prophets, who saw the reliance on military power as symbolic of the people's straying from God.

His son Solomon was "a man of peace," but he preserved that peace by establishing huge standing forces, including professional cavalry and charioteers. Solomon was also militarily allied to Egypt. All of this was in gross violation of the Deuteronomic Code on kingship. The heavy taxation required to maintain such a force split Solomon's kingdom in two after his death, but the tradition of kings leading large standing professional armies continued.

Ultimately this policy came under withering critique by **the prophets**, who saw the reliance on military power as symbolic of the people's straying from God. *"Woe to those who go down to Egypt for help, they rely on horses, and put their trust in chariots for they are many and in horsemen they are very strong! They do not rely on the Holy One of Israel, nor seek the Lord!"* thundered the prophet Isaiah.[63] The prophet's recommendation is: *"In ease and rest shall you be saved; in quietness and confidence shall be your strength — but you did not wish it."*[64] The sentiment is echoed by Zechariah, the prophet of the return to Zion after the Babylonian exile: *"Not by might nor by force —*

but by My spirit, says the Lord" — the words read out to this day in the Haftorah of the Shabbat of Hanukkah!

Second Temple Models: Martyrdom or Self-Defense?

The Babylonian destruction of Jerusalem in 586 BCE brought on a change of heart. Jewish military power and alliances had proved to be "a broken reed."[65] When Jews in Babylon were threatened with persecution they dealt with it in a new way — **martyrdom**. Stories began to be circulated about Daniel in the lions' den, about the three Jewish leaders who were cast into a fiery furnace and were not burned. These stories received their final literary forms in the book of Daniel, a book, many scholars maintain, which took its final form during the persecutions of Antiochus. The message of the book to the suffering Jews of Judea was clear — remain steadfast in refusal to bow to foreign gods, risk your life and miraculous salvation will come eventually. To reinforce this message the book of Daniel ends with an apocalyptic vision — all the persecutions are part of the drama of "the End of Days." The date for the final upheaval has been sealed and is near: *"Happy is he who waits."*[66]

This was the background of those **Hasidim** — pious families who took refuge in the desert caves. They were not pacifists or total religious quietists like latter-day Quakers or Amish. They had arms and were willing to defend themselves — but not on Shabbat. The observance of Shabbat was what distinguished their warfare from secular warfare. It showed decisively that their ultimate trust was not in their weapons, but in God — and this demanded vivid physical proof. When the crunch came, they chose martyrdom — calling heaven and earth to witness their loyalty. Such dramatic manifestations must ultimately call forth the divine mercy.

---

63. *Isaiah* 31:7   64. *Isaiah* 30:15
65. *Isaiah* 36:6   66. *Daniel* 12:12

The Greek Armies flee the Maccabees. *(Medieval manuscript)*

The **Hasmonean** fighters with Mattathias faced the same dilemma — but responded differently. They shared the cultural and religious world of the desert martyrs — but the extreme nature of the crisis, the sense that the very survival of Torah was at stake, called forth a new decision: the decision that God's warriors would fight on the Shabbat — but only to defend themselves. This decision meant that military force could be used in the real world — without necessarily leading to the arrogance of "the strength of my hand."

One sees this concern in the actions of Mattathias' successor — his son, Judah the Maccabee. Before battle Judah called his troops together.[67] They fasted and brought out the Torah scrolls. Those afraid to fight or newly betrothed, etc., were sent home, according to Deuteronomy 5:5-8, in spite of the fact that the Jews were already numerically inferior to their enemies. Then Judah, as priest, addressed the troops, reminding them of Biblical examples of God's miraculous deliverance of the strong into the hands of the few. Then after fasting, prayer and exhortation — Judah cleverly made use of every ruse and tactical ploy to outsmart the Greek commanders and achieve victory. It is fitting therefore that Judah and his victories should be commemorated on Hanukkah with the emphasis not on military prowess — but on their pure, religious motivation symbolized by the kindling of the menorah lights.

In using military power to further God's cause, the Maccabees had crossed their Rubicon. From then on they played the diplomatic game with increasing skill — finally achieving political independence after a struggle of over 20 years. The Hasmonean successors maneuvered less skillfully or more brazenly, and the Hasmonean state succumbed to Rome. Significantly, Josephus relates that the Jews defending the Temple Mount against Pompey's Roman soldiers in 63 BCE would defend themselves on Shabbat if directly assaulted — but would not prevent the Romans from raising earth-works around the Temple Mount on Shabbat. The Romans took advantage of this Jewish scruple, and in Josephus' opinion only this allowed them to conquer the fortified Temple Mount.[68]

The Rabbinic Tradition: Legitimizing Military Power

Perhaps this is what led to a further change — the legitimation of **offensive** military operations on Shabbat. In Rabbinic literature this legitimation is ascribed to Shamai the Elder (Hillel's intellectual sparring partner), who lived under the Roman-Herodian rule while the Temple still stood (20 BCE). Shamai interpreted Deuteronomy 20:20 — *"And you shall build the siege against the city which is making war on you — until you reduce it."*

---

67. *I Maccabees* ch. 3-4
68. *Jewish Wars I*, 146

Shamai noted that the end of the verse "until you reduce it" is unqualified, and he commented — "even on Shabbat." Thus offensive war could be pursued, and as later legal discussions made clear, even *initiated* — on Shabbat. Indeed this is what took place during the great Jewish Revolt against Rome (66-70 CE). The Jews attacked the Romans mercilessly on Shabbat the same as any other day, giving the Romans no advantage. There is no record of any Rabbinic criticism of this practice.

With the Temple destroyed and Jewish military power crushed, we might have expected the Jews to revert to a position preferring martyrdom over fighting. But this is not what happened. The post-Maccabean tradition was too strong. Instead the Rabbis systematically worked out a legitimation of Jewish military power, taking David as their paradigm, not Gideon. The Deuteronomic restrictions on the king's aggrandizement of horses, money, etc., were held to apply only to the king's private use, not to the accumulation

Diaspora position, threatened occasionally by messianic activism, and overthrown in the hearts of most Jews by secularization, political Zionism, and finally, the Holocaust. **Zionism and the State of Israel have led to the re-emergence of the Maccabean tradition.** The Israeli army suspends training and other non-operational activities on Shabbat, while maintaining total military vigilance and, when deemed necessary, initiating military action on Shabbat. All this is done with the blessing of the Army Rabbinate, and with the full cooperation of Shabbat-observing soldiers and officers. At the same time, in its prayers for the soldiers' welfare, the religious community affirms that military power alone is not what brings security. Victory is ascribed to God's help — but God is conceived of as acting through human agents. If the religious/ secular polarization is a deep-seated threat to Israel's existence — the ability of religious and secular soldiers to live side by side on Shabbat in the Israeli army, each carefully distinguishing their military duties as soldiers from their own individual "leisure time," is a bright and encouraging phenomenon.

> The post-Maccabean Rabbis systematically worked out a legitimation of Jewish military power, taking David as their paradigm, not Gideon.

---

of resources for the state. The Babylonian Talmud specifically says the king may maintain a surplus of horses and monies for security needs, and need not be limited by any religious concerns about minimalization.[69] Halacha allowed active war to be continued on Shabbat — including pre-emptive offensive action, if an enemy attack seemed imminent.[70]

However while the Rabbis in theory legitimized "realistic" war waged by the ruler of a powerful Jewish state even on Shabbat, in practice they took up the Book of Daniel's position — waiting for a supernatural divine redemption.[71] This was the traditional

Two Competing Conceptions of Shabbat

The Maccabean decision can also be seen as a turning point in the understanding of the Shabbat. The Shabbat celebrates God's refraining from Creation. After six days of activity, it is the hallowed day of rest. However this can be understood in several ways. One can view Shabbat as the anti-thesis of creation, a day of rest and harmony, a day of quiet protest against the jostling, uprooting creativity of the human race and their aggressive dominance over nature. Shabbat can also be a leap into another dimension of reality, "a taste of the world to come," a fundamentally other-worldly experience.

In this conception, Shabbat must not

69. T.B. *Sanhedrin* 21b
70. T.B. *Eruvin* 45a, *Shulchan Aruch O.H.* 330:6
71. T.B. *Ketubot* 111a

> On the sectarian Shabbat no use of fire or light was permitted. It was a day of abstinence, of sitting in darkness and eating cold food.

compromise with life. Shabbat announces a superior ethic, one of total dedication to God through total renunciation of the demands of the world. This is how many Jewish sectarians saw Shabbat, from the Qumran Dead Sea sect to the literalist Karaites of the Middle Ages. On the sectarian Shabbat no use of fire or light was permitted. It was a day of abstinence, of sitting in darkness and eating cold food. One could leave the house only to attend synagogue. From such a perspective it is easy to see how preserving the Shabbat could take precedence over the preserving of human life for the martyrs of the Maccabean period.

Rabbinic Judaism, which emerged from the Pharisaic movement, took a different path. The Rabbis upheld not only the strict Torah prohibition of work on Shabbat, but also the demand of Isaiah the prophet[72] that the Shabbat be a day of joy and honor. In explicit opposition to their Sadducean opponents, the Rabbis ordained the lighting of candles just before Shabbat — and explained that the purpose of the candle-light meal is *"shalom bayit,"* peace in the home, the intimate enjoyment between husband and wife. Three full meals were Rabbinically ordained for Shabbat, as well as sexual relations between the couple. One must wear fine clothes, use the best dinnerware and thoroughly clean the house and oneself beforehand. Shabbat became a celebration of creation, of life itself. Not only work and creative activity were important, but rest and enjoyment as well. Shabbat was not world-denying, but world-affirming — the created world is "very good" and can be sanctified. It is a day to step back and appreciate, to become aware of what we have and not what we lack, to spend a day feeling as if "all one's work has been completed."

Shabbat and the Sanctity of Life

In this atmosphere it is clear that loyalty to Shabbat cannot violate human life. Indeed the Rabbis ruled that even the slightest doubt as to whether a life-threatening situation existed, required the suspension of normal Shabbat prohibitions. The Talmud ruled that if either a sick person or a doctor felt that life was endangered — the Shabbat must be suspended. The opinion of two doctors who felt danger existed took precedence in Jewish law over the opinions of 100 doctors who felt otherwise.[73] Similarly the Talmud ruled that even if 100 doctors believed there was no danger, if the sick person maintained that s/he felt endangered, then the Shabbat must be suspended — "for the heart knows its own trouble."[74] The actions in violation of the Shabbat were not to be shunted off to gentiles, children, women or ignorant people. In life-threatening situations, they were to be performed by "the great ones of Israel" to show one and all that in this case the mitzvah is to violate the Shabbat.[75] The Jerusalem Talmud was even more emphatic: "[In life-threatening situations when the Shabbat must be violated] the one who acts quickly is praiseworthy, the Rabbi who is asked his opinion deserves blame, and the one who asks the Rabbi is a spiller of blood." The commentators explain that the Rabbi deserves blame because he did not sufficiently educate his congregation that if any possibility of endangerment exists, one must immediately call a doctor or an ambulance — and not waste precious time seeking Rabbinic permission.

The Talmud[76] relates that once the great Rabbis of the early 2nd century were walking along the road and the following question was put to them: "From whence do we learn that even doubtful danger to life suspends the Shabbat?" The Talmud records seven learned answers to this question, each Rabbi citing a

---

72. *Isaiah* 58:13   73. *Shulchan Aruch O.H.* 618:4
74. *Proverbs* 14:10, *T.B. Yoma* 83a   75. *T.B. Yoma* 84b
76. *T.B. Yoma* 85a

different proof-text. The impression is however, that these texts are cited after the fact. The suspension of Shabbat prohibitions in order to prevent even a possible threat to human life had been decided long ago and had become an essential part of the Rabbinic ethos.

Even so, two of the answers given are especially noteworthy. "Rabbi Yonatan ben Yosef said: *'For the Shabbat is holy **unto you**'*[77] — it is handed over into your hands, and you are not handed over into the Shabbat's hand." Here we have the fundamental principle: holiness must serve human needs, and not the other way round. The other answer is

---

The fundamental principle is that holiness must serve human needs, and not the other way round. *"'You shall observe my statutes and my laws which a person must perform and **live by them**'* — and not die by them!"

---

given by a Babylonian scholar, Shmuel: *"'You shall observe my statutes and my laws which a person must perform and **live by them**'*[78] — and not die by them!" Shabbat, and mitzvot in general, come to affirm life, not cause death. And in the summation of the Talmudic discussion, flaws were found in all the proof-texts — except for that of Shmuel — *"and live by them."*

It was left to the great codifier of Jewish law, Maimonides, to sum up this great principle. Maimonides' legal language is famously terse and to the point — but on the issue of violating the Shabbat to preserve life, he suddenly becomes expansive and passionate:

It is forbidden to hesitate in violating the Shabbat for the sake of a sick person whose life is in danger, as it is said: "That a person must perform and live by them — and not that one should die by them." Thus you have learned that the laws of the Torah are given, not as an act of Divine vengeance to

the world — but an act of mercy, loving-kindness and peace for the world. And those sectarians [the Karaites] who say that this is desecration of Shabbat and forbidden — of them it is written *"Also I have given them statutes which are not good, and laws they cannot live by."*[79,80]

The Karaites, like other sectarians before them, were filled with genuine religious zeal. Theirs was an ideal of self-sacrifice, of self-immolation, and the rigorous understanding of Shabbat gave this practical expression. Better to die than to violate the Shabbat. But, according to Maimonides, they had missed something fundamental about the relation of God to Israel through mitzvah. Shabbat, the holiest day, was to be suspended if it threatened life. God's law comes not to crush humanity, not to overwhelm people with Divine majesty, but to ennoble and enhance human life. And this, stresses Maimonides, is symbolic that **all the laws of Torah are not vengeance in the world — but mercy, loving-kindness, and peace in the world.**[81]

---

77. *Exodus* 31:14
78. *Leviticus* 18:5   79. *Ezekiel* 20:25
80. Maimonides, *Laws of Shabbat* 2:3, *Mishne Torah*
81. The writer might be accused of ignoring the Rabbinic laws which do mandate martyrdom in certain situations. Without going into detail, it may be said that the Rabbis made *"and you shall live by them"* into the fundamental rule regarding mitzvah, and all exceptions had to prove their validity. Exceptions were established for three basic prohibitions considered so heinous that one should die rather than violate them: idolatry, adultery/incest, and murder. There were also special stipulations for times of intense religious persecution when dramatic steps were called for. But these were reactions to exceptional situations created by evil oppressors, in contrast to the fundamental rule, as Maimonides understood it.

Although the Biblical and Rabbinic theory and practice of war share a great deal with the principles common to their period, there are several features of Jewish law and thinking about war which offer us alternative insights. A few examples:

1. Channeling the Soldier's Sexual Power: "The Captive Woman"[82]

By the ancient laws of war women were considered war booty to be used and disposed of in any way the captor saw fit. Rape, systematic extermination, enslavement and sale were typical. The Torah, however, explicitly limits the soldier's choices: either make her your legal wife with full rights or let her go. A thirty day "cooling off" period provided for a transition for the soldier and his female booty, allowing her to mourn her lost parents and to prepare to marry her captor. During the mourning period the grieving woman looked so unattractive that the captor might well decide to let her go free. The Rabbis understood the Torah's willingness to allow the soldier to take sexual advantage of the captive in highly limited fashion, as a necessary concession to *yetzer hara*, the evil instinctual inclinations released by war. They further required that the woman captive convert by free consent before any marriage could be performed, thus re-enforcing the dignity and freedom of a captive woman who by the "normal" laws of war was merely sexual booty.

2. Ecology Versus the Scorched Earth Policy of Warfare: "Don't destroy the trees"[83]

Fruit-bearing trees are not to be cut down during a siege. From this Biblical law the Rabbis learned the prohibition of wanton destruction of any natural resources — whether in war situations or in normal domestic relations.

3. Morale and Motivation in War: "The Speech of the Priest"[84]

The priest addressed the army before battle reminding them of the holy cause they were fighting for, and warning them that success depended on their righteousness in the eyes of God. Spiritual and moral motivation, not the desire for glory or loot, was considered an essential part in the education of a soldier.

4. The Duty to Disobey Unjust Orders

The Rabbis praised Avner and Amasa, King Saul's senior officers, for refusing his direct order to massacre the priests of Nov whom Saul unjustly suspected of aiding David's escape from Saul's assassins. Later when David was king, David's general, Yoav, was excoriated by the Rabbis for obeying David's orders to deliberately place Uriah (Bat-Sheva's cuckolded husband) in a place of extreme danger on the battlefield. Jewish law held that any command by King or officer in violation of the Torah was null and void and must be disobeyed. **That is still the law in the Israeli army today. Any soldier who chooses to obey an obviously immoral order, such as shooting unarmed civilians, may be tried for a crime even though s/he was "only following orders."**

5. Pursuing Peace Precedes Conducting War

God directly commanded Moses to attack Sihon who barred the entrance to the land of Israel.[85] Instead, Moses sent messengers requesting peaceful passage. Only when Sihon refused and attacked Israel did Moses conquer him. The Rabbis saw this as a praiseworthy act of *"seek peace and pursue it"*[86] — not only being prepared to make peace, but to actively seek it out and foster it. According to the midrash[87] God was delighted at Moses' "disobedience" — and learned from Moses to establish a permanent law: *"When you approach an enemy city to make war on it, first call upon it to make peace."*[88]

---

82. *Deuteronomy* 21   83. *Deuteronomy* 20
84. *Deuteronomy* 20   85. *Deuteronomy* 2
86. *Psalms* 34:15   87. *Deuteronomy Midrash Rabbah* 5:13
88. *Deuteronomy* 20:10

Mothers Martyred.
"Jewish mothers with newly circumcised babies are flung headlong from battlements by occupation troops.   The women who had circumcised their children were put to death under the decree, hanging the babies around their necks, and destroying their families and the men who had circumcised them." (I Maccabees 1:60, 61)

(Copper etching from an early 19th century French Bible)

5.

THE MARTYR'S CONVICTION

A SOCIOLOGICAL ANALYSIS

by Eugene Wiener[89]

This is [an essay] about the linkage between convictions and the willingness to die for them, between the belief in a cause and the willingness to commit oneself totally to it. Conviction is necessary in human life. It gives meaning to the course of human existence and provides answers to the central questions of life.

In the modern western world, the psychological climate discourages total commitment and martyrdom. Individuals willing to martyr themselves for a cause strike us as irrational and motivated by psychological problems. Their convictions do not appear to be the expressions of free will and considered judgement. In an age of loosening communal and family ties, the individual who is irrevocably committed to particular convictions seems needlessly inflexible.

In addition, so many people have been sacrificed for what appear to be stupidities, that there is considerable suspicion about the sacrifice of life for any cause. This is the age of the "martyrs of Jonestown" and the bloody martyrs of Khomeini. Consequently, the act of sacrifice often generates in us a feeling of despair at the waste of precious life. This is particularly true in an age when "conviction contests" have become too dangerous. The stakes are too high. Viewing adversaries as representatives of Evil Empires may bolster our morale, but it creates the conditions for a

89. Eugene Wiener, *The Martyr's Conviction: A Sociological Analysis*, pp. 1-3, 39-46, 131-138. Scholar's Press, reprinted by permission of the publisher, Brown University Judaica Series (1989), and the copyright holder, Brown University.
    Rabbi Eugene Wiener is a sociologist in Haifa University.

showdown which could destroy the world.

How can anyone still believe in causes when the twentieth century has been witness to a series of the most horrendous mass murders in the name of worthy principles? People are rightfully suspicious of the moral

---

So many people have been sacrificed for what appear to be stupidities, that there is considerable suspicion about the sacrifice of life for any cause.

---

demands of causes. For modern sensibilities, the martyr's dramatic struggle between good and evil, between victory and defeat, appear to be the conflicts of the stage, not the stuff of everyday life.

However, it is our contention that, without the element of conviction, it is difficult to create a world we ourselves can value. It is our thesis that culture and values are only plausible when there is the possibility of dying for them. Although convictions arouse our deepest suspicions and represent a great danger to the human life, we cannot construct worlds of meaning without them. These are the martyr's dilemmas. This is also the predicament of modernity, for strong value convictions are simultaneously essential for the human spirit and yet dangerous to the human community.

The Roots of Western Martyrdom: The Willingness to Die for a Cause

Martyrdom first entered the arena of western consciousness during the ancient encounter between Greek and Israelite culture. Martyrdom was originally developed by the Israelites in response to the religious persecution of Antiochus Epiphanes (167 BCE).

Considering the significance of the Mosaic code to the Israelite society, the willingness to die is not too difficult to understand.

(1) First, the Mosaic action-guide was perceived as a **sacred covenant** between God and his chosen people.

(2) Second, the prescriptions of the code were intimately linked with a comprehensive interpretation of reality, including a **cosmology** of the structure of the universe and a cosmogony of its origins.

(3) Third, the code was tied in with a proud national heritage and a sense of **collective identity**. In short, the Mosaic law was the axis upon which the Israelite's world revolved. Through the observance of its ordinances, one attained meaning, order, dignity, identity and sanctification and forsook a chaotic, meaningless and polluted realm. Martyrdom is a response to the challenged integrity of the group. The act of the martyr proclaims that life is not worth living if the values of the group are denied.

(4) It is important to note that at the time of the Antiochan suppression, there were strong **apocalyptic currents** circulating among the Judean populace. Many Jews believed that the persecutions were merely a final drama before the eschaton [the end of the world which is marked by a violent final judgment day]. At that time the "remnant of the faithful" would be delivered, while the apostates and the heathens would be smitten. In addition, the Antiochan persecution prompted the Israelite writers to speak of **collective resurrection** for those who die in defense of the law.

(5) Another view which undoubtedly contributed to the plausibility of self-sacrifice was the notion of **a battle between opposing deities**. This concept, taken over from Iranian religion, may have led some Israelites to see their persecutors as messengers of an evil force opposed to God. In the last chapter of Daniel, Antiochus himself is seen not merely as a hostile ruler but as a contrary power to God. He was cast for a supernatural, demonic role, the first antichrist. In the writer's view, the struggle between Judaism and Hellenism becomes part of a cosmic drama, at the end of which the

victims would rise from the dust of the earth and shine as stars in the heavens and their opponents, the Hellenizers and apostates, would awaken to shame and everlasting contempt. Judgement would award each according to his merits.

(6) [The choice of martyrdom was not passive or pessimistic, but active and optimistic. It was expected to turn the tide in favor of one's camp either by arousing **God's vengeance** on the perpetrators or by appeasing God's anger at his people that had led God to abandon them to the persecutor's wrath.]

[In the *Testament of Moses*,[90] written in this same period, the main character, the martyr Taxo, tells his children: "Let us fast for the space of three days, and on the fourth let us go into a cave which is in the field and let us die rather than transgress the commands of the Lord of Lords, the God of our ancestors. For if we do this and die, our blood will be avenged." In addition, the Maccabean martyr

---

Without the element of conviction, it is difficult to create a world we ourselves can value. It is our thesis that culture and values are only plausible when there is the possibility of dying for them.

---

was viewed as an innocent sacrificial offering designed to atone for the sins of the people. The idea of **vicarious atonement** through sacrifice had been firmly established in the consciousness of the Israelite populace through the rituals of animal sacrifice in the priestly code. Vicarious atonement is based on a fairly simple metaphysical assumption. It is presumed that sin produces divine anger, which inevitably leads to punishment. Through the ritual of sacrifice, God's anger is directed away from the sinner toward an innocent, whose vicarious suffering absorbs the sinner's punishment.[91] Given all these ideas circulating in the Judean orbit, Antiochus clearly erred when he forced Israelites to choose between forsaking their

law or dying for it. By forsaking the law, the Israelite stood to lose both his present world and his hopes for the future. By sacrificing oneself for the law, one could die a holy and meaningful death, thus assuring oneself a happy future in the age to come.

The Greek Motif in Jewish Martyrdom

From the world of the Judean nationalists, we now shift to the Hellenist Jews living on the periphery of Palestine several generations after the Maccabean insurrection. Unlike their compatriots in Judea, the Jews living in Antioch [in Syria] and Alexandria [in Egypt] lived as a tiny minority in a world dominated by Hellenism. Within this context, the Jews carved out a "cognitive compromise" with their polytheistic neighbors. "Hellenistic Judaism" was the compromise produced by a creative synthesis between Greek and Israelite culture. We find several works written by Hellenist Jews recounting the events of the Judean revolt. It is in these works that the concept of martyrdom first comes to fruition. As the image of the martyr comes into focus, the zealot fades into the background. In *First Maccabees* [written in Judea, the zealous] Mattathias and his sons are responsible for Israel's salvation. In *Second Maccabees* and *Fourth Maccabees* [written in Egypt], by contrast, the death of the martyrs marks the turning point which arouses God to end his people's persecution.

In the mindset of Hellenistic Jews, three key social types contributing to the emergence of martyrdom can be isolated. The first is the figure of the **warrior-athlete**, a heroic individualist who faces pain and even death in order to overcome his opponent. The second is the **philosopher** (exemplified most perfectly by Socrates), who stoically stands by his rational principles, regardless of the personal expense. Finally, there is the **tragic figure** (e.g. Antigone) who chooses to die rather than forsake a normative principle. These

---

90. IX:1-7   91. p. 41

The Confrontation that creates the Martyr
BY EUGENE WIENER

Classical martyrdom is often accompanied by a dramatic confrontation between a ruler with visions of his own divinity and a group with deviant convictions. Martyrdom and self-sacrifice flourish when rulers make megalomaniacal demands for displays of total loyalty from their subjects. These demands produce anger and counter-displays of loyalty to convictions which are forbidden. It is the centrality of the villain as tyrannical persecutor which is used to explain the role that Antiochus, Caligula, Hadrian, Decius and Diocletian played in the development of Jewish Hellenistic and early Christian martyrdom.[92]

A martyrological event, in the ideal sense, requires a confrontation between two types of individuals or groups. There is generally a dissenting, deviant, non-conforming person or group, with an alternative set of convictions and a dominant powerful person or group willing to exercise its power. Martyrdom as an event is created out of the confrontation between the two.

From an examination of the classical sources, the components of **an ideal martyrological confrontation** include the following elements [in the ideal scenario]:

(1) A dissident individual is threatened with punishment if he or she persists in holding certain beliefs and convictions and behaving in ways that are proscribed by the ruling powers.

(2) The confrontation with the ruling powers, who persecute the dissident individual, takes place in a public setting.

(3) The individuals who are to undergo the agony of the test make a statement justifying their persistence in the proscribed belief or practice.

(4) The persecutor states his willingness to desist in applying punishment for non-conformity to established norms if the martyr will only recant and renounce his convictions.

(5) The martyr issues a statement of defiance, which affirms the preference of death to the betrayal of the espoused cause or principle.

(6) The established powers question the sanity or wisdom of the martyr-designate.

(7) The martyr rejects the services of mediators who attempt to blur the sharp differences between the victim and the persecutor(s).

(8) The martyr rejects all devices designed to achieve the ruse of symbolic betrayal of his cause and create the impression of his subordination to the persecutors.

(9) The martyr restates the purposes and convictions that justify the sacrifice of his life.

(10) The sufferer issues a profession of faith coupled with an expression of hope for his ultimate vindication.

(11) The martyr-designate is put to death.

Then the martyrological narrative — a literary tradition — immortalizes the martyr's story and makes it the basis for teaching group norms, as on Hanukkah.

---

92. Tcherikover, 1959

---

three images, together with the Greek notions of an afterworld and a disembodied soul, were the crucial elements of consciousness needed to consolidate the figure of the martyr.

It is thus hardly a coincidence that the first martyrologies were created by Hellenistic Jews. [In *Second Maccabees*, Elazar the elderly scribe chooses a painful martyrdom on the wheel of fortune rather than eat unclean foods.]

Making a high resolve, worthy of his years and the dignity of his age which he reached with such distinction and his admirable life even from his childhood, and still more of the holy and divine legislation, [Elazar told his persecutors] to send him down to Hades at once. "For," said he, "it does not become our time of life to lead many young people to suppose that Elazar, when ninety years old, has gone over to heathenism, and to be led astray through me, for the sake of this short and insignificant life, while I defile

Greek soldiers killing a woman (500 BCE)

and disgrace my old age. For even if in the present I escape the punishment of men, yet whether I live or die I shall not escape the hands of the Almighty. **Therefore by manfully giving up my life now I will prove myself worthy of my great age, and leave to the young , a noble example of how to die willingly and nobly for the sacred and holy laws."**[93]

Elazar is portrayed as a true "philosopher," patterned after the figure of Socrates, and Hannah is described in terms reminiscent of the Greek Iphigenia. The actions of the martyrs are depicted as a battle on behalf of virtue, or an athletic contest to be endured. The moral of the book is that the Jews are a nation of martyr-heroes with deep religious convictions. In [Hellenistic] Judaism, the combination of philosophy and martyrdom is seen as the most genuine form of Jewish heroism. The martyr's decision to sacrifice his or her life is often based on a rationally grounded belief that the principle he or she represents will live because of the sacrifice.

The martyr is held up as a role model for all Jews suffering from persecution. He or she is seen as a virtuoso of religious conviction who will be rewarded with eternal glory in the afterworld. The martyr's death is perceived as an innocent sacrifice, which will atone for the sins of the Israelite people and thereby expedite divine deliverance.

Our Modern Ambivalence about Martyrdom: The Psychologically Self-Absorbed Individual versus the Self-Sacrificing Hero of Conviction

Unlike the classical examples of martyrological conviction, which we have discussed, contemporary western man has been characterized as preoccupied with **the self**. Indeed, as community structure and family bonds weaken, it is the self, which is regarded as the new center. For contemporary man it is important to develop a mindset, which tries to keep options open at all times and thereby avoid commitments.

93. *II Maccabees 6*

According to this point of view, there are no absolute or intrinsic hierarchies of goals and values and it is important to maintain multiple perspectives. Psychological clarity about oneself supersedes commitment to any societal value.

This ideal of 'hanging loose' and seeing the self and its dictates as the center is echoed in

---

It seems to be particularly difficult to believe in causes nowadays. The psychological climate discourages commitment and the media present us with a constant debunking, so that frequently, yesterday's cause is today's fraud.

---

some of the popular forms of therapy. It is summarized in **Fritz Perls**' Gestalt Therapy Prayer:

> I do my thing and you do your thing.
> I am not in this world to live up to your
>   expectations
> And you are not in this world to live up to
>   mine.
> You are you and I am I.
> If, by chance, we find each other, it's
>   beautiful.
> If not, it can't be helped.

What this "prayer" connotes is a firm denial that we are here to live up to each other's expectations. Unlike the martyrs who sacrifice their lives for the group and its convictions, we are not here to live up to traditions handed down to us through culture or religion. Quite the contrary, the only worthwhile struggle is to free ourselves of each others' grasp, in order to turn around and "by chance" find each other again. According to the analytical attitude, for modern man the highest good is an affirmation of "my thing," and the ability to reject what is asked and found unsuitable. With this solipsistic faith in the centrality of the self, there can be no certainty that meaningful connections can be made with others.

In a hypothetical meeting between a martyr and a psychologically oriented individual with an analytic attitude, one finds a meeting between two individuals with very different commitments. Most immediately blatant is **the contrast between a commitment to knowing and feeling one's inner essence, and a commitment to the fulfillment of a moral purpose**. The dispute between them would be over "self" or "cause" as the central object of conviction. **To the psychological personality,** clarity about oneself supercedes devotion to an ideal as the model of right conduct. From his perspective, the martyr appears to be fanatically escaping from the self-examination which should be his major preoccupation.

The martyr appears in his eyes as a fanatic with unresolved psychological problems, which have forced him to close his options. The martyr's conviction represents a premature closure. Perhaps a better cause will come along tomorrow. Perhaps the cause will be discredited or demonstrated to be a psychological aberration, a fraud or a dangerous illusion. Besides, why be so morbid and give up the good things in life?

For the martyr, of course, the cause is the central issue, not the options available or the process of identifying with that cause. The martyr would see the psychological man as hopelessly fragmented and in search of guidance from a fickle self. He is unstable and set on a quest, which is doomed to failure. When nothing is held dear and all options are open, there are no absolute values with which to give meaning to the world. Although maintaining open options appears to represent such a choice, it is a choice which lacks moral vigor. The good that such a position affirms has no specific content and has no staying power against evil other than the commitment to free options. In addition, a concentration exclusively on the self as life's quintessential project precludes all other commitments, because the layers of the self do not lead into the world, but just ever deeper into the self.

Although the martyr is generally depicted

as other-worldly, from this interchange it appears that this is not the case. The martyr's path must lead through this world even though its destination is posthumous existence. It is the psychological man who, in the end, is more world-denying. In reality, the self is as much an abstraction and a mystic entity as the world to come. No one has ever seen or touched the self, and it is a social convention which barely existed for much of recorded history. The irony is that the project of psychological man, although self-affirming, is ultimately world-denying, while the martyr, who is self-denying, is ultimately world-affirming.

The **martyr** is not a pluralist, nor a relativist, particularly when it comes to his own convictions. It is not objective detachment, which the martyr seeks, but passionate commitment— to be possessed by some great and transcendent purpose. The **psychological personality**, on the other hand, seeks to survive and is skeptical about the worth of ultimate commitments. These are two very different worldviews and life perspectives.

Maimonides on Martyrdom: When to Defy and When to Compromise

Surprisingly, the mourner's kaddish is based on the mitzvah of kiddush hashem (sanctifying God's name in the world) — if necessary, by martyrdom. Our God exists independent of the world, yet the Divine concern to create a just and holy civilization on earth makes God dependent on human cooperation. The name of the Creator is profaned if the creation is corrupt, ruled by cruel and idolatrous tyrants. However, when human beings undertake to accept God's law, God's kingdom of justice on earth, then God's name is sanctified and God is in effect the actual ruler of the world. We mourn the death of any human being who embodied the image of God and upheld the Divine values in God's kingdom on earth by reinforcing the now weakened kingdom of holiness embodied on earth.

In a world that neglects the Divine plan, then it is the Jewish people as an exemplar of humanity that is commanded to keep the ideal going by voluntarily embodying this idea. When tyrants try to force us to violate basic values of human life, sexuality and worship, then one must be willing to become a "martyr," literally to bear witness to our loyalty to God's law over corrupt human authority. However in all other areas when saving one's life means compromising Jewish practices, then we are commanded to transgress Jewish law and to live, as long as that does not involve rape, murder and idolatry.

In the days of Antiochus and of Hitler, however, the tyrants sought not only to use Jews to kill and to rape, but they sought to abolish Judaism and wipe out God's name. In those cases martyrdom is an obligation whatever the transgression involved.

MAIMONIDES: THE LAWS OF MARTYRDOM — DEFINITIONS AND RESTRICTIONS

All the members of the house of Israel are commanded to sanctify the great name of God, as it is said, *"But I will be sanctified among the children of Israel."*[94] They are furthermore cautioned not to profane it, as it is said, *"Neither shall you profane My holy name."*[95]

How are these precepts to be applied? If an idolater coerces a Jew to violate any one of the commandments mentioned in the Torah under the threat that otherwise the Jew will be put to death, the Jew is to commit the transgression rather than suffer death; for concerning the commandments it is said, *"which, if a human does them, s/he shall live by them:"*[96] **"Live by them," — and not die by them.** That means that if one suffered death rather than commit a transgression, one is to blame for one's own death [because in most cases it is a mitzvah to prefer life over observance].

This rule applies to all the commandments, except the prohibitions of **idolatry, adultery or incest, and murder**. With regard to these: if a Jew is told: "Transgress one of them or else you will be put to death," one should suffer death rather than transgress.

The above distinction only holds good if the idolater's motive is personal advantage; for example if the idolater forces a Jew to build him a house or cook for him on the Sabbath, or forces a Jew to cohabit with him, and so on.

But if the idolater's purpose is to *compel the Jew to violate the*

Greeks forced Jews to sacrifice pigs to pagan gods in a manner portrayed on this vase drawing
(450 BCE)

Our Nostalgia for Martyrs

It seems to be particularly difficult to believe in causes nowadays. The psychological climate discourages commitment and the media present us with a constant debunking, so that frequently, yesterday's cause is today's fraud. Widespread skepticism is not only a response to the media, but to both the history of the 20th century, with its mass murders and final solutions, and to an awareness that the stakes are too high for an apocalyptic showdown between antagonistic convictions. Nothing

There are other things that are a profanation of the Name of God. When a person, great in the knowledge of the Torah and reputed for piety, does things which cause people to gossip, even if the acts are not express violations, one profanes the Name of God. As, for example, if such a person makes a purchase and does not pay promptly, provided that one has means and the creditors ask for payment and one puts them off; or if one indulges immoderately in jesting, eating, or drinking . . . or if one's mode of addressing people is not gentle, or one does not receive people affably, but is quarrelsome and irascible.

The greater a person is, the more scrupulous one needs to be in all such things, and do more than the strict letter of the law requires. And if a person has been scrupulous in one's conduct, gentle in conversation, pleasant toward fellow-creatures, affable in manner when receiving them, not retorting, even when affronted, but showing courtesy to all, even to those who treat one with disdain, and if one conducting one's commercial affairs with integrity and devotes oneself to the study of the Torah . . . and does more than one's duty in all things (avoiding, however, extremes and exaggerations) — such a person has sanctified God, and about such a person the Bible says, *"You are My servant, O Israel, in whom I will be praised."*[99]

ordinances of the religion, then if this took place privately and ten fellow-Jews were not present, one should commit the transgression rather than suffer death. But if the attempt to coerce the Jew to transgress was made in the presence of ten Jews, one should suffer death and not transgress, even if it was only one of the remaining commandments that the idolater wished the Jew to violate.

When one is commanded to transgress rather than be slain, and suffers death rather than transgress, s/he is to blame for his death.

When one is commanded to die rather than transgress, and suffers death so as not to transgress, he sanctifies the name of God. If one does so in the presence of ten Israelites, he sanctifies the name of God publicly, like Daniel, Hananyah, Mishael, and Azaryah, Rabbi Akiva and his colleagues. These are the **martyrs**, above whom none ranks higher. Concerning them it is said, *"But for Your sake are we killed all the day long; we are accounted as sheep for the slaughter."*[97] And to them also, the text refers, *"Gather my saints together to Me, those that have made a covenant with Me by sacrifice."*[98]

94. *Leviticus 22, 32*   95. *Leviticus 22:32*   96. *Leviticus 18:5*
97. *Psalms 44:23*   98. *Psalms 50:5*   99. *Isaiah 49:3*

THE RABBIS' HANUKKAH   183

seems worth such a risk.

And yet, without convictions we cannot live a life of meaning. Without a dedication to values neither culture nor religion is plausible, and our doubts about the purpose of life go unanswered. **Without our convictions, we are less than human.**

One could, in fact, make a case that **martyrs are particularly valued in a world that has become susceptible to the ethic of self-interest and personal fulfillment**. As moral certainties crumble under the influence of the therapeutic society there is a nostalgia and growing fascination with those who sacrifice their lives willingly for their convictions. As we feel ourselves becoming morally impoverished we tend to idealize those who had proven their moral courage.

The therapeutic era can be seen as a form of disenchantment with all causes beyond the individual. The retreat to self as the context in which to find the highest good is born out of a disappointment with causes. Introspection, the exploration of the inner world of feeling, the cultivation of private states and the communication of these inner space discoveries to others who value them,

become the essence of life. But what follows is disappointment. For however much the subjective world is changed and enriched by insight and however much one's personal sphere of social engagements become more satisfying, the world at large remains much the same. In the end it would appear that there is no way to make things a bit better in the world than by formulating a goal and devising a method to achieve it.

In this task, martyrs and other people of conviction have much to teach us. However, if their enthusiasms do not include self-awareness and self-respect they cannot become models of behavior for those in the enlightened world. The best of the martyrs from the past teach us how serious and fateful our duties are, while the behavior models of the therapeutic world teach us our personal rights to happiness. This would appear to be our situation. We move between these two worlds, uncomfortably sensing the disparity between them, for they are indeed very different. Both personal rights and personal duties are necessary to maintain a balance which we can sustain. We don't seem to have much of a choice.

The Martyrdom of Hannah and her Seven Sons. (II Maccabees 7:20-23)
by *Julius Schnorr von Carolsfeld (1860)*

184

6

AL HANISSIM

DO I REALLY BELIEVE IN MIRACLES?

by Noam Zion

An ancient ceramic cruse of oil and lamp (3rd-4th century CE)

Candle lighting on Hanukkah is about proclaiming the miracles that occurred. But how do we explain miracles to ourselves, let alone to our children? As modern "believers" in the scientific lawfulness of nature (even if we do not "understand" the theory of relativity and the Heisenberg uncertainty principle or how electro-magnetic fields pass through our houses and our bodies bringing us television images), we are usually embarrassed by traditional "believers" in supernatural interventions into the natural world. Yet we know that since the Middle Ages when the Greek understanding of the lawful structure of nature was accepted by religious people, the belief in God has meant both that God created the world order and the God can at will violate that order. The world as seen by the scientist is not "the whole truth," and other dimensions exist that sometimes encroach on our orderly world. To believe in miracles is to believe in these other dimensions, yet how do we reconcile religious beliefs with scientific ones?

Interestingly enough, it is easier to reconcile religion and science today than ever before. Both religious and scientific beliefs have changed greatly since the Middle Ages. We have completely rejected the Aristotelian science taken for granted then and replaced it first with Newtonian and then with Einsteinian physics. Today many scientists would qualify the "lawfulness of nature" by saying these are merely useful hypotheses, partial

---

Interestingly enough, it is easier to reconcile religion and science today than ever before.

---

models that help predict physical events, until we come up with better models. It is thought best to use multiple models simultaneously even if they appear intuitively contradictory (like the particle and the wave theory of light). Today our picture of reality as law abiding is less secure. Miracles are not as inconceivable as they once were when we took the scientific picture of the world literally.

Still our street-sense as moderns tells us that it is irrational and unhealthy to educate our children that a benevolent God creates anomalies in nature (like splitting the Red Sea) specifically to help the chosen people. It is not only the "belief in miracles" that threatens "our belief in nature" but the kind of person we imagine believes in supernatural occurrences seems weird whether s/he is an ultra-Orthodox Jew, a born-again Christian or a New Age occultist. To open up ourselves and our children to a life-giving faith in God's surprises means not only holding scientific hypotheses with less self-confidence, as in fact many scientists do today, but to ask what the faith in "other dimensions" will do to our everyday life. What kinds of miracle beliefs do we wish to explore and what kinds of believers are dangerous and crazy?

Let me map out some of the possible

approaches to miracles and on such a map you may be able to locate your own beliefs. I too will express my preferences. Today's science and philosophy cannot totally exclude any of these views of miracles, so it is a matter of choice which one we want to adopt when "proclaiming the miracle of Hanukkah." Rejecting certain options will be as important as adopting others, as we sort out our beliefs.

What kinds of miracle beliefs do we wish to explore and what kinds of believers are dangerous and crazy?

Option #1

Public miracles usually violate the laws of nature because that is how God teaches us to look beyond the physical to a higher realm of reality.

Korah, Datan and Abiram, the desert rebels, accused Moses of making up the whole project of the Promised Land, of pulling off a Wizard-of-Oz hoax on the whole people. Then Moses called upon God to "prove" that he had been chosen, by "making a miraculous creation" like the earth opening its mouth to swallow them up.[100] In fact, earthquakes do occur, but not usually when predicted in advance to prove a point at a particular time. The miracle is not necessarily a violation of natural law, but it is a "sign" felt by the people to be a decisive message from another dimension. Miracles of this sort, like Moses turning his staff into a snake before Pharaoh, come to establish credibility, to prove a point, to end speculation.

One might object to such miracles on several grounds:

(1) Uncertainty is preferable in the realm of faith since it refers faith to one's personal choice rather than "forcing belief" on us by powerful and threatening "tricks."

(2) The relative certainty of the natural order is more reliable in most cases. One should not build a worldview on bizarre exceptions.

(3) To cite supernatural miracles is to open up the field to charlatans who claim authority for their dangerous belief systems based on exotic so-called miracles.

Personally speaking, I do not believe literally in the supernatural variety of miracles as actual occurrences in the present or the past. Even if they occurred, I do not think they would "prove" something to me, that is, convince me of a certain religious worldview. Yet they do make great stories and they do teach lessons in a dramatic, literary way that I appreciate because I deeply believe that what appears invincible (like Pharaoh at the Red Sea or even a powerful cancer) can sometimes be vanquished in unpredictable ways. "God" is my name for that surprising power when the forces of good are victorious. I choose to believe in that God of surprising moments of reversal, but I also choose to be skeptical of particular "tricks," as I see them, which strike me as trivial, even if I cannot explain them away scientifically.

Option #2

Private miracles, the hidden coincidences, that sometimes change the direction of our lives because of amazing timing, are guided by Divine destiny.

The concept of the "hidden miracle" is developed by Nachmanides (13th century Spain) in his explanation of the ups and downs and ups again of Joseph's life in the Bible. Even though God never speaks to Joseph — not even in dreams — and never violates any laws of nature to cast him down into the pit via his brothers' jealousy or to raise him up by his ability to analyze the future and make a plan to preempt a famine, Joseph is convinced, in retrospect, that it is the hand of Divine destiny that has shaped his roller coaster existence and given it meaning.

But one might object on three grounds:

(1) You cannot "prove" the existence of an invisible hand of God, because it is only a

---

100. *Numbers 16*

matter of interpretation.

(2) One might become passive awaiting God's miracles whether public or private.

(3) Living in a world of existential uncertainty offers more moral grandeur and harsh honesty than the childish world of Divine providence.

Personally, I have great respect for an existentialist Camus-like stand that there are no Divine safety nets and that accidents may determine one's fate in the most indifferent way. Yet in a world of uncertainty I do not want to be dogmatic either in accepting or denying the possibility of personal, private miracles. It is a matter of interpretation and it is not provable one way or the other. When I choose to interpret coincidences as miracles, as a personal sense of destiny, then it gives me a strength to make meaning out of my life. I feel like Queen Esther who decides to reveal her Jewishness to the King in order to appeal to save her people from Haman, because *"who knows if just for this opportunity I became queen."* We, like Esther, cannot know for sure but we can wager on the possibility that God has

The God of Surprise!   BY RABBI DAVID HARTMAN

Central to the Exodus story and the Pesach seder is the recounting of the ten plagues. As moderns educated in natural science, the lawful order of the world, the story strikes us as childish, as primitive, as mythological. Yet we may be missing the point of these extraordinary events if we understand it as ancient superstition. Instead the miracle is a symbol of spontaneity in history, a faith in the changeability of oppressive regimes. What appears as fate, the necessity of a small people subject to an invulnerable empire, is revealed as an illusion. The language of the supernatural miracle is the Bible's way of undermining the acquiescence of humans to the "way things have to be," to the political "facts of nature" created by powerful dictators.

There is an unpredictable Power present in the universe. For a people arising from helplessness, utter destruction and complete impoverishment, the movement from Egypt to the desert was a radical leap. It was not a steady process, not a gradual development. The plagues and the crossing of the Red Sea signaled the breaking in of Power that confronted tyrannical hegemonies, which refused to accept ultimate divine Sovereignty.

Belief in miracle is the basis of the "hope model" of Judaism. Exodus becomes a call to revolutionary hope regardless of the conditions of history. The act of protest against their environment can occur, because the Jews possess a memory bank that structures what they think is possible. The Exodus becomes vital, because it tells people that they are able to hope. The order that people observe in the cosmos is not irreversible. Tomorrow will not necessarily be like today.

Belief in the doctrine of creation reinforces the belief in miracle. Creation means that the world that came about at a certain moment could be recreated in a new constellation if God so wills it. **Spontaneity and surprise characterize divinity.** Not everything is a recurring pattern. The cosmos is not a Nietzschean wheel of eternal recurrence. Creation and the miracles of Exodus protest against the despair of the book of Ecclesiastes. The Preacher of Ecclesiastes proclaims that the world is *hevel*/vanity. Nothing really changes; all is endless repetition. A generation comes, a generation goes. A child dies, a wife, a father . . . all is in vain, without significance.

The Exodus provided the memory that made hope a very real possibility. Being is not inalterable. Becoming marks a human being's ontology. Radical surprise becomes an important feature. New possibilities are always present; history can change.

Life is not just the present. A future is real. Without spontaneity and without creativity the future would be just a repetition of what already was. The Exodus introduces the dimension of a radically new tomorrow. That is the idea of Messianism. The belief in a Messiah proclaims a radical futurism; a new separate concept in human consciousness of time. Life is not exhausted by endless cycles. Once our story is told as our beginning through revolution, then history is a wide-open book.

Hanukkah is the Festival of Lights. It commemorates an ancient Jewish rebellion against oppression, during which the Temple in Jerusalem was miraculously recaptured from pagan hellenizers and rededicated to the worship of God. The candles of Hanukkah celebrate that rededication. They also help brighten the long winter nights.

But **I remember a Hanukkah when darkness almost overpowered the light.** It was the first week of November 1938. The final years of the Depression lay like a polluting mist across the streets of New York. On afternoons when it did not rain I would play on the sidewalk in front of the plate-glass window of the candy story near our apartment house. The bubble of darkness on the other side of the world bumped only vaguely against my consciousness. I was very young then, interested more in Flash Gordon and Buck Rogers than Adolf Hitler.

One afternoon I was near the candy store, in the cardboard box that was my rocket ship, when an elderly couple walked slowly by; I caught some of their frightened words. Before supper that evening I saw my mother standing over the kitchen sink, her head bowed, and heard her whispering agitatedly to herself. Later, my father came home from work, drenched in weariness; he turned on the radio and became wearier still.

That night I lay awake in my bed and saw the pieces of the day come together and form a portrait of terror: "A Jewish boy had shot a German [official in Paris]," the old people had said. "We will pay dearly for it, very dearly." "The boy had been sent by his parents to live with his uncle in Paris," my father had murmured. "Then the boy's parents were deported to Poland [by the Nazis in Germany]."

"The boy went out of his mind," my mother had said in a voice full of fear. "He did not know what he was doing."

I lay very still in my bed, thinking of the boy who had shot the German and wondering what the Germans would do to the Jews. Two days later the [German official] died, [then came ***Krystal Nacht***, the pogroms called the **Night of the Broken Glass, November 9, 1938**].

In the weeks that followed I dreamed about the synagogues that were burning all over Germany, about the Jews who were being sent to concentration camps, about the looted stores and smashed shop-windows. One day I stood in front of our apartment house and imagined our street littered with glass, shattered glass everywhere, the plate-glass window of the candy store splattered across the sidewalk, the store itself burned and gutted. I imagined the entire block, the neighborhood, the city heaped with broken glass and thick with the stench of fire. The days of that November and December began to go dark, until it seemed all the world would soon be shades of darkness: dark sun and dark moon, dark sky and dark earth, dark

offered us or called us to take an initiative in a significant "**window of opportunity**" that may just transform history "miraculously." We can become active partners with Divine destiny by regarding key junctures in our life, so-called "accidents," as pregnant with meaning. That is how we rewrite and reinterpret our lives as a purposeful narrative.

Option #3

The laws of nature are themselves a miracle created by God and worthy of wonder.

As the Jewish philosophers Maimonides (12th century) and Heschel (20th century) argue, the fact of order can itself be seen as Divine. As the prayerbook phrases it, "we thank you God for miracles of the everyday" such as our success in processing our wastes without diarrhea or constipation. In experiencing the beauty of order in the snowflake and in the glacier, in the human mind's innovative wisdom and in the lawfulness of the everyday, we discover the miracle of what exists, rather than the miracle of the anomaly and of the bizarre. Though the miracle of Hanukkah celebrates the extraordinary, in which we may be reticent to believe, we can still have faith in the miracle of the ordinary, the amazing patterns of order in a world created by God out of chaos.

night and dark day. I was a child then, but I still remember that darkness as a malevolence I could touch and smell, an evil growth draining my world of its light.

My world seemed thick with that darkness when Hanukkah came that year on the twenty-fifth of December. I remember my father chanting the blessings over the first candle on the first night of the festival. He was short and balding, and he chanted in a thin, intense voice. I stood between him and my mother, gazing at the flame of the first night's candle. The flame seemed pitiful against the malignant darkness outside our window. I went to bed and was cold with dread over the horror of the world.

The next night two candles were lighted. Again my father chanted the blessings before the lighting and the prayer that follows when the candles are burning: "We kindle these lights on account of the miracles, the deliverances, and the wonders which You did for our ancestors . . . During all eight days of Hanukkah these lights are sacred . . . We are only to look at them, in order that we may give thanks unto Your Name, for Your miracles, Your deliverances and Your wonders."

I wanted a miracle. But there were no miracles during that Hanukkah. Where was God? I kept dreaming of burning synagogues.

On the eighth and final night of the festival I stood with my parents in front of the burning candles. The darkness mocked their light. I could see my parents glancing at me. My mother sighed. Then my father murmured my name.

"You want another miracle?" he asked wearily.

I did not respond.

"Yes," he said. "You want another miracle." He was silent a moment. Then he said, in a gentle, urging voice, "I also want another miracle. But if it does not come, we will make a human miracle. We will give the world the special gifts of our Jewishness. We will not let the world burn out our souls."

The candles glowed feebly against the dark window.

"Sometimes I think man is a greater miracle-maker than God," my father said tiredly, looking at the candles. "God does not have to live day after day on this broken planet. Perhaps you will learn to make your own miracles. I will try to teach you how to make human miracles."

I lay awake a long time that night and did not believe my father could ever teach me that. But now, decades later, I think he taught me well. And I am trying hard to teach it to my own children.

---

101. Reprinted by the generous permission of Rabbi Chaim Potok from an article originally published in McCalls' Magazine, 100, No. 3, Dec. 1972, p. 30

The Biblical miracles are always associated with historical redemption because they point not to the violation of natural order which is seen as Divinely beautiful, but to the violation of human order which is so often corrupt and oppressive.

This is an insight I owe to my teacher Rabbi David Hartman. Miracles in the Bible are often not merely proofs of religious dogmas (as in the case of Elijah on Mount Carmel), but also contributions to undermining totalitarian oppressors. For example, at the Red Sea the Jews needed not only a military miracle to be saved from Pharaoh's chariots, but a psychological-political miracle to be liberated from their paralyzing fear of Pharaoh, their self-deified master. When Pharaoh is so amazingly defeated before their very eyes, then they can begin to believe in their own potential as free human beings and to give their allegiance to a God of liberation.

The violation of nature is the *form* the miracle took in the eyes of the people because for them the absoluteness of the rule of Pharaoh, his invincibility, seemed as solid as the laws of nature. Many of the ten plagues are described as events that had never before occurred since the foundation of Egypt.

Thus described, they served to undermine the mental hold on the slaves who believed the ancient kingdom of Egypt could never be shaken. But the message of the miracle is about people's mistaken belief that the power of an empire is absolute and eternal. I believe in this message which liberates me from the totalitarian propaganda of the oppressor, even if I regard the supernatural form of the miracle as a rhetorical device, a kind of educational gimmick, to shake me out of my habitual defeatism about "the way things are and always will be."

CHOOSING OUR HANUKKAH MIRACLE

With these options in mind, we return to the Hanukkah narratives. The Rabbis speak of two different kinds of miracles that the menorah proclaims. We must decide whether to believe in and propagate either.

A. Miracle Oil

The miracle recalled in the Talmud speaks of a cruse of oil that burned for eight days instead of one. That is a supernatural miracle violating the laws of nature. Taken literally it promotes a belief in supernatural intervention. It may even denigrate human effort. Perhaps that kind of belief explains why Lubavitch Hasidim refused to wear gas masks during the Iraqi missile attacks on Israel in 1991 when chemical warheads were feared.

However David Hartman argues that the miracle of oil is only a symbol that arouses human faith. When human beings are willing to believe that more is possible than meets the eye, then they will invest in historical projects like the Maccabean Revolt and the Declaration of the Independence of Israel in 1948 even against all odds. Our presupposition that a cruse of oil cannot burn for eight days, that it is a natural impossibility, is only a symbol of the mistaken belief in the historical impossibility of change.[102]

B. The Miracles of the Few Against the Many

Even if we cannot embrace the miracle of the cruse of oil, the Rabbis offered a different kind of miracle to celebrate. The Rabbinic prayer for Hanukkah, *Al HaNissim*, ignores the miracle of the oil and speaks of a general phenomenon possible in every generation whereby God helps human beings to bring about miraculous rescues from historical oppressors. This belief in God's miracles does not undermine human effort but causes it to redouble. The miracle is "natural" within the realm of historical possibility, yet inconceivable and unattainable by oppressed peoples who don't believe in its possibility.

In the Exodus from Egypt, God initiates the miracles for a passive, despairing people of slaves. However on Hanukkah, first the martyrs like Hannah and then the zealots and the warriors initiate the redemptive process. In a world where God seems eclipsed, where there are no supernatural signs and no prophets, where the leading priests accepted Hellenism as a boon, the Maccabees bear witness to another dimension. They evaluate the world differently and they believe in a Divine power whose hidden will becomes manifest. The Rabbis celebrated the political and military manifestation of God's miracle in the Maccabees' victory.

Personally, I prefer the miracle of the few against the many. I need to reject the miraculous long-burning cruse of oil lest I be understood as an anti-rationalist or passive Jew. But perhaps beyond my polemic against the childish legend, I need to mature and to reinterpret both kinds of miracles as opening me up to other dimensions, to possibilities in myself and in my world that I have too quickly foreclosed. Believing in miracles is another way of learning to keep my options open and letting myself be surprised.

---

102. See David Hartman, "Trusting in a New Beginning," in the companion volume, *The Hanukkah Book of Celebration*, p. 195.

CHAPTER V

Scientists' and Kabbalists' Thoughts on Lights and Lamps

A giant synagogue menorah

(Sefer Minhagim, Amsterdam, 1662, Jewish National and University Library, courtesy of Beit Hatefusoth Photo Archive, Tel Aviv)

Scientists' and Kabbalists' Thoughts on Light and Lamps

*Exploring the scientific conception of physical light, the light of Creation,
and Jewish understandings of the menorah*

The Bezalel Art Institute's Menorahs.
The new art institute in Jerusalem at the turn of the 20th century
aimed to revive the visual arts in Jewish tradition. The Zionist
national renaissance used art nouveau to develop a new shape to
the ancient seven-branched menorah as the emblem of Judea.
The students' creations are displayed in the following pages.

INTRODUCTION

LIGHT AND LAMPS

The weave of topics in this chapter is surprising, interdisciplinary and associative. In a playful, exploratory way we sought to view the major symbol of Hanukkah — light emanating from a candle placed in a menorah — in a broader perspective. For the light of the Hanukkah menorah can be understood as a subset of a larger field of associations:

(1) the use of light as a metaphor in Jewish tradition and of course other cultures;

(2) the conceptual understanding of the processes of producing and disseminating light both according to modern physics and traditional Kabbalah;

(3) the history of the particular lamp called a "menorah," both in the world of Jewish law and the history of lamps in countries where Jews have lived; and

(4) the use of the menorah of the Temple as a national emblem for Judaism and the Jewish people in contrast with the star of David.

Casting our net widely we hope to expand the meaning of the Hanukkah lamp beyond its historical memories to its spiritual and physical significance. Yet this chapter will provide only a taste of physics, of Kabbalah, of Jewish ceremonial art, and of Zionist history — to whet your appetite.

LIGHT AND LANGUAGE
PROVERBS AND PARABLES ABOUT LIGHT AND LAMPS

Light glides easily from the realm of the physical to the symbolic in all languages and cultures. In the following proverbs and parables drawn mainly from Jewish tradition but also from other Western sources, you will find beautiful turns of phrase and delightful play of imagination. Find one that speaks to you and share it with others, perhaps as part of the candle lighting ceremony on Hanukkah.

Proverbs & Parables

When God began to create heaven and earth — while the earth was still unformed and void and darkness was spread over the surface of the deep — a Divine wind swept over the water. Then God said:"Let there be light," and there was light. God saw that the light was good, and God separated the light from the darkness.

— **GENESIS 1:1-3**

The Holy One created light out of darkness.

— **RABBI BERECHIA** (LEVITICUS RABBAH 31:8; 3RD CENTURY)

I form the light and create the darkness,
I make peace and create evil.

— **ISAIAH THE PROPHET IN THE NAME OF GOD** (ISAIAH 45:7, 6TH CENTURY BCE)

Zohar: The Hidden Light [1]

God said, "Let there be light!" and there was light.
God saw how good the light was
and God separated the light from the darkness. [2]

Rabbi Isaac said,

"The light created by God in the act of Creation flared from one end of the universe to the other but then it was hidden away, reserved for the righteous in the world that is coming, as it is written: *'Light is sown for the righteous.'* [3] At that time the worlds will be fragrant, and all will be one. But until the world-to-come arrives, it is stored and hidden away."

Rabbi Judah responded,

"If the light were completely hidden, the world would not exist for even a moment! Rather, it is hidden and sown like a seed that gives birth to seeds and fruit. Thereby the world is sustained. Every single day, a ray of that light shines into the world, keeping everything alive; with that ray God feeds the world. And everywhere that Torah is studied at night, one thread-thin ray appears from that hidden light and flows down upon those absorbed in her. Since the first day, the light has never been fully revealed, but it is vital to the world, renewing each day the act of Creation." [4]

Before the world was created, an impulse arose in the Divine mind to create a great shining light. A light was created so bright that no creature could control it. When God saw that no one could bear it, He took one-seventh of the light and gave it to humans in its place. The rest He hid away for the righteous for the time that would come, saying, "If they prove worthy of this seventh and guard it, I will give them the rest [of the hidden light] in the final world." [5]

---

1. The parables from the Zohar (1:31b; 2:148b), Moshe Cordovero and Azriel of Gerona are translated by Daniel C. Matt and reprinted from *The Essential Kabbalah* (1995) p. 90, 38, 110, and 193 by permission of HarperCollins publishers.
2. *Genesis* 1:3-4   3. *Psalms* 97:11   4. *Zohar* 1:31b; 2:148b   5. *Sefer Bahir* 160

Imagine that You are Light

Whatever one implants firmly in the mind becomes the essential thing. So if you pray and offer a blessing to God, or if you wish your intention to be true, imagine that you are light. All around you — in every corner and on every side — is light. Turn to your right, and you will find shining light; to your left, splendor, a radiant light. Between them, up above, the light of the Presence. Surrounding that, the light of life. Above it all, a crown of light — crowning the aspirations of thought, illumining the paths of imagination, spreading the radiance of vision. This light is unfathomable and endless.[6]

The Ein Sof and the Colors of a Ray of Sunlight

In the beginning *Ein Sof*, the kabbalist Infinity of God, emanated ten *sefirot*, which are of its essence, united with it. It and they are entirely one.

To help you conceive this, imagine water flowing through vessels of different colors: red, green, and so forth. As the water spreads through those vessels, it appears to change into the colors of the vessels, although the water is devoid of all color. The change in color does not affect the water itself, just our perception of the water.

So it is with the *sefirot*. They are vessels, known, for example as *Hesed*, *Gevurah* and *Tiferet*, each colored according to its function, white, red, and green, respectively, while the light of the emanator — their essence — is water, having no color at all.

Better yet, imagine a ray of sunlight shining through a stained-glass window of ten different colors. The sunlight possesses no color at all but appears to change hue as it passes through the different colors of glass. Colored light radiates through the window.

Just so the *sefirot*. The light that clothes itself in the vessels of the *sefirot* is the essence, like the ray of sunlight. That essence does not change color at all, neither judgment nor compassion. Yet by emanating through the *sefirot* — the variegated stained glass — judgment or compassion prevails.[7]

The Prophetic Spirit as a Candle

"God descended in a cloud and spoke to Moshe. In the process, the prophetic spirit that dwelt on Moshe emanated on the 70 elders and just as it poured out on them, they began to speak ecstatically, as prophets."[8]

How shall we explain this? It is like a human being lighting one candle from another. It is analogous to someone doing a favor for others, without suffering loss. One benefits but the other does not lose out.[9]

---

6. *Shaar Ha-kavannah*, attributed to Azriel of Gerona, 13th century Spain
7. Moshe Codovero, *The Light of the Candles*, 6:1-6, 16th century Eretz Yisrael
8. *Numbers* 11:2   9. *Midrash Bemidbar Rabbah* 13

Side column quotes:

Light and shade go together in this world.

— **MENDELE MOCHER SEFORIM**
(HEBREW AND YIDDISH WRITER, 19TH CENTURY, EASTERN EUROPE)

I sense how meaningless is light, without darkness,
How lauded righteousness exists, only because of wickedness . . .
What is the image of God without Satan at His back?

— **ZALMAN SCHNEOR**
(HEBREW POET, 1903)

Light that makes things seen, makes things invisible. Were it not for night and the shadow of the earth, the noblest part of creation had remained unseen and the stars in heaven invisible.

— **SIR THOMAS BROWNE**
(ENGLISH POET)

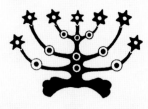

The first creation of God, in the works of the days, was the **light of senses**; the last was the **light of reason**; and his Sabbath work, ever since, is the **illumination of the spirit**.

— FRANCIS BACON
(ENGLISH PHILOSOPHER, 16TH CENTURY)

Your words are a lamp for my feet and a light on my path.

— PSALMS 119:105

The mitzvah is a lamp and the Torah, a light.

— PROVERBS 6:23

The life breath (the soul) of a human is the lamp of God. With it, God searches all the hidden chambers.

— PROVERBS 20:27

Let us walk in the light of God.

— ISAIAH 2:5

Light is sweet and it is good for the eyes to be able to see the sun.

— ECCLESIASTES 11:7

Lord, may it be Your will to place us on the side of Light.

— RABBI HAMNUNA (BABYLONIAN TALMUD, BERACHOT 17A)

Light a Menorah for God?

"When you light the lamps, the seven lamps shall illuminate the menorah."[10]

Israel asks incredulously: "You light the whole world and tell us to light the menorah?"

"Let us see light in your light!" says the Holy One, "The little lights of your menorah are more precious to me than the lights of all the stars I have placed in the sky."[11]

This may be compared to a king who had a beloved friend and told him one day, "I intend to come to your home for a meal. Please make preparations."

His friend hurried to set up the house, arranging his simple table and lamp. The king came to visit surrounded by his entourage, preceded by a servant bearing a lamp of gold. When the friend saw all the honor of the king, he became embarrassed, and hurriedly hid all he had prepared, for it was all so plain and common.

The king entered and said, "Didn't I tell you I was coming? Why is nothing prepared?" Said his beloved friend, "I saw all your honor and was embarrassed, for all I prepared for you was common and simple."

Said the king, "I swear to you! I reject everything I have. Out of love for you I want to share only your simple things."

So too — the Holy One is all Light, yet He tells Israel to light a menorah! And as soon as they light the menorah, the *Shechina* (the Divine presence) arrives.[12]

Does He then need our light? Rather, it is testimony to all on earth that the *Shechina* depends on the people of Israel.[13]

The Teacher: The Lamp of Israel

King David is called by his followers *"Ner Yisrael"* — the lamp of Israel — and so also is Rabbi Yochanan ben Zakai. When his students came to visit, they greeted him: "The lamp of Israel, the right hand pillar, the powerful hammer!"

10. *Numbers* 8:1
11. *Midrash Tanhuma Tizaveh* 2
12. *Bamidbar Rabbah* 15:8
13. *Talmud Bavli Shabbat* 22b

Sunrise is like Redemption

At dawn Rabbi Chiya and Rabbi Shimon ben Chalafta were walking in the valley beneath the Arbel Mountain (that rises above the Sea of Galilee / Kineret). They saw the morning star's light break through. "That," said Rabbi Chiya, "is like the process of redemption of Israel. First it emerges a little at a time, and the more it continues, the greater the light increases."[14]

The Borrowed Light and Your Own Light

A rabbi once poured out his heart to the Rizhiner Rebbe (19th century) saying: "What shall I do? As long as I am studying Torah and commentaries, I feel myself

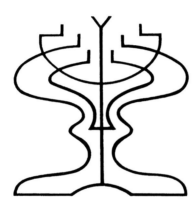

encompassed by holy light. However as soon as I halt my studies, I feel chilled and surrounded by darkness. Can I ever make this light my own?"

The Rizhiner Rebbe replied, "Whenever you are not occupied with Torah, then occupy yourself with a mitzvah, then the light will not fail you." He explained, "The light you feel surrounding you as you study is a **light borrowed** from the souls of great scholars. However, a light derived from your performance of a mitzvah is **your own light** and it will never fail you."

The Hidden Diamond

The Rizhiner Rebbe explained how in the midst of the plague of darkness in Egypt, *"All the children of Israel had light in their homes."*[15]

"Each one of us possesses a Holy Spark, but not everyone exhibits it to best advantage. It is like a diamond, which cannot cast its luster if buried in the earth. However when our Divine spark is disclosed in its appropriate setting, after being suitably cut and polished, there is light, as from a diamond, in each one of us."

---

14. *Jerusalem Talmud, Berachot* 1:1
15. *Exodus* 10:23

The Lamp / Menorah of Imperfections

by Rabbi Nachman of Bratzlav (19th century Eastern Europe)

This is the tale of one who left his father's house and the land of his birth and went forth to distant parts to learn a craft. In time he returned to his land and to his father's house. His father asked: "What skill have you learned in distant lands, my son?"

The son said: "I have learned to fashion a hanging lamp that is a wonderful piece of art. And if you please, my father, assemble all the masters of this art that live in the land and I will show them the lamp that I have fashioned by the skill of my hands."

So the father assembled all the masters of that art living in the land to show them the great accomplishments his son had mastered in his years abroad. The son brought forth the wonder lamp and displayed it before the large gathering. They looked at it and it did not please them. And when the father asked them for their opinion of the lamp, they all answered as one, that it was extremely misshapen, for they did not wish to hide the truth from him.

As soon as the visitors left the house, the father said to his son: "Listen, my son, your fellow craftsmen all agreed as one that the lamp is misshapen. Wherein then lies its greatness?"

"This is its greatness, that in this lamp I have combined all the imperfections that are to be found in the work of my fellow craftsmen gathered in our house today. Look, father, the work of every craftsman has some imperfection of its own. One craftsman excels in making one part of an object while he fails in another; a second craftsman turns out one part of his work with exquisite beauty, whereas in another it is truly ugly. What is good with the one is faulty with his fellow, and just what is ill-made and ungainly with his fellow turns out graceful in his own hands. And I have a lamp that is a combination of all their imperfections, in order to inform and advise them all that they have not attained perfection. My lamp/menorah is a reminder to each of his imperfections."

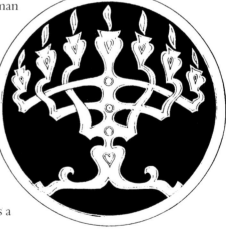

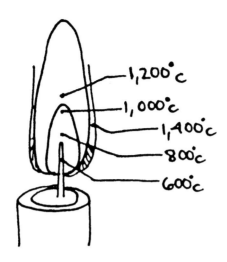

Albert Einstein

2.

THE SCIENTIFIC MIRACLE OF LIGHT AND ITS JEWISH ANALOGIES

by Sherman Rosenfeld and Noam Zion

In this interdisciplinary section, we explore light as a paradigm for both science and the Jewish tradition. We set the stage with a brief biography of the Jewish hero of light — Albert Einstein — and then present the topic of candles and flames from several points of view: chemistry, biology and Jewish sources. Finally, we dip very lightly — and hopefully tantalizingly — into two extremely abstract worlds of system building — modern physics and Kabbalah. The dialogue between a science educator, Sherman Rosenfeld, and a Jewish educator, Noam Zion, in search of analogies between such disparate realms should serve as an initiation to those who wish more knowledge from scientists and from scholars of mysticism.

"The most incomprehensible fact about the universe is that it is comprehensible."

— ALBERT EINSTEIN

"God does not play dice with the world. God is subtle, but He is not malicious."

— ALBERT EINSTEIN

"In the time left to me to live, I just want to reflect on the essence of light."

— ALBERT EINSTEIN

ALBERT EINSTEIN, HERO OF LIGHT
PHYSICIST, ZIONIST, HUMANIST (1879-1955)

"What is a Jew? Judaism is interested primarily in the moral stance toward life. Therefore the life of the individual has meaning only insofar as the individual helps to make the life of every creature more noble, more beautiful.

"However Judaism includes an added element, something expressed in the Book of Psalms — a kind of intoxication and amazement with the beauty and magnitude of the universe. From this feeling true scientific research draws its spiritual nourishment, but it is also expressed in the songs of the birds. Therefore Judaism honors so greatly every intellectual aspiration and spiritual effort. **The desire to know for its own sake, an almost fanatic love for justice and the passion for personal independence are the characteristics of Jewish tradition** *which lead me to thank my destiny that I am connected to them.*

"Those in our world today [the Nazis] who rebel against the ideals of reason and freedom of the individual and who are trying to establish a slave state lacking in spirit, by the cruel use of force, see us absolutely justifiably as their uncompromising enemies."

— ALBERT EINSTEIN

The first scientific superstar known by the person in the street all over the world was Albert Einstein, even though his theories were way over people's heads. His selection by Time Magazine as "Person of the Millennium" reinforces that status today. That status was well earned, for Albert Einstein as a theoretical physicist deserves to be called a "hero of light" in two ways. In his scientific research, his insights about the nature of light revolutionized modern physics and won him a Nobel Prize. His method, as well as his results, were extraordinary. Einstein "threw light" on the topic of light, by using a visualization technique, in which "thought experiments" preceded mathematical and verbal thinking. In other words, he "illuminated" difficult problems by non-verbal insights that only later were translated into equations and words. So by better understanding Einstein's life, one might better understand not only the nature of light but also the value of using visual thinking as a tool for "enlightenment."

At the same time, it is important to go beyond his scientific life; Einstein was also a moral "source of light," particularly as a Zionist and as a humanist.

Albert Einstein was born in Ulm, Germany, on March 14, 1879. From an early age, he disliked school but enjoyed playing the violin and learning about physics and geometry, particularly in his spare time. Einstein rejected the Germanic school structure designed to "pour knowledge" into students' heads, and followed his own interests. Following the completion of his Ph.D. in physics, Einstein applied for a university position, but was rejected. Instead, in 1903, he accepted a position as patent official at a Swiss Patent office. While this was a low-ranking job, it gave him time to think and write about topics that interested him. Then, in 1905 at the age of 26, out of the clear blue (from the point of view of the scientific establishment), Einstein published four classic papers: on the size of sugar molecules, on Brownian motion, on the photoelectric effect, and on the special theory of relativity. This tremendous burst of intellectual energy signaled the beginning of a long career of scientific contributions about the nature of matter, energy and the fundamental physical forces of the universe.

Throughout his life, Einstein made a number of original insights into the nature of light, such as the following:

(1) When photons (the "packets of light" that constitute light waves) bump into metal atoms, they stimulate a discharge of electrons. This is called the **"photoelectric effect"** for which he won the Nobel Prize in 1922. One of the uses of this effect is the "electric eye," used to open and close some automatic doors. Imagine the entrance to a building. Parallel to the door, a beam of light from one side of the entrance hits a metal receiver on the other side. When a person's body blocks this beam of light, the "electric eye" sends an electrical signal to the door to open.

(2) At speeds close to the speed of light, the size of an object decreases and time slows down (as measured by an observer at rest). This insight is part of the special theory of relativity, which represents a major revolution over Newtonian physics. Einstein conceived of the world in four, rather than three, dimensions — the usual spatial dimensions — height, width and depth, and the fourth dimension, time.

Caricature of Professor Einstein visiting America in 1919

Einstein conceived of the world in four, rather than three, dimensions — the usual spatial dimensions — height, width and depth, and the fourth dimension, time.

One way Einstein arrived at this insight was through a visual "thought experiment." He imagined that he was "riding on a beam of light," flashlight in hand. How fast would the light from the flashlight travel? Twice the speed of light? No, if you assume that nothing can go faster than the speed of light. So Einstein reasoned that at speeds close to the speed

of light, distance contracts and time expands. As experiments showed, Einstein was right. As an example of Einstein's general theory of relativity, imagine two twins, each with a clock. One stays on Earth while the other takes off on a space ship traveling very close to the speed of light. Two hours later (from the ship's perspective), the space traveler returns to find the other twin over 80 years older!

(3) Matter and energy are not distinct but in fact are related by the speed of light. More specifically, a tiny bit of matter can be converted into a huge amount of energy, and vice versa. Einstein's expression of this idea is his famous equation, $E=mc^2$. To better understand this insight, consider that "c" equals the speed of light, which is a huge number, about 300,000 kilometers — or 186,000

miles — per second. Now multiply this number by itself and you get an even HUGER number (this is the c^2 in the equation). Multiply THIS number by a teeny tiny bit of matter (which is the **m** or mass in the equation) and this equals a HUGE amount of energy (which is the **E** in the equation.) In other words, every bit of matter in the universe contains in it the potential for releasing tremendous amounts of energy.

This insight led to the creation of atomic bombs, as well as electric power plants based on atomic energy. However, Einstein's relationship to atomic energy was ambivalent. On one hand, during World War II, he wrote an influential letter to President Roosevelt which resulted in the formation of the Manhattan Project, which in turn produced the atomic bombs used to win the war. On the other hand, after the war, he became chairman of the Emergency Committee of Atomic Scientists and lobbied for outlawing atomic and hydrogen bombs.

Einstein not only thought a great deal about light, but he did so in a visual manner. In fact, the "brilliance" of Einstein's intellect was largely due to the exceptional ability he had to think in non-verbal ways. He used many visual **"thought-experiments"** to investigate his questions (as illustrated above in the example of "riding on a light beam"). When asked to reflect about how he thought, Einstein claimed that he reasoned with a combination of mental images, which were of a "visual and muscular type." Later, to communicate his insights, Einstein would "translate" the content of these non-verbal images into words and mathematical equations. As he wrote:

> "The words or the language, as they are written or spoken, do not seem to play any role in my mechanism of thought. The psychical entities which seem to serve as elements of thought are certain signs and more or less clear images which can be 'voluntarily' reproduced and combined."

Recent brain research supports the notion that Einstein excelled in non-verbal thought. Neuroscientists have discovered that certain areas of the brain — the lower bulge of the inferior parietal lobes — are the "home" of spatial reasoning and abstract mathematical thought. A study of Einstein's brain showed that these areas were unusually large. (You may wonder, how could a recent development in the theory of the brain be tested on the long-dead Einstein. In fact, after his death a colleague removed his brain, the physical remains of the greatest scientific genius of this century, and preserved it for later scientific research).

The Public Conscience: Zionist and Humanist

In his lifetime, Albert Einstein not only contributed enormously to our understanding of light but also acted as a "beacon" on moral issues. He not only dedicated his efforts to solve the mysteries of the universe but also was actively involved in the social and political world around him. As a result of his superstar standing, Einstein's public pronouncements carried weight.

In particular, he was a proud member of his people who defended their right to be different, to be Jews even in a hostile world during the worst period of anti-semitism in history. Einstein repudiated the anti-semitism of Germany and left his native land in 1932. He revoked his own citizenship as well as his membership in the Prussian Academy of Sciences, an organization that led the way in persecuting Jewish scientists and in condemning the false "Jewish physics promoted by Einstein." As soon as Hitler came to power, Einstein's life was often threatened by German nationalists. One organization put a $5000 price on his head, encouraging assassins to murder him. In May, 1933, the Nazis staged a book burning at the end of a torch parade in which 20,000 volumes were soaked in kerosene. This is how the newspaper described the event:

"A tall, middle aged Nazi held a large picture of Einstein in his right hand and a burning torch in his left. Then he cast the picture on the pile and in an instant all 20,000 books were aflame as the crowd cried: 'Away with traitors!'"

Einstein never forgot that he was a refugee and extended his assistance to many people who asked for his help. He worked tirelessly to raise money, speak and write articles on behalf of refugees and other worthwhile causes. He became an active supporter of the

---

In 1923 Einstein visited the future campus of the Hebrew University and spoke in his opening words in Hebrew on Mount Scopus:
"I am very happy to be able to lecture in this land from which emerged Torah and light to the whole enlightened world and before this building that will be a center of wisdom and science."

---

unpopular Zionist cause for an independent Israel. In 1921 he took his first break from scientific research to go across America speaking and raising money for the nascent Hebrew University in Jerusalem. "I am doing this only for the Zionist cause to raise dollars for education in Jerusalem. For this occasion I must play the role of a minor god [the revered genius] and serve as a trap [for potential donors]."

In 1923 Einstein visited the future campus of the Hebrew University and spoke in his opening words in Hebrew on Mount Scopus: "I am very happy to be able to lecture in this land from which emerged Torah and light to the whole enlightened world and before this building that will be a center of wisdom and science." Though he vigorously supported Zionism, he did so from a critical point of view. For example, he thought that Chaim Weizmann, also an eminent scientist in his own right — and later to become the first president of Israel — was too much of a *"Realpolitiker"* (Weizmann, of course, thought

that Einstein was an impractical idealist!). Later, in 1952, Prime Minister David Ben-Gurion invited Einstein to be Israel's second president. However he declined, saying, "I know a little about nature but almost nothing about human beings."

As a humanist, he was a courageous believer in the moral imperative of international peace in a warring world. In fact, his scientific search for intellectual unity in physics parallels his search for international harmony. It is fitting to close on the note that the physicist who struggled for so long to develop a "unified field theory" (including all of the fundamental forces of the universe) was also very active in working for the cause of world peace. He believed that the only solution to this issue was on a supranational basis, as promoted by the World Federalist Movement. Although the achievement of world peace eluded Einstein and his colleagues — as did his attempt to develop a unified field theory — it focused a great deal of his own energies. One might conclude that part of Einstein's legacy — as physicist, Jew and humanist — is the commitment to achieve these two noteworthy goals.

$$E=mc^2$$

CANDLES AND FLAMES

A SCIENTIFIC PERSPECTIVE ON LIGHTING THE MENORAH

On Hanukkah, we light wax candles or oil lamps for eight days. By doing so, we illuminate the darkness. But what exactly is a flame? A candle? How does a solid, cold mass of wax turn into a flame, giving off heat and light? And how does one burning candle — a *shamash* — ignite another?

On this holiday we also eat lots of fatty, oily foods, like potato pancakes ("latkas"). Then we need lots of exercise to "burn off the fat." Are our bodies somehow related to burning candles, and if so, how?

In order to investigate these questions, we will first look at the amazing process that turns fuels (like wax or oil) into light and heat. Then we will see how the cells in our body act as "slow-burning candles." We will explore the origin of the energy found in both the candle's fuel and our body's food. Finally, we will try to understand how the *shamash* can ignite the other candles, without diminishing its own flame.

1. What is the Chemical History of a Candle?

If you look at the flame of a candle, you will notice that it has three distinct regions, each with its own color. A black area surrounds the wick, a blue area surrounds the base of the flame, and both seem to give rise to a bright yellow area in the rest of the flame. What is the significance of these three areas of the flame? Moreover, why does a candle need a wick? What happens there?

The great physicist, Michael Faraday (1791-1867), asked these and other questions in a series of six lectures — "The Chemical History of a Candle" — given to young people at the Royal Institute in London, during each winter season in the 1860s. Faraday, one of Albert Einstein's heroes, is best known for his discovery of the principle of electrical induction, which is the basis of harnessing electricity as an energy source. And yet, Faraday chose to focus his "Christmas Lectures" on the old-fashioned source of light, the candle, because he felt that most scientific laws in the universe are somehow connected to this subject.

Faraday pointed out that a flame is telling a complex chemical story. Here is a brief summary of that story: energy-rich wax and oxygen react to release energy (in the form of heat and light) as well as energy-poor carbon dioxide and water.

And here's the same story again, this time in more detail: (1) the solid wax of the candle melts, near the wick. (2) The liquid wax moves up the wick, and as it does, the candle's heat turns it into a gaseous mixture; (3) this gaseous mixture combines with oxygen in the blue area of the flame, giving rise to heat, light, water and carbon dioxide. (4) The same gaseous mixture doesn't combine with oxygen in the dark area of the flame; instead, carbon particles are formed here. (5) In the yellow area of the flame, the same carbon particles (soot) become incandescent, continue to give off light and heat, and (6) eventually, around the yellow area of the flame, carbon dioxide and water vapor are released.

In short, each burning candle has a history — a chemical history — which takes place very quickly. In a burning candle, each fraction of a second, billions and billions of wax molecules are transformed from solid to liquid to gaseous form, moving up the wick and through the flame. In this process, they produce many intermediary products — with the help of oxygen — in a series of complex chemical chain reactions, eventually releasing light, heat, carbon dioxide and water vapor.

In his lectures, Michael Faraday illustrated different aspects of this chemical process via simple demonstrations and experiments *(see diagrams below)*.

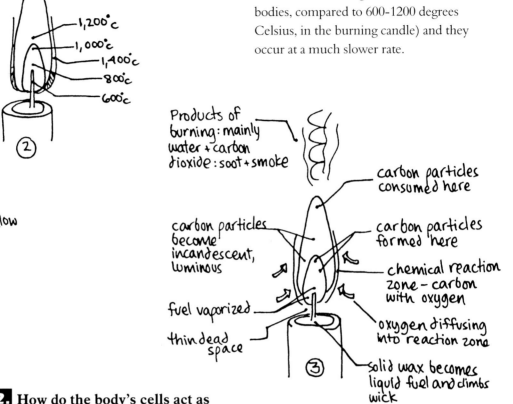

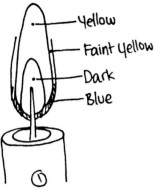

Three Diagrams of the Burning Candle

by Tanya Zion

after Michael Faraday

carbon dioxide and water. So, when you're digesting a potato pancake (and, in fact, when you're simply living), you're actually going through the same overall process as a candle. But there are two big differences: in our bodies, these biochemical reactions occur at much cooler temperatures (98.6 degrees Fahrenheit or 37 degrees Celsius in our bodies, compared to 600-1200 degrees Celsius, in the burning candle) and they occur at a much slower rate.

2. How do the body's cells act as "slow-burning candles"?

All living things need energy in order to exist. The ultimate source of energy in our bodies is the food we eat. Although the specific biochemical processes which break down this food are very different from those which break down the wax molecules of a candle, the overall reactants and products are the same. Energy-rich molecules react with oxygen to give off energy (usually in the form of heat and special molecules, which can be stored to power later biological reactions),

3. Where did all of this energy originate?

In the food we eat, as well as in the candles, all this energy had to come from somewhere. From where? As it turns out, from light! In the living world, plants "capture" light energy from the sun, which drives a reaction, which transforms this light energy into the chemical energy found in candles and our food. The resulting chemical energy, located in the sugars, is then transformed in biochemical reactions within the plants — and when we eat them, within our bodies — to produce other products, including fats and oils. There

Michael Faraday chose to focus on the old-fashioned source of light, the candle, because he felt that most scientific laws in the universe are somehow connected to this subject.

are other ways for the fuel needed for candles to be formed — beeswax, paraffin from petroleum products, and the like — but in each case, the ultimate energy source for these fuels is light energy from the sun.

So here's the big picture. In an "energy-capturing" process (called **photosynthesis**) sunlight, water and carbon dioxide react in a plant to produce organic matter and oxygen. The reverse "energy-releasing" process (called **combustion**) takes place in a candle: oxygen combines with organic matter to release energy, in the form of light and heat, along with carbon dioxide and water. In each of our body's cells, a similar "energy-releasing" process (called cellular respiration) occurs, though at a much lower temperature and at a much slower rate.

4. **How can the *shamash* ignite another candle, without losing its own energy?**

As every good Boy Scout knows, there are three requirements for a fire: (1) a fuel source, (2) oxygen, and (3) a high temperature which starts the process ("igniting temperature"). As pointed out above, each candle has its own fuel source and oxygen is all around it. So, all that is needed to turn the "potential energy" of a cold Hanukkah candle into light and heat, is the high igniting temperature, which is provided by the *shamash*. In essence, the *shamash* (from the root word meaning "to serve"), initiates the combustion process in the Hanukkah candle. Then that ignited candle is on its own, releasing energy from its own wax.

Candles and Flames as a Source of Jewish Inspiration[1]

The Jewish tradition is rich with metaphors and analogies based on the symbols of candles and flames. Here are some examples:

◆ Just as the *shamash* lights other candles with its heat without diminishing itself, so Moshe is described as passing his prophetic and leadership spirit on to the seventy elders in the desert. *"God emanated from the spirit that was on Moshe on to the seventy elders. As the spirit rested upon them, they began to prophesy without end."*[2] Rashi, the medieval commentator, suggests an analogy: "To what may Moshe be compared? To a candle burning in a menorah (lamp) from which everyone may be lit without diminishing the light of the original candle."[3]

◆ Lubavitch Hasidism uses this analogy in describing every Jew as a candle with its own potential inner light. The Jew's mission is to ignite the flame of enthusiasm (*hitlahavut* — literally flaming energy) in him/herself and in all whom they meet.

◆ A different imagery is used in the poem *Happy is the Match* by Chana Szenes, the young Israeli female paratrooper who volunteered to jump behind Nazi lines into occupied Hungary during the Holocaust. She wrote what became a famous poem just before her capture and eventual execution by the Nazis. In the poem she compares herself to a match, which unlike the *shamash*, is consumed in igniting another candle, as a martyr whose sacrifice is not for naught. Her life served as such a match in sparking the heroic efforts of her generation of Israelis to defend and rebuild the Jewish people after the war.

Happy is the match consumed in igniting the flame.
Happy is the flame that burns deep in the hearts.
Happy are the hearts with the strength to stop beating,
    to sacrifice themselves for the sake of honor.
Happy is the match consumed in igniting the flame.

◆ On Hanukkah it is important to appreciate the role of one family, Mattathias and his five sons who single handedly inspired and led the Maccabean Revolt over 25 years until their final victory. When the Greeks "snuffed" out the life of one brother then there was a second and a third to replace him. They served as the *shamash* which literally and figuratively relit the *ner tamid,* the menorah in the Temple and in their people.

1. Michael Faraday, *The Chemical History of a Candle* and Jearl Walker, "The Amateur Scientist" from *Scientific American*, April, 1978.
2. *Numbers* 11:25   3. *Midrash Sifrei* on *Numbers* 11:17

EIGHT WAYS OF LOOKING AT THE NATURE OF LIGHT

AND ITS ANALOGIES TO THE JEWISH IMAGERY OF LIGHT

A candle (or a cruse of oil) that burns longer than normal violates our usual expectations of the laws of nature. A military victory of a few against an entire empire violates our sense of historical laws of power. In a similar way, as illustrated below, the very nature of light befuddles our usual categories. This makes light a perfect symbol for Judaism to use, both to represent the miracle of creation as well as to illustrate the miracle of redemption in history against incredible odds.

Each of the following topics will be presented first in a scientific perspective and then in one or more perspectives from the Jewish tradition. These eight possible analogies between the imagery of light in modern physics and the Jewish, in particular kabbalist, symbolic imagery of light, are not meant to be comprehensive, nor are they meant to present these very different ways of thought as identical systems. Certainly we are not claiming that modern physics "proves" Kabbalah or that Kabbalah prophetically predicts Einsteinian physics. However, human modes of thought are interrelated as we seek, by the power of imagination, to make sense of our universe at its most basic. The analogies of these world constructions may enlighten one another even if the parallels are at best very partial. In both modes of thought — Jewish mysticism and modern physics — there is a sense of stretching human understanding to the limits in the face of what is felt to be miraculous, at the edges of or beyond human conception. Both systems of symbols force us to look carefully at the light of the Hanukkah candles and to see them as a microcosm reflecting the basics of the spiritual and physical universe.

Light is Paradoxical and Transcends our Usual Conceptions

SCIENTIFIC PERSPECTIVE: What is light? The term usually refers to the part of the electromagnetic spectrum which people can see. (Parts of the electromagnetic spectrum which people cannot see include x-rays, microwaves, and radio waves). Light exists as both particles and waves. This is a rather strange idea. Our daily experience tells us that waves cannot be particles and particles cannot be waves. But there are some experiments in which light "behaves" as if it were made up of particles (called "*photons*"), and other experiments in which light "behaves" as if it were made up of waves. In the history of science, scientists have argued about whether light is a wave or a particle. Quantum mechanics, a central theory of twentieth century physics, shows that light is simultaneously "wave-like" and "particle-like." In fact, today scientists say everything in the universe has wave-like properties and particle-like properties, just in different degrees.

JEWISH PERSPECTIVE: The Kabbalah has always described the *Ein Sof*/Divine Infinity in paradoxical terms as the dark light which is invisible, immaterial and indescribable. Yet through the *sefirot* (the ten aspects of the Divine, the world and the human) the *Ein Sof* emanates into the physical world with its visible, differentiated vessels containing opposite, yet dialectically complementary, attributes like mercy and judgment or feminine and masculine.

Light is Unity within Diversity

SCIENTIFIC PERSPECTIVE: Each element in nature emits its own special light. It is commonly understood that white light contains all the colors we can see. If you take a prism and shine white light through it, a rainbow of colors will result. This "visible spectrum" is continuous and ranges from red to orange, yellow, green, blue and violet. What is not so commonly known is that each element in nature, when heated to a certain

---

Reminiscent of the scientific notion that every substance is identifiable by a unique spectrum fingerprint of light, the Kabbalah thought of each human soul as having a unique aspect of the complete human soul created for Adam.

---

temperature, emits its own special light, something like its own "**spectrum fingerprint**." For this reason, astronomers can analyze the light from different stars in the sky and conclude what elements exist on those stars!

JEWISH PERSPECTIVE: The scientific perspective envisions white light as a basic entity that can be differentiated into what appear to be separate entities, white light being broken down into seven colors.

The Light of the Divine Face   BY SHERMAN ROSENFELD

What's the meaning of "divine light"? For one answer, check out the daily prayer for "*shalom*," in the Jewish prayer book: "Bless us . . . all of us . . . with the light of your Face, because you have given us the light of your Face: the living Torah, the love of kindness, *tzedaka*, *bracha* (blessing), *rachamim* (compassion), *chayim* (life) and *shalom* (peace)."

Jews pray to God for "the light of Your face" and then the text lists a series of seven "attributes" of this divine light: "the living Torah, the love of kindness, *tzedaka*, *bracha*, *rachamim*, *chayim* and *shalom*." So you can think of this prayer as a prism of "divine light," just like the diffraction gradient above is a prism of white light.

Similarly, the kabbalist Moshe Cordovero[4] describes the *Ein Sof* as a kind of water or a kind of light that is differentiated into separate vessels whose characteristics are apparently opposites but are in fact all the same substance and not really contradictory but dialectically and dynamically related.

He compares the *Ein Sof* and the *sefirot*, the Divine infinity and the ten vessels of the world, to water pouring into vessels of different colors such as white, red, green and so forth. So the water, which is in fact colorless, appears to have the hues of the vessels. Similarly, light passing through a prism suddenly appears to be made of seven colors.

Reminiscent of the scientific notion that every substance is identifiable by a unique spectrum fingerprint of light, the Kabbalah thought of each human soul as having a unique aspect of the complete human soul created for Adam. The 16th century Italian kabbalist, Moshe Zacuto, regarded the unique *nitzoz*/spark within each of us as defining our destiny: "Every human being should know the root of one's own soul, so as to perfect it and to restore it to its origin, which is the essence of its being." If everyone develops his or her own soul roots, then humankind and the cosmos will be redeemed.

 Light is the Basic Building Block of the Universe: Life is Energy, Energy is Matter and Matter is Energy

SCIENTIFIC PERSPECTIVE: According to Einstein's famous equation $E=mc^2$ even a tiny quantity of mass can produce an enormous amount of energy *(see biography of Albert Einstein, page 200)*. This theoretical equation has been verified and utilized in many ways, such as in the creation of the atomic power which runs some electrical power plants. In essence, the equation says that matter (**m**) and energy (**E**) are not two

---

4. Safed, 16th century

distinct entities, but are interconnected by the speed of light (**c**). Light is the primary substance. The accepted scientific theory today is that the universe started with the "Big Bang," a singular event, which generated unimaginably huge amounts of light. According to this view, this light eventually turned into the countless galaxies that make up the universe.

JEWISH PERSPECTIVE: Like Einstein, kabbalist thought imagines a world made out of an infinite magnitude of light which is then divided up into ten vessels or *sefirot* which make up the visible world but do not constitute static fixed entities. The spiritual and the physical are not radically different but simply the same substance conceived under different perspectives simultaneously.

 Light is the Basis of Life

SCIENTIFIC PERSPECTIVE:

Energy comes in many different forms, such as light, heat, electricity, movement and chemical energy. Often, these forms of energy can be converted into other forms of energy. For example, the chemical energy in the battery of a flashlight can be converted into light energy. While we may not think of light in these terms, light is a form of energy. In fact, life on Earth is completely dependent upon the light energy of the sun. Without the sun's energy, life could not exist.

Like Einstein, kabbalist thought does not make a fundamental distinction between the organic and inorganic. There is a dynamic flow of energy through both, which is essential to the life of the universe. Any blockage in the flow causes chaos.

Plants have the ability to convert the energy from sunlight into the chemical energy stored in sugars, in a process called *photosynthesis*. In this process (driven by sunlight), carbon dioxide and water are converted into sugars

Can You Produce Water from a Candle?!

*C*an fire produce water, when these two seem to be opposites? Can water, which extinguishes a flame, be contained within a burning flame?

At first, it may not seem to make sense, but it's true! When a candle burns, water is produced. You can demonstrate this for yourself by placing a dry glass container over the top of a candle. Within a few seconds, you will notice that water vapor has moistened the inside of the container. In the process of cellular respiration, our body also burns food — at a much lower temperature — and produces carbon dioxide and water. We exhale the carbon dioxide and part of the water in our breath.

and oxygen. The food of all animals — people included — ultimately comes from this process which depends on light.

JEWISH PERSPECTIVE: Like Einstein, kabbalist thought does not make a fundamental distinction between the organic and inorganic. There is a dynamic flow of energy through both, which is essential to the life of the universe. Any blockage in the flow causes chaos. As the light of the Divine emanated into objects and continues to flow to them giving them life, it can also reverse its direction and change these temporary objects back into the light from whence they came. The flow outward and back is the dialectical process of the life of the universe and of God. The connection between the divine energy usually associated with the universe and the organic life of the individual human being is expressed in the oft-quoted proverb, *"The candle of God is the soul of the human."* [5]

---

5. *Proverbs* 20:27

Light Carries Information — Light is Knowledge

SCIENTIFIC PERSPECTIVE:
Everything we see in the physical world comes to us through the vehicle of light. Without light, we cannot see a thing. Think about it. When you look at something, all you see is the information carried by the light. In fact, light is the only thing you can see. We may think that we "see" various objects, but in reality all we see is the light that is reflected from those objects, light which carries information to our eyes and brains. Bob Miller, an artist who worked for many years at the Exploratorium, a science museum in San Francisco, has this to say: "My eye intercepts the

The Guiness Book of Records: What is the most powerful lamp in the world?

In Vancouver, Canada, in 1984, a high-pressure argon arc lamp was produced which has the power of 1,200,000 candles.

Professor Daniel Matt, author of *God and the Big Bang* and the translator and commentator of a future new edition of the Zohar, read this curious fact about the 1,200,000 candle power of the most powerful lamp. He was reminded of the Talmudic passage from the *Babylonian Talmud, Shabbat* 88a:

> Rabbi Simlai expounded: "When Israel said *'We will do'* before *'We will listen'*[7] [thereby demonstrating true faith by committing themselves to fulfill God's word before hearing the details], 600,000 ministering angels came down to grant each and every Israelite two crowns, one for *'We will do,'* and one for *'We will listen.'* As soon as Israel sinned, 1,200,000 angels of destruction descended and removed them, as it says: *The children of Israel were stripped of their ornaments from Mount Horeb.*"

In other words, both the Jewish people at Sinai and the most powerful lamp in the world have 1,200,000 crowns of light!

little bit of light that's going through this little area in space, and I see the world out there with all its textures and colors. But all I'm really seeing is just that little bit of light. That's all I can see. And in some mysterious way, I 'project' this visual perception back on the real world. To me, that's miraculous."[6] In a sense, the human mind is the instrument of self-consciousness by which nature comes to know itself, and the eye is the an important source for that self-knowledge.

Light as perceived by the human eye carries an enormous amount of knowledge. Today, lasers of light can carry much more information than any telephone wire and the amount of brain space and computer memory needed to store visual information is much greater than that needed to store verbal knowledge. A picture is still worth a thousand words.

JEWISH PERSPECTIVE: In the Biblical creation story light serves this cognitive function and therefore before God creates anything else he says, *"Let there be light."* This light pre-exists the sun and moon whose light is more functional. By this light God sees the world, names it and evaluates it. The Rabbis analogize this first light to Torah, which they call in Aramaic *"oraita"* — a word interpreted as referring to light. They imagine God looking in the Torah of primordial light as a blue print for the creation. The mystics maintain that when a soul brings its unique aspect to illuminate an aspect of the Torah to which that soul corresponds, then it also, in turn, illuminates itself and illuminates the Torah and thereby the world.

The Hanukkah candle is also a medium to convey information and to propagate a message — ***pirsum hanes***. Therefore the Hanukkah candle may not be used to provide light or heat but only to proclaim to passersby the miracle of the light. While lighting the candle is important, observing it and decoding its message is even more important.

---

7. *Exodus* 24:7

---

6. *Exploratorium Quarterly*, Volume 11, Issue 4

The eye and the visual power of the brain are the key to cognition of the information conveyed by light — both symbolic and physical.

Light is Self-Propagating

SCIENTIFIC PERSPECTIVE:

Imagine an electric bell ringing in a glass container. Now imagine that the air inside the glass container is slowly removed by a vacuum. As the air is removed, the ringing would become fainter and fainter until no sound would be heard. Sound waves are transmitted though a medium, in this case the particles that make up air. (Other mediums through which sound can travel include water, wood, rock and metal.) Without a medium, no sound can travel. But light does not need a medium in order to be transmitted. The electro-magnetic waves are self-propagating, which is why we can see the

light from stars millions of light years away from us, even though there is no air (or any other medium) in space. If a flashlight were placed alongside the ringing bell in the same glass container, we would still see the light after all the air had been removed, even though we wouldn't be able to hear the bell.

JEWISH PERSPECTIVE: Although Torah is compared to light, its propagation according to the Rabbis is totally unlike the self-propagation of light through a vacuum. Torah's knowledge is transmitted through the medium of the active human learner who necessarily refracts the light absorbed. Comparing study to the smashing of a hammer on a rock (Torah) that splits off

sparks in every direction, the Rabbis saw the active role of the learner. In fact, Torah's light self-propagates in the biological — not the physical sense. For Torah is "fruitful and multiplies" itself in being transmitted through the human mind's eye. There is no principle of the conservation of Torah energy, rather the opposite is true, the more Torah is studied, the more is created; the more energy is spent on learning, the more energy there is for learning.

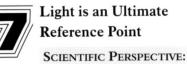

Light is an Ultimate Reference Point

SCIENTIFIC PERSPECTIVE:

From the scientific point of view, the speed of light is an important point of reference. In Einstein's famous equation, $E = mc^2$ (where **E** is energy, **m** is matter, and **c** is the speed of light), the speed of light is the "conversion factor" of energy and matter. Light is also a reference for what it means for something to be "straight," and it is used to create our most precise clocks.

Let's look at the first point of reference. One of the most surprising discoveries of the 20th century is that distance and time are not absolute, but merely relative to the speed of light!

This principle, part of Einstein's "theory of special relativity," can be illustrated by one of Einstein's famous "thought experiments." Imagine that you're traveling on a beam of light and someone on the side (an "observer") is watching you. In your hand is a flashlight. Now, while traveling on that beam of light, you turn on the flashlight. From the point of view of the "observer," how fast would *that* light travel? Our day-to-day logic tells us that the "observer" would see that light from the flashlight travels *twice* the speed of light. However, as it turns out, nothing can travel faster than the speed of light. On the contrary, *time and distance themselves* must change in relation to the constant speed of light. In other words, as an object travels at speeds closer to the speed of light (186,000

There is no principle of the conservation of Torah energy, rather the opposite is true. The more Torah is studied, the more is created. The more energy is spent on learning, the more energy there is for learning.

---

miles per second, or about 300,000 kilometers per second), time expands and distance contracts. As fantastic as this sentence sounds, it is true and verifiable. Fortunately, objects that can travel close to the speed of light are sub-atomic, so we normally don't experience this reality.

JEWISH PERSPECTIVE: In the Biblical creation story light is the measuring rod for each object created. By it everything is evaluated by Divine sight, *"God saw that it was good."* The Hebrew term for something just and good is *"yashar"* — straight in one's eyes, just as in physics light defines straightness.

 The Interplay of Opposites Makes the World Discernible

SCIENTIFIC PERSPECTIVE: According to many physicists, the universe began when all matter and energy were condensed together into a tiny point. Then, in a singular event, a "Big Bang" explosion sent mass and energy shooting in all directions, forming galaxies as

well as molecules and atoms. The distribution of space, matter and energy — in regard both to outer space as well as to the inner space of atoms — is central to our conception of the world. Opposites play off one another to bring about contrast to the universe as we know it: "space" is the absence of matter and "darkness" is the absence of light. These "sets of opposites" (and others like them) work paradoxically to constitute reality for us.

JEWISH PERSPECTIVE: Sixteenth century Lurianic Kabbalah envisioned the creation of the world as beginning with a radical withdrawal of all light from the empty space which became the space of the universe. The Divine infinity/*Ein Sof* underwent a process of self-contraction called *tzimzum* and then its light went shooting back into the space (without filling it completely). The infinite light became finite material light that entered ten vessels, *sefirot*, which themselves broke, spreading the light even more. The description of reality for both Lurianic Kabbalah and modern physics involves the playoff of relatively empty space and energy/mass or, in other terms, darkness (as the absence of light) and light. World building, or *tikkun olam* as the kabbalists call it, involves gathering divine energy/ sparks of light which were dissipated in empty space in the original creation process (the kabbalist "Big Bang," so to speak) and redirecting them into different vessels.

SCIENTIFIC PERSPECTIVE: Darkness plays an equally important role in the realm of the psycho-biology of the eye. Our eyes are structured so that they respond to different amounts of light. A quantity of light which "makes a difference" is called a JND ("just noticeable difference"). As it turns out, starting with complete darkness, our eyes perceive a "just noticeable difference" with only a very small amount of light. The next JNDs involve increasingly greater amounts of light. Ironically, however, in terms of our perception, "discerning darkness from light" takes much less light energy than "discerning light from light." The more light we see, the more light energy is needed to produce a "just noticeable difference." Paradoxically, when an area is flooded with light, our eyes are less able to discern differences than when the same area has less light.

JEWISH PERSPECTIVE: The conception of darkness as mere absence of light, not as a

> The description of reality for both Lurianic Kabbalah and modern physics involves the playoff of relatively empty space and energy/mass or, in other terms, darkness (as the absence of light) and light. World building, or *tikkun olam* as the kabbalists call it, involves gathering divine energy/ sparks of light which were dissipated in empty space in the original creation process (the kabbalist "Big Bang," so to speak) and redirecting them into different vessels.

malevolent or inertial substance of its own, helps us make sense of the Hasidic proverb of the Baal Shem Tov: *"A little bit of light can illumine a great deal of darkness."* This is reminiscent of Eleanor Roosevelt who said, "Instead of cursing the darkness, light a candle." Yet darkness continues to play a positive role even in its absence. In the Biblical creation God does not eradicate darkness when light is created. Rather, darkness receives its place — night — and light its place — day. The dialectics of light/darkness and matter/space are keys to understanding our spiritual and physical worlds.

Light and the Electromagnetic Spectrum
BY SHERMAN ROSENFELD

One of the most fascinating features of all electromagnetic waves, including light, is that they are "self-propagating." These waves are composed of two alternating fields of energy — an electric field and a magnetic field — which propagate each other even without a medium, such as air or water. (For a while, scientists argued that light — like sound — needs a medium in order to travel and they mistakenly postulated the existence of an "ether" to fill this function.)

A variety of electromagnetic waves make up what is called "the electromagnetic spectrum." These waves differ in their wavelengths, ranging from short wavelengths (such as x-rays, which are fractions of millimeters long) to longer wavelengths (such as radio waves, which are kilometers long). And there is another difference: the only electromagnetic waves which are visible to the human eye are light waves. Yet all electromagnetic waves have several common features: they are "self-propagating," they travel at the "speed of light" (186,000 miles or about 300,000 kilometer per second), and they have a dual nature, i.e., they exist simultaneously as both waves and as particles (photons). By contrast, sound waves, which can only travel through a medium like air, travel at only approximately 1100 feet (335 meters) per second in air.

Most of the light we see originates from very hot objects, like the sun, the surface of which reaches 6000 degrees Centigrade (10,000 degrees Fahrenheit). When humans discovered how to make fire, they simultaneously discovered how to produce light. The colors of a flame (or parts of the same flame) usually indicate different temperatures. For example, from lower to higher temperatures, the flame color moves from red to yellow to white and finally to blue.

White light is composed of the wavelengths of many colors. As Isaac Newton first demonstrated, when white light passes through a glass prism, it defracts and separates into a series of different colors, called the visible spectrum. Physically speaking, each different color represents a different wavelength and a different amount of energy. Longer wavelengths (less energy) are more reddish and shorter wavelengths (more energy) are more bluish or violet. For example, after a rain — or while running your sprinkler — a rainbow results when sunlight is refracted through droplets of water. From top to bottom, the colors of the rainbow are red, orange, yellow, green, blue, indigo, and violet.

Incidentally, don't confuse the "colors of light" with the "colors of pigments" (the latter are found not only in paints and plants but also in our clothes and most every object around us). These two sets of colors recombine differently. For example, the primary "colors of light" are red, green and blue light; when recombined they produce white light. The primary "colors of pigments" are yellow, blue and red; when combined they produce a dark brown color.

Why do these two sets of colors act differently? The source for both sets is visible light. But when white light hits an object, some of that light is absorbed and some is reflected. The reflected light is what we actually see as the "color" of that object; but all the other colors in the visual spectrum have been absorbed by the object. (For example, we see that most leaves are green. This means that all the other colors — mostly red and blue — are absorbed. We see "green" because it is the color NOT absorbed.) So "colors of pigments" act differently, when they are recombined, than "colors of light" do.

DESIGNING A HANUKKAH MENORAH

HISTORICAL AND HALACHIC GUIDELINES
FROM THE MENORAH TO THE HANUKKIYAH

by Noam Zion

For years I was confused by the term "MENORAH." The menorah in our home was the nine-branched Hanukkah candelabrum for wax candles. In the Bible menorah means either a plain lamp of any kind or the seven-branched oil candelabrum lit only by the priest and only in the portable Tabernacle or the Jerusalem Temple. Now I have begun to sort things out with the help of an article by Bracha Yaniv, "The Influence of Halacha and Custom on the Design of the Hanukkah Menorah,"[8] which provided the research summarized in the following pages.

The Hanukkah menorah as a special candelabrum was developed only in the later Middle Ages. Until then the only Jewish menorah was the seven-branched Temple menorah, which went out of use in 70 CE when the Temple was destroyed. At home on Hanukkah and Shabbat Jews used the same kind of lamps as the general population in whatever land they resided. For example, in the Talmudic era in the area around the Mediterranean and until the 20th century in Persia and Afghanistan, each of the eight oil candles for Hanukkah was a separate oil dish. On Hanukkah eight dishes were lined up. Sometimes a stone circular star was used with separate compartments. When using simple pottery dishes, it was forbidden to light a used candle. New disposable pottery dishes were purchased or made specifically for Hanukkah. As the Talmud stipulated, "If no new one is available, then the old one must be cleaned very, very well with a flame."[9]

In medieval Europe the general and the Jewish population used a circular, metal, star-shaped lamp (with multiple wicks) that hung from the ceiling. Later when in the 16th century the general population switched over to tallow and wax candles and their appropriate candelabra, the star-shaped hanging oil lamp was associated specifically with the Jews who continued to prefer oil over wax candles for Shabbat and Hanukkah. The star lamp was then known as the *"Judenstern"* — the Jewish star — and it was manufactured with eight separate compartments in a circle.

In the Middle Ages a uniquely Jewish Hanukkah menorah began to be developed in conformance with Jewish law and local materials. Here are the key halachot and their influence on the design of the Hanukkah menorah.

A Lamp for the Doorway or the Windowsill

The Rabbis of the Mishna established:

"It is a mitzvah to place the Hanukkah candle outside of the doorway of one's home. If one lives upstairs, then one places it in the window opening nearest the public domain. In time of danger one places it on one's table (inside) and that is adequate."

Rava added: "The Hanukkah candle should be placed within a handsbreadth of the doorway, to the left [as one enters], so that the Hanukkah candle is to the left and the mezuzah to the right."[10]

Therefore, outdoor menorahs need to be protected from the wind (today with glass walls). In 13th century Germany the menorah was hung from the outside door, so it required a hook and a backing to protect the wooden door from the flames. In Morocco the menorah's backing was inscribed with the verse appropriate for the doorway: *"Blessed are you as you come in! Blessed are you as you go out."*[11] Menorahs placed inside the window need legs to raise the level of the candle so it can be seen from the outside.

---

8. *Minhagei Yisrael: Hanukkah*, p. 121-161, edited by Daniel Sperber
9. *Babylonian Talmud, Soferim* 20a
10. *Babylonian Talmud, Shabbat* 21b-22a
11. *Deuteronomy* 28:6

The Double Function of the *Shamash*: the Ninth Candle

The Hanukkah candles are purely symbolic and therefore their light, unlike Shabbat candles, may *not* be used for any practical purposes. After the candles are lit, many families sing *"Hanerot Hallalu"* — "These candles are holy and so we are not permitted to use their light."[12] Therefore beginning in the 16th century the menorah was often inscribed with this song.

Ravah[13] rules: "One needs another candle whose light is to be used."[14] In the pre-modern period when oil lamps or wax candles lit the home, it was also a problem to distinguish between the lamps for lighting and the lamp for Hanukkah. In the modern era when the electric lights are extinguished for the lighting of the menorah, one may end up using the light of the Hanukkah candles to see or to read. Hence an added lamp or candle — the *shamash* — separated off from the other lights became standard.

Some Babylonian Rabbis also forbade the use of one Hanukkah candle to light the others. Rav said: "One may not light one Hanukkah candle from the other," though Shmuel says: "One may light one from the other."[15] In the 17th century we can see a woodcut of a man lighting an oil menorah (see page 191) using two wax candles — one to give light and one to light the oil — which is in accordance with Rav's ruling.

The Afghani menorah: Nine little brass saucers in a row.

(20th Century)

Later a special place for the oil shamash was added to the menorah to give light, while a wax candle was used to light the other candles. The custom of Habad, Lubavitch Hasidim, is to use a wax candle for the shamash and oil candles for the 8 nights, in order to distinguish the two types of candles and to reflect the fact that oil is the recommended fuel only for the Hanukkah lights themselves.

Fuels: Olive Oil? Wax? Electricity?

The Rabbis of the Mishna argued about the type of fuel appropriate for Hanukkah candles:

Rabbi Tarfon said: "Only olive oil may be lit (for Hanukkah)." But Rabbi Yehoshua ben Levi (whose view became dominant) ruled: "All the oils are good for Hanukkah candles, though olive oil is the most commendable."[16]

In the Mediterranean in the days of the Bible and the Talmud, **vegetable oils** were used exclusively for indoor lighting in a candelabrum called simply a menorah. In the 16th century **wax**, whether from animal tallow or beeswax or vegetable fats, became readily available in high quality and inexpensive candles. However, menorahs designed for wax candles specifically for Hanukkah were not invented until the 19th century. Generally wax candles were white until 20th century American Jews began preferring multi-colored candles.

In the 20th century there was a debate over electric menorahs and many rabbis disqualified electric Hanukkah menorahs. However, a contemporary Israeli rabbi for religious soldiers, Rabbi Rabinowitz, holds that in situations of possible danger, flashlights are acceptable as Hanukkah candles, though a blessing should not be said over them.

Round Menorahs and Line Menorahs

Although each home needs only one candle for Hanukkah, the Rabbis encouraged *"hidur mitzvah"* — going beyond the minimum to beautify the mitzvah — by lighting an extra candle for each night per home (8 for the 8th night) and/or by a separate candelabrum for each person in the home. Often Jews used one oil container with multiple wicks. Rav

---

12. *Babylonian Talmud, Soferim* 20:6; *Shabbat* 23a
13. the 3rd century Talmudic scholar
14. *Babylonian Talmud, Shabbat* 21b
15. Babylonian Talmud Shabbat 22a
16. *T.B. Shabbat* 23a

Hana ruled: "One (oil) lamp with two wicks counts for two people."

Rava refined that ruling: "If one fills a bowl with oil and surrounds it with many separate wicks (in a circular fashion), then if a cover is put over the bowl with separate openings for each wick, then it counts for many people lighting their own candle. If there is no such cover, it will appear like a "bonfire" *(medurah)* and it will not count as a candle for anyone."[17]

In the Middle Ages there were many circular menorahs with separate multiple wicks as in the hanging star-shaped European "Jewish star" lamp. However, in the later Middle Ages menorahs were usually designed with rows of candles. **Still, as long as it does not appear like a bonfire, a round menorah is perfectly halachically kosher.**

The "Jewish Star" German hanging lamp

Three-Tiered Menorahs and Portable Menorahs

In Afro-Asian and Sephardic homes only one Hanukkah menorah is lit and that by the head of the household for the whole family. In Ashkenazi homes one often tries to provide a separate menorah for every family member. Therefore in the German Rhine Valley special two and three-tiered menorahs with eight rows each of candles could be used by two or three family members simultaneously.

What about the guest who is not a family member? The Babylonian rabbi, Rav Sheshet,[18] ruled: "The boarder is obligated to light his/her own Hanukkah lamp."[19] In the 19th century, yeshivot in Eretz Yisrael sent out official fundraisers to wander the world collecting contributions, some carrying their own portable menorah.

Free-Standing Giant Synagogue Menorahs

Though the halacha requires that each home light its own menorah, it became a medieval custom to light a synagogue menorah as well. As the notion of the synagogue as a "micro-Temple"/*mikdash m'at* became popular, it was natural that the Hanukkah menorah that recalls the Temple's seven-branched menorah be celebrated in the micro-Temple itself. Rabbi Yaacov Ben Asher[20] rules: "In the synagogue the Hanukkah menorah should be placed on the southern wall so as to recall the Temple menorah that stood in the southern part of the Temple."[21]

Therefore 18th century European Hanukkah menorahs were designed as free-standing oil candelabra, decorated with organic motifs like those described as part of the Tabernacle's menorah in *Exodus* 25 and with reliefs of Aaron the priest lighting the Temple candles. Later smaller home menorahs were also designed to stand up high on a table.

In summary, the confusion between the Temple menorah and the Hanukkah menorah may be resolving itself. Initially there was no Hanukkah menorah at all but just a series of pottery dishes with a wick. Then in the late Middle Ages as special Hanukkah menorahs were first designed, especially for the synagogue, they came to resemble the seven-branched original menorah. However, in the 19th-20th century many menorahs are designed specifically for wax candles — clearly different from the Temple's oil lamp.

In Israel a new name has been invented for the Hanukkah menorah — **"hanukki-yah**."[22] This word was invented in 1897 by Hemda Ben Yehuda in an article she wrote in her husband's Hebrew newspaper. Her husband's name was Eliezer Ben Yehuda, the reviver of modern Hebrew, however Eliezer Ben Yehuda may not have liked his wife's invention since he never included it in his own classic Hebrew dictionary. However, today's Israeli children clearly distinguish a "hanukkiyah" used for Hanukkah's candle lighting and the Temple's seven-branched "menorah," now the official symbol of the State of Israel.

17. *Babylonian Talmud Shabbat* 23b   18. 3rd century CE
19. *Babylonian Talmud Shabbat* 23a   20. 14th century
21. *Tur Orach Hayim* 671
22. Reuven Sivan, "First Words," *Etmol,* 1977

4.

IN SEARCH OF AN APPROPRIATE NATIONAL SYMBOL

THE MENORAH OF JUDAH THE MACCABEE OR THE STAR OF DAVID?

by Noam Zion

THE INVENTION OF THE "JEWISH" STAR: FROM ALCHEMY TO ZIONISM

In the 19th century, for the first time in Jewish history, the six pointed star was universally called the "Shield of David" and identified by Jew and anti-Semite alike as the Jewish symbol. Previously known as "Solomon's seal" or David's shield, the hexagram was used extensively in Moslem, Jewish and Christian magical literature. Although the decorative symbol of the hexagram appears in Jewish contexts as early as the sixth century BCE, it appears next to a swastika and neither decoration seems to have a particular Jewish meaning. By the same token the hexagram appears on many medieval churches without any religious significance. In alchemy, for example, it denoted the harmony between antagonistic elements of water and fire. In the mystical messianic movement of Shabbtai Zvi (1665) the Shield of David is called "the Seal of the Messiah son of David." However, originally the meaning of the term *"Magen David"* referred to God who is David's shield, just as in the prayer book God is called *"Magen Avot"*(Shield of the Ancestors). The *Magen David* first became a public symbol for the Jewish people in Prague where the Jewish community earned the privilege of flying its own banner called "King David's flag" (1354).

However, it is only in the 19th century, **when Jews of Western Europe were struggling to fend off assimilation into Christianity, that the *Magen David* was adopted as an answer to the Christian symbol of the cross**. It then appeared on the coat of arms of the newly ennobled Rothschild family (1822) and Lord Moses Montefiore.[23] Gershom Scholem[24] notes that

23. E.J. Vol. 11:695-696
24. "The Star of David: History of a Symbol" in *The Messianic Idea in Judaism*, p. 256 ff, 1971, Schocken and Luah Haaretz (Tel Aviv, 1948), 148-63.

The Menorah
Atop Israel's First Art School

When the first modern Zionist school of art was created in Jerusalem in the early 20th century by Boris Shatz, it was topped by a menorah which became a symbol of Jewish artistic creation. That school was named Bezalel after Bezalel ben Or (Uri), the inspired artisan of the Tabernacle in the desert in the days of Moses, who forged the very first menorah and whose father's name means "Light/Or."

the construction of synagogues played a special role in the dissemination of the *Magen David* as the Jewish symbol. Alfred Grotte, in his day one of the most famous synagogue builders, wrote in 1922:

> "When in the nineteenth century the construction of architecturally significant synagogues was begun, the mostly non-Jewish architects strove to build these houses of worship according to the model of church construction. They believed they had to look around for a symbol which corresponded to the symbol of the churches, and they hit upon the hexa-

The Shield of Judah the Maccabee
and the Menorah Psalm 67

In 12th century Germany the tradition of Jewish magic spoke of a protective shield *(Magen)* belonging to Judah the Maccabee. The shield derived its power from the inclusion of God's 72 names and a hexagram with the angelic name Metatron. In 14th century Spain the Magen David was "written" not as a star but as a seven-branched menorah using the words of Psalm 67. Sometimes David's magical shield is inscribed with the same verse associated with the acronym of Judah the MaCaBY's name — *Mi Chamoch Ba-eyleem YHWH = Who is like You among the gods?*[25] The scholar Gershom Scholem notes that about 1580 a booklet appeared in Prague entitled *The Golden Menorah*. It concludes with this illuminating comment: "This psalm [67] together with the menorah alludes to great things . . . When King David went out to war, he used to carry on his shield" this psalm in the form of a menorah engraved on a golden tablet and he used to meditate on its secret. Thus he was victorious."[26]

gram. In view of the total helplessness (of even learned Jewish theologians) regarding the material of Jewish symbolism, the *Magen David* was exalted as the visible insignia of Judaism. As its geometrical shape lent itself easily to all structural and ornamental purposes, it has now been for more than three generations an established fact, already hallowed by tradition, that the *Magen David* for the Jews is the same kind of holy symbol that the Cross and the Crescent are for the other monotheistic faiths."

Concurrent with the rise of modern European anti-semitism, Jews and non-Jews alike began to see themselves in national or ethnic terms. Since distinctive ethnic dress and religious observance were in decline, members of the various groups sought secular national symbols. These symbols took on increasing importance especially in the new age of mass literacy, newspapers, and political propaganda.

Theodor Herzl wrote admiringly of the power of symbols to transform disparate Catholic and Protestant German-speaking principalities into Otto Bismarck's creation of a powerful united modernized German empire. He saw such tactics as being highly applicable to the even more ambitious Zionist endeavor:

> "The exodus to the Promised Land presents itself practically as an enormous job of transportation unparalleled in the modern world.

> "Beforehand, prodigious propaganda is necessary: the popularization of the idea through newspapers, books, pamphlets, travel lectures, pictures, songs. Everything directed from one center with purposive and far-sighted vision.

> "Finally, I would have had to tell you what flag to unfurl and how. And then you would have asked in mockery, 'A flag, what is that? A stick with a cloth rag?' No, a flag is more than that. With a flag you can lead men where you will — even to

---

25. *Exodus* 15   26. See *Encyclopaedia Judaica*, Vol. II, p. 695

Theodor Herzl's sketch of the Jewish national flag. Herzl imagined a white field with seven golden stars, six of the stars form the Star of David, and the seventh floats above it.

(ca. 1896)

the Promised Land.

"Men live and die for a flag; it is indeed the only thing for which they are willing to die in masses, provided one educates them to it.

"Believe me, the policy of an entire people — especially one that is scattered all over the world — can only be made out of imponderables that float high in the thin air. Do you know out of what the German Empire sprang? Out of reveries, songs, fantasies, and black-red-and-gold ribbons — and in short order. Bismarck merely had to shake the tree, which the visionaries had planted.

"What, you do not understand an imponderable? What then is religion? Consider, if you will, what the Jews have withstood throughout two thousand years for the sake of a vision. Visions alone grip the souls of men. And whoever does not know how to deal in visions may be an excellent, worthy, practical-minded person, and even a benefactor in a big way; but he will never be a leader of men and no trace of him will remain."

— Theodor Herzl's Diaries *(1895-1896)*

The early Zionist movement adopted the blue and white flag whose colors and stripes suggested the traditional *"tallit"* (which in the Biblical and Rabbinic age still was dyed with a special blue dye derived from a now nearly extinct sea creature) and placed a Star of David in the middle of the stripes. However, this new symbol — even if it was misleadingly called the "Star or the Shield *(Magen)* of David" — in fact, lacked historical or spiritual depth. The great 20th century Zionist and historian of mysticism, Gershom Scholem, speaks of "the magnificent career of emptiness associated with the 19th century *Shield of David.* It expresses no idea, arouses no spiritual reality."

Perhaps secular Zionists, intent on rejecting the old religious baggage that prevented the growth of an activist modern nationalist movement, were drawn to this history-less symbol whose content they could shape. Nevertheless, secular and religious Zionists also wanted to root their new form of national existence in a romantic restoration of the ancient mythic essence of their people. Early on, the Temple's menorah was the unofficial companion of the Star of David in Zionist literature. In 1904 E. M. Lillien, the Jugendstil European artist joined the Zionist movement in response to Martin Buber's call

Hasmonean Gelt — left, King Mattathias Antigonus' coins, 40 BCE; and right, Israeli ten "cent" coin

The Maccabees, the Menorah, and Hasmonean "Gelt"

Over 100 years after the Maccabean revolt the last of Hasmonean kings, Mattathias Antigonos (40-37 BCE), minted a coin in his name with a seven branched menorah imprinted on the silver coin. Both his name (named after the original rebel, Judah's father, Mattathias) and his coin reflect the compromise (or perhaps symbiosis) reached between the Hellenistic culture and the Jewish culture of the Hasmoneans. On one side it says in Hebrew: *"Matityahu the High Priest and Friend of the Jews"* and on the other in Greek, *"King Antigonos."* [27]

Judaea Capta — "Judea is captured," the motto written on coins produced by the victorious Romans after the defeat of Judea.

68CE (Israel National Medallion)

27. Daniel Sperber, *Minhagei Yisrael: Hanukkah*, p. 171-173

for a restored and renewed national art. He created a collage of stars of David integrated with seven-branched Temple menorahs — Lillien juxtaposed the new star and the old menorah in the same way he often juxtaposed the secular youthful farming pioneer *(halutz)* in Eretz Yisrael and the old religious Jews imprisoned in Europe praying and yearning for redemption. **The future and the past welded through a cultural transformation of old religious symbols with new activist nationalist symbols.**

The Arch of Titus.
Titus's soldiers bring the Temple's menorah
as a trophy to Rome.

The Arch of Titus and the National Emblem

On July 15, 1948, soon after the establishment of the State

Titus' Captured Menorah: A Pagan Base to a Temple Menorah?

The Temple candelabrum reproduced on the Arch of Titus (81 CE) in Rome presents the historic menorah originally made by Judah the Maccabee in 164 BCE. However its base differs from the Rabbinic descriptions of a three-legged base and the other artistic representations of the menorah. In fact, the decorations on the Roman portrayal of the base include pagan symbols like two eagles holding a wreath of leaves and two sea dragons which are expressly forbidden in Rabbinic law. It seems that the original three-legged stand broke or was removed to make it easier to transport the massive gold menorah. The design of the replacement of the base is based on the podium of the god Zeus-Didyma in the Temple in Asia Minor dedicated to the violent Roman warrior god — Jupiter. Or perhaps the pagan style base was ordered by King Herod (37 CE) who rebuilt and remodeled the Temple in contemporary style. When the State of Israel chose as its symbol the menorah with the pagan base rather than the three-legged menorah, Chief Rabbi Herzog (father of Chaim Herzog, who later became President of the State of Israel) protested. However, it is the Roman portrayal of our menorah which has left its mark in the national memory, however it acquired its pagan base.

of Israel (but while Jerusalem was still under siege by the Arabs) the temporary Israeli National Assembly began a competition to choose a national emblem to accompany their blue and white flag which had long been the flag of the modern Jewish nationalist movement. A national emblem was essential to complete their application for membership in the United Nations. The committee for proposing a national emblem specified that it include a seven-branched menorah and the seven stars which Theodor Herzl had envisioned for the original Zionist flag. While the menorah represented the most ancient symbol of the Jewish commonwealth, the seven stars represented Herzl's vision of the Jewish state as a progressive European state limiting the working day to seven hours per day.

The blue color of the Israeli flag — originally the flag of the Jewish people chosen by the Zionist movement in the early 20th century — originates from the *techelet*/blue color of the *tzitzit*/fringes mandated by the Torah on the corners of whatever four-cornered garment is worn.[29] But where do the stripes come from?

As we know from Roman and Greek dress, many distinguished persons in the Greco-Roman world dyed their four-cornered sheet-like togas with a colored stripe. For example, Roman senators, as well as Jews, wore a distinctive "royal blue" stripe. Later Christian clergy adopted and continued to wear a colored stripe.

Much later in the Middle Ages when togas were out of fashion, Jews wore special four-cornered garments over or under their clothes so as to continue to observe the mitzvah of *tzitzit* (though the special blue dye for *techelet* was no longer available). Ashkenazim added a blue or black stripe to their "*tallit*" (Hebrew for a toga one throws on) and the European Zionists used that stripe as a part of their national flag. More recently the source for this rare blue dye has been rediscovered and reintroduced by some Jews on their *tzitzit*.

28. Daniel Sperber, *Minhagei Yisrael: Hanukkah* p. 207-208.
29. *Numbers* 16:38

David Remez, from the Ministry of Education, argued that the design of the menorah be based on the relief on the Arch of Titus in Rome. Similarly, he urged that the first coins of the State of Israel bear the inscription *"Judea Restituta"* just as the Roman coins of 70 CE bore the motto *"Judea Capta"* (Judea is captured).

The arch was constructed (after 81 CE) by the Emperor Titus to celebrate his victory as a general over Judea (70 CE) in a hard-fought battle ending with the burning of the Temple and the capture of its gold ritual utensils including the seven branched menorah. Though the secular Zionists did not want a purely religious symbol for their new state, the Temple's menorah was considered appropriate because the Temple did not stand merely for a house of worship. It represented the place of the decisive battle of the previous War of Independence, fought from 66 to 70 CE against the Roman Empire.

Ner Tamid — The Intermittent Eternal Light

While modern synagogue architecture includes an Eternal Light that burns continuously night and day, the original "eternal light" burned from evening until morning only. The High Priest prepared and lit the oil candles nightly[30] in the golden menorah in the Tabernacle and later in the Temple.

30. *Leviticus* 24:3; *Exodus* 27:20

The Prophet Zecharia's Golden Menorah

The menorah was not merely another ritual object in the service of God. As early as the Second Temple period in the prophecy of Zecharia, the menorah became a symbol of the Divinely aided restoration of the Jews to their land after the Babylonian Exile. One of the last of the biblical prophets, Zecharia received his revelation during the struggle of the newly returned community of Persian and Babylonian Jews to Jerusalem to rebuild the Temple under the auspices of the liberal Persian Emperor Cyrus (from 539 BCE). Cyrus and the Persians displaced the descendants of Nebuchadnezar, the Babylonian who captured and burned the Temple in 586 BCE. Exactly 70 years later, as predicted by Jeremiah, the Temple was rebuilt, though political independence was not restored. Nonetheless, the high priest did become the civil and political as well as religious governor of the Persian province of Judea.

Zecharia had a vision of a golden menorah surrounded by two olive branches, representing the two messianic leaders of his time, Zerubbavel and the High Priest Joshua:

> The angel who talked with me came back and woke me as a man is wakened from sleep. He said to me, "What do you see?" and I answered, "I see a menorah all of gold, with a bowl above it. The lamps on

The Blue Star and the Yellow Star

Both Zionist and anti-semitic national political movements have used the *Magen David* to represent the Jewish people in the press and the propaganda. The *Magen David*, the hexagram, not the menorah, was chosen for this purpose. Gershom Scholem sums up his essay on the Jewish star by attributing the high status of the *Magen David* in our modern consciousness to the Nazis. "Far more than the Zionists have done to provide the Shield of David with the sanctity of a genuine symbol has been done by those who made it for millions into a mark of shame and degradation. The yellow Jewish star, as a sign of exclusion and ultimately of annihilation, has accompanied the Jews on their path of humiliation and horror, of battle and heroic resistance. Under this sign they were murdered; under this sign they came to Israel. If there is a fertile soil of historical experience from which symbols draw their meaning, it would seem to be given here. Some have been of the opinion that the sign, which marked the way to annihilation and to the gas chambers, should be replaced by a sign of life. But it is possible to think quite the opposite: the sign which in our own days has been sanctified by suffering and dread has become worthy of illuminating the path to life and reconstruction. Before ascending, the path led down into the abyss; there the symbol received its ultimate humiliation and there it won its greatness."

it are seven in number, and the lamps above it have seven pipes. Next to it there are two olive trees, one on the right of the bowl and one on its left." I, in turn, asked the angel who talked with me, "What do these things mean, my lord?"

"This is the word of the Lord to Zerubbavel: **Not by might, nor by power, but by My spirit**, says the Lord of Hosts. Whoever you are, O great mountain in the path of Zerubbavel, turn into level ground! For he shall produce that excellent stone; it shall be greeted with shouts of 'Beautiful! Beautiful!'"

And the word of the Lord came to me: "Zerubbavel's hands have founded this House and Zerubbavel's hands shall complete it. Then you shall know that it was the Lord of Hosts who sent me to you. Does anyone scorn a day of small beginnings? When they see the stone of distinction in the hand of Zerubbavel, they shall rejoice . . . ."

[What are those seven stars in the vision?]

Not a Star, but a Shield: The Origin of the "Magen David"   BY THEODORE GASTER[31]

The Shield of David (Hebrew, Magen David) — that is, the hexagram formed by two inverted triangles — is today the universally recognized symbol of Judaism. It is frequently emblazoned on the walls and windows of synagogues, on ritual implements and vessels. It is the central element of the Israeli flag. It surmounts the graves of fallen Jewish soldiers and is the official badge of the Jewish military chaplain. In the Holy Land, the Red Shield of David is the equivalent of the Red Cross elsewhere. This widespread use of the symbol is, however, of comparatively recent date. Back of it lies a long and complicated history, woven of many strands.

Not until the twelfth century do we hear of the hexagram as the Shield of David. Nobody knows for certain how and why this peculiar name came to be adopted. The most probable conjecture would seem to be that it was originally designed as a complement to the familiar Seal of Solomon, which was a popular designation of the pentagram. In a legend recorded in

the Koran, it is said that the seal in question came down from heaven engraved with the all-powerful name of God. It was partly of brass, partly of iron. With the brass part, Solomon sealed his orders to the good spirits; with the iron, to the bad. This seal is mentioned frequently in ancient magical texts as an instrument of power efficacious in controlling or banning the princes of darkness.

Possibly we can go a step further, for the fact is that it was common practice in antiquity to name particularly powerful charms after Biblical or other heroes. A famous Hebrew book of spells, for instance, was entitled The Key of Solomon, and another went under the name of The Sword of Moses.

On this analogy, the "Shield of David" would have seemed a peculiarly appropriate name for a magical sign.

---

31. Theodore Gaster, *Customs and Folkways of Jewish Life*, p. 221-222; William Sloan Publishers © 1955 by Theodore Gaster, cc. 55-7551.

"A person may not make a house after the design of the Temple, or a porch after the design of the Temple-porch, a courtyard after the design of the Temple-court, a table after the design of the table [in the Temple], or a candelabrum after the design of its candelabrum. He may, however, make one with five, six, or eight [branches], but with seven one may not make it even though it be of other metals. R. Jose b. Judah says: Also of wood one may not make it, because thus did the Hasmoneans make it. [The Rabbis] said to him: It consisted of metal staves overlaid with tin. [The Talmud resolved the dispute by explaining:] When [the Hasmoneans] grew rich they made one of silver, and when they grew still richer they made one of gold![32]

---

32. *Babylonian Talmud Avodah Zara 43a*

"Those seven are the eyes of the Lord ranging over the whole earth."[33]

Judah the Maccabee's Menorah

What Zecharia had in mind was the menorah first fashioned by Bezalel for the mishkan (Tabernacle) in the desert. It was placed in Solomon's Temple (1000 BCE) and despoiled by the Babylonians (586 BCE) and returned in 539 BCE by Cyrus of Persia.[34] Perhaps the repatriated utensils included the seven-branched menorah.

However the founders of Israel in 1948 had a different vision of the menorah. It was the menorah represented on the Arch of Titus after the destruction of the Second Temple

The First Proposal for an Israeli National Symbol. This suggestion includes a seven branched menorah, seven stars representing Herzl's dream of the seven hour workday and olive branches mentioned in the prophecy of Zecharia.

(The Shamir brothers, 1948)

(70 CE) which was definitely ***not*** the original menorah. It was most probably Judah the Maccabee's menorah. For in 169 BCE Antiochus the IV, Emperor of the Greek Syrian empire, confiscated "the gold altar and the menorah" from the Temple in order to use it to pay off his political debts:

"Antiochus entered the Temple in his arrogance and took the golden altar, the menorah, etc. Taking them all he carried them away to his own country. He massacred people and spoke most arrogantly. Great was the sadness in Israel."[35]

The shame of the plunder of the Temple evoked the deepest anguish in Judah the Maccabee's father, Mattathias, one of the priests of the period:

"Wretched am I, why was I born to behold
The dissolution of my people and the
　　destruction of the holy city,
To sit idly by while it is given into the hand
　　of its enemies,
The sanctuary into the hand of foreigners?
Her people have become as a man without
　　honor,
Her glorious treasures captured, taken
　　away;
Her infants have been killed in her streets,
Her young men, by the sword of the
　　enemy.
What nation has not shared
And what kingdom has not seized her
　　spoil?
All her adornment has been taken away,
Instead of a free woman, she has become a
　　slave.
Look, our sanctuary and our beauty,
And our glory have been laid waste!
The Greeks have profaned them.
Why then should life continue for us?"

Mattathias and his sons tore their clothes, put on sackcloth, and mourned bitterly.

When his son Judah succeeded in recapturing and rededicating the Temple in

---

33. *Zecharia* 4: 1-14　　34. *Ezra* 1:7

35. *I Maccabees* 1:21 *ff*

In Germany, the hexagram received the intriguing name of Drydenfuss and was regarded as representing the footprint of a *trud* or *incubus* — a special kind of demon. It could serve alike to conjure demons or to keep them at bay, and it is mentioned frequently in the magical charms attributed to the celebrated Doctor Faustus. Sometimes its efficacy was further enhanced by its being combined with the sign of the Cross!

Moreover, even in modern times, a common German charm against dangers and hazards was to carry upon the person a small hexagonal amulet covered with the skin of a lamb that had been torn to pieces by lions or bears. This was known specifically as a "David's Shield," and the practice was justified by reference to the words of *I Samuel*,[38] *"Your servant (i.e.*

David) killed both the lion and the bear, and this uncircumcised Philistine (i.e. Goliath) shall be like one of them, seeing he has defied the armies of the living God!"

Just why the hexagram came to be used as a magical symbol is again a problem. Perhaps the most plausible answer yet advanced is that the design originated as a combination of the familiar alchemical symbols: a triangle with base down ▲ = fire, and a triangle with base on top ▼ = water. In Hebrew, these elements are called respectively *esh* and *mayim*, and it was fancifully supposed that together they composed the word *shamayim*, "heaven," a recognized paraphrase for God.

37. Theodore Gaster, p. 219-220
38. 17:34

---

165 BCE, he ordered "that new holy utensils be manufactured and a new menorah, incense altar and table be installed in the Temple." [This was a personal tribute to his father Mattathias.][36]

The Menorah of the State of Israel and its Olive Branches

As we noted, Israel chose in 1949 to make the menorah portrayed on Titus' arch the symbol of the new state. The choice of Judah's menorah for the Israeli emblem was no accident, as we have seen. The new Israeli government felt its sense of mission in reversing the historic wrongs of 70 CE and in reviving the spirit of the Maccabees of 165 BCE. Since the War of Independence had just been completed as the new emblem was approved on Feb. 11, 1949, Israel chose to emphasize its peaceful intent by using the olive branches of Zecharia to flank the menorah.

What do those olive branches connote? First, those olive branches symbolize peace. Some of the rejected designs for the emblem included the phrase "Peace over Israel" that

appears under a menorah on a mosaic floor of a 6th century CE synagogue uncovered in Jericho. Secondly, perhaps the olive branches also recall the end of Noah's long journey after the apocalypse of his era, the Flood. In 1949 the Jewish people were home from 2000 years of dispersion, after an unspeakable "flood" — the Holocaust — and after 2000 years of political servitude. Finally, the organic imagery of the olive branches was also attractive to a generation enamored of the return to agriculture in its own land. In the original menorah in the Bible there is organic imagery in the "branches" which are described as resembling the stem, the bell and the flower of a plant native to Israel. Some scholars hold that this organic imagery connects the menorah to the ancient Near Eastern Tree of Life.

All of this contributed to the choice of the menorah with olive branches to signify the miracle of 1948. Out of desecration and death the menorah and its people were revived and began to give off a new light. The base of the menorah has its roots in the past, while its branches are its present growth and its flames represent its future light unto the nations.

As we have seen, the hexagon, the seal of

---

36. *I Maccabees* 4:49

Solomon, later known as the Star of David, which had become a Jewish national symbol only in the 19th century, came to adorn the flag of the new nation state. But the official emblem of the old-new Jewish land became the seven-branched menorah whose roots go back to the Bible and whose model was taken from the menorah of Judah the Maccabee. Ironically, we often think of the eight or nine-branched Hanukkah menorah as the symbol of the Maccabees, but for Judah as for the modern State of Israel, the seven-branched Temple menorah, later captured by Titus, is the authentic symbol of Jewish revival.

Designing the Jewish Flag[39]

How did the national movement of the Jewish people get the familiar blue and white flag now identified with the State of Israel?

The early Russian Zionist Hibbat Zion Societies[40] (1882) inscribed the word "Zion" in a star of David as their symbol. The Zionist flag in its present form — two blue stripes on white background with a Shield of David in the center — was first displayed in Rishon le-Zion in 1885. Theodor Herzl, who was not aware of the emblem used by the Hibbat Zion movement, made the following entry in his diary (June 12, 1895):

> "The flag that I am thinking of is perhaps a white flag with seven gold stars. The white background stands for our new and pure life; the seven stars are the seven working hours: we shall enter the Promised Land under the sign of work."

This was also the flag that he proposed in *The Jewish State* (1896). However, under the influence of the Zionist societies he accepted the Shield of David as the emblem for the Zionist movement. But Herzl insisted that the six stars should be placed on the six angles of the Shield of David, and the seventh above it. In this form, with the inscription *"Aryeh Yehudah"* (The Lion of Judah) in the middle, the Shield of David became the first emblem of the Zionist Organization.

Ultimately, the Zionist activist David Wolfsohn created the flag of Zion on the model of the tallit, which, as he pointed out, was the traditional flag of the Jewish people, adding the Shield of David. This was also the flag, which, by a special order issued by Winston Churchill, became the official flag of the Jewish Brigade Group in World War II.

The combination "blue and white" as the colors of the Jewish flag is first mentioned in the latter part of the 19th century. In his poem, "The Colors of Eretz Yisrael," written about 1860, the poet L.A. Frankl writes:

> "All that is sacred will appear in these colors:
> White — as the radiance of great faith
> Blue — like the appearance of the firmament."

---

39. Based on *E.J.* Vol. 6:1335-1337.
40. *L'Or HaMenorah*, Rachel Arbel, "Between the Menorah and the Shield of David: the Crystallization of a Zionist Symbol," p. 187 (Israel Museum, 1998).

Gallery:
Menorahs at the Temple, at the Knesset, and at Home

King Antiochus plunders the Second Temple Menorah, 169 BCE
(Courtesy of the Library of the Jewish Theological Seminary of America)

The Arch of Titus — 70 CE

The Roman general Titus destroyed Jerusalem after a four-year battle ending in 70 CE and carried off the Temple utensils including the menorah to Rome. The stolen menorah was probably the one fashioned by Judah the Maccabee in 164 BCE for the first Hanukkah, since the earlier menorah had been plundered by Antiochus IV. The Arch of Titus was built in honor of Titus in 81 CE after he had already become the Roman Emperor.

(An engraving by Francois Perrier 1695, after the bas-relief on the Arch of Titus)

The Menorah — Into Exile and Back Home

The Symbol of the New State of Israel, 1949 CE.

Ben-Gurion and the Cabinet Return the Menorah to Jerusalem

Cartoonist A. Navon, portrayed the transfer of the Knesset from Tel Aviv to Jerusalem, 1949, as a reversal of the famous procession of Titus removing the menorah from Jerusalem two thousand years ago. David Ben-Gurion, identifiable by his balding head and bushy white hair, and Golda Meir, the only woman in the picture, are carrying the new symbol of the State of Israel, a menorah designed to resemble the captured menorah on the Arch of Titus in Rome. Prime Minister David Ben-Gurion's pose recalls King David who brought the ark up to Jerusalem (circa 1000 BCE) accompanied by musical instruments like the shofar and the flute.

Declaring Jewish Sovereignty from the Rooftop

The menorah atop the Israeli Knesset with the traditional blessing for miracles, "in those days and in our own era."

(December, 1950, Central Zionist Archives, Jerusalem)

The Persian Rose Menorah

This circular menorah, made of stone, was used for Hanukkah and for everyday use in 19th century Persia.

Traditional Menorahs at Home

Ancient Oil Menorahs/Lamps

(from the Schlesinger Collection of the Archeology Institute and the Hebrew University, displayed in and photographed by the Israel Museum)

The German Jewish Menorah

For use on Shabbat and Hanukkah

(Germany, 18th century)

The New Knesset Menorah

The New Knesset Menorah

This Menorah was given to the State of Israel by the British Parliament in 1956.

The relief panels review significant Jewish moments such as the exiled Jews weeping in Babylon, Ezekiel's vision of the dry bones revived, the Maccabees' Revolt, and the Warsaw Ghetto Uprising.

Zechariah's prophecy about the golden menorah is inscribed on the menorah: "Not by might and not by power, but by my spirit, says the Lord."

(The artist was Benno Elkan.)

"In the mountains the question arises: 'Whom will I send?' Send me! To serve the good and the beautiful! Will I be able to do this?" "God, if you have given me fire in my soul, let me be able to burn and to provide a worthy light in my home, the House of Israel! And let these words be not just flowery formulas but a mission for my life. To whom are these words directed? To the goodness in the world, of which there is a spark in me."

— Chana Szenes, Diary

Chana (Anikó) Szenes, aged sixteen, ready for her first ball, in Budapest, Hungary, 1937.

(Courtesy of the Senesh family)

CHAPTER VI

Profiles in Modern Jewish Courage

In 1965 Dr. Martin Luther King, Jr., is presented an award by his old friend Rabbi Jack Rothschild who organized the first official interracial dinner in Atlanta, in honor of King's winning the Nobel Peace Prize. (Courtesy of the Ida Pearle and Joseph Cuba Community Archives and Genealogy Center, of the William Breman Jewish Heritage Museum.)

Profiles in
Modern Jewish Courage

Raoul Wallenberg

Marshall Meyer

Yossi & Kalman Samuels

Chana Szenes

Yoni Netanyahu

INTRODUCTION

> "There is a time for everything under heaven . . . a time to embrace."
>
> — ECCLESIASTES 3:5
>
> If you see a group of **tzaddikim** — Good People — standing near you, stand up and hug them and kiss them, and kiss them and hug them again.
>
> — ECCLESIASTES RABBAH 3:5, 1

Why should there be a large collection of **modern Jewish profiles in courage** in a book on Hanukkah? After all, these heroes do not belong to the period of the Maccabees nor do their stories take place on Hanukkah. Most of them demonstrate courage in areas very different than the military daring of Judah the Maccabee, the brilliant tactician.

The answer is that, for the authors of this anthology, Hanukkah is not only about commemorating the ancient past nor exclusively about victories in battle. The point of the remembrance is to identify the kind of courageous faith that showed itself in the Maccabean Revolt but continues to express itself in other realms in the contemporary era. In the *"Maccabees' Megillah"* at the beginning of the companion volume, *The Hanukkah Book of Celebration*, we retold the historic tales of the Jews who faced Antiochus and the Greeks. Now we wish to recall the most dramatic moments in the lives of Jews and a few Righteous Gentiles who lived in our era and who can be role models for us.

These particular people were chosen not only for the inspiring tales of their confrontation with military enemies, but for their overall struggles with human oppression, physical illness and moral dilemmas. Uniquely, many of them have left us their introspective reflections on the quandaries of courageous living. These extraordinary people have left us a partial record of their doubts, struggles and insights about their vocations in life. We can learn about a heroism which is expressed not only on the battlefield by those with absolute conviction, but in everyday life as well as in moments of extremity by persons whose mixed motivations are accessible to us.

The realms chosen reflect some of the great public causes of the Jewish people in the last one hundred years. In no sense is the roster of heroes complete or representative of the vast variety. Considerations of accessibility and readability dominated the selection process. First, there is the political struggle. *In the Cause of Human Rights: Acts of Civil Courage*

COURAGE, BRAVERY AND COWARDICE: DEFINITIONS AND FAMOUS QUOTATIONS

Definition: **Courage**

Courage comes from the Latin *cors, cord* (heart as in "cardiac") and it means "to have heart," that is "to be courageous," while "to lose heart" is to be disheartened, to be discouraged. When hearts are together, then there is "accord" (*cors*). Originally courage, like heart, referred to all of one's inner emotions, but after the 17th century the term courage was narrowed to apply to bravery.

portrays the Jewish part of the democratic revolution in the world. Jews have been activists both because they were often victims of discrimination themselves and because they continued to believe in the prophetic tradition of justice for all. The examples are taken from the American Civil Rights Movement as well as the struggle against the murderous dictatorship in Argentina. Two rabbis — one Reform and one Conservative — and one secular Jew are represented.

The second grouping is *In the Service of Human Needs: Tzedakah Heroes and Miracle Workers*. These are exceptional people, in so-called ordinary times, who met challenges that we experience daily and acted extraordinarily. Two of the heroes are ultra-Orthodox Jewish parents who moved from North America to Jerusalem, where their son became a special needs child. The others are younger, a 12 year old girl and a young man of 23. Age is no impediment to becoming a *Tzedakah* hero. At any age one can work to change the way human needs are met in one's society. These people can be called "Miracle Workers" and should be honored on Hanukkah, the holiday of small and great miracles.

The third field of endeavor is defined by the Nazi threat to Jewish survival, *In Defiance of the Nazis: Spiritual and Military Resistance*. These four heroes include a resourceful, selfless Catholic priest and three Jews with literary ability as well as courage. Janusz Korczak is the father of orphans who wrote magnificent children's stories before and during his ultimate test in the Warsaw Ghetto.

Rabbi Leo Baeck was a German Jewish spiritual leader who kept up the highest level of civilization in the midst of Nazi barbarism in the Czech ghetto Terezin. The youthful Chana Szenes, who parachuted into Nazi-occupied Hungary, was also a poet whose poems became popular songs after her death.

The final area of particular significance to twentieth century Jews has been the rise of the modern State of Israel. The heroes in *Courage in the Cause of Israel's Survival: A Physical and an Ethical Struggle* include an American rabbinic smuggler and an Israeli anti-terrorist commando. Their concern was not only the physical survival of the Jewish people, but its intellectual and moral strength. For example, Yoni Netanyahu, brother of former Prime Minister Benjamin Netanyahu, not only participated in the Entebbe rescue of hostages, but wrote touching and revealing letters about the struggles of a young man caught between his private aspirations and his public calling.

For those interested in a general conceptual treatment of courage we have collected some brief but very enlightening essays about Jewish and Greek notions of the hero as well as a very insightful psychological profile of the Righteous Gentiles who rescued Jews in the Holocaust. These principles open the chapter in the section entitled *Cultures of Heroism*.

We believe that the celebration of Hanukkah and the enhancement of human courage in pursuit of higher causes will be served by this inspiring collection of dramatic contemporary tales.

Definition: **Bravery**

Bravery comes from the Latin *barbarus* (the wild, uncivilized, savage barbarian) still implicit in the term "Indian brave." But the wildness came to mean bravery in war or more negatively *bravado*, meaning boastful or threatening behavior, an ostentatious display of boldness.

Definition: **Cowardice**

Cowardice comes from the Latin *cauda* or *coda* (tail) and seems to mean someone who runs away like a dog with its tail between its legs.

CULTURES OF HEROISM

PREFACE — JEWISH, GREEK AND PSYCHOLOGICAL FACES OF THE HERO

> "Mankind's common instinct has always held the world to be essentially a theatre for heroism."
>
> — **WILLIAM JAMES**, PSYCHOLOGIST
>
> "Each cultural system is a dramatization of earthly heroics; each system cuts out roles for performances of various degrees of heroism: from the 'high' heroism of a Churchill, a Mao, or a Buddha, to the 'low' heroism of the coal miner, the peasant, the simple priest; the plain, everyday, earthy heroism wrought by gnarled working hands guiding a family through hunger and disease."
>
> — **ERNEST BECKER**, THE DENIAL OF DEATH

The Greeks and the Jews contributed different aspects to the Western notions of heroism. Without attempting to survey the complex history of the idea of the hero, we would like to highlight three perspectives before presenting the nuanced stories of courageous Jews and Righteous Gentiles collected below.

*One perspective is the **Rabbis' hero**, which focuses primarily on the internal struggle for control of our instinctual drives in the name of higher values. The twentieth century Jewish philosopher Yeshayahu Leibowitz summarizes this view which combines Rabbinic thought with the ethical theory of the German philosopher Immanuel Kant. Leibowitz is known as a fearless social critic whose observance was strictly Orthodox and who earned multiple doctorates in natural sciences as well as philosophy. His outspoken nature respected neither Orthodox nor academic nor Zionist consensus.*

In this piece he lashes out against the commonly held belief that military heroism is the highest form. (The editors do not necessarily agree, but we do enjoy his sharp wit that forces us to reexamine traditional views).

*The second perspective is the **Greek tragic hero** epitomized by the ancient Athenian playwright Sophocles, author of Oedipus. The third perspective — neither Rabbinic nor Greek — is a **social psychological study of the righteous gentiles** who rescued Jews during the Holocaust. We conclude this introductory chapter on heroism with Ernest Becker's portrayal of the **contemporary crisis of heroism in Western Society**.*

FAMOUS QUOTES ON HEROES, COURAGE, COWARDICE AND GREAT LEADERSHIP

Many a great hero is the product of great vision combined with a strong will to go it alone and the power to lead others.

✸

He who wills something great is in my eyes a great man — not he who achieves it. For in achievement luck plays a part.

The most remarkable of all things is when a man never gives up.

— **THEODOR HERZL**, FOUNDER OF THE ZIONIST MOVEMENT

✸

The hero has a generous concern for the good of mankind and the exercise of humility.

— **JOSEPH ADDISON**, ENGLISH POET

THE RABBIS' HEROISM: SELF-CONQUEST

by Yeshayahu Leibowitz[1]

> "Who is a Hero? One who overcomes his urges"
>
> — PIRKEI AVOT 4:1

The first words of the *Shulhan Arukh*[2] are: "One should pull oneself together" (lit., "overcome oneself," *lehitgaber*, from the root *g-b-r*). Heroism (*geburah*, from the same root) is one of the most significant terms relating to man's consciousness, will, and behavior. It is very difficult to define formally. We may say that conceptually heroism is always linked with the struggle between a man's choice of values, which is conscious and which he decides to exercise, and an urge arising from his nature and operating within him without his knowledge and even against his will. If in such a struggle the individual stands his ground in keeping with his decision and against the promptings of his nature, that is heroism; it is the meaning of the Rabbis' words: "Who is a hero? One who overcomes his urges."[3]

All heroism is the resistance of temptation. For this reason, heroism may be embodied in a person's behavior in every sphere of existence in which his nature impels him to strive for gain, pleasure, or achievement, when between them and him is interposed an imperative or principle that he considers a binding value. If this sense of obligation is not imposed upon him from without but arises from his own consciousness, and if for this consciousness the person must pay by forfeiting gain, pleasure, or achievement, that is heroism — the devotion of self to a value that does not "give" one anything (in any objective sense) but rather demands something of him.

A greater urge, greater perhaps than that for possessions, honors, or power, and even greater than the sexual urge, is the urge for physical existence, one's clinging to life, fear of death, and recoiling from mortal danger. **Values are measured in terms of what a person is willing to pay for them.** The price may be life itself, as in *kiddush ha-Shem* [sanctifying God's name], the sacrifice of an individual's life for the sake of others, for his country, for liberty, justice, or honor (or what one perceives as liberty, justice, or honor). That heroism, consisting of risking one's life, even to the point of sacrificing it for the sake of something that is acknowledged to be a supreme value, may be found in every aspect of life. Consider the person who enters a burning building to rescue a baby trapped inside, or who leaps into a raging river to save a drowning man. Yet the prevailing opinion in most nations and cultures links the concept of heroic death with death in battle. This linkage, prevalent in the State of Israel today, has excited a great deal of study and discussion.

What has the soldier's death in common with the other forms of heroism? From the standpoint of the meaning and value of heroism, there would seem to be no difference between the heroism of the person who risks or sacrifices his life in order to save another human life and the heroism of the

---

1. *Contemporary Jewish Religious Thought* edited by Arthur Cohen and Paul Mendes-Flohr (p. 363-369) is reprinted by permission of Free Press/MacMillan, a division of Random House, © 1987.
2. *OH* 1:1   3. *Pirkei Avot* 4:1

Few will have the greatness to bend history itself, but each of us can work to change a small portion of events. . . . It is from numberless acts of courage and belief that human history is shaped.

— ROBERT F. KENNEDY,
U.S. ATTORNEY GENERAL

The leader has to be practical and a realist, yet must talk the language of the visionary and the idealist.

The leader personifies the certitude of the creed and the defiance and grandeur of power. He articulates and justifies the resentment damned up in the souls of the frustrated. He kindles the vision of a breath-taking future so as to justify the sacrifice of a transitory present. He stages a world of make-believe so indispensable for the realization of self-sacrifice and united action.

— ERIC HOFFER, SOCIAL CRITIC

soldier who risks or sacrifices his life for his people or his country. Furthermore, in ordinary life, even without the risk or sacrifice of one's life there may arise situations that require spiritual heroism that is in no way inferior to that required in sacrificing one's life in war. Nonetheless, there is something special about fighting, for in all the other acts of heroism, the individual battles with himself ("conquers his urge"), and if he finds that he must sacrifice his life, he sacrifices only his own life. By contrast, in war the individual battles with another, and alongside his willingness to sacrifice his own life he also, and even primarily, intends to deprive the other individual of his life. Yet it is precisely this form of heroism that makes the deepest impression on the common man.

Military heroism is the least worthy kind of heroism. For it is the only one that is to be found among the masses and in every people and culture in every period in history regardless of the spiritual, moral, or social level of those who possess it. This is certainly not the case with regard to the heroism of controlling the natural urges, for it has always been rare in every time and place. Nor have we found, either in history or in present-day life, that the good and the spiritually and morally superior have a monopoly on military heroism. Rather, it occurs with the same frequency among the inferior. **Hence it is easier for the average person heroically to stand the test of risking his life in battle against the temptations of the urge for possessions or power, sexual pleasure,**

and so on. Heroism in battle is no indication of a person's stature as a human being. If one is a hero in the military sense (an excellent soldier), it is no guarantee that he is a superior person, either in terms of wisdom and intelligence or in honesty and integrity. On the other hand, a person who has heroically withstood urges arising from envy, hatred, or lust is certainly one of the elite few.

Judaism, as represented in its literary sources and in the existential civilization of scores of generations from ancient Israel up to, but not including, the generation of the mid-twentieth century, rejects war, yet is not pacifistic. Judaism recognizes war as a fact of human life, because mankind, to which the Jewish people belongs, exists in an imperfect world. This is the realism, at times even the brutal realism, of Jewish religious law (*halakhah*), which relates to the world as it is and not as it should be according to the messianic vision. Judaism does not marvel particularly at military heroism. Yet at present in Israel, the reverence for a man principally because of his excellence as a soldier is rampant, and bravery on the battlefield is thought to atone for serious character defects, and even for intellectual or moral inferiority.

A leader is one who, out of madness or goodness, volunteers to take upon himself the woe of a people.

— JOHN UPDIKE, NOVELIST

The leader is one who breaks new paths into unfamiliar territory.

— GERALD WHITE JOHNSON

Leadership is to get good out of all things and all persons.

— JOHN RUSKIN, ENGLISH SOCIAL CRITIC

The final test of a leader is that he leaves behind him in other men the conviction and the will to carry on.

— WALTER LIPPMANN, JOURNALIST

The leader is the other side of the coin of loneliness, and he who is a leader must always act alone. And acting alone, accept everything alone.

— FERDINAND E. MARCOS, EXILED PRESIDENT AND DICTATOR OF THE PHILIPPINES

THE CHANGING FACE OF THE RABBIS' HERO

by Noam Zion

For the Bible, courage is often the straightforward courage of a military leader inspired by the Divine spirit. As the Jews emerged from slavery and forty years of Divine care in the desert, Joshua was asked to transform them into soldiers and settlers who have to take care of themselves. Unlike the long period in the desert during which God intervened supernaturally on a daily basis, now God's aid would consist chiefly of strengthening their will and their self-confidence in battle:

> *"Be strong and of good courage, don't quake or fear, for I, your God, am with you."*[5]

However, later biblical Proverbs and Rabbinic wisdom shifted the focus from external military conquest to internal moral self-control. Punning on the Hebrew word for "hero," *gibor*, which means both to overcome and to be manly, they redefined manliness and virility in non-violent ways.

Ben Zoma says:

"Who is a *gibor* (a hero who conquers his enemy)? One who conquers his/her urges (inclinations/instincts)." As the Biblical proverb[6] states: *"Better patient self restraint of one's anger than conquest; better one who rules his/her spirit, than one who captures a city."*[7]

In addition, conquest of the enemy could be achieved without violence.

"Who is a *gibor* (hero, conqueror)? One who turns an enemy into a friend."[8]

A Hasidic story of the Tzaddik of Lublin refocuses the heroic struggle on the breaking of one's desires:

Once in the middle of a harshly cold winter night, Emperor Napoleon slept in his tent covered with many warm blankets. Then he awoke with a great thirst for water. But he felt too lazy to get out from under the covers and face the cold. Then he pulled himself together and argued with himself: "So I am a lazy bum, am I? You, Bonaparte, are a lazy coward! What difference is there between me, the great hero, and other mortals?"

With that he mobilized his will, stood up, dressed and walked in the cold night to the other side of the camp to the water barrel. However when he arrived, and filled his cup, he began to debate in his mind: "For a little bit of water I expended so much effort and made such a fuss? Can't I even overcome my thirst? So, what difference is there between me, the great hero, and other mortals?" Therefore Napoleon emptied the cup on the ground, mastered his thirst and went back to bed.

That, said the Rebbe, is what I call a hero (*gibor*)!

In the 18th-19th century, Jews who had not been soldiers or defenders of their own land for centuries were often viewed as cowards and weaklings. However the great writers, Goethe in Germany and Mark Twain in America, argued that the very opposite was the case, though the Jewish courage they praised was not necessarily military.

---

5. *Joshua* 1:9   6. *Proverbs* 16:32   7. *Pirkei Avot* 4:1   8. *Avot d' Rabbi Natan* A 23

ON PERSONAL COURAGE

✺

One of the most courageous things you can do is identify yourself, know who you are, what you believe in, and where you want to go.

— SHEILA MURRAY BETHEL

✺

Moral courage is a more rare commodity than bravery in battle or great intelligence.

— JOHN F. KENNEDY,
PRESIDENT OF THE U.S.

✺

Personality is the supreme realization of the innate individuality of a particular living being. Personality is an act of the greatest courage in the face of life, the absolute affirmation of all that constitutes the individual.

— CARL JUNG, PSYCHOLOGIST

"The Israelite people never was good for much, as its own leaders have a thousand times reproachfully declared; it possesses few virtues and most of the faults of other nations. But in cohesion, steadfastness, **courage and obstinate toughness,** it has no match. It is the most perseverant nation."

— *J. W. Goethe*[9]

"If the statistics are right, the Jews constitute 1% of the human race. Properly, the Jew ought hardly to be heard of; but he is heard of, has always been heard of. He has made a **marvelous fight** in this world, in all ages, and he has done it with his hands tied behind him."

— *Mark Twain*[10]

In both Israel and North America the **spiritual heroism**, given priority by Goethe, Mark Twain and of course Rabbinic culture, still competes with the traditional **physical bravery** typical of Judah the Maccabee. In my judgement, both kinds of courage have their origins in a spiritual outlook and both involve a willingness to undergo pain or loss, in the short term, in the hope of attaining victory, in the long term.

---

9. *Wilhelm Meister's Travels*, Chapter 11, 1829
10. "Concerning the Jews," Harper's Magazine, 1898

THE GREEK TRAGIC HERO

by Bernard Knox[11]

Greek civilization, like the Biblical world, begins with **heroism of the warrior**. In fact the term "hero" is a Greek concept for a semi-divine class of noble soldiers like Achilles and Hercules. However, just as Rabbinic culture critically transformed the struggle with the external enemy into the battle to conquer the "internal enemy," one's urges, so the Greek tragedians recast the hero as a human being, rather than a god, whose heroic status is achieved through moral tests. The Greek tragic heroes often "fail" by the usual criteria of success, but the fame achieved grants them immortality.

The traditional legendary hero, against which the tragedian rebels, is described as follows:

These **legendary heroes** belong to a princely class existing in an early stage of the history of a people, and they transcend ordinary men in skill, strength, and courage. They are usually born to their role. Some, like the Greek Achilles, are of semi-divine origin, unusual beauty, and extraordinary precocity.

War or dangerous adventure is the hero's normal occupation. He is surrounded by noble peers, is magnanimous to his followers and ruthless to his enemies. He is a

---

11. *The Heroic Temper: Studies in Sophoclean Tragedy* by Bernard Knox (p. 3-6, 27, 34, 56). Used by permission of the University of California Press and the copyright holder, the Regents of the University of California, 1964.

Every human being on this earth is born with a tragedy, and it isn't original sin. He's born with the tragedy that he has to grow up. A lot of people don't have the courage to do it.

— **HELEN HAYES, ACTRESS**

God, give us the serenity to accept what cannot be changed.

Give us the courage to change what should be changed.

Give us the wisdom to distinguish one from the other.

— **REINHOLD NIEHBUR, PROTESTANT THEOLOGIAN**

What a lawyer needs to redeem himself is not more ability, but the moral courage in the face of financial loss and personal ill-will, to stand for right and justice.

— **JUSTICE LOUIS BRANDEIS, LEADER OF AMERICAN ZIONISM**

man of action rather than thought and lives by a personal code of honor that admits of no qualification. His responses are usually instinctive, predictable, and inevitable. He accepts challenges and sometimes even courts disaster. (Thus baldly stated, the hero's ethos seems over-simple by the standards of a later age.) He is childlike in his boasting and rivalry, in his love for presents and rewards, and in his concern for his reputation. He is sometimes foolhardy and wrong-headed, risking his life — and the life of others — for trifles.[12]

*However the tragic hero cuts a very different figure. The first Greek tragedian, **Aeschylus**, describes him as **one with the capacity to learn through suffering**. Suffering need not be embittering but can be a source of knowledge and growth. Not the "man of action" but the human who has increased self-knowledge is the victor in what otherwise appears as a tragic defeat.*

However, Sophocles develops the tragic hero in new ways, different than his predecessor Aeschylus and his successor Euripides, whose heroes are usually passive victims of blind fate.

The Sophoclean Hero

The Sophoclean play is the medium for a vision of human existence, which differs fundamentally from that of **Aeschylus**. Sophocles did not share Aeschylus' belief in a Zeus who worked through the suffering of

---

12. *Encyclopaedia Britannica*, Vol. 18, "Hero"

mankind to bring order out of chaos, justice out of violence, reconciliation out of strife. Aeschylus imagined that the sweep of history affords us a perspective for the suffering we see on stage, and offers us consolation by giving it meaning. Human beings, involved in an action too great for them to understand, are warned or encouraged, judged or defended, by gods, from afar and eventually in person. Human suffering, in this all-embracing vision, has a meaning, even a beneficent purpose; it is the price paid for human progress. In the end the tragedy has a happy ending.

But the **Sophoclean** play rules out the future, which might serve to lighten the murk and terror of the present. The Sophoclean hero acts in a terrifying vacuum, a present which has no future to comfort and no past to guide, an isolation in time and space which imposes on the hero the full responsibility for his own action and its consequences. It is precisely this fact which makes possible the greatness of the Sophoclean heroes; the source of their action lies in them alone, nowhere else; the greatness of the action is theirs alone. Sophocles presents us for the first time with what we recognize as a "tragic hero": one who, unsupported by the gods and in the face of human opposition, makes a decision which springs from the deepest layer of his individual nature, his *physis*, and then blindly, ferociously, heroically maintains that decision even to the point of self-destruction.

[For **Euripides** tragedy lacks heroism]. The characteristic Euripidean hero suffers

---

rather than acts. They are victims rather than heroes. The Sophoclean characters are responsible, through their action and intransigence, for the tragic consequences, but in Euripidean tragedy disaster usually strikes capriciously and blindly, and it comes most often, not from the reaction of his fellow men to the hero's stubbornness, but from the gods themselves.

Between these two views of the human situation, the Aeschylean and the Euripidean, these poles of hope and despair, Sophocles creates a tragic universe in which man's heroic action, free and responsible, brings him sometimes through suffering to victory but more often to a fall which is both defeat and victory at once; the suffering and the glory are fused in an indissoluble unity. Sophocles pits against the limitations on human stature great individuals who refuse to accept those limitations, and in their failure achieve a strange success. Their action is fully autonomous.

The hero is faced with a choice between possible (or certain) disaster and a compromise, which if accepted would betray the hero's own conception of himself, his rights, his duties. The hero decides against compromise, and that decision is then assailed, by friendly advice, by threats, by actual force. But he refuses to yield; he remains true to himself, to his *physis*, that "nature" which he inherited from his parents and which is his identity.

In Sophocles, it is through this refusal to accept human limitations that humanity achieves its true greatness. It is a greatness achieved not with the help and encouragement of the gods, but through the hero's loyalty to his nature in trial, suffering, and death; a triumph purely human then, but one which the gods, in time, recognize.

For Sophocles, **the hero is a lonely figure**: "alone," "abandoned" and "deserted." The hero is isolated, but not only from men; he also abandons, or feels himself abandoned by, the gods. **The hero offered the ancient Greeks the assurance that in some chosen vessels, humanity is capable of superhuman greatness, that there are some human beings who can imperiously deny the imperatives which others obey in order to live**. It is not that the hero is worshipped as an example for human conduct; he is no guide to life in the real city man has made or the ideal city he dreams of. But he is a reminder that a human being may at times magnificently defy the limits imposed on our will by the fear of public opinion, of community action, even of death, may refuse to accept humiliation and indifference and impose his will no matter what the consequences to others and himself.

✳

I am tired of hearing about men with the "courage of their convictions." Nero and Caligula and Attila and Hitler had the courage of their convictions . . . But not one of them had the courage to examine their convictions or to change them, which is the true test of character.

— **Sydney Harris**

✳

Courage is mastery of fear — not absence of fear.

— **Mark Twain**, novelist

✳

The coward calls himself cautious.

— **Publilius Syrus**, Roman philosopher

Man's tragic destiny is that he must desperately justify himself as an object of primary value in the universe; he must stand out, be a hero, make the biggest possible contribution to world life, show that he *counts* more than anything or anyone else.

[Humans need] a mythical hero-system in which to earn a feeling of primary value, of cosmic specialness, of ultimate usefulness to creation, of unshakable meaning. People earn this feeling by carving out a place in nature, by building an edifice that reflects human value: a temple, a cathedral, a totem pole, a skyscraper, a family that spans three generations. The hope and belief is that the things that man creates in society are of lasting worth and meaning, that they outlive or outshine death and decay, that man and his products count.

Heroism is first and foremost a reflex of the terror of death. We admire most the courage to face death; we give such valor our highest and most constant adoration. It moves us deeply in our hearts because we have doubts about how brave we ourselves would be. When we see a man bravely facing his own extinction, we rehearse the greatest victory we can imagine.

Man will lay down his life for his country, his society, his family. He will choose to throw himself on a grenade to save his comrades; he is capable of the highest generosity and self-sacrifice. But he has to feel and believe that what he is doing is truly heroic, timeless, and supremely meaningful.

The crisis of modern society is precisely that the youth no longer feel heroic in the plan for action that their culture has set up. They don't believe it is empirically true to the problems of their lives and times. We are living **a crisis of heroism**, that reaches into every aspect of our social life: the dropouts of university heroism, of business and career heroism, of political-action heroism. The rise of anti-heroes, those who would be heroic each in his own way or like Charles Manson [the mass murderer] with his special "family," those whose tormented heroics lash out at the system that itself has ceased to represent agreed heroism.

The great perplexity of our time, the churning of our age, is that the youth have sensed — for better or for worse — a great social-historical truth: that just as there are useless self-sacrifices in unjust wars, so too is there an ignoble heroics of whole societies. It can be the viciously destructive heroics of Hitler's Germany or the plain debasing and silly heroics of the acquisition and display of consumer goods, the piling up of money and privileges that now characterizes whole ways of life.

In our culture anyway, especially in modern times, the heroic seems too big for us, or we too small for it. Tell a young man that he is entitled to be a hero and he will blush. We disguise our struggle by piling up figures in a bankbook to reflect privately our sense of heroic worth, or by having only a little better home in the neighborhood, a bigger car, brighter children. But underneath throbs the ache of cosmic specialness, no matter how we mask it in concerns of smaller scope.

If history is a succession of **immortality ideologies**, then the problems of men can be read directly against those ideologies — how embracing they are, how convincing, how easy they make it for men to be confident and secure in their personal heroism. What characterizes modern life is the failure of all traditional immortality ideologies to absorb and quicken man's hunger for self-perpetuation and heroism. **Neurosis** is today a widespread problem because of the disappearance of convincing dramas of heroic apotheosis [deification] of man.

Modern man became psychological because he became isolated from protective collective ideologies. He had to justify himself from within himself. Or, put another way, psychology has limited its understanding of human unhappiness to the personal life-history of the individual and has not understood how much individual unhappiness is itself a historical problem in the larger sense, a problem of the eclipse of secure communal ideologies of redemption.

13. Ernest Becker, *The Denial of Death* (p. 4-7, 11-12, 190-193).
   Reprinted by permission of Free Press/Simon and Schuster.
   © 1973.

THE RIGHTEOUS GENTILES:
THE PSYCHOLOGY OF THE RESCUERS
AND THE ORIGINS OF MORAL COURAGE

based on **Samuel and Pearl Oliner**[14] **and Krzysztof Konarzewski**[15]

Samuel and Pearl Oliner have researched the kind of moral hero associated with the rescuers of Jews during the Holocaust. They have called their psychological research a study of the altruistic personality.

In summing up their interviews they distinguished four motivational models:

(1) the autonomous, rational individualist;

(2) the empathetic, caring human being;

(3) the loyal member of an ethical community;

(4) the angry protester

*(1) The **autonomous individualist** is motivated by abstract universal principles of justice and disdains both emotional appeals and social norms. The Rabbinic Midrash about Abraham, who was brought up as a pagan, discovering God by rational philosophic inquiry, then breaking the idols, and preaching his universal truth to others despite the threat of persecution by the pagan king, is a perfect example of the autonomous individualist.*

The emphasis on autonomous thought as the only real basis for morality continues to enjoy widespread acceptance. The **lonely rugged individualist**, forsaking home and comfort and charting new paths in pursuit of a personal vision, is our heroic fantasy — perhaps more embraced by men than women, but nonetheless a cultural ideal. His spiritual equivalent is the moral hero, arriving at his own conclusions regarding right and wrong after internal struggle, guided primarily by

intellect and rationality. It is this vision that underlies much of Western philosophy and psychology.

In a culture that values individualism and rational thought most highly, a morality rooted in autonomy is considered most praiseworthy. Those who behave correctly — ethically, in fact — but do so in compliance with social norms or standards set by individuals or groups close to them or because of emphatic [emotional] arousal are presumed to be in some way morally deficient. That few individuals behave virtuously because of autonomous contemplation of abstract principles has not deterred advocates of independent moral reasoning from advancing it as the most morally admirable style. In some sense, rarity may even confirm its virtue, since it conforms to our cultural notion of the hero as a rather lonely person. But this is also a dispiriting view, for if humankind is dependent on only a few autonomously principled people, then the future is bleak indeed.

Furthermore, the venerators of autonomously principled individuals often fail to acknowledge that such individuals may not in fact extend themselves on behalf of people in distress or danger. Ideology, grand vision, or abstract principles may inure them to the suffering of real people.

Just as there are multiple styles of cognition and affect, so there are multiple styles for arriving at moral decisions. The virtue that may arise out of attachments of **(2) care and empathy**, or of **(3) affiliations** with other

---

14. *The Altruistic Personality: Rescuers of Jews in Nazi Europe* by Samuel and Pearl Oliner (p. 143, 217, 204, 49, 59-60). © 1988. Reprinted by permission of Free Press/Simon and Schuster.

15. K. Konarzewski, "Empathy and Protest" and Victor Seidler, "Rescue, Righteousness and Morality," P. Oliner, *Embracing the Other*, NYU Press 1992, p. 22-25, 64. Interspersed comments in italics are from the editor.

❁ Cowards die many times before their deaths.

The valiant never taste of death but once.

—SHAKESPEARE, JULIUS CAESAR

❁ Courage is doing what you're afraid to do. There can be no courage unless you're scared.

You gain strength, courage and confidence by every experience in which you really stop to look fear in the face. You are able to say to yourself, "I lived through this horror. I can take the next thing that comes along." You must do the thing you think you cannot do.

— ELEANOR ROOSEVELT, SOCIAL REFORMER AND FIRST LADY, WIFE OF PRESIDENT F. D. ROOSEVELT

Raoul Wallenberg, the Swedish delegate to Nazi Hungary, provided thousands of Swedish transit passes to help save Jews from deportation. Here Raoul Wallenberg stands in his office in the Swedish embassy at Budapest (November 26, 1944). The candle on his desk was there due to frequent blackouts. Though he survived the war, Wallenberg disappeared right after the war, when the Soviet Union liberated Hungary. Perhaps he was murdered by the Soviet police.

(Photographed by Thomas Veres, courtesy of USHMM Photo Archives)

people is no less meritorious or reliable than that which arises out of **(1) autonomous abstract thought**.

(2) The **empathetic human** *is moved precisely by an inclusive emotional solidarity with the other, seeing and being moved to action by a fellow human being's pain. The Dutch rescuer Louisa explained:*

"We helped people who were in need. Who they were was absolutely immaterial to us. It wasn't that we were especially fond of Jewish people. We felt we wanted to help everybody who was in trouble."

The interests of individuals may be subordinated to the greater good, as demonstrated in the following

---

The coward threatens only when he is safe.

—**J.W. Goethe, German poet**

Money lost, nothing lost.
Courage lost, all is lost.

—**Yiddish proverb**

I no more believe any man is born a coward than that he is born a knave. Truth makes a man of courage, and guilt makes that man of courage a coward.

—**Daniel Defoe, novelist**

Whether I shall turn out to be the hero of my own life, or whether that station will be held by anybody else, these pages must show.

— **Charles Dickens, from David Copperfield**

incident when Louisa put her son at risk, out of the greater concern for all in her charge:

"We saw a big car in front and knew it was the Germans. It was a big official Ford. Everyone ran out the back door and into the tunnel and disappeared with my husband. But our Jewish children were taking a nap upstairs. I knew we could not all run. I stayed because I was the last one anyway. I picked up the papers [files on people in hiding] and put them in the sweater that my nine-year-old son was wearing. I said to him — a terrible thing to say — "Try to get out of here quietly and disappear with the papers." He said "yes." In the end [the Germans did not search the house or arrest me and thus we were saved].

"Later my mother said, "I don't think you have the right to do this. Your responsibility is for the safety of your own children." I said to her that it was more important for our children to have parents who have done what they felt they had to do, even if it costs us our lives. It will be better for them — even if we don't make it. They will know we did what we felt we had to do. This is better than if we think first of our own safety."

*(3) The **loyal member of an ethical community** belongs to a particular identity — religious or ethnic or ideological — and follows faithfully the ethical dictates of that community because that is one's moral duty. For example, a Jew who helps a widow, orphan or stranger because "you know the heart of the stranger since you were strangers in the*

land of Egypt" is motivated by empathy but also by the particular identity and Divine commands of Jewish tradition. Raw emotion and humanitarian concern may play a lesser role than a religiously based moral duty and a particular communal identity. Many Calvinist Christians in Holland acted in compliance with their Christian sense of duty inspired by their reading of the Bible.[16]

*(4) The heroism originating in an **angry protest** responds not to universal principles or heart-rending pain but to the enemies' arrogant willfulness. Hate rather than love, anger rather than empathy is the motivating force. A young Dutch rescuer explained:*

My main motivation was because I was a Dutch patriot. I was for my country. I was for law and order. The Germans robbed people of their freedom. And when they started taking the Jewish people, that really lit my fire. They took them like sheep, throwing them into trains. I couldn't stand it anymore. I really became full of hate because they took innocent people — especially when they took little kids. That was the worst. They took innocent people and I wanted to help. As a small nation, we always had pressure from Germans who had tried to advance northward for more than one thousand years. My grandfather and great-grandfather told me that we must hate the Germans because someday they would try to take over. We had an anti-German feeling — not person-to-person but nation-to-nation.

---

16. See the companion volume, *A Different Light: The Hanukkah Book of Celebration*, page 60.

INSPIRATIONS TO ACTION — COLLECTED BY DANNY SIEGEL[17]

To be is to stand for.

— ABRAHAM JOSHUA HESCHEL, JEWISH PHILOSOPHER

To be is to do.

— MYRIAM MENDELOW, FOUNDER OF THE YAD LAKASHISH WORKSHOP FOR THE ELDERLY IN JERUSALEM

The opposite of love is not hate, it's indifference. And, the opposite of life is not death, it's indifference. Because of indifference one dies before one actually dies.

— ELIE WIESEL, HOLOCAUST SURVIVOR AND NOVELIST

---

17. Danny Siegel, *Heroes and Miracle Workers* (1997), by permission of the author

EDUCATING MORAL HEROES

by Krzysztof Konarzewski

Krzysztof Konarzewski has developed two proactive strategies for educating toward moral heroism based on the Oliners' psychological studies of gentile rescuers during the Holocaust.

These rescuers more frequently highlighted two kinds of moral principles — **the principle of justice** (the right of innocent people to be free from persecution) and **the principle of care** (the obligation to help the needy). Those motivated by the principle of justice tended to exhibit different emotional characteristics than did those who were motivated by the principle of care. They usually had more impersonal relationships with those they assisted and reserved strong emotions (anger and hate) for those who violated the principle of justice they held clear. Rescuers motivated primarily by care, on the other hand, usually focused on the subjective states and reactions of the victims. Kindness toward the victim was the dominant theme, while hate and indignation toward the violators were more transitory. In some cases the rescuer was even ready to extend help to the enemy if he was in pain or danger.

Empathy and Protest: Conceptual Distinctions

From the Oliners' interpretations two hypotheses may, I believe, be extracted. The first explains altruism by empathy, the second, by protest. Conceptually they are quite distinct from one another: the first considers altruism as an act *on behalf of* somebody or something.

The hypothesis of **empathy** says that an individual shows an inclination to help another person as if that person has been "incorporated into himself" in the sense that the fear and pain of another becomes his own fear and pain. He rescues others as he would rescue himself if he were in a similar situation. The other becomes the vicarious self. Rescuing of the other is rescuing **the self-in-the-other**.

The hypothesis of **protest** says that the tendency to help another person stems from disagreement with the existing state of affairs or the social order. An individual may disagree either with the world itself or his position in it. The world in which lawlessness is rampant, brute force is the last resort, and innocent people are condemned to torture and death — that world may elicit the protest in various forms, among them, altruistic protest.

At the core of altruistic motivation, according to the first hypothesis, lies the unfortunate other who may be physically or symbolically present. According to the second, this position is occupied by the world that has been pulled out of its proper form by the hostile forces. Hence the altruistic acts may not be dependent on the presence of the persecuted other. In fact, such persons may be actively sought. There is another, equally obvious difference between the two hypotheses. While the first requires the victim to be personally attractive to the potential rescuer, and considers love as the surest way to altruism, the second makes no claim of that sort. One may come to the victim's aid even if he personally dislikes him and would have quit the relationship had the victim been in a more favorable situation.

"There is a time for everything under heaven . . . a time to embrace."
— **ECCLESIASTES 3:5**

If you see a group of **tzaddikim** — Good People — standing near you, stand up and hug them and kiss them, and kiss them and hug them again.
— **ECCLESIASTES RABBAH 3:5, 1**

Most of the things worth doing in the world had been declared impossible before they were done.
— **JUSTICE LOUIS BRANDEIS**

God says: Just as I create worlds and bring the dead back to life, so you, human beings, are also capable of doing the same.
— **MIDRASH PSALMS 116:8**

Psychological Prerequisites: Inclusiveness or Independence

The two hypotheses assume different psychological prerequisites of altruistic behavior. According to the first, it is **inclusiveness** — that is, perceiving of other people as essentially similar to the self, regardless of the ways they are socially categorized. As the Oliners put it, we would expect a person involved in the act of altruism to be one whose "ego boundaries were sufficiently broadened so that other people were experienced as part of the self." The main obstacle to altruism is everything that splits people into separate categories, makes them different from others.

The second hypothesis assumes **independence** as the basic prerequisite of altruism. The opposition of the independence, and hence the main enemy of altruism, is conformity to current leaders and movements.

Education for Inclusiveness and Independence

The two psychological prerequisites of altruism are acquired in different educational settings. **Inclusiveness** requires an education that creates the climate of universal solidarity of men on the, so to speak, biological basis. It can be achieved by the rejection of all social categories in introducing people to the child. Such an education consists of making the child interact with others — regardless of their gender, ethnicity, social class, religious affiliation, and the like — by means of setting tasks, modeling, suasion, etc.

What can be said about **independence**? It grows, I believe, in educational contexts that require the child to reflect on the validity of various claims set up for him by other people, and teach him to resist the claims regarded as unjustifiable. Basic means of such education are examples of moral examination of the mutual claims in the family and the practice of appropriate reasoning in the course of everyday life.

Konarzewski believes that moral heroism can be taught. It is not the exclusive domain of extraordinary people. Perhaps the profiles below can reveal how such people emerge and how they can be accessible models for us all.

Shimon [the son of Rabban Gamliel] says: It is not what one says, but rather what one does, that makes all the difference in the world.

— PIRKE AVOT 1:17

Never doubt that a small group of thoughtful, committed citizens can change the world: indeed, it's the only thing that ever does.

— MARGARET MEAD, ANTHROPOLOGIST

Charismatic leaders make us think, "Oh, if only I could do that, be like that." True leaders make us think, "If they can do that, then . . . I can too."

— JOHN HOLT, EDUCATOR

From day to day, the activities of most of the rescuers were more mundane than glamorously heroic. For each dramatic act of rescuing a Jew from incarceration, there were months and years of ongoing activities to feed, shelter, and clothe him or her.

A Suitcase of Model Teeth

As Jews were forced to evacuate their places of residence, several rescuers stored personal items for them: jewelry, silverware, a prized cabinet, a grand piano, or even food. Such items were sometimes related to the victim's profession — one family kept a suitcase full of models of teeth for a Jewish dentist. Sometimes items were simply valued personal memorabilia: religious objects such as a prayer shawl or phylacteries.

Rescuers who stored such items expressed a strong sense of obligation regarding their safekeeping, even after it became clear that their owners would not be returning. An Italian priest agreed to store some valuable gold coins for a Jewish couple who did not return after the war. Considering them a sacred trust, he still had them in his possession forty years later. Shortly before his death, he gave them to the Roman Jewish community, which, in turn, decided to use them to launch a study of Italian rescuers, a fitting tribute, they felt, both to the Jewish couple and the priest.

Helping for Free

A French priest tells of his encounter with a Jewish refugee accustomed to pay for everything. "You are the first," he said to the interviewer, "to hear this story":

"It's about a couple and their three children. I can see their faces in front of me now. They came to see me in August, a pretty warm day. The man wore a black suit. I received them in my office, the husband and the wife. We talked for a long time, and he asked for my help. I had already been denounced in Vichy [the capital of the pro-Nazi French government] for my illegal activities, but I said to them: "Okay, I will take care of you. Tonight, be at this place." Then they stood up to leave. The man put his hands in his pocket and took out a bundle of bills. He offered them to me. I looked at him and said nothing. He put the money back in his pocket and left. Years went by.

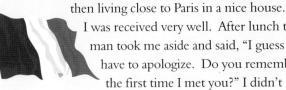

"After the war — I don't remember exactly how long after — we ran into each other one day. He was very glad to see me and invited me to lunch at his house. He was then living close to Paris in a nice house. I was received very well. After lunch the man took me aside and said, "I guess I have to apologize. Do you remember the first time I met you?" I didn't remember exactly, so he told me the story of the money. He said, "Listen to me, Father. We were used to paying for everything. You were helping us, me and my family. You were providing us with the greatest gift of all — our lives. Nothing I have would be mine except for you. You were the first priest I ever met. You taught me that priests can help for free."

The "Ordinariness" of the Righteous Gentiles

by Samuel and Pearl Oliner

While we have placed the "righteous gentiles" and other moral heroes on a pedestal as the "exceptional" people who we wish to praise, we may simultaneously be removing them from the models for emulation who set standards for all of us to follow.

The rescuers themselves claim to be "ordinary" and refuse to be "treated as anything special. They are clear that what they did others could have done. They do not want to be placed on some kind of pedestal as 'righteous gentiles.' That is to miss the point. **To treat them as moral heroes is to deprive the rest of us of the responsibility for what we do and fail to do in our everyday lives.** To remove those who rescued into a separate moral sphere is to avoid crucial issues of individual guilt and responsibility."[18]

Rescuers were and are "ordinary" people. They were farmers and teachers, entrepreneurs and factory workers, rich and poor, parents and single people, Protestants and Catholics. Most had done nothing extraordinary before the war nor have they done much that is extraordinary since. Most were marked neither by exceptional leadership qualities nor by unconventional behavior. They were not heroes cast in larger-than-life molds. What most distinguished them were their connections with others in relationships of commitment and care. It is out of such relationships that they became aware of what was occurring around them and mustered their human and material resources to relieve the pain. Their involvement with Jews grew out of the ways in which they ordinarily related to other people. [It was wholly consistent with] their characteristic ways of feeling; their perceptions of who should be obeyed; the rules and examples of conduct they learned from parents, friends, and religious and political associates; and their routine ways of deciding what was wrong and right. They

---

18. Victor Seidler, "Rescue, Righeousness and Morality," *op. cit.*

Raoul Wallenberg, on the right with his hands clasped, stands between the Hungarian police and a Jew holding a Swedish Schutzpass issued by Wallenberg to protect him from deportation from Budapest (November 1, 1944).

(Photographed by Thomas Veres, courtesy of USHMM Photo Archives)

inform us that it is out of the quality of such routine human activities that the human spirit evolves and moral courage is born. They remind us that such courage is not only the province of the independent and the intellectually superior thinkers, but that it is available to all through the virtues of connectedness, commitment, and the quality of relationships developed in ordinary human interactions.

They also highlight the important truth that interpretations of events are human inventions, and that what and how we choose to see shape our responses — and thus the future. "Situations defined as real are real in their consequences." If we persist in defining ourselves as doomed, human nature as beyond redemption, and social institutions as beyond reform, then we shall create a future that will inexorably proceed in confirming this view. Rescuers refused to see Jews as guilty or beyond hope and themselves as helpless, despite all the evidence that could be marshaled to the contrary. They made a choice that affirmed the value and meaningfulness of each life in the midst of a diabolical social order that repeatedly denied it. Can we do otherwise?

Relentless Follow up in Nazi-Occupied France BY SAMUEL AND PEARL OLINER

A French woman, who describes herself as "really a very shy and timid person," reported:

"I was in Toulouse when I learned a Jewish woman whom I knew had been arrested and that she had probably been taken to Du Vernet camp. I heard that there were some possibilities in exceptional cases to get out of the camp. I had a cousin, a very nice guy, who had been a soldier and had escaped from prison. During the first month after his escape, he worked for the Vichy government, dealing with the files of people from the camps. So I took the train and went to Vichy to see him. He told me he would be able to arrange it because he had just helped a policeman, and the policeman owed him someone. He assured me he would take care of it. So I came back to Toulouse, but I could not rest. I told myself that I really couldn't trust the administrative staff. I don't know exactly what got into me, but I decided to go and see the prefect of Toulouse.

"When I arrived at headquarters, I was told that he was attending a meeting that would probably be over in a few minutes. I didn't know what the prefect looked like. I had a small amount of money with me and went over to the usher, paid him, and asked him to point out the prefect to me when he left the meeting. He pointed to this tall man, and I watched him walk up the steps. I followed.

"I entered his office without an invitation and simply sat down. I said: 'Sir, we are very surprised in Vichy — surprised that you are not following orders here.' And then I gave a big speech on the fact that it was not surprising that we lost the war and that there were lots of stories about how orders were not being followed. He asked me what was going on. I said: 'What is happening is that the field marshal gave specific instructions that a certain woman in whom he is particularly interested be released, but this has not been done.' He said, 'Okay, it will be taken care of. Just give me the name of the person.' I said, 'No, that's not enough. You are the superior of the man in charge of the camp. I would like you to call him and tell him to release the woman.' He agreed and called the man in charge. I said, 'I will report back to Vichy what you have done,' and I left.

"But I was still not satisfied and said to myself, 'That's not enough.' So I got on the train again and went to Du Vernet camp. There I was told that instructions had been received and that the woman would be released. When I saw her, she didn't recognize me at first and thought that I was simply another person who had been arrested. I signaled to her to make her understand. A policeman escorted us out of the camp and even offered us free train tickets. On the way, we also took out a baby in a basket."

IN THE CAUSE OF HUMAN RIGHTS: ACTS OF CIVIL COURAGE

During the Emancipation of the Jews over the last 200 years, Jews have struggled not only to advance their own civil rights, but have been leaders in the forefront of the fight to expand democracy for all. Generally they have understood this activist impulse as an expression of their prophetic Jewish as well as their Western democratic legacy.

*We have chosen to highlight three American Jewish heroes who showed **civil courage** and a mastery of democratic means to fight oppression in North and South America. Two of them are rabbis — one Conservative and one Reform — and one is a secularist who nevertheless used the Bible to reeducate clergy to the realities of power and the beneficial effect of mobilizing self-interest and fear, for empowerment of the oppressed.*

Rabbi Jack Rothschild *led his very reluctant southern Temple in Atlanta into the struggle for civil rights hand-in-hand with Martin Luther King. His struggle almost cost him his Temple when it was blown up by white supremacists in 1958.* ***Saul Alinsky*** *was the community organizer who was the gray haired hero of the 1960s — a radical without left-wing ideology who taught people to believe in their ability to defend themselves and to rejuvenate democracy. His sense of humor in creative protests was raucous and usually very effective.* ***Rabbi Marshall Meyer*** *went south to Argentina where he and his family confronted the government reign of terror (1976-1983) and defined anew what a Biblical prophet in modern garb can achieve.*

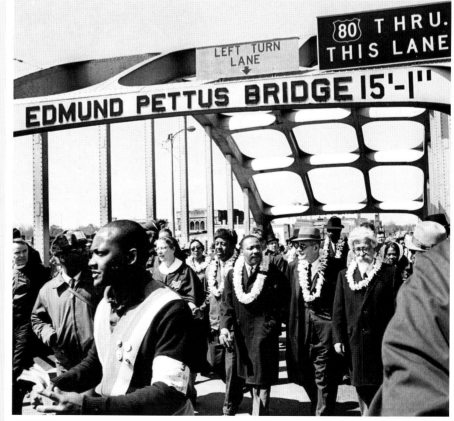

Marchers cross the Edmund Pettus Bridge, Selma, Alabama, March 21, 1965. From the left, starting under the "S" on the bridge, march leaders include Ralph Abernathy, Martin Luther King, Ralph Bunche, and Rabbi Abraham Joshua Heschel. Only two weeks earlier, Alabama state troopers had used tear gas, clubs and horses to turn civil rights marchers back at this same bridge, so the crossing itself was a triumph. These events led to the passage of the Voting Rights Act of 1965, which ended nearly 100 years during which African Americans across most of the South could not vote.

For Heschel, politics and theology were always intertwined. After the civil rights march in Selma, he said, "I felt my legs were praying." Even as social protest was for him a religious experience, religion without indignation at political evils was impossible.

Heschel reflected later, "I felt again what I have been thinking about for years — that Jewish religious institutions have again missed a great opportunity, namely, to interpret a civil rights movement in terms of Judaism, in terms of the prophetic traditions."

In spring 1968, Dr. King had made plans to join the Heschel family seder. But King was assassinated several days before Passover, and Heschel spoke at his funeral instead.

(photograph © 1965 Robie Ray; used by permission)

1.

THE PROPHETIC PREACHER

RABBI JACK ROTHSCHILD AND THE TEMPLE BOMBING (ATLANTA, 1958)

by Melissa Fay Greene[18]

"I don't like being told it's not my fight . . . [A rabbi] must himself have a deep dedication and a pervading commitment to the ideal of equality and dignity for all men. And he must be prepared to involve himself in every facet of community and congregational life that will translate his commitment into the minds and hearts of those whom he would lead. He must do so with patience and forbearance and tact — but there must never be the slightest doubt about what he believes or where he stands."

— RABBI JACK ROTHSCHILD

"The ultimate measure of a man is not where he stands in moments of comfort and convenience, but where he stands in times of challenge and controversy," said Coretta Scott King, quoting from her husband's sermon *On Being a Good Neighbor*. "The true neighbor will risk his position, his prestige and even his life for the welfare of others." These words could be applied as a fitting tribute to my husband Martin Luther King's good friend, Rabbi Jacob M. Rothschild."

— CORETTA SCOTT KING

---

18. Melissa Fay Greene, *The Temple Bombing*, 1996, Random House (pp.4-7, 8-9, 33-36, 79-83, 188-190, 378, 381-383, 420-425, 428-429, 435-436). Reprinted by the gracious permission of the author.

THE PREFACE:
THE TEMPLE BOMBING, OCTOBER 12, 1958, 3:37 AM

Fifty sticks of dynamite in the middle of the night blew apart the side wall of the Temple, Atlanta's oldest and richest synagogue, which stood in pillared, domed majesty on a grassy hill above Peachtree Street.

From May 17, 1954 — the day the Supreme Court ruled in *Brown v. Board of Education of Topeka* that states could not lawfully segregate schoolchildren by race — until the end of the 1950s, hundreds of homes, schools and houses of worship across the South exploded.

Across Dixie, some of the fights over racial prominence involved not only white against black and black against white, but Christian-born white against Jew. Where Jewish people were available, whites aimed at blacks *through* the Jews. Ten percent of the bombs from 1954 to 1959 were cast at Jewish targets — synagogues, rabbis' houses and community centers. The chief target of the Atlanta bombing was a Pittsburgh-born Reform rabbi, Jacob M. Rothschild.

A Northern Rabbi
Comes to Atlanta, 1946

Young Rabbi Jack Rothschild was the sort of man who, in a public forum, would clear his throat and then raise the ethical question, the very question he had turned over and over in his mind for many weeks, while slumped in front of TV baseball in his den or seated alone in his study, snapping down cards in solitaire. This he would stunningly and eloquently say, and heaven help those who were not ready for it.

He had arrived in Atlanta in 1946. In 1947 he had begun to speak on the Negro question, and by 1952 the Negro question occupied so great a portion of his time and thoughts that — near the end of his life — he would say it had been his greatest cause, that without it his pulpit would not have been worth as much. Rabbi Rothschild, in short, supported integration and said so publicly and repeatedly in sermon and speech and editorial. And he had invited black speakers onto his pulpit and black dinner guests into his house.

And what stood behind it all, one felt, was not muscle or rugged good looks, the kinds of things that would do you some good in a crowd. Among the tall, handsome, silver-templed Atlanta ministers, Rothschild looked somewhat the four-eyes, the egghead, the bookworm. But he had seen bloodshed on Guadalcanal [in World War II in America's bloody battle with Japan], and had sat with dying boys, Jewish and Christian, in hospital tents as bombs fell, the first Jewish chaplain to come under fire in World War II. What stood behind the eloquence and the quietly revolutionary actions was a clarity of mind and a history of having not flinched under fire.

The South into which Rothschild traveled in 1946 was like another country. Across its five-story cities and whistle-stop towns, its pine barrens and cotton fields, its cotton mills and red clay roads lay an invisible checkerboard of alternating white and black squares — landing places for white and landing places for black, forbidden places for white and forbidden places for black — where the citizens hopscotched, careful not to step on the lines nor rub shoulders in passing.

He saw them first at the train station: *White Waiting Room. Colored Waiting Room. Men. Women. Colored.* As he bumped along through the city, he sighted more; and in the days to come, riding the streetcar to the Temple, he saw more. Thrown off balance by the signs and by other marks of the Jim Crow system five minutes after arrival, he never regained his footing. He never got used to it and he never accommodated himself to it. He began to lay down a different moral geometry than he had ever lived by.

He was stunned by the signs. So were many outsiders. There were refugees in Atlanta who had been denied seating on German park benches labeled *Nur Fur Arier* (Aryans only), and who ended by fleeing for their lives. When these Jewish refugees read the *White Only* signs displayed matter-of-factly in Atlanta at restrooms and drinking fountains, restaurant and theater entrances, park benches and public libraries, they

The Temple in Atlanta.
This bastion of southern Reform Judaism takes the form of a Colonial, Byzantine, Romanesque, Gothic, Neo-Classical building with an Ionic portico.
Here the bar mitzvah was replaced by confirmation, and the kippah, the tallit and kashrut were removed completely, while the organ and the non-Jewish
choir were added as essential parts of the worship.

protested to their new American friends: "But this is like Hitler."

No native southerner had to be instructed that the clean, locked restroom, the one with an aura of disinfectant rising from under the door, was for Men or Ladies; that the filthy, stinking restroom, with the brown toilet clogged and the door hanging from a single hinge, was for the Coloreds. Even young southerners could tell with their eyes closed that when entrances to hotels, theaters, train stations, or movie houses had double doors under a marquis, were carpeted, or were flanked by potted palms or by black doormen in absurd epaulets, they were entrances for whites. Those for blacks were around back, off the alley, or at the top of steep fire-escape stairs screwed precariously to the brick. The signs, in short, were pedagogical in purpose; they were like bright hand-printed labels in a first-grade classroom — DESK, WINDOW, FLOWER. Locals did not rely on the signs; only fools, "uppity niggers," or Yankees needed signs to tell them which was which. And every courtroom in Georgia was provided, by state law, with two Bibles; one for white witnesses, the other for black witnesses.

No Segregation in this Temple

[In 1954 the Supreme Court ruled that all public schools must be integrated.] Rothschild was driving his young son, Bill, home from Sunday school one day and made a remark that pierced the child's memory. "We were listening to the radio," said Bill Rothschild. "Some local civic leader was saying that the public schools ought to remain open and we ought to obey the law because it would be good for business, and Dad kind of looked at me and sort of half looked out the front windshield and said, 'Why don't they do it because it's right?'"

"The Talmud asks the pertinent question," said Rothschild in a sermon in 1954: "'Why did God create only one man — Adam — when he made the world?' And answers its own question in these words: 'So that no man could one day claim, 'My father is better than

yours, hence I am superior to you.'"

When he felt the congregation silently quailing at his words, wishing he would keep his voice down, fearing retribution, fearing an impairment of relations with white Christian Atlanta, Rothschild stormed at them. The congregants bowed their heads and endured the spray of his syllables and his tongue-lashings, and surreptitiously slid their sleeves up to check their watches. "I don't mind them looking at their watches," the rabbi once said. "It's when they tap them, then hold them up to their ears that I get concerned."

"[Rothschild] brought his congregation kicking and screaming into the twentieth

The Columbians: Post-War America's First Neo-Nazi Group
BY MELISSA FAY GREENE

On the home front, as World War II veterans returned from overseas, the Jewish war was not quite over. In the summer of 1946, the *Columbians*, postwar America's first neo-Nazi group, was founded in Atlanta. Brown-shirted rank-and-file Columbians marched and drilled in public streets and parks, preparing for the overthrow of the existing government. "Their central motivation was hatred of the Jews," wrote the *Atlanta Constitution* journalist and historian Harold Martin, "and [their] members wore armbands bearing the drunken thunderbolt design once worn by Hitler's Elite Guard."

Atlanta's whites were encouraged to phone in on a sort of racial-911 whenever they spotted a black family trying to move into a white or mixed neighborhood and to report "generally troublesome Negroes." A library of fifty volumes contained *Mein Kampf* and histories of the Nazi movement.

The Columbians had a simple recruitment strategy. They asked three questions of prospective members:

1. Do you hate Negroes?
2. Do you hate Jews?
3. Do you have three dollars?

Apparently, given the eight hundred applications for membership found in their headquarters, the strategy was an effective one.

Ralph McGill at the *Atlanta Constitution* accused the

Columbians of "starting a cut-rate war in the hate racket by charging three dollars for membership instead of the ten dollars charged by the Klan." One day he reported in his column that, according to his informants, he himself had been the subject of debate at a recent Columbian's meeting. "Should they lynch McGill or simply waylay him one night and give him a good slugging?" the members had debated. The vote had been in favor of beating him up. McGill publicly thanked them in his column: "Always grateful for small favors."

A Columbian leaflet in October 1946 read: "The Jews, who do the greatest part of advertising in newspapers, hate us because we had the courage to come out and tell the truth about how the Jews are taking all the wealth and money in the nation." "The Jews and the newspapers are afraid of us because we are organizing the white people of the South."

"Everybody in America is free to hate! Hate is natural. It's not un-American to hate. Why does the Jew think that he alone is above criticism and being hated?"

Against Jews, the organization sponsored speakers, printed a newspaper, and distributed leaflets revealing the Jewish plot for world domination. Against African Americans they unleashed violence rather than propaganda: they beat up black citizens, picketed their neighborhoods, and dynamited their houses.

century, both on Zionism and on civil rights," said one congregant. "He was a lonely man. I think it was difficult for him. They criticized him violently when on Friday nights or the holidays he talked about civil rights. They said they wanted him to talk about the *Bible*. Then they'd have fallen asleep."

In 1955, the Temple Sisterhood invited Rothschild's friend, Dr. Benjamin E. Mays, the president of Morehouse College, a nationally known black clergyman and educator, to speak at a Temple luncheon, and then, accompanied by Mrs. Mays, to sit down and *eat*. The Sisterhood was "bombarded with protests and dire predictions of what would happen should such a meeting be allowed to take place," said Janice Rothschild.

"Don't you know that mixed eating is against the law in this state?" said a furious congregant in an early-morning phone call to Rothschild's study.

"No, no, no, you've been misinformed, Sam," said the rabbi. "The Sisterhood luncheon isn't going to be integrated."

"Is Mays coming after lunch, to spare us the embarrassment?"

"Not at all. Both Dr. and Mrs. Mays will be with us for lunch, but they're going to be seated at the center of the head table and all us white folks will be segregated around them."

Janice Rothschild began to fear for her husband's safety, as he persisted in accepting speaking engagements to gentile groups and black groups around Atlanta and across the South. "Bombings have shocked and bewildered us," Rothschild said in a Friday night sermon in May, 1958, entitled "Can This Be America?" — "Synagogues and centers have been bombed . . . What shall be our course of action?" he asked them, knowing they silently prayed for his answer to be that perhaps he ought to refrain from making integration speeches all over the place from now on. Of course, this was *not* his answer. "Our first duty is not to allow ourselves to be intimidated." The congregation sighed. "We are a vulnerable

minority. What we do makes no difference in how we are treated. Whether we speak our conscience, or hide and remain silent — we will be attacked."

[On October 12, 1958, the Temple was bombed during the night.] The bomb that blew a hole in the Temple's outer wall broke into the psyche and dream life of the congregation for years to come. This most private place, this place where they gathered in order to be among Jews and to behave as Jews, had been stalked.

In Alfred Uhry's play *Driving Miss Daisy*, the Atlanta Jews particularly loved — and howled with self-recognition at — one line (a line deleted by Hollywood for the movie). Told that the Temple has been bombed, Miss Daisy, annoyed and bewildered, snaps: "Don't they know we're *Reform*?" by which she means: "Don't they know that we're really quite similar, in our lives and religious practices, to them, unlike our Orthodox brethren, who really are, it must be admitted, a little extreme?"

The bombing had launched Rothschild briefly into national prominence, and he would continue, until the end of his life — growing year by year a little heftier, a little balder, a little more acerbic — to be a strong, clear voice for social justice within the Jewish world, in high demand as a speaker, sought after as an author of articles and resolutions, and a role model for a new generation at Hebrew Union College. If he had seemed unflappable before the bombing, deaf to the threats ricocheting in his general direction from across the South, then after the bombing he was positively a marvel. He simply never flinched. He did not change his ways. He was as pushy, demanding, and unsympathetic to the moral plight of his congregants after the bombing as before it. In this he defied the main course of human nature, for a great many souls act publicly in support of an ideal; far fewer return after the first spray of gunfire or clubbing by the opposition.

A Daring Dinner with Coretta and Martin Luther King (1960)

In 1960, Martin Luther King, Jr., moved home to Atlanta, prompting Governor Ernest Vandiver to observe: "Wherever M.L. King, Jr., has been there has followed in his wake a wave of crimes including stabbings, bombings, and inciting of riots, destruction of property and many others. For these reasons, he is not welcome in Georgia." Jack and Janice Rothschild, on the other hand, invited him and his wife to dinner. Sitting down to a meal together was a great racial experiment of the era, and only the most intrepid of both races dared.

"It was to be my first experience with a purely social biracial function," Janice recalls. "I wanted to tell people, to brag about it. When I could resist the urge no longer, I did mention it to a few carefully selected friends, only to discover that some of them had already entertained guests of both races in their homes together. They appeared to be as relieved as I was to have broken the silence about it.

"You know it was all very strange and new, how to act. I mean, when you had black guests, did you introduce them to your maid? So we did, and I remember the maid was so impressed that we introduced her, because these were people she wanted to meet.

"My Daddy, the Negro Doctor"

"My father was one of the first black doctors of his generation," said Alice Washington. "His first patient came as a referral from a white pharmacist and it was a white couple. In those days, it was completely illegal for a black physician to treat white patients. But, as the story goes, the white pharmacist said to this white couple (in an emergency situation), 'No, we don't have a doctor. There is a black doctor in town. If you want to see what he would do, all right.' So this young white couple came to my daddy, and fortunately for them, he was at home. He said to them, 'It's against the law for me to treat you, but I have just taken the oath that says I will serve as I am needed.' My father always finished telling this story by saying, 'Fortunately for me, the patient lived.'"

"I remember a joke going around during the early days of the civil rights movement: The lady of the house and her maid sat down together in the kitchen and had lunch. And the lady says to the maid, 'I bet where you worked before you didn't sit down and have lunch with your employer, did you?' And the maid says, 'No ma'am. I always worked for high-class people before.'"

[On the night of the dinner visit] "the Kings arrived much later than the others," Janice recalled. "No explanation was necessary, but Martin apologized anyhow and explained that they had been delayed trying to find our house. (The street was poorly lighted and the numbers were hard to read.) They finally had to drive up to one of the other houses to inquire. As Martin told us this, he quickly added, 'But we were careful not to embarrass you with your neighbors. I let Coretta go to the door so they'd think we were just coming to serve a party.' I still have a lump in my throat when I think of it."

A Nobel Prize Dinner with Martin Luther King (1964)

Coretta Scott King wrote: "Rabbi Rothschild shared in Martin's Dream as a basic tenet of his own religious teaching. He had the courage to proclaim his belief publicly long before it became expedient or even physically safe to do so in a Southern city. He was in great measure responsible for the Atlanta dinner honoring Martin as recipient of the 1964 Nobel Peace prize, an occasion that heralded a new era in race relations in our city."

It was unheard of. It was outlandish. It was titillating. Simply spearing and munching a curl of one's lettuce or cucumber side by side with black people munching on theirs was a singular experience for the white upper echelon. "There was the natural uneasiness that would come at a first biracial gathering such as this," said Mayor Allen.

That night it was as if the African American people were from another country; since they

Educating His Son to Think for Himself

Rabbi Bill Rothschild, Jack's son, recalls how a prize-winning Atlanta journalist described his father's courage during the Temple bombing and the Civil Rights movement: "He had guts when it took guts to have guts." Rothschild was a widely respected Southern clergyman, so his invitation to the thirty year old young black minister M.L. King, Jr., to come to his home was a much appreciated sign of recognition.

Bill recalls how his father taught him to act morally in the face of the callous orders of authorities. When Bill was approximately eight years old the maid became very upset at their dog making a mess in the house. She ordered Bill to put the animal out of the house in the cold. Bill was upset so he called his father to consult. Rabbi Rothschild told him, listen to the maid and put the dog out. Bill followed his instructions. When the Rabbi came home he saw the shivering little dog freezing in the cold. He asked his son, who had followed the Rabbi's instructions against his own inclination, "Why did you listen to me? Didn't you see I was wrong?"

were, abruptly, to be treated with respect and the appearance of equality, it was as if each were the ambassador to the United States from some exotic, far-off kingdom, from Niger or Ethiopia. By the time the main course was served, whites and blacks were babbling at each other animatedly and passing the rolls hand to hand. The conversations took place on a plane that simply had not existed the night before and did not exist on this night anywhere else in the South.

Mayor Allen recalled, "Martin Luther King, Jr., was winner of the Nobel Prize, giving him every reason in the world to be somewhat bitter or pompous toward people who had spent much of their past lives fighting what he had dedicated his life to do. But he was a big man, a great man. He had arrived late for dinner, and I remember his leaning over and apologizing to me."

"'I forgot what time we were on,' he said with a grin.

"'How's that?' I said.

"'Eastern Standard Time, CST, or CPT.'

"'CPT?'

"'Colored People's Time,' he said. 'It always take us longer to get where we're going.'"

Rabbi Rothschild opened the festivities. He praised the assembly for being there:

> You attest the truth that goodness and righteousness do reside in the human heart. You give the lie to the canard that prejudice is always stronger than decency, that hate is more powerful than love.
>
> You — rich and poor, Jew and Christian, black and white, professional and lay, men and women from every walk of life — you represent the true heart of a great city. You are Atlanta. You — and not the noisy rabble with their sheets and signs now slogging sullenly the sidewalks beyond these doors. Here is a truth we must resolve never to forget. Let none of us ever again fear to summon this truth so simply, so eloquently and so forcefully brought home to us tonight by our presence here.

After other speakers honoring King spoke, Rothschild had the floor again, since the presentation of the city's gift fell to him. He told a story from Jewish tradition, the legend of Adam terrified by darkness at the end of his first day of life. God tells him to grab two stones, the rock of Despair and the rock of Death, and to rub them together. As Adam does so, the friction sends up sparks and the first fire is lit.

> We are coming to understand that our hands, too, must seize the cold stones of Darkness and Despair and from them strike the flame that will guide mankind from the gloom of despair to the radiance of hope. We pray that together you and we — and all decent men everywhere — may bring dignity of soul, nobility of heart, and tranquility of spirit to every child of God — and thus ensure brotherhood and peace in all the world.

"At [the] end," said Rothschild, "almost fifteen hundred people — white and black,

Jew and Christian, rich and poor, humble workers and great ladies — rose, joined hands and sang 'We Shall Overcome.'" The whites, rather remarkably (perhaps it was from having seen TV footage) knew the melody and verses. Coretta Scott King would remember that moment as "the most surprising of all the tributes" connected with the Nobel Prize. "It was tremendously moving," she wrote, "the spirit of it. We had overcome a major barrier for a southern city. We felt, for that night at least, it was really 'black and white together' in Atlanta."

"That dinner proved to be an indescribably magnificent event," Rothschild later said. "I remember this occasion vividly and speak of it with pride and warmth because even though it may seem a small thing, it was for us the

---

When he walked on that pulpit and he opened his mouth, it was as if Amos, Isaiah, Jeremiah, they were all right there. It was hands-on: do what we can to make it right.

---

climactic event of triumph and hope after years of struggle and heartache."

[Many recalled Martin Luther King's speech] eighteen months earlier, standing before the Lincoln Memorial in Washington, D.C. above a dark sea of people: **"I have a dream that one day on the red hills of Georgia, the sons of former slaves and the sons of former slaveowners will be able to sit down together at the table of brotherhood."** That night they turned up at the door, found their tables, pulled out their chairs, sat down, and ate. They ate at the table of brotherhood. And in a great many ways that night altered Atlanta, and thereby the South, forever.

An Epitaph for a Reform Prophet

"As I think of Jack Rothschild, I think of the civil rights movement, and I think of the prophets," said Rabbi Alvin Sugarman. "His was an absolute prophetic course. When he walked on that pulpit and he opened his mouth, it was as if Amos, Isaiah, Jeremiah, they were all right there. It was hands-on: do what we can to make it right. So his source — his rabbinic authority — and his human authority merged.

"And that had an incredible impact on the congregation and on my life, notwithstanding that for many, many years, walking out after services you heard, 'He's talking about civil rights again.' So there was this subtext of murmurs, and some of it probably wasn't so quiet. After his death, you heard: 'Our rabbi, he had the courage to stand out and fight, speak up and do the right thing. He was a force in the civil rights movement.' It was like an artist whose works, after his death, became masterpieces. For me there was an incredible blending: when you heard him speak, it was Jack Rothschild, it was Amos."

Rothschild in his last guest sermon at Hebrew Union College in Cincinnati said, "For these many years I have labored to bring about the fulfillment of **the prophetic ideal: one God in Heaven, one humanity on earth.**"

THE COMMUNITY ORGANIZER, SAUL ALINSKY

"LET THEM CALL ME REBEL"

by Sanford Horwitt[19]

"Let them call me rebel and welcome, I feel no concern from it;
but I should suffer the misery of devils, were I to make a whore of my soul."

— THOMAS PAINE, AS QUOTED BY SAUL ALINSKY

"The **Organizer**, there is no higher calling in a free and open society! It is the Organizer's job to build People's Organizations which are all inclusive. It can be done only by those who believe in, have faith in, and are willing to make every sacrifice for the people. Those who see fearlessly and clearly; they will be your radicals.

"Sound it now. Whether it be the hoarse voice, the bell, the written word or the trumpet, let it come. Sound it clear and unwavering. Reveille for Radicals."

— SAUL ALINSKY

INTRODUCTION:
THE RADICAL COMMUNITY ORGANIZER AS HERO

Saul Alinsky first burst upon the national scene in 1945 with a best selling book, **Reveille for Radicals**, a passionate account of how he had established "People's Organizations" in industrial slums, most notably in Chicago. Alinsky took a phrase from the dull vocabulary of social work — "community organization" — and turned it into something controversial, important, even romantic. "We the people will work out our own destiny" was the rallying cry and motto of the Neighborhood Council, which Alinsky organized in the summer of 1939. During the next four decades, he and his lieutenants taught people in other communities throughout the country how to organize to better their lives and working conditions. Everywhere they went they won fame for their efforts to help poor people and others help themselves.

Indeed, Alinsky had invented a new political form, and in the 1960s, his star rose to new heights amid the turmoil of that decade. Alinsky-style community organization came to suggest David-and-Goliath struggles marked by colorful, confrontational tactics: dumping a mound of garbage in front of a tavern owned by the wife of an alderman to protest his unresponsiveness to complaints of inadequate garbage pickup, or dispatching black tenants of a run-down tenement to picket the white suburban home of the slumlord who had refused to make necessary repairs. He also pioneered the use of stockholdings by churches and others to help promote socially responsible policies on the part of corporations. Alinsky's **urban populism** was immensely attractive and successful, but idiosyncratic as the man himself.

The Measure of a "Man":
Young Alinsky's First Test

"I was born in one of the worst slums in Chicago. We were poor — my parents were Russian immigrants, Jewish and very orthodox. [My mother] was only seventeen when she had me. As a kid I remember living in back of a store. My idea of luxury was to live in a apartment where I could use the bathroom without one of my parents banging on the door for me to get out because a customer wanted to get in."

In the 1920's Saul remembered invading gangs of Polish boys "storming into our

19. Sanford Horwitt, *Let Them Call Me Rebel: Saul Alinsky — His Life and Legacy*, pp. 167, 174, 176, 221, 467, 540-541. Reprinted by permission of Alfred A. Knopf, © 1989.

neighborhood and we'd get up on the roofs with piles of bricks and pans of boiling water and slingshots, just like a medieval siege. I had an air rifle myself. There'd be a bloody battle for blocks around and some people on both sides had real guns, so sometimes there'd be fatalities." Gangs of Jewish boys would retaliate by invading the Polish territory.

In Alinsky's final analysis it came down to a question of manhood. **The measure of a man was his bravery, his fearlessness, his courage, his strength.** Ten-year-old Sollie, whose own father was such a weak, forlorn figure, would go into the pool hall on Twelfth Street, around the corner from Alinsky's apartment, where the older, tougher neighborhood guys hung out. One of the older guys would tell the ten-year-old to raise his arm and flex his muscle and, feeling it, would say to Sollie, "No, you're not ready yet, kid, to fight the Polacks." This little ritual went on for several years, until one day, when Sollie was thirteen or fourteen, one of the guys in the pool hall felt his muscle and told him he was ready now, that he had made it. It was a day Saul Alinsky never forgot, the day he became a man.

When he was twelve years old and living on the old West Side, one day a friend was jumped and beaten by three kids from the nearby Polish neighborhood west of Crawford Avenue. "So naturally we went on the hunt and found a couple of Poles," Alinsky remembered. "We were merrily beating them up when the police suddenly appeared and arrested all of us." The boys were taken to the police station, where their mothers soon appeared, screaming as to how the boys had disgraced their families and would be punished when they got home.

But Alinsky's mother first took her son to their rabbi, and the rabbi lectured him about how wrong he was. Young Sollie defended himself. "'They beat my friend up,' I said. 'So we beat them up. That's the American way. It's also in the Old Testament: an eye for an eye, a tooth for a tooth. Beat the hell out

of them. That's what everybody does.' The rabbi answered, 'You think you're a man because you do what everybody does. Now I want to tell you something the great Rabbi Hillel said: *"Where there are no men, be thou a man."* I want you to remember that.' I've never forgotten it," Alinsky said, a lifetime later.

Saul in the Footsteps of Moses

*When Moses had grown up, he went out to his brothers and witnessed their suffering. He saw an Egyptian beating a Hebrew, one of his brothers. He looked this way and that way and saw that **there was no man**. So he struck the Egyptian and hid him in the sand. When Pharaoh learned of the matter he sought to kill Moses. Moses fled . . . .*[20]

By 1935, after graduating the University of Chicago, twenty-six-year-old Saul Alinsky seemed to be on his way to a career as a criminologist. He had done a splendid job working with delinquents on the streets of the near West Side. Then he got a job within the establishment in the Joliet prison [but he didn't stay there long].

One story that Alinsky told to friends was that he was kicked out of Joliet prison because he physically attacked a prison guard in an angry rage. Seeing the guard, a burly two-hundred-pounder, giving an unmerciful beating to a young, scrawny inmate, Alinsky jumped on the guard's back, slammed him down, and beat his head to the floor repeatedly. Alinsky said he might have killed the guard if someone hadn't pulled him off. The incident, Alinsky told friends, forced an internal investigation of sadistic behavior by prison guards — but also forced Alinsky's exile from the prison system. [The story sounds like the young Moshe who beat and killed an Egyptian taskmaster and then fled to the desert. There he received a revelation and returned to Egypt with a plan and some powerful Divine backing.]

Alinsky once asserted that in ancient times

Never doubt that a small group of thoughtful, committed citizens can change the world: indeed, it's the only thing that ever does.

— MARGARET MEAD, ANTHROPOLOGIST

20. *Exodus* 2:11-15

men of action [like Moses] periodically went off into the wilderness to reflect on their experiences. "Well, my wilderness turned out to be a jail in a Middle Western city where I was organizing people living in a miserable slum. There was this police captain who was very anti-labor who figured my mere presence would contaminate his town. So whenever I walked down the main drag a squad car would pull up and I'd be invited in. They never booked me — just tossed me in the clink for safekeeping. I got used to it. I'd say to the jailer, 'Will you please phone my hotel and tell them to expect a late arrival.' I had a very good deal in that jail — I didn't suffer at all. I had a private cell; they treated me very nicely. Now there's no place that is better designed for reflective thinking and writing than a jail. The only way you can escape is mentally. So you're attracted to writing. It becomes a compulsion. I wrote *Reveille for Radicals* in that jail. Sometimes the jailers would tell me to get out when I was in the middle of a chapter. I'd tell them, 'I don't want to go now, I've a couple of hours more work to do.'"

Voter Registration and The Chicago Machine (1961)

After successfully organizing Irish Catholic neighborhoods, Alinsky became the first man to

What's the Difference Between a "Radical" and a "Liberal"?

Radicals are not to be confused with liberals, who do not have the passion, the unfettered commitment to the underdog and downtrodden. "Liberals like people with their head" was the kindest thing Alinsky could say about them. "Radicals like people with both their head and their heart."

Or since there are always at least two sides to every question and all justice on one side involves a certain degree of injustice to the other side, liberals are hesitant to act. Their opinions are studded with "but on the other hand." Caught on the horns of this dilemma they are paralyzed into immobility. They become utterly incapable of action. They discuss and discuss and end in disgust.

organize an African American slum. The neighborhood was called Woodlawn and his community worker was Nicholas von Hoffman. Alinsky knew that an organization needs inspiration and a dramatic case. He found the inspiration in the Freedom Riders and the concrete cause in voter registration in the all-white corrupt political machine in Cook County, Chicago.

[In 1961 the Freedom Riders were an interracial group organized after] the Supreme Court had outlawed segregation in interstate transportation, including bus and train terminals, but the decision was being widely ignored in much of the South. The **Freedom Riders** traveled through several Southern states without major incident until they arrived in Anniston, Alabama, where a mob burned one bus and beat up the passengers in another. When more Freedom Riders arrived in Montgomery, they were greeted with even worse violence — an ax-and-chain-wielding crowd circled the bus terminal and attacked the Freedom Riders as they got off their Greyhound bus. Attorney General Robert F. Kennedy shortly dispatched five hundred federal marshals to Montgomery to protect both them and Martin Luther King, Jr. By the time the Freedom Ride ended in Mississippi, it had become one of the most dramatic episodes yet of the civil rights movement, the courage and determination of the Riders inspiring blacks and sympathetic whites throughout the United States. [Later three Freedom Riders, one black and two Jews, were murdered and their case is the basis of the dramatic movie "*Mississippi Burning.*"]

Saul Alinsky spotted an opportunity to capitalize on — and test — the growing identification of Woodlawn residents with the civil rights movement in the South — a Voter Registration Drive. As a consequence of a partisan feud in the Illinois state legislature over charges of vote fraud in Cook County, the voter registration lists were wiped clean and every eligible voter in Chicago had to register again before he could vote in the next election. The moment that Saul heard about

A young Protestant clergyman who worked with Caesar Chavez and the California migrant workers describes Saul Alinsky's training sessions and his use of Biblical examples for the clergy of the Migrant Mission:

"Saul's basic question was, 'Who is calling the shots [in a community] and how do they call them?' His discussion helped us all to grow into an understanding of what the real world was all about." "Most of us were raised nice middle-class boys, and [in our experience] everybody likes everybody else, nobody gets too mad at anybody — and the people in the Migrant Ministry were probably like that." Alinsky was more than willing to disabuse them of any expectation that Christian love would dissolve the differences between migrants and the growers. Alinsky was teaching them tough-mindedness as much as teaching techniques. "It was just getting accustomed to the fact that there was an enemy out there and that the enemy was willing to use all kinds of methods to attack you personally, to attack your organization, to try and take your financing away, all the things that the growers did."

Alinsky was also determined to smash illusions the ministers had about their own motives. "He felt very strongly that if you are a do-gooder, you're never going to make it, and don't kid yourself that you are committed to helping others, because you are primarily interested in helping yourself. You had better get to the root of your own motives, because you are not going to save yourself by helping somebody else."

Alinsky's humor, wit, and playful irreverence enlivened his meetings with clergy. He would tell the clergy that the Bible ought to be read as an organizer's training manual and that much could be learned from Moses and Paul, two terrific organizers (Alinsky admitted his bias for Moses). Then, with tongue partially in cheek, he would spin out an analysis of, say, an exchange between Moses and God when the Jews had begun to worship the Golden Calf. Moses, like any good organizer, never relied only on facts or ethics to persuade. "Moses did not try to communicate with God in terms of mercy or justice, when God was angry and wanted to destroy the Jews," Alinsky explained, noting that:

A great organizer, like Moses, never loses his cool as a lesser man might have done when God said, *"Go

it, Alinsky and [his community organizer] Nicholas von Hoffman invented their own version of the Freedom Ride. They would organize a large bus caravan from Woodlawn to City Hall to register voters. Of course, success depended entirely on getting a huge turnout of black voters.

Most of the organizing for the bus caravan was crammed into several weeks, and much of the energy went into fund-raising. "The Woodlawn Organization never put up any money for [this] because you knew that you'd never fill a bus unless the people who are going to ride in the bus pay for it," von Hoffman says. "So we had these endless fund-raisers for the buses. One apartment house after another. We had chicken dinners, barbecues, we even had hookers running fund-raisers." As the Saturday of the big event drew near, Alinsky and von Hoffman did not want anything left to chance. "We wanted a list of every name, of every person who was going to be on every bus. And their address," von Hoffman remembers. With only several days to go before the buses were to roll, von Hoffman's hopes and fears gyrated wildly. He had upped the number of buses that he ordered to twenty, then to thirty, and finally to more than forty. The lists of people were looking good, but the complexity of the operation scared him.

On the morning of the event, hundreds of people were scheduled for wake-up phone calls and buses had to make pickups at specific places and times, though many drivers did not know the area. "In many instances, we were working with people who had never been in any organization bigger than a crap game," he says. With the final preparations in place, the first near-disaster struck when the Chicago Transit Authority, under the control of City Hall, called to down! Your people, whom you brought out of the land of Egypt, has sinned." If Moses had dropped his cool, one would have expected him to reply, "Where do you get off with all that stuff about *my* people whom *I* brought out of the land of Egypt? . . . Who started that bush burning, and who told me to get those people out of slavery, and who pulled all the power plays, and all the plagues, and who split the Red Sea?" But Moses kept his cool, and he knew that the most important center of his attack would have to be on God's prime value — that God wanted to be No. 1. All through the Old Testament one bumps into *"There shall be no other gods before me," "Thou shalt not worship false gods."*

At this point, trying to figure out Moses's motivations, one would wonder whether it was because he was loyal to his own people, or felt sorry for them, or whether he just didn't want the job of breeding a whole new people, because after all he was pushing 120 and that's asking for a lot. At any rate, he began to negotiate, saying, "Look, God, you're God. Whatever you want to do you can do. But you promised them not only to take them out of slavery, but that they would practically inherit the earth. Yeah, I know, you're going to tell me that they broke their end of it so all bets are off. But it isn't easy. The news of this deal has leaked out all over the joint. The Egyptians, Philistines, Canaanites, *everybody* knows about it. But go ahead and knock them off. What do you care if people are going to say, 'There goes God; you can't make a deal with him. His word isn't even worth the stone it's written on.' But after all, you're God and I suppose you can handle it." . . . *"And the Lord repented from doing the evil which he had spoken against his people."*

As much fun as all this was, many of the clergy found it difficult to accept Alinsky's theory that nobody operates outside of his self-interest, and many of them were troubled by his ideas about the use of conflict. If you are going to arouse people who are demoralized and apathetic — whether in a meat-packing plant or a community — **you have to "agitate to the point of conflict,"** he would say bluntly, "fan resentments" and "rub raw the resentments." His trinity was conflict, organization, and power. But I still think "that Saul was one of the biggest idealists there ever was."

cancel all the buses it had agreed to rent. A mad scramble ensued, with von Hoffman scrounging buses from suburban transit systems and from the archdiocese.

[Finally when von Hoffman came to] the morning's rendezvous point, his eyes fixed on "the most satisfying scene I have ever seen in my life. As far as the eye could see, buses, all jammed with black persons. Every bus was draped with a banner saying 'Better Housing' or 'Jobs' or 'Vote'." The caravan headed toward City Hall with forty-six buses and more than 2,500 black passengers.

> Suddenly and unexpectedly, the black cops were confronted by a posse of white Irish cops. Father Egan sprang from the car in full priestly attire, smoothing things over and averting still another possible disaster.

The first stop the bus caravan made on its way to City Hall had been planned so that the *Chicago Daily News* reporter who was in the lead bus, could phone in a story to meet an early deadline. The second stop was not planned. The caravan was escorted by black motorcycle cops and behind them were a convertible filled with black leaders, von Hoffman, white Father Jack Egan and a bus carrying a generous number of nuns. In tight situations in Chicago, you couldn't be too Catholic, was Alinsky's commonsense philosophy. Suddenly and unexpectedly, the black cops were confronted by a posse of white Irish cops. Father Egan sprang from the car in full priestly attire, smoothing things over and averting still another possible disaster.

But as the contingent came within sight of City Hall, they saw more police who seemed eager to do battle on this otherwise quiet late-summer Saturday. In fact, City Hall was ringed by policemen, and Jack Egan had heard a rumor that many more heavily armed reinforcements were at the ready in the basement of City Hall. As the buses were parked and the riders started to get out, von Hoffman spotted Marshall Korshak, the usually unflappable, hard-bitten Democratic committeeman of the 5th Ward. Von Hoffman hollered to him: "Hey, what are you going to do, Marshall, machine-gun the nuns? These people are all your voters." "It's a mistake, it's a mistake," Korshak chanted, a kind of political prayer, it seemed, in the circumstances. "Yes, it is a mistake," von Hoffman said, "and you better do something about it. They haven't come here to burn the place down, which they should do. Maybe next time they will, but this time they want to register to vote — even the nuns."

The parked buses surrounded City Hall, too. Inside, it took most of the day for Election Commissioner and forty-five extra clerks to register everybody. It was the largest single voter-registration event ever at City Hall. If one understands that Chicago's religion is politics, then one can also appreciate why the capacity to deliver votes in unprecedented numbers might attract as much of the city's attention as other supernatural acts — such as, say, the capacity

"Do you know that one of your neighbors is a slum landlord?" the picket signs and flyers asked. "He is Julius Mark, 2409 East Seventy-third Street. He leases and won't fix a slum at 6434 South Kimbark, where the tenants are so mad they've called a rent strike."

to walk on water. It was not something that the mayor could ignore. (In 1960, Richard J. Daley's efforts had helped to elect John F. Kennedy as President. Kennedy won Illinois by only 8,858 votes. Woodlawn's plurality for Kennedy was about 17,000). No, the mayor could not ignore a forty-six-bus caravan of 2,500 Woodlawn voters.

Tracking Down the Slumlords

A new tactic which the Woodlawn Organization used to pressure slum landlords was quintessentially Alinsky. In addition to rent strikes, they began to picket the (often white) landlord who refused to repair heating systems or broken water pipes, but instead of picketing in front of the slum building in Woodlawn, a delegation — black people, mostly, with only a few white clergy sprinkled in — traveled to the landlord's white neighborhood to picket his house and pass out flyers to his neighbors. "Do you know that one of your neighbors is a slum landlord?" the picket signs and flyers asked. "He is Julius Mark, 2409 East Seventy-third Street. He leases and won't fix a slum at 6434 South Kimbark, where the tenants are so mad they've called a rent strike."

Like all the other demonstrations, the residential picketing was carefully planned. Von Hoffman called the police in advance to tell them that there would be peaceful picketing. The media were notified. Later, in recounting the psychology of the tactic to reporters, Alinsky remarked, deadpan: "For this assignment, we practically used a color chart in Woodlawn to recruit pickets. We wanted to use only the darkest Negroes." The residential picketing by blacks usually produced results. Not only was the landlord embarrassed but his neighbors were furious if not hysterical. Once again, Alinsky and his organizers used white fear and loathing of blacks to best advantage. **For every positive there is a negative, and vice versa: this was one of Alinsky's fundamental operating principles. If blacks suffered discrimination because of their skin color, then, he said, there must be a way to "flip the coin" to their advantage.**

Alinsky also capitalized in other ways on white phobia about blacks intruding into their space. He forced banks, for example, to reveal the names of slum landlords who had tried to conceal their ownership by using corporate fronts. One of Saul's activists reported:

First the clergy would go in, with their collars on, for an appointment with the bank president. A very important part was when they would say, "Thank you gentlemen, but we're sorry, we can't help you." We'd say, "Thank you, Mr. President. Just remember we've been here and we asked nicely." That's it, and we'd leave. No sassiness, no threats. And then a group of our citizens would come and say, "The clergy were here and you wouldn't help them. What about us? We're homeowners in the area. Will you help us?" "Well, it's against bank policy." We'd have it all documented, how many times we went into these places. We used the regular methods for being open, thoughtful, decent, kind, all of the Boy Scout virtues, and everybody told us to go to hell. So we'd say, "All right, we have to use another way of communicating."

Alinsky's Message to the College Campus

In Cincinnati, Rabbi Levi Lauer recalls, the college students asked Alinsky how they could convince big grocery store chains to stop buying non-union grapes picked by corporate fruit growers in California who exploited the migrant Mexican workers paying very low salaries and refusing to give them any social benefits at all. The students were willing to picket the stores so long as they did not get themselves arrested. No, said Alinsky, don't bother to picket. After a grocery store chain refuses to cooperate on the boycott of non-union grapes, just send 16 students into a key store at the busiest time, have them collect mounds of items in their baskets, line up at every check out counter to clog up the store. Then let them "discover," to their chagrin, that they have "accidentally" forgotten to bring money and then just leave all the items at the counter. The confusion and client irritation at the delays promised to keep buyers away. Quickly the grocery store agreed to buy union grapes only, as long as there were no more problems at the checkout counter.

In Bob Jones University, the Bible-belt school in the South, students complained they weren't allowed to hold hands with their girl/boy friends in public and that public protest was forbidden. "What is permitted?" Alinsky asked. "Chewing gum," they said. "So warn the school and then ask everyone to chew 20 sticks of gum per day and stick them everywhere." After only four days the school gave in to their demands.

Saul said that there was a very simple way to do that. You just line up people to open new accounts in the bank, and you fill up the bank lobby, and do it peacefully. Train your people carefully. And you do that for two or three days, and tie up their business, and of course you scare the hell out of every white person coming to that bank when they see all these black people in there. We only had to do it once to one bank, and every other bank knew what would happen if it didn't cooperate. And they had been warned.

And that's how we did the bank thing. That's how we found out where those slum landlords — "slumlords" we called them — lived."

Because of this process, black pickets went into white communities [to challenge slumlords where they lived. The black activists did not] feel self-conscious about a publicity stunt, but acted with dignity, righteousness, and purpose in fighting for just a cause.

Charles Silberman in his famous expose *Crisis in White and Black* called Alinsky's Woodlawn project "the most important and the most impressive experiment affecting Negroes anywhere in the United States." Silberman went on. "A major part of the 'Negro problem' lies in what the last three hundred and fifty years have done to the Negro's personality: the self-hatred, the sense of impotence and inferiority that destroys aspiration and keeps the Negro locked in a prison we have all made." Alinsky's work in Woodlawn is the prime example of how poor blacks themselves could break the psychological shackles that inevitably limited their progress.

The Repertory Theater of Protest: The 1960's and the IgNobel Prize

Saul Alinsky was a true believer in the possibilities of American democracy as a means to social justice. He saw it as a great political game among competing interests, a game in which there were few fixed boundaries and where the rules could be changed to help make losers into winners and vice versa. He loved to play the game and had a special flair for it. During a lifetime of action and experimentation, he created a set of new tactics and strategies for playing the game — and, most important, excited the imagination of a succeeding generation of players to carry on. Alinsky's influence, relevance, and legacy live on in no small part because he effectively advanced the great American radical ideal that democracy is for ordinary people.

In using the media to best advantage, Alinsky could be counted on for a good one-liner, or a zinger deflating some pompous politician, or controversial broadsides that few others would deliver on the record. And he always made good copy. When he came to Rochester, New York, invited by white churches and the black community to build a community organization after the bloody race riot there in 1964, he infuriated executives of the Rochester-based Eastman Kodak firm with the line that "Kodak's only contribution to race relations was the invention of color film." A fan of his own mischief-making, Alinsky later recalled with delight the community uproar in Rochester that greeted his suggestion as to what might be the only way for poor blacks to get the attention of the smug, self-righteous establishment: they should purchase a large bloc of tickets to a performance of the Rochester symphony — but, just before arriving, they would all get together for a huge baked-bean dinner so that at the symphony, Alinsky deadpanned, their presence could not be ignored.

Saul's Weakspot: Fundraising

Generally Saul Alinsky's tactics worked better in political confrontations than in philanthropic fundraising, because he had the courage to tell off a donor — from Hollywood, for example. Alinsky recalls:

I found it was impossible to raise money among the picture people for this kind of work unless I spent five or six weeks selling them on the idea.

They were not too interested because there was no social prestige attached to making a contribution to the work, and they seemed to be a little frightened of the ungentlemanly tactics employed by our organizations. One picture person after another uses the term "Oh, well, so and so wasn't *important*." People out there are judged like chattels on the basis of their income or social position. I blew up with a producer, after he had used that phrase. I said, "I have never believed that there could be so many physically grown up people who are mentally adolescent, who are pathetically insecure, who are damnably maladjusted, and who are completely inhuman as yourself and those that are associated with you and your industry." I walked out without a contribution.

[An] important picture guy [with a] very cynical look on his face said, "Alinsky, you're talking about all these poor people and how you feel about them. You seem to be well dressed and as a matter of fact. I noticed the wristwatch you are wearing. If I'm not mistaken, that's an Audemar Piquet, which happens to be one of the most expensive watches made in the world." He then leaned back and literally leered. I glanced down at the face of my watch. Then without a word I unstrapped the watch and handed it to him with the back side up and waited until he read the inscription, *"To Saul Alinsky from Chicago's Packinghouse Workers,"* etc. etc. I then reached over, took the watch back, looked at his face, which was the color of a full-ripened cherry, turned around and walked out. I guess I don't have the tact for money raising.

College student activists in the 1960s and 1970s sought out Alinsky for advice about tactics and strategy. On one such occasion, in the spring of 1972, at Tulane University's annual week long series of events featuring leading public figures, students asked Alinsky to help plan a protest of a scheduled speech by George Bush, then U.S. representative to the United Nations, a speech likely to include a defense of the Nixon administration's Vietnam War policies. The students told Alinsky they were thinking about picketing or disrupting Bush's address. That's the wrong approach, he rejoined, not very creative — and besides, causing a disruption might get them thrown out of school. He told them, instead, to go to

The organizer's goal [is] to create a setting in which victimized people could experience and express their self-worth, power and dignity.

hear the speech dressed as members of the Ku Klux Klan, and whenever Bush said something in defense of the Vietnam War, they should cheer and wave placards reading "The KKK Supports Bush." And that is what the students did, with very successful, attention-getting results.

[As Saul Alinsky taught, in each situation you need to show the seemingly powerless side that they actually have leverage over the so-called powerful side.] "You need [the opposition] for a very important organizing tactic which I call mass *jujitsu*," Alinsky explained. Recalling recent episodes in the civil rights struggle, he said:

A Bull Connor with his police dogs and fire hoses down in Birmingham did more to advance civil rights than the civil rights fighters themselves. The same thing goes with the march from Selma to Montgomery. Imagine what would have happened if instead of stopping the marchers that first day with clubs and tear gas, chief state trooper Lingo had courteously offered to provide protection and let them proceed. By night the TV cameras would have gone

back to New York and there would have been no national crises to bring religious leaders, liberals, and civil rights fighters from the North into Selma, Alabama. I've always thought that just as King got the Nobel Prize there should be an IgNobel prize for people like Governor Wallace of Alabama and Governor Barnett of Mississippi.

[All these antics were part of Alinsky's heroics. His book] *Reveille for Radicals* was aimed at would-be **hero-organizers**. One could almost envision Alinsky's organizer flying high in a Superman cape, swooping into a forlorn industrial community, ready to fight for "truth, justice and the American Way!" Clearly, Alinsky saw the organizer — especially himself — in heroic terms, leading the "war against the social menaces of mankind." **There was much in his concept of the organizer that *was*, indeed, heroic, for fundamentally the organizer's goal was to create a setting in which victimized people could experience and express their self-worth, power and dignity.**

Saul Alinsky with his protégé Nicholas von Hoffman in Alinsky's office, late 1950s.

The Epitaph for Saul Alinsky:
"'Here lies the man who antagonized more people than any contemporary American' — He would consider it high praise."

— Irv Kupcinet, Chicago columnist

"Silence is Deadly"

Rabbi Marshall Meyer and Argentina's Reign of Terror (1976-1983)[21]

> "It is a religious obligation. If you accept the Bible, then human rights is an obligation. You cannot take the thrust of the biblical literature and keep quiet."
>
> "In order for new ideas to be born, new actions have to be forged in the smithy of our souls, we have to be prepared to rethink our positions with regard to many things even some of our most cherished ideas. Genuine creativity is reserved for those **brave souls** who are capable of changing their minds and their feelings. Who is willing to risk changing hatred to love, inflexibility to patience, elasticity and understanding."
>
> — Rabbi Marshall Meyer

Renewing Judaism in Argentina

In 1959, Meyer, a 29-year-old New York-born rabbi, arrived from the United States with his wife, and a book on elementary Spanish. He intended to stay for two years, but he stayed until 1985 during the most morally challenging period in Argentinian history when a right wing anti-semitic military government terrorized its people.

"I am an anti-Establishment man," said Marshall Meyer. By nature outspoken and political, he was regarded by the Jewish "establishment" with a mix of hostility, envy, and amazement. At the time of Meyer's arrival, Jews who wanted to affiliate had few options. Almost all temples were Orthodox, with rabbis who had superb Talmudic training, but who lacked secular higher education. As a result, most Jews avoided synagogues. But underneath was spiritual yearning. Meyer, they say, was like a gift from God. His services galvanized the community, particularly the young. A protege of [the American spiritual and moral leader Rabbi] Abraham Joshua Heschel, Meyer founded the first Conservative rabbinical seminary (Seminario Rabbinico) in Latin America (later renamed in his honor) and the unprecedented Bet El, a synagogue rooted in the Prophetic Tradition and Liberation Theology. [M.F.]

Rabbi Meyer's example became a beacon of hope for Jewish youth and their families. His integrity and moral conscience became a force, which brought many into the synagogue and Seminario. **He permanently changed the image of the Latin American rabbi.** In those dark days of the military juntas, few in the Jewish community spoke out as openly and as often as he did. His position gave him a public platform for articulating his views. Meyer certainly was not alone among the Jewish leadership in decrying the actions of the military governments, but his public pronouncements were constant and distinctive, and he was unique in his calls for justice and action based in the teachings of Judaism. The Friday evening service at Bet El during this period was more than a religious service, it was a religious

---

21. This biography is a composite of several sources used by permission:

M.F. = Margarite Feitlowitz, "Life Here is Normal," *A Lexicon of Terror*, by permission of Oxford University Press, p. 99.

R.F. = Richard Freund, From "Somos Testigos — We are Witnesses: The Jewish Theology of Liberation of Rabbi Marshall T. Meyer," Conservative Judaism, 47:1, Fall, 1994, p. 36. Professor Richard Freund is the Maurice Greenberg Professor and Director, Greenberg Center for Judaic Studies at the University of Hartford. He directed the Seminario Rabinico Latinoamericano in Buenos Aires, Argentina from 1983-1986.

L.R. = Louis Rapport, used by permission of the Jerusalem Post, Dec. 10, 1982.

M.T. = Moshe Tutenauer's personal recollections.

G.M. = Gabi Meyer's personal recollections of his father, paraphrased from the editor's interview with him in 1999. Gabriel and his mother Naomi Meyer were very helpful in preparing this profile and in providing photographs.

Marshall Meyer
(courtesy of Naomi Meyer)

revival with nearly a thousand in attendance most weeks. Meyer's actions and words defined what would be the continuing Seminario **legacy of the rabbi: a person of courage, conscience, and action**. [R.F.]

A Prophetic Voice from the Pulpit

From his pulpit, Meyer openly denounced the generals and their Dirty War. Services overflowed, and not only with Jews: Catholics, Protestants, atheists, and of course members of the Secret Service came to hear Meyer's views. He received death threats every week, but still met with relatives of the disappeared, visited jails and marched with the Mothers of the Plaza de Mayo. Yet he agonized

that he was endangering the community. He meditated on his mentor, Heschel, who had angered some Jews by marching on Shabbat [for civil rights] with Martin Luther King. **"I'm praying with my feet,"** Heschel replied to those who charged that he should have been in *shul*. "So how could I stop?" Meyer asked, rhetorically. "I knew that my teacher, a *tzaddik* [a righteous man], would have told me, **'You'll endanger their souls if you are silent.'**"

"My political position," stated Meyer, "was very clear, and I said it to the leader of the Argentine Jewish Community: 'You don't have cordial relations with Hitler.'"

"It's not that I think the Jewish leaders were evil, but

they were silent, acquiescent. They are guilty of sins of omission, which in Jewish law are as bad as sins of commission." The **specter of acts omitted** — and committed — by the leadership still haunts the Jewish community. [M.F.] Marshall remarked: "Silence is deadly. Where certain Jewish organizations made a mistake was in counselling silence — not out of cowardice, but because they didn't read the barometer correctly. Their policy was not to get involved with the 'disappeared.' I believed it was not a question of quiet diplomacy. I believed it required every ounce of one's strength. And it was in response to everything that I understood to be sacred and primary in Judaism, which is the sanctity of human life, whether they were Jews or Christians or atheists or whatever." [L.R.]

Like Amos and Isaiah, Marshall's concerns went beyond the politically persecuted to the poverty-stricken who suffered under the regime of unrestrained economic capitalism in Argentina. When Marshall established his popular synagogue — Bet El — in a fashionable Jewish neighborhood, he insisted that money should simultaneously be raised both for the synagogue and the construction

---

When Marshall established his popular synagogue — Bet El — in a fashionable Jewish area, he insisted that money should simultaneously be raised both for the synagogue and the construction of a clinic in a poor shanty town.

---

of a clinic in a poor shanty town. Every week Marshall joined the local priest to drive out to that town and serve the poor people. When the synagogue construction had progressed and it was time to bring in the Torah scroll and deposit it in the new *aron kodesh* (the ark), the rabbi first demanded that the doctors in the synagogue join him in opening up the clinic in the shanty town. No ritual Torah scroll was sufficient without a living Torah of justice and mercy. [G.M.]

My Father: "If not a prophet, then the son of a prophet"
based on an interview with Gabriel Meyer, Marshall's son

I was born in Buenos Aires in 1966 and lived under the military regime (1976-1983). I remember that my parents would receive telephone calls — probably from right-wing vigilante groups — saying: "Your son Gabriel walks home from school at 4 p.m. every afternoon. He will disappear tomorrow." On the walls of the buildings were big antisemitic posters which said ominously: "Freud, Marx and Einstein — what do they have in common?" During the military regime anyone whose personal telephone book contained the number of someone who was accused of being connected to "subversive" activities could be arrested, tortured and then disappear without a trace.

When I visited my father's office I often found *"las madres de la Plaza de Mayo"* — the mothers of "the disappeared," those suspected activists kidnapped by the government and its right-wing gangs. These mothers wore a white kerchief on their head with the name of their "disappeared" son or daughter embroidered on it. Every Thursday they marched in silent but illegal protest in the Mayo Square before the dictators' headquarters.

They were pleading to know the whereabouts of their children and carried placards with pictures of the disappeared. One of the few to join the mothers of the disappeared regularly was my father. These mothers told me over and over what an angel my father was. He was one of the few with the courage to protest with them, one of the few who would really listen to their tales of anguish, and the first Jew they had met who as a Jew, as a rabbi, stood up for human rights of all faiths. When asked why he risked his own life with his behavior, my father merely insisted that as a Jew and a rabbi he had no choice: "If the Jews are no longer prophets, at least they are still the sons and daughters of prophets."[21]

At times my father's total identification

Gabriel Meyer (center) at demonstration of the Movimiento Judeo por los Derechos Humanos — Buenos Aires, 1983. *(courtesy of Naomi Meyer)*

discover contraband but really to humiliate him. All the time they insulted him with typical antisemitic epithets. Often they confiscated his Siddur or Tanach, claiming it was a form of subversive propaganda. On the walls he saw adoring pictures of Hitler and beyond the walls he heard the screams of tortured victims. One guard whispered ostentatiously, "that son-of-a-bitch will walk in here one day and he won't walk out."

Once inside the prison my father purposely tried to stray beyond the designated visiting areas in order to meet other prisoners, write down their names and stories and report back to their families who only knew they were missing. Once a 15 year old Jewish girl, whose brother had been executed at their home in front of her eyes, was arrested, tortured and imprisoned for three years merely because she had been a witness to this vigilante execution. When my father helped arrange for her release and travel abroad, he invited me to join him on the trip to the airport to see her off.

My family and friends would ask, "Aren't you afraid?" My father replied, "Yes, of course I am always afraid for myself and for my family. But I am not paralyzed by fear. I must act because I am a Jew who is commanded, *'justice, justice shall you pursue.'*"[22]

On Shabbat, my father's favorite time, he had loved to sing *nigunim*, tell stories and play with us. However the increasing persecutions took a special toll on him and his family. After a grueling week of listening to these terrible stories of persecution, Marshall would come home tired and deeply saddened and "unload" these accounts on his family and then at the synagogue on his congregation. Someone must listen, he felt. His congregants often complained that he ruined their Shabbat spirit. Some members of the congregation asked him to curtail his political activities and get back to the job of serving the Jewish community for which he had been hired. Marshall, who founded the shul, just

with the pain of the dictatorship's victims invaded the whole personal space of our family. Often there would be strangers sleeping on the living room floor. By the next night they were gone, soon to be replaced by others. This was one of the stops in the **"underground railroad"** that helped Argentines whose lives were in danger, to escape beyond the borders, often by virtue of connections carefully cultivated by my father with diplomats from abroad.

During the week, my father would visit some of the prisons using a permit he had extracted from the president on one of my father's many forays into the palace of the government to challenge the authorities. At the prison entrance the resentful guards would strip him naked, supposedly to

21. *Talmud*   22. *Deuteronomy* 16:20

shrugged and said, "Let them complain, or look for another rabbi. I have no choice about how to be a Jew in the world. They just do not understand the nature of my 'job.' The Mishna says, 'one who saves one human life is considered as if s/he had saved the entire universe.'"[23]

The price of my father's fame and infamy was sometimes exacted from us, his children. At age twelve I had been a popular outgoing boy in a Jewish elementary school. But then some of the parents of my schoolmates became fearful lest their children play with "the son of the human rights activist" for fear of guilt by association. My sisters were fearful about the possible consequences. But they were always proud of our father's actions and understood the real meaning of what living a Jewish life meant.

On the week of my Bar Mitzvah in 1979, I laid *tefillin* for the first time on Thursday and then on Friday my father took me to a unique initiation into adult responsibility. My father took me to meet the great Jewish journalist and critic of dictatorship — Jacobo Timmerman. Timmerman was under house arrest after having been tortured in jail. I remember his home-cum-prison surrounded by Ford Falcons, the car of the police. Inside were police living in Timmerman's home, eating from his refrigerator, reading his newspaper on his sofa and denying him any semblance of

private life. Later Timmerman was released and moved to Israel where he dedicated his book, *Prisoner without a Name, Cell without a Number,* "To Marshall Meyer, a rabbi who brought comfort to Jewish, Christian and atheist prisoners in Argentine jails."

[In educating his children, Marshall was trying to live up to Abraham's mandate: *"For I have singled him out, chosen him, to instruct his children and his household after him to keep the way of the Lord, the way of justice and right."*[24]] When I was 16 towards the end of the rule of the dictatorship, I myself became an activist campaigning for a civil rights lawyer running for parliament. The principal in my Jewish school warned the other students to ignore my "exaggerated rhetoric and dangerous ideas."

In those days I helped my father set up the first explicitly Jewish civil rights organization and organize the first-ever public demonstration against antisemitism in Catholic Argentina. As many in Argentina know, anyone could be arrested for suspected terrorist leanings — with or without any basis in evidence — but the Jews were more likely to suffer from worse beatings and degradation than anyone else. When my father and other Jewish activists approached important leaders of the Communist, Peronist and Socialist parties about the massive demonstration against antisemitism to be held in the center of town, all the parties agreed readily to join them. My father had proven that Jews would worry about any victim of the dictatorship no matter what their political or religious background. At the head of the demonstration stood the head of the "Mothers of the Mayo Square" and the Argentine Nobel peace prize winner, Adolfo Perez Esquivel, alongside my father, Rabbi Marshall Meyer. [G.M.]

After the Fall of the Dictatorship (1983)

In 1983 Marshall Meyer was the only non-Argentine named to the new democratic government's "National Commission on the Disappeared staffed by *outstanding citizens.*"

"I believe in the God of Rabbi Meyer"
BY RICHARD FREUND, PROFESSOR OF JEWISH THOUGHT

Marshall Meyer's influence during this period was profound. In 1985 I visited Tucuman, Argentina, a city some 1,000 miles north of Buenos Aires which had been one of the hottest spots of confrontation between the "terrorists" and the government. I had been invited to speak on "Modern Jewish Theology." During the question and answer period a man stood up and said: "My son disappeared under the last military regime. Rabbi Meyer came here in the midst of the repression in 1982 and stood where you are standing now and told me that God suffered because of my suffering and that [Rabbi Meyer] suffered because of my suffering. I tell you that even until this day **I believe in the God of Rabbi Meyer**."

---

23. *Sanhedrin* 4:5   24. *Genesis* 18:19

276

Marshall recalled: "I was informed of my nomination by a call from the President, Alfonsin. I told him I hoped it would not present any problems for him because I was an American citizen. He replied: 'I'll change the law.' I said: 'It's not necessary to do that. I'll collaborate anyway.' But he insisted that I must be on the National Commission on Disappeared Persons. Within three hours the law was rewritten so that 'outstanding citizens' was changed to 'outstanding personalities.'"

"The commission functioned for 18 months and presented to Dr. Alfonsin a 50,000-page report with incontrovertible proof of butchery, murder and disappearance of some 10,000 people (including more than 500 Jews) —

some of the most horrifying pages of human cruelty that one could read after the literature of the Holocaust. People being thrown alive from helicopters, people being drowned, tortured to death, pregnant women having their babies cut by cesarean section from their wombs, and the women being left to bleed to death while the babies were sold. (There was a black market in children). The book that the commission prepared is called *Nunca Mas* (Never Again), which, interestingly enough, was the call of the ghetto survivors."

"The perpetrators of the crimes have yet to be punished. It remains a kind of curse on the land. For example, a 15-year-old boy in my congregation went scuba diving in the

Rabbi Abraham Joshua Heschel and Prophetic Sympathy[25]

Marshall's mentor was no less than Rabbi Abraham Joshua Heschel, the neo-Hasidic theologian of modern life who taught at the Jewish Theological Seminary in NYC. Marshall served as his personal secretary and imbibed the theory and practice of the prophets, but he also learned the art of *chesed* — lovingkindness — from Heschel.

Once when Marshall had no place to go for seder except back to his bachelor apartment on the west side of Manhattan, he returned home to discover his revered teacher cooking soup and talking with Marshall's mother on the telephone trying to learn her recipe for *kneidlach*.

Heschel, who had lost his family and his whole Hasidic world in the Holocaust, took up the lonely path of the prophet in the United States as a very early activist for Soviet Jewry, for the civil rights movement and for the anti-Vietnam War Movement. In all these, he and his disciple Marshall Meyer tried to live up to the ideals of the prophet as Heschel described them:

✦ The prophet is a man who feels fiercely. Prophecy is the voice God has lent to the silent agony, a voice to the plundered poor, to the profaned riches of the world. It is a crossing point of God and the human. God is raging in the prophet's words.

✦ In contrast to the Stoic sage who is a *homo apathetikos*, the prophet may be characterized as a *homo sympathet-*

ikos. The pathos of God is upon him. It moves him. It breaks out in him like a storm in the soul, overwhelming his inner life, thoughts, feelings, wishes, and hopes. It takes possession of his heart and mind, giving him **the courage to act against the world**.

✦ Like a scream in the night is the prophet's word. The world is at ease and asleep, while the prophet is hit by a blast from heaven. No one seems to hear the distress in the world; no one seems to care when the poor is suppressed. But God is distressed, and the prophet has pity for God who cares for the distressed.

✦ A single crime — to us it is slight, but to the prophet — a disaster. The prophet's scream, which sounds hysterical to us, is like a subdued sigh to him. Exaggeration to us is understatement to him.

✦ The unique feature of religious sympathy is not self-conquest but **self-dedication**; not the suppression of emotion but its redirection; not silent subordination, but active cooperation with God.

✦ Sympathy is an act in which a person is open to the presence of another person. Prophetic sympathy is no delight; unlike ecstasy it is not a goal but a sense of challenge and a commitment.

25. From Fritz Rothschild's Selected Writings of A.J. Heschel entitled, *Between Heaven and Earth* (p. 125-126), which includes quotations from Heschel's *The Prophets*. Reprinted by permission of HarperCollins Publishers, © 1962.

Tigre River not long ago and swam into an inner circle of hell, discovering dozens of bloated bodies encased in concrete jackets. Shock treatment hasn't yet helped the youth to regain his mental health. I remember the reaction of a pregnant woman when her husband, a helicopter pilot, told her that he had dumped bodies into the sea: She broke a bottle and slit her throat in front of him."

"At my Conservative synagogue, a man who had survived Auschwitz came into the office and banged on the desk. He pleaded to say *Kaddish* — the prayer for the dead — for both his missing sons, a chemist and a physicist. I had to tell him that according to Jewish law, you can't say *Kaddish* if you don't know if your sons are dead or alive."

By 1984 after Marshall had completed 25 years in Argentina, he was a tired hero. When asked to explain why he left in 1984 he said: "I felt it was a rabbinic duty not to leave my people at a time when they were running the risk of being slaughtered. I've buried people under the right-wing regimes, and I've buried people killed by left-wing terrorists. I attended mothers during this period — if I were to take a count, I attended more Christians than Jews, but **I never asked a person who was in tears and agony whether she was Jew or Christian**. [But now that the danger is over I admit to:] "Exhaustion — spiritual, emotional, nervous, physical — exhaustion of all kinds. I just couldn't stand the pressure any longer. I had spent eight years visiting prisons, receiving mothers, and marrying and burying." [L.R.]

Back in NYC: Establishing a New Brand of Synagogue

When Marshall returned to New York City in 1985, he sought to apply insights from his experience with Argentine Jewry to revive a moribund synagogue on the West Side of Manhattan — the first Ashkenazi synagogue built in New York. The services at Bnai Jeshurun ("B.J.") were transformed with song and spirit, accompanied by a synthesizer and a Latin American beat.

Together with music and spirituality and his charisma, Marshall tried to build his renewed synagogue based on social commitment. His shul became a refuge for the homeless of New York, for the victims of AIDS and their families, and a center for political refugees, as well as a spiritual center for unaffiliated and single Jews seeking a more meaningful Jewish experience.

It grew from 30 to presently 1700 members with two Friday night services led by Marshall's Argentine successors.

"What am I doing here?"   BY RABBI MOSHE TUTENAUER

By the time I arrived, in August of 1983, the worst was over in Argentina. The military was about to give up power and elections were scheduled for October of that year, but the kidnappings and terror went on.

It was a warm spring day in September. I persuaded Marshall that we could have our conversation on the streets as well as in the office. So Marshall and I went for a walk. He, not I, spotted several gray cars, speeding around a corner and screeching to a stop about 100 yards from us. Marshall quickened the pace. He began to bark instructions to me. The cars, he said, were secret police. They were, he said, about to arrest someone. Marshall's plan was to pass by the cars just as the prisoner would be forced in. As we approached the parked cars, Marshall gave me my instructions: Remember the license number of every car on the left side of the street, remember what the police were wearing, remember how tall and heavy they were. Remember whatever you can about the one being arrested. Walk by, look sharply and keep going.

Two thoughts occurred to me as I listened to Marshall. The first: what am I doing here? This can be very dangerous and it is definitely not my fight. The second: what a brave man this is! He could have said: "These are Argentines and I am an American, these are Gentiles and I am a Rabbi." But for Marshall, these were human beings in trouble and he had a religious obligation to help them.

IN THE SERVICE OF HUMAN NEEDS: TZEDAKAH HEROES AND MIRACLE WORKERS

"The Good People"
by Danny Siegel[26]

The Good People everywhere
will teach anyone who wants to know
how to fix all things breaking and broken in this world —
including hearts and dreams —
and along the way we will learn such things as
why we are here
and what we are supposed to be doing
with our hands and minds and souls and our time.
That way, we can hope to find out why
we were given a human heart,
and that way, we can hope to know
the hearts of other human beings
and the heart of the world.

PREFACE: A TZEDAKAH HERO

Over two decades ago, the North American Jewish poet and Jewish educator **Danny Siegel** *began to use the evocative power of words to introduce young Jews to the poetry of "Tzedakah heroes." He identified and described movingly the individual efforts of incredible people — Jews and non-Jews, in Israel and North America — to help people in need. Not only did he seek to personalize the giving of* tzedakah, *which has become too institutionalized in organizational fund raising, but he wanted people, especially teenagers, to discover new Jewish role models. Danny discovered that the "ordinary" people who create and maintain* tzedakah *projects for the handicapped, the ill and the needy are heroic in their human dimensions. Yet basically anyone who desires to can step into their shoes and begin to be "tzedakah heroes."*

Ultimately Danny formed an independent tzedakah *fund called ZIV (which means "light") to gather support for these personal initiatives in* tzedakah *and gemilut chassadim (acts of lovingkindness). In this anthology we have told the tales of three of Danny's "discoveries:"* **Malky and Kalman Samuels** *who founded Beit Shalva, a center for mentally handicapped children, in Jerusalem;* **David Levitt**, *a sixth grader who created a massive leftover-food donation program in Florida (See page 67 in the companion volume,* The Hanukkah Book of Celebration); *and* **Jay Feinberg**, *a leukemia patient, whose family created an international donor registry for bone marrow transplants. In addition, we have included a story about* **Dawn Krieger**, *who like David Levitt, was 12 years old when she suddenly became a mature* tzedakah *hero. The story is written by Kathy Levin Shapiro who created a project to bring together teenagers and the elderly in nursing homes for a transformatory human relationship of give-and-take and friendship across the generations.*

---

26. Danny Siegel, gifted speaker, author of *Heroes and Miracle Workers* (1997) and *Tell Me a Mitzvah* and founder of Ziv Tzedakah Fund, Inc., a non-profit, tax-exempt corporation, administered by Naomi Eisenberger, 384 Wyoming Ave., Millburn, NJ 07041, 201-763-9396 (phone), 201-275-0346 (fax), naomike@aol.com (e-mail), www.ziv.org.

What seems to be true for all these tzedakah heroes, as Danny Siegel emphasizes, is that they do not feel they are extra-ordinary nor do they feel that they have been altruists sacrificing themselves for others. Rather they feel that they are doing what anyone can and should do and that they have received so much personally from the so-called beneficiaries of their help that there is no real self-sacrifice involved. In fact, the more energy one expends on"giving," the more energy one seems to have available to give.

4.

BEIT SHALVA'S FOUNDERS

MALKY AND KALMAN SAMUELS AND THE DREAM HOUSE FOR SPECIAL NEEDS CHILDREN (JERUSALEM, 1999)

by Sherry Makover[27]

For months, a newly religious painter covered the walls and the ceilings of the new Shalva Center with magical fairy tale themes. The artist, a former musician in an army troupe, has brought the walls to life with his cartoon characters and made this seven-story building in Jerusalem a wonder palace.

With only two million dollars, Kalman and Malky Samuels have created a paradise for children. The Samuels, who have themselves raised a blind deaf child, are aware of the difficulties involved in raising a handicapped child. They dreamt of a beautiful activity center for handicapped children to enhance their lives and the lives of their families by partially easing the burden.

Malky, 44, a homemaker, outlined the dream; Kalman, 47, a computer consultant for a scientific firm, has traveled all over the world seeking financial support. Friends and neighbors made fun of the Samuels' big dreams and small pockets. Kalman himself had his doubts. "I don't know that I can do it," he said to his wife Malky, but she, an unbelievable woman, answered by saying "I didn't ask if you could do it, I asked if you want to do it."

The construction of the new Shalva center with all its specialty rooms (especially the Sensory Room that translates the child's movements into music or colors) took three years to build. Malky, with no formal training, designed the building and supervised the furnishing, insisting that all would be today's most exciting design. Malky's supervision assured that all equipment is the latest in its field, in order to enrich the lives of these handicapped children. She was in the final stages of pregnancy, a tired mother of a hyperactive handicapped child that has six other siblings. Yet she made time to run from artisan to artisan, from merchant to merchant, from company to company, unwilling to settle for second best. Malky pointed out slight defects, and insisted that even the most remote corner be reached, "because I said to my husband, either we are a small cog in a machine, which is something that I do not want, or we are really doing something big here, and we are doing it wholeheartedly to perfection." When the final touches were put on the building, many neighborhood parents wanted their children to play at Shalva. However the Samuels allowed entrance by one criterion only, only the mentally handicapped may join Shalva.

---

27. Sherry Makover, "Malky and Kalman," by permission of Maariv (April 20, 1999, special section of Israeli heroes for the 51st anniversary of Statehood).

Yossi and his father Kalman at the Seder *(Courtesy of Beit Shalva)*

The First Contact
Through Sign Language

How did the idea for Shalva get started?

The credit goes to Yossi, Malky and Kalman Samuels' second child, who was born as a normal healthy baby. He was bright, responsive, and quite well developed. His parents called him Yossele, and thought that he was the most marvelous child in the world, actually, they still think so. At the age of 11 months Yossi received a standard vaccination. When Yossi got home his eyes began to twitch and his fever rose. "My wife cried that this was not her son," Kalman recalls, "but the doctor said that it was a simple virus and if the fever does not go down, go give the baby aspirin." Two weeks later, a neurologist found irreversible brain damage because of the vaccination, and Yossi, the healthy child, became blind, deaf and brain-damaged.

This all happened in 1977 when routine vaccinations caused a wave of brain damaged children across the country. When the cause of these injuries was discovered, the Ministry of Health stopped all vaccinations for a three-month period at which time, the supplier of this batch of tainted vaccinations was changed. For Yossi the change was too late.

For eight years Yossi lived in his own closed world; no one was able to penetrate his bubble. Because of his blindness and deafness, he developed slowly, while suffering from additional disabilities. Kalman recalls: "There was a severe feeling of 'we have lost our sweet clever child,' so much sorrow. Our lives changed completely. Our lives revolved completely around Yossi and we did not have one moment of peace and quiet. We were obligated to protect Yossi from himself and from others, but the most difficult part was to see him desolate and locked up in his own private world. A small child, lonely, with whom we could not communicate."

Malky remembers: "Many, with only the best intentions, said to us: 'Have mercy on your family and admit Yossi to an institution. He will harm your healthy children, and will make it very difficult to find a *Shiduch*' (a marital match for your other children within the Ultra-Orthodox world). 'Why ruin the entire family?' What they did not understand is that Yossi did quite the opposite. He united our family. Even then, when I did not know that this would be the case, I would attack anyone who dared suggest that Yossi be institutionalized. I said, 'As long as I live, Yossi shall live with me.' Simultaneously, we raised our other children, while explaining how special Yossi is, how loved and how wanted. The children absorbed this message, and would fight over the chance to take him for a walk, to play with him, to take him out for a pizza or a hamburger."

"It was difficult raising Yossi," says Malky, "Even the neighbors that knew him, thought that I was raising an E.T. (Extra Terrestial being) at home — a creature from outer space. One afternoon, Yossi ran into the

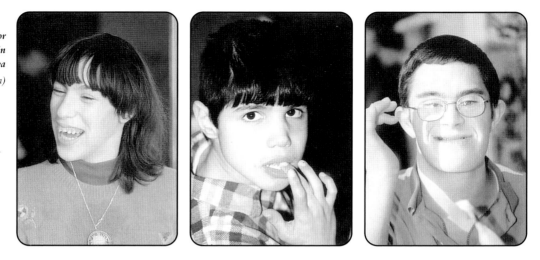

neighbor's garden and their children threw sand and water on him making him into a mud doll. When he came home, I saw only his tiny eyes peeking out of the mud and tears. Words cannot describe the utter despair that I felt. Then, I remembered the words a Rebbe once used: '*If it doesn't kill you — it strengthens you.*'"

"Malky cried a lot," says Kalman, "and through her tears she swore that if she succeeded in breaking through to Yossi's inner world, she would help parents of children in similar situations."

"Then, when Yossi was eight years old, in walked Shoshana Weinstock, a special education teacher for the deaf. She was the first one to break through Yossi's wall of silence, and teach him to communicate via sign language. I remember that day.

Shoshana was working with Yossi and she suddenly got up and started running and shouting: 'He understands! He understands!'

Shoshana was working with Yossi and she suddenly got up and started running and shouting: 'He understands! He understands!' When she calmed down, we learned that Yossi succeeded in connecting the Hebrew word "table"/*shulchan*, when signed to him in sign language, to the table itself. From that day, everything speeded forward. Yossi began

learning sign language. He was curious, and had a phenomenal memory. He immediately understood all that he newly learned. He enriched his language, and wanted to learn everything. He spoke to us freely, in sign language, and told us what he went through during the 'dark' years when communication was impossible. We talked, and cried, and cried and talked, we could barely grasp the extent of **our private miracle**." [This story is reminiscent of Anne Sullivan whose patient work and faith in Helen Keller suddenly opened Helen Keller up to the world.]

Round-the-Clock Care

This major change in Yossi's life greatly eased the Samuels' life. Malky remembered her promise and asked Kalman to help her open a unique care center for special children, to enable their parents at least a few hours of rest daily. Malky explains: "Only the parent of a handicapped child can understand why I thought mainly of the parents' time. A handicapped child must be protected, defended, comforted, loved, cherished and trained. This round-the-clock care takes so much physical and spiritual energy that many parents simply break."

So, in a small room, in a rented apartment, the Shalva Center was born — in its first format. Six handicapped children were invited for two hours daily. Malky was the driver that brought the children to Shalva and took them home, and the Samuels' children served as the escorts.

Slowly the hours of activity at Beit Shalva increased and became an entire afternoon. More and more children joined the activities. Kalman and Malky organized a small crew of volunteers and hired professional paramedical staff. The handicapped children and their parents had "Beit Shalva," a House of Tranquillity, a special social environment where they enjoyed many enriching activities. Later the children were also trained for future employment in a normal surrounding.

Two years later, Malky wanted more. She said, "If our goal is to allow parents to recharge their physical and emotional batteries in order to allow them to continue caring for their special child, we must have an overnight respite program and we must have summer camps. We need a large building and many specialty rooms." For three years, Malky had been planning the new "Beit Shalva" in her mind. "I have the center all planned. Now you take care of the financial backing," she said to her husband.

Malky sketched the plans for the five-story structure on stationary. She had no training as a designer or as an architect, but she knew intimately the special needs of the children, for whom the home was being built. Upon completion, the sketch was sent abroad, where Kalman was at his ill father's side in Canada. A few days later, Kalman met an old acquaintance while at the local synagogue, a wealthy Jew whose mother had just passed away. Kalman gathered his courage, pulled Malky's sketch out of his pocket, showed his

Hanukkah Candle Lighting at Beit Shalva-Beit Nachshon.
The new campus of Beit Shalva was named for Nachshon Wachsman, an Israeli soldier kidnapped by terrorists and killed in a daring attempt to free him. His brother attended Beit Shalva at an earlier location and therefore the new building was dedicated to Nachshon's memory. In the photograph at the extreme left is Nachshon's mother wearing a hat and next to her is Nava Barak, wife of Prime Minister Ehud Barak.

friend and told him of his wife's unrealistic dream. Like the Talmudic mystics who peeked in the Heavenly Garden of Eden and were captivated, the man fell in love with Malky's project. He told Kalman that he would provide the seed funding for this dream, if Kalman would promise that although he is very busy in his job, he would not hand this project over to others, but Kalman himself would take care of it.

The rest was easier. Kalman traveled all over the world, recruiting donations[28] to complete the building. Malky worked hand in hand with the building crew. Three years later the new Shalva Center was complete, all five floors. One hundred retarded children, Down Syndrome, autistic, CP, deaf and

---

One hundred retarded children, Down Syndrome, autistic, CP, deaf and hyperactive children — all streamed to Shalva and happily filled the many rooms in this multi-level structure.

---

hyperactive children — all streamed to Shalva and happily filled the many rooms in this multi-level structure. A staff of 65 professionals and volunteers await them to play with, guide, assist and teach them. The gates are open to all: ultra-Orthodox, secular, right wing and left wing. "I personally am religious," said Kalman Samuels, "but we do not force anything; people of their own accord respect each other."

"We too are Special"

"Every child in Shalva is a star," says Malky. But the most brilliant star in this marvelous place is without a doubt, Yossi Samuels. Today, Yossi is 22, blind and deaf, but remarkably intelligent. He communicates with children, family members and the world via sign language — slight finger movements on the palm of his hand, each movement is another letter. Yossi asks that the daily newspapers be read to him. He is interested in politics and current events, and he responds to them all. He is composing a personal diary on the computer. He types on a regular, not a Braille keyboard. Yossi plays with children, treating them with friendship and respect. When he speaks, his words are not clear, they make a humming sound, but his parents, siblings, and, of course, the Shalva children easily understand what he says. "The ear becomes accustomed to his speech," says his mother, "Spend one day here with him and you too will understand."

Parents come to Shalva, they cry and kiss the Samuels. They say, "you just cannot imagine how much Shalva helps us." "I," says Kalman, an emotional man, "chuckle to myself because anyone that says such a thing does not know our personal history, or Yossi. I say to those people: You are so right. No one from outside could possibly understand."

"My biggest feeling of pride," says Malky, "is that normal healthy children come here with their parents to pick up their siblings, and they want to stay here and play. But we do not allow other children to play here. Shalva belongs only to these special children, the handicapped. The healthy children start to cry and say to us: "We too are special" and the Shalva children answer with pride: "Excuse me — we are the special ones.""

---

28. Tax deductible contributions may be sent to Shalva, attention Kalman Samuels, POB 35199, Evan Denan Street 6, Jerusalem, 91351, fax.972-2-653-5787, tel. 972-2-651-9555, info@shalva.org, or to American Friends of Shalva, 1720 51st Street, Brooklyn, NY 11204, tel. 718-438-8928.

5

JAY FEINBERG: THE HERO WITH BAD BLOOD
by Danny Siegel[29]

THE FACTS

Jay was 23 years old and already working for the Federal Reserve Bank of New York for about a year after graduating from college, when he was diagnosed with chronic myelogenous leukemia. In the cancer circles, this is called "CML," the first of many euphemistic abbreviations I would hear from Jay. It was June of 1991.

There was a lot of bad news. For CML, standard chemotherapy wouldn't do any good. It would only delay the inevitable. The only hope was a bone marrow transplant, but even that disheartening prospect was worse than expected. His DR10 — which Jay explained as a site on the surface of a white blood cell — was extremely rare. The odds on a match of 6 out of 6 antigens were worse than the normal mathematical odds.

Since this is all about genetic matches, a person who needs bone marrow from someone else starts with family members. One of Jay's earliest low points was when his two brothers, Eddie and Steven, were tested and matched each other, but didn't match with Jay. To an outsider such as myself, the despair is beyond imagining.

And then there is the horrifying historical fact of how many Jews died in the Holocaust. All of those people and their descendants who could have been tested, could have been part of a larger gene pool, are gone. Nevertheless, Jay and his family engaged in an enormous genealogical research effort to test as many relatives as possible, no matter how distant — to the point where they found relatives they never knew they had. They even discovered a Holocaust survivor and his family in Australia, all of them Jay's cousins. They, too, were tested.

Then Jay said, let's try an Unrelated Donor Search of national and international bone marrow registries, searching databases around the world. They found a dozen potential matches of 4 out of 6, and of those 12 preliminary matches, some were not eligible or ready, and the rest did not match on the remaining antigens. A match of only 4 out of 6 is in and of itself a bleak situation.

In September, 1991, the Feinbergs launched a campaign called *"Friends of Jay"* (now called **Gift of Life**). It was an attempt to get massive numbers of people tested so that someone, somewhere, might turn up as a good or perfect match for Jay and many others in similar desperate circumstances. After all, the results went into an international pool, to benefit anyone seeking a life-saving donor. More than 55,000 people have been tested since Jay and his people have launched their campaign. Dozens of matches have been found as a result of the campaigns, and the Feinbergs continue to hear of more matches. Two of my friends even spent weeks in the Former Soviet Union, in Sapotskin and Minsk in Belarus, and other nearby sites, hoping that someone from Jay's ancestral home was a distant cousin or otherwise somehow close enough to his genetic make-up to provide a good match.

The Transplant

At 2:00 a.m. on July 28, 1995, at the Fred Hutchinson Cancer Research Center in Seattle, Jay finally got his transplant. By most estimates, his time had already run out, but once the decision was made, the family went out to Seattle, preparing to receive the bone marrow from the best-available match. That match was from a young woman in Brooklyn

29. Danny Siegel, *Heroes and Miracle Workers* (1997) (p. 40)

who had been tested at a drive in Jerusalem. While they were there, in one of those last-minute events in the Divine Plan, a slightly better donor was found at the very last *Friends of Jay* donor drive in Wisconsin. She was the last donor tested, a volunteer from Chicago, and though hers was not a perfect match, this one was definitely better than the one Jay had been prepared to receive. This very-last-minute marrow is the one that they gave him. It was a "5 and 5" match, 5 of Jay's antigens, and 5 of the donor's, and, from the standpoint of potential rejection, a much better match, though it was still a mismatch by one antigen.

Today, December 9, 1996

Jay is making plans to return to work. The Federal Reserve Bank told him that his job is waiting for him whenever he can come back. He has begun moving his things to an apartment. Last August, one year after the bone marrow transplant, he was officially

---

Jay would insist, of course, that the true hero of this story is his heroic donor, that remarkable young woman from Chicago.

---

declared "in remission." There's this other jargon-term in the cancer business called disease-free survival. The custom is that only after five years do they use terms like "cured." Jay can live with that.

More important: the drives continue. Many people are alive today because of Jay's efforts, the efforts of the Feinberg and Atlas families, the faithful volunteers, and the hundreds of others who have been out in the field organizing, publicizing, and urging people to get tested. **The Gift of Life Foundation**,[30] Jay and his parents, get calls all the time asking for insight, advice,

strategies for their own search to find an appropriate match. People from other ethnic groups inquire about organizing campaigns, about the technicalities of matches, about the politics of bone marrow transplants. They need Jay's expertise, learning from his experience and research. And they need to hear from Arlene and Jack Feinberg, Jay's parents, not only about the technical side of bone marrow transplants, but also about the terrors and dislocations in family life during the process. They need to talk to someone who's been through it.

Jay, The Hero

Is Jay a hero? Jay would say it isn't so. He would say the heroes are all those people who organized the campaigns, who gave of their time and money and who rolled up their sleeves to make it happen, to save dozens of lives. He would insist, of course, that the true hero of this story is his heroic donor, that remarkable young woman from Chicago. On those counts, I will grant him his non-heroic status. I will agree with him that this is the story of hundreds of heroes.

But I disagree on this: all along, even in the worst of times when everything was working against him, he insisted that the campaign continue. We — his friends, his family, and those who only know him by the picture on the posters — we knew that meant, "Even if I die, the campaign must go on." That's good enough for me — Jay is a hero.

---

30. Gift of Life Foundation (Friends of Jay Feinberg), c/o Arlene and Jack Feinberg, 4740 Yardarm Lane, Boynton Beach, FL 33436, 800-9-MARROW (962-7769), fax: 800-707-5343, e-mail: registry@hlamatch.org, Website: www.Giftoflife.com.

6

DAWN KRIEGER, *MAGIC ME,* AND THE ELDERLY

by Kathy Levin Shapiro[31]

"God said, Just as I create worlds and bring the dead back to life, so you human beings are also capable of doing the same."

— *Midrash Psalms* 116:8

In the 1980s Kathy Levin from Baltimore, MD, created what became a nationwide project to build relationships between what seemed the least likely population groups — the seriously declining elderly often forgotten in nursing homes and the everyday teenagers of schools of all sorts. The point was not to become do-gooders singing and performing for the elderly or bringing them food. Rather the goal was to build two-way human relationships, which might become long term intergenerational friendships. Kathy explains, **Magic Me** is a program designed to help preteens address their fears and concerns about the elderly in nursing homes. Magic Me is designed to transform visits to nursing homes from cookie drop-offs, performances for the elderly where the youngsters are staring at the elderly with fear and wonder and the elderly are stuck in wheelchairs at a distance being performed for, into real, honest time together where old and young work and create together. Magic Me invites youngsters to dare to break down the barriers and to approach the elderly person to person.

When I, the editor, was invited to visit Magic Me in action, I met director Kathy Levin, a beautiful, vivacious, strong-willed blond woman, at the seventh grade of an African American inner city school. Her task was to prepare the class for their first visit to the local nursing home, and I watched a miracle occur which she called "Magic Me." Kathy began by having the children air their real fears about the old and infirm, about contagious disease, about the awful smell of urine, about the hideous deformities and so on. Then without explanation, with thick shipping tape, she closed shut one student's mouth and pinned a big boy's arm behind him so they could neither speak nor move freely.

In the course of the discussion Kathy explained that adolescents and the elderly have something in common — a bizarrely changing body and a precious, hidden Magic Me. People are "turned off" by and sometimes ridicule the teenager who suddenly grows tall and awkward, with face pimples and hormonal rushes. Those teenagers often feel that their bodily changes, over which they have no control, alienate them from a society that judges them by looks alone. Society misses the deep inner "me" so ready to give and receive love. "Well," says Kathy, "that is how the elderly feel when their bodies begin to deteriorate, even though their inner selves, their souls, remain intact." The elderly feel as if their mouths have suddenly been taped shut or their arms have become disabled for no reason other than the aging process. Their bodies are not under their control, in fact, they misrepresent them every time they meet someone new. Therefore the elderly also suffer from stigmatization, but you teenagers can reach the Magic Me of these elderly by reaching out with your often-misunderstood Magic Me.

Kathy then prepared the students to visit the elderly in order to play catch with them, to help them do their hair, to talk to them about what interests the kids and even — believe it or not — to "break dance" with them. I followed the students down the block to an understaffed public nursing home and watched, mouth-open, as they literally "break danced" with the elderly, even with those in wheelchairs. Each one did what s/he could and without patronizing. The teenagers had a great time with the elderly, cherishing every attempt of these disabled people to move a part of their body to music these children loved. Now I believe in **miracle workers** like Kathy.

On the next page is a story of one of Kathy's proteges, Dawn Krieger, a Jewish teenager and her bosom buddy Agnes.

---

31. Kathy Levin, founder of *Magic Me*, went on to create a musical stage play about these complex but real intergenerational relationships. Broadway composers including Stephen Schwartz *(Pocahantas)*, Comden and Green *(Singing in the Rain)*, Marvin Hamlisch *(A Chorus Line)*, Kander and Ebb *(Cabaret)*, each contributed an original song. For information contact magicme8@aol.com.

DAWN KRIEGER: "YOU JUST HAVE TO"

by Kathy Levin Shapiro

One young girl, aged 12, Dawn Krieger, a student at the Bryn Mawr School in Baltimore, found her life transformed as she became a volunteer in *Magic Me*. Tall and delicate, Dawn could barely stand the discussion in the classroom before the group went to the nursing home. The children were discussing their fears, honestly and openly. One child offered, "I'm scared, scared they're going to . . . you know . . . die . . . on me!" Dawn was crying silently to herself. But she decided to join the group on the first visit to the nursing home, anyway.

Dawn recalls, "I'll never forget the day I met Agnes. She's soooo little and has the most beautiful face of anyone." To most people who walk through the nursing home, Agnes is all but invisible. Perhaps it's her size, or that she never, never utters a sound. Her head is a halo of wooly, white wisps of hair. To Dawn, "Agnes is the most beautiful woman I've ever seen. The way she looks up at me with those big black eyes. She's so innocent, like a baby."

While the other girls in her class were scouting the malls on the weekends, you could find Dawn in the nursing home perched on Agnes' bed, braiding her hair. "I love touching her head. It's all warm. And when Agnes smiles at me, I know everything's going to be OK." Dawn visited Agnes weekly for a year.

But once when Dawn came into the nursing home with a holiday basket she made for Agnes, there wasn't anybody in her chair. "Where's she? In the bathroom? Down the hall? Nurse! Where's Agnes?" Finally a young nurse informed Dawn that Agnes had been taken to the hospital. "Why didn't you tell me? Why didn't you call me?"

That afternoon, after school, Dawn and her Mom rode over to the hospital. When Dawn saw Agnes in the bed, she was overwhelmed at how little Agnes seemed in that big, white bed. The hospital gown was hanging off her skeletal body. As Dawn tiptoed toward the bed, she squealed, "Oh, my goodness, it's the heart necklace! She's wearing the heart necklace." Her Mom was filled with tears; it was the heart necklace Dawn saved up for and bought for Agnes last year. Dawn immediately took this stick of a woman and clutched her in delicate, young arms. She kissed silent Agnes on the forehead and placed her limp body back down on the sheets to rest. Dawn knelt down and held her. Agnes died about an hour later. Dawn gave the eulogy in the black Baptist funeral home.

Dawn reports, "There were tons of people out there." To Dawn, "It was the scariest thing I'd ever done in my life. I was shaking and crying up there and started thinking about Agnes, her warm head and those eyes, and then I couldn't finish telling all those people how much she meant to me. I said: 'Agnes, I miss you so much and I love you.'"

Dawn's mother listened. She had never realized until this moment that Dawn was already becoming a young woman.

Dawn says, "The hardest part was going back to the nursing home." She called and asked for permission not to have to go. The following week, when the bus was ready to leave school for the nursing home, Dawn decided to step inside. The other children hugged and cheered for her. When she arrived at the nursing home, she slowly walked down the hall and spotted Agnes' empty corner and stopped. Her voice got caught in her throat. She looked around the hall and saw an exceptionally frail woman, drooling, sitting alone in her wheelchair facing a blank wall. She took a long, deep breath and, very slowly, started toward her. "You just have to . . . ," said Dawn to herself.

While the other girls in her class were scouting the malls on the weekends, you could find Dawn in the nursing home perched on Agnes' bed, braiding her hair.

The *Magic Me* Prom:
Samantha Bow   BY KATHY LEVIN SHAPIRO

amantha was a real *Magic Me* girl (who started at age 12, just like Dawn Kreiger who was one of her friends). She kept up her relationship with her favorite senior citizen, Mr. Bill, all the way through high school and even college. At her high school prom, she couldn't think of a better "date" than Mr. Bill. When she found out that he had never gone to a prom in his life, she was convinced "he was the guy." To boot, she decided to convince her entire class of some hundreds of 17- and 18-year-olds to transform their Senior Prom to a **Seniors' Prom**. You can see that this girl doesn't take "no" for an answer. The long and short of it is that the kids all brought nursing home elders as their dates and decided to decorate the nursing home and to hold the dance there. That was one of the best nights of my life. To see the youngsters transformed into elegant young adults and the elders into suave and beautiful people in tuxes and ball gowns!

But Samantha and Bill were **The Couple**.

Samantha and her date to the High School Prom, Mr. Bill

(Photos courtesy of Kathy Levin Shapiro)

D.

IN DEFIANCE OF THE NAZIS:
SPIRITUAL AND MILITARY RESISTANCE

*T*he *nature of totalitarianism, especially as practiced by the Nazis, is to destroy human solidarity and to erase the civilized meaning of human existence. Therefore resistance, whether expressed in military or spiritual terms, required a difficult act of cognitive heroism in which one goes beyond the Nazis' demeaning perception of the victim and reinstates the humanity of oneself and of others.*

Alongside other Holocaust related stories in this book, we have brought four more examples of such courage. **Father Andre** *was a Belgian priest who had the motivation, the "guts" and the incredible adroitness to be a double-dealing host. Simultaneously he wined and dined Nazi officers in the front room, while giving hospitality to hundreds of Jews, who passed through his bedroom.* **Janucz Korczak** *is the well-known "father of the orphans" who chose to accompany his children in the Warsaw Ghetto to the gas chambers in 1942. The special quality of his heroism is revealed not only in the final act of his life but in his career decision to devote his life to teaching orphans to respect themselves. Using literature Korczak brought insight and comfort to thousands. Literature served him in three ways:*

(1) the **diary** *he wrote and encouraged his children to write to express their tormented inner world,*

(2) the **children's stories** *he wrote to give child and adult alike a window into the misunderstood child, and*

(3) the **play** *his orphans put on in the Warsaw Ghetto in 1942 that prepared them and all the adult audience for death.*

His wisdom in life has so much to teach us, even more than his courage in death.

Rabbi Leo Baeck, *the German Jewish spiritual leader, refused to abandon his community in Germany after 1933 and was sent to Terezin, the "model" ghetto in Czechoslovakia. There he not only survived but kept alive the highest level of philosophical and religious culture in the midst of Nazi attempts at dehumanization.*

Finally, we turn to an armed response to the Nazi threat — **Chana Szenes,** *the Hungarian immigrant to Eretz Yisrael who volunteered to join the British paratroops and return to Budapest in 1944 to try to save her mother and her people. Mordechai Anielewicz, the leader of the Warsaw Ghetto Uprising (1943), is perhaps a more "heroic" figure in the military sense, but unfortunately we have no diaries and few eyewitnesses to reveal the inner world of his courage. Therefore we have chosen that young woman and poet, Chana Szenes (pronounced Senesh) because she has shared with us her hopes and her doubts, making her heroism nuanced and more humanly accessible to us.*

In the context of reading about heroism during the Holocaust on Hanukkah, it is appropriate to recall how this children's holiday became a source of Jewish courage during the persecutions in Germany in the 1930s. The great Liberal Rabbi Joachim Prinz recalls that even the most assimilated or even baptized Jews began to come to the synagogue during the rise of Nazism. They sought in the traditional holiday resources to strengthen them against the virulent anti-Jewish propaganda. Hanukkah was one of the most important holidays in this regard.

Prinz explains: "The German Jews had adjusted Hanukkah to Christmas, and it had become really little more than the giving of gifts and the joyous acceptance of them by children. The Christmas tree was displayed, after all, in many German Jewish homes. The Hanukkah menorah was shown almost in the manner of Christmas, with gift packages around it, and it looked very much like a Christmas celebration."

"But now under Hitler, quite naturally, it was the Hanukkah story which interested us most. The battle

of a handful of Jews against overwhelming majorities. Jews are not cowards, we said. Here is the story of the Maccabees, and it is proof of Jewish courage and stamina, and above all, of their ability to be victorious. Never mind that Germany is so powerful. Never mind the uniforms of the Storm Troopers and the SS, and the German army. Don't overestimate the weaponry, for we say in the Haftorah of Hanukkah, "Not by might and not by power." So a perfunctory holiday, which used to satisfy Jewish children and teach them not to be envious of their Christian neighbors, now returned to its original meaning. When we placed the menorah on the windowsills in accordance with Jewish tradition, we wanted to proclaim loudly and clearly and visibly that this house was inhabited by Jews, and we were proud of it."   [LB 194]

7.

THE BED OF A RIGHTEOUS PRIEST

FATHER ANDRE (BELGIUM, 1940-45)

by Herbert Friedman[32]

When Chaplain Herbert Friedman was sent by the U.S. Army to Namur, Belgium, in 1945 soon after the end of the Nazi occupation of Belgium, he heard about an amazing local clergyman.

Walking down the narrow main street, I saw a Star of David hand-drawn on the dusty window of an abandoned store. The door yielded, and beyond the empty front room, I found another room containing some chairs, a small cabinet, a framed picture of a priest, and Monsieur Burauck, sitting behind a small table. The place was dim and dingy, but the smile spreading across his pinched face as he recognized the Tablets of the Law, [the emblem of the Jewish chaplain], on my uniform gave a glow to what turned out to be a tiny synagogue.

M. Burauck was its caretaker, one of Namur's very few Jewish survivors. He showed me the Torah scroll in the Ark and then I noticed, pinned to the wall, below a priest's picture, faded flowers and the inscription, "This man is one of the saints of the world." It was written in Flemish, an exact translation of the Hebrew phrase *"Chasidei oomot ha-olam,"* which is applied to non-Jews who, at mortal danger to themselves, have saved the lives of persecuted Jews.

(In Israel today, such persons are greatly honored by the government. They are presented with a medal and asked to plant a tree at Yad Vashem, the National Holocaust Memorial Museum. The foot of each tree bears the name and nationality of the person so honored. These Righteous Gentiles are nominated by Jews whom they actually saved. Each case is investigated as carefully as possible. The total number of Righteous Gentiles has reached, at the time of this writing, 14,706.)

When I remarked that it was most unusual to find the picture of a Catholic priest on a synagogue wall, M. Burauck offered tea and told me a fabulous story. Father Andre was Namur's parish priest. His parish house was located in the center of town, right alongside the hotel. When the German armies overran Belgium in 1940, the Gestapo requisitioned the hotel and used it as a headquarters. Approximately 40 Gestapo officers lived and worked there, and many of them, professing Catholics, became friendly with the priest next door.

32. Rabbi Herbert Friedman, *Roots of the Future* (1999) (Gefen Publishing House, gefenbooks@compuserve.com) pp. 47-49, 51, 55-67. Reprinted by generous permission of the author and publisher.

Rescuing Jewish DP's and Providing "German" Hospitality (1945)

BY RABBI HERBERT FRIEDMAN

As an American Jewish Chaplain in the fall of 1945, in occupied Germany, my purpose was to rescue wandering, homeless, traumatized Jews who had survived Hitler's horrors — gas chambers, mass shootings, incinerators — and were now seeking places of refuge. They were hungry, weary — and for good reason — frightened.

To carry out this singular rescue mission, we drove our trucks slowly along back roads, picking up survivors, 50 to a load. We then found a barn, shed, partially destroyed house, garage, stable, or any other place of shelter, and left the refugees there under the care of one of our armed men, until we could find a larger place to hold the several truck-loads we brought together for better security. Next, we supplied our "guests" with food, water and blankets, obtained from quartermaster supplies. This constituted "rescue" in the most elementary meaning of the word.

In the ensuing weeks, we picked up hundreds and hundreds of Jews. Some were so gaunt, weak, and listless that they didn't care what was happening to them. We were merely uniformed men who were putting them in trucks, and for them that was all too familiar.

We also found children, as young as ten. I once encountered two of those, a boy and girl, walking slowly along a farm road, filthy clothes in tatters, holding hands, not talking. As our truck approached, and they saw we were slowing down, they started to run, jumping off the road into a ditch, he pulling her with all his strength, which wasn't much, across a plowed field, zigging and zagging as though searching for a place to hide. I walked, rather than ran, trying to indicate by stance and gesture that I did not intend to capture them, but was a friend. Gradually the distance between us narrowed, they tired and slowed down, and I overtook them. They held hands again, as though to go together to whatever lay in store.

I told them my name and asked theirs. They did not know. Nor did they know where they were born, how old they were, what camp they had been in, or how long they had been on the road. They were completely amnesiac. Eating the bread I gave them, they followed me back to the truck, to be hugged and kissed by the burly soldier-driver who was crying because these kids reminded him of his own, who were home safe and sound.

Whether adults or children, the main problem to be solved with the refugees we found was where to put them. We placed as many as possible in established camps. But they were all filling up rapidly, because Munich, the capital of Bavaria, was the destination of choice for refugees from all over Germany and Austria. We were looking for any place with four walls and a roof; three walls would also do. The smaller towns and villages offered the best prospects because they were not so badly bombed.

A large barn would accommodate 100 people; a small hospital building, 200. I remember once coming upon a Rathaus (City Hall), neither grand nor large, but intact and possessing a heating system that worked. I estimated that we could fit in 300 people if we threw out all the German clerks and their filing cabinets and turned the entire structure into a dormitory. There were two lavatories in working order, and that would do.

I strode into the mayor's room, struck an aggressive pose, drew my Colt .45, slammed the butt hard on his desk, and informed him in my best college German that this place was now requisitioned by authority of the American Army. I wanted it empty and perfectly clean by 8 o'clock the following morning. The speech ended with another slam of the Colt. Period. The ploy worked perfectly. The mayor started to protest, thought better of it, and asked meekly what he was supposed to do with his personnel and records. I answered over my shoulder, on my way out, "That's your problem, not mine."

At 8 the next morning, the Rathaus staff of about 20 lined up in front of the empty, immaculately clean building — German efficiency put to good use. My crowd of about 100 ragged, unruly refugees jumped off the trucks and surged inside. The place was thoroughly dirty before the next 8 a.m. arrived. Never mind, they were warm, fed, and safe.

In an effort to win his friendship and confidence, they invited him to their quarters and in turn forced their presence on him in his refectory. Father Andre permitted the intrusions and accepted the invitations, because he had a well-hidden motive of his own. He was one of the leaders of the underground in that part of Belgium, and his apparent friendship with the Gestapo served as a marvelous cover for those activities.

Under the very noses of his Gestapo neighbors, the priest gave refuge and food to the terrified victims who had been directed to the haven of his four walls.

One of the most important aspects of the underground's work was to help Jewish and other refugees escape from the Nazi murderers. Father Andre's parish house became a way station on that underground railroad. Under the very noses of his Gestapo neighbors, the priest gave refuge and food to the terrified victims who had been directed to the haven of his four walls.

It became his custom to shelter these fugitives in his own bedroom, often in his own bed. On one occasion, he had 22 refugees in his house awaiting nightfall, so they could move on to the next underground station. Suddenly, in the middle of the afternoon, three of the Gestapo officers entered his house without warning, seeking a bottle of cool wine. With calm courage, he stalled them at the entrance hall long enough to enable the refugees to hustle into his bedroom. The three Nazis then sat in his courtyard drinking for an hour, and he stayed with them so they would not go wandering through the house. If they had found the Jews, it would not only have meant their and Father Andre's deaths but also the destruction of a link in the chain of underground stations and workers who were fighting the Holocaust.

On another occasion, some 15 officers

were sitting around Father Andre's refectory table, carousing and drinking, when a servant slipped up to him and whispered that at the back door stood five Jewish children who would have to be smuggled into the house and kept overnight. The priest excused himself from the table, brought the children through a corridor in the cellar and took them into his bedroom, where they found a few hours of rest and managed to fall asleep in spite of the drunken shouts of their sworn enemies in the next room.

When Belgium was at last liberated and the Nazis driven out, Father Andre could finally admit the work he had been doing. A tabulation revealed that he had harbored in his own home more than 200 Jewish refugees, most of them children under the age of 15. Shortly after the end of the War, when the priest's birthday came around, the tiny remnant of Namur's Jews gathered to decide on the most suitable birthday present for this beloved man. One sunny morning, in a large cart, they carried it to his house — a new bed! It was, they explained, a symbol of their appreciation for the fact that for several years he had almost never slept in his own bed, giving it to others at great risk. A new one would now launch him into a new era of freedom and peace.

As a final gesture, the small group of Jews asked for Father Andre's photograph to enshrine in their holiest place — on the wall of the synagogue, right next to the Ark. Father Andre came to the synagogue the day they hung the picture, and as they tearfully thanked him for what he had done, he replied that he had simply been doing the will of the Lord in helping his neighbors.

Moral courage is a more rare commodity than bravery in battle or great intelligence.

— JOHN F. KENNEDY, PRESIDENT OF THE U.S

8

JANUSZ KORCZAK

THE KING OF CHILDREN (1878-1942)

by Betty Jean Lifton and Yitzchak Perlis[33]

> "One of my ancestors may well have known the Hasmoneans who raised the banner of revolt and may have even shared in their struggle."
>
> "The lives of great men are like legends — difficult but beautiful."
>
> — JANUSZ KORCZAK

INTRODUCTION — WHO WAS HENRYK GOLDSZMIT?

His legend began on August 6, 1942, during the early stages of the Nazi liquidation of the Warsaw Ghetto, though his dedication to destitute children was legendary long before the war. When the Germans ordered his famous orphanage evacuated, Janusz Korczak was forced to gather together the two hundred children in his care. He led them with quiet dignity on that final march through the ghetto streets to the train that would take them to "resettlement in the East" — the Nazi euphemism for the death camp Treblinka. He was to die as Henryk Goldszmit, the name he was born with, but it was by his pseudonym that he would be remembered.

It was Janusz Korczak who introduced progressive orphanages designed as "just communities" into Poland, founded the first national children's newspaper, trained teachers in what we now call moral education, and worked in juvenile courts defending children's rights. His books *How to Love a Child* and *The Child's Right to Respect* gave parents and teachers new insights into child psychology. Generations of young people had grown up on his books, especially the classic *King Matt the First*, which tells of the adventures and tribulations of a boy king who aspires to bring reforms to his subjects. It was as beloved in Poland as *Peter Pan* and *Alice in Wonderland* were in the English-speaking world. During the mid-1930's he had his own radio program, in which as the "Old Doctor," he dispensed homey wisdom and wry humor. Somehow, listening to his deceptively simple words made his listeners feel like better people.

It wasn't that Korczak glorified children, as did Rousseau, whom he considered naive. **Korczak felt that within each child there burned a moral spark that could vanquish the darkness at the core of human nature. To prevent that spark from being extinguished, one had to love and nurture the young, make it possible for them to believe in truth and justice.** When the Nazis materialized out of that darkness with their swastikas, polished boots, and leather whips, Korczak was prepared to shield his Jewish children, as he always had, from the injustices of the adult world. [L 3-4]

> The child — a skilled actor with a hundred masks: a different one for his mother, father, grandmother or grandfather, for a stern or lenient teacher, for the cook or the maid, for his own friends, for the rich and poor. Naive and cunning, humble and haughty, gentle and vengeful, well behaved and willful, he disguises himself so well that he can lead us by the nose.
>
> — JANUSZ KORCZAK,
> HOW TO LOVE A CHILD

---

33. Selections quoted from P (Perlis) in *Janusz Korczak: The Ghetto Years 1939-1942* including "Final Chapter — Korczak in the Warsaw Ghetto" by Yitzchak Perlis (translated by Avner Tomaschoff), reprinted with the permission of the Ghetto Fighters House and HaKibbutz HaMeuchad (1978);

and from L (Lifton) in Betty Jean Lifton, *The King of Children* (1989), Random House. Permission was requested from the publisher and the author's literary agent.

Janusz Korczak poses with his orphans at a summer camp in Poland, August, 1938

(Courtesy of the USHMM from Beit Lohamei Haghettaot; photographer Szlomo Nadel)

Janusz Korczak — From Child to Father of the Orphans: A Childhood of Rejection by his Parents and Empathy for Poor Children

I am a butterfly drunk with life. I don't know where to soar,
but I won't allow life to clip my colorful wings.

— JANUSZ KORCZAK, CONFESSIONS OF A BUTTERFLY

The boy heard repeatedly from his mother that poor children were dirty, used bad language, and had lice in their hair. They fought, threw stones, got their eyes poked out, and caught terrible diseases. But he saw nothing wrong with the janitor's son and his friends. They ran about merrily all day, drank water from the well, and bought delicious candy from the hawkers whom he wasn't allowed to go near. Their bad words were actually funny, and it was a hundred times more inviting to be down there with them than in that boring apartment with his French governess and his little sister. "A child is someone who needs to move," he would write one day; to forbid this is "to strangle him, put a gag in his mouth, crush his will, burn his strength, leaving only the smell of smoke."

"That boy has no ambition," his mother said when she saw him playing hide and seek with his sister's doll. She didn't understand that while searching for the doll, he moved into dimensions beyond the narrow confines of his apartment. "The doll wasn't a doll, but the ransom in a crime, a hidden body which had to be tracked down." "Children's games aren't frivolous," he would write. "Uncovering a secret, finding a hidden object, proving that there is nothing that cannot be found — that's the whole point."

His father (who later developed a genetic mental illness and died in an asylum) flew into a rage, calling him a "a clod, fool, or an idiot," when he saw him sitting for hours with his building blocks. He didn't understand that Henryk was constructing the solitary towers that would appear in *King Matt the First* and his other books as a symbol of refuge for the orphaned and the lost. "Feelings that have no outlet become daydreams," he wrote. "And daydreams become the internal script of life. If we knew how to interpret them, we would find they come true. But not always in the way we expect."

It was also considered bad manners for a child to hang around the kitchen, but sometimes when his parents were out, Henryk would sneak in to ask the cook to tell him a story. This imaginative woman knew when to pause to let him catch his breath, when to rush on. He never forgot the warmth of her style, the dramatic suspense, as natural to her as the rhythm of her fingers kneading the dough. He would always be grateful for her patience when he interrupted with a question, the respect she had for both the tale and the listener. It was she, he knew, who was responsible for the magical ingredients that went into his own talent as a storyteller. [L 13-14]

A Child Discovers the Barrier between Jews and Christians

Henryk did not know that the puppet shows and Nativity Christmas plays had religious as well as cultural significance. By stressing the ethical rather than the ritual part of their Jewish heritage, his parents had not yet made him aware of that "mysterious question of religion." It took the janitor's son and the death of his canary to do that.

The canary had been the boy's closest friend, caged as they both were, neither allowed to fly free. But one day he found the canary lying stiff on the bottom of the cage. He picked up the little body, put the beak in his mouth, and tried to breathe life into it. It was too late. His sister helped him wrap the dead bird in cotton and put it into an empty candy box. There was no place to bury it except under the chestnut tree in the forbidden courtyard below. With great care he constructed a little wooden cross to put over the grave. "You can't do that!" The maid told him. "It's only a lowly bird, lower than man." When tears streamed down his face, she added, "It's a sin to cry over it."

But Henryk was stubborn, even then. He marched down to the courtyard, his sister tagging behind him, and began digging the little grave. Then the janitor's son came

The Many Strategies
of the Master Educator of Orphans   BY BETTY JEAN LIFTON

In 1910, Dr. Korczak changed professions again and gave up a successful medical practice and literary career to become the director of an orphanage for Jewish children. In fact, Korczak managed to combine all his talents to serve his passion for poor children which had developed in his difficult childhood.

The doctor became the "Father of Orphans" combining his storytelling and his medical talents into a new kind of progressive educator. "I am a doctor by education, a pedagogue by chance, a writer by passion, and a psychologist by necessity."

Janusz Korczak used venerable strategies from his "pedagogic arsenal." If one strategy didn't work, he pulled something else out:

Strategy #1 — Boxing Matches

Korczak credited much of his skill in disciplining the wild beast in himself to his observations of how animals were trained at the circus: "The work of a trainer is very straightforward and dignified. The fury of wild instincts is overcome by the force of man's unflinching will." And he added, "I do not require that a child surrender completely. I just tame his movements." So he used to set up boxing matches among children who got into fights.

He knew that in requiring two hotheads to set a date for a future fight, he gave them time to cool off, to reconsider the importance of their quarrel, and, in the process, to learn how to choose their battles. [L 61]

Strategy #2 — Betting You Can Improve

It is Friday afternoon. A long line of children waits in the main hall outside the small supply room, which Korczak transforms every week into a gambling casino with one croupier — himself. "What do you bet?" He asks Jerzy, an eight-year-old rascal who is first in line. The idea is for the children to place a bet on some bad habit with the goal of overcoming it, and winning a few candies in the bargain. "I bet I'll only have one fight this week," Jerzy says. "I'm not sure I can accept that," Korczak responds, without looking up from the ledger where he keeps his records. "It would be unfair to you." "Why?" "Because you will clearly lose. You beat up five boys this week, and six the week before, so how can you stop so suddenly?" "I

can do it." "Why not try four fights?" "Two," Jerzy argues. After some more bargaining, they compromise on three. Korczak records the bet in the ledger and slips Jerzy a chocolate from the candy basket in good faith. If Jerzy manages to win, he'll collect three more. [L125]

Strategy #3 — Calling Children "Bad Names"

Believing that an educator should also be part actor, Korczak might pretend to lose his temper with an incorrigible child. He would shout, his face and bald pate turning bright red, but his words were not the obvious admonitions — "Shame on you!" or "Don't do that!" Reaching into his "jar of strong scolding expressions," he would pull out: "You torpedo! You hurricane! You perpetual motion machine! You rat man! You lamp! You table!" Knowing the power of an expression, he was constantly expanding his repertoire, borrowing words from nature or the arts: "You rook! You bagpipe! You dulcimer!" He also experimented to find just the right word that would get through to a particular child. One scamp on whom he tried everything else, became subdued for the rest of the day when Janusz called out to him "Ah, you F-major!"

However, beyond those techniques, Korczak had a great effect on the children because he respected their inner world since he too knew the value of his own inner world. Everything children collected was also important to Korczak — from the smallest bits of string to tramcar tickets and even dry leaves. Everything might have a story connected to it or be emotionally priceless: "They all hold memories of the past, or yearnings for the future." He had harsh words for the disrespectful teacher who had the nerve to throw out these treasures as if they were rubbish: "A gross abuse of power, a barbarous crime. How dare you, you boor, dispose of someone else's property?" To protect the property of his orphans, Korczak provided everyone with a little drawer of his own, complete with a lock and a key. [L 125-127]

along, took in the scene shrewdly, and objected to the cross for a different reason: the canary was Jewish. And, what was worse, so was Henryk.

It was a moment of revelation he never forgot: "I, too, was a Jew, and he — a Pole, a Catholic. It was certain paradise for him, but as for me, even if I did not call him dirty names, and never failed to steal sugar for him from my house — I would end up when I died in a place which, though not hell, was

---

One mother entered the sickroom to find both her child and the doctor missing; when she cried out in alarm, they both poked their heads out from under the bed.

---

nevertheless dark. And I was scared of the dark." Death-Jew-Hell. A black Jewish Paradise. Certainly plenty to think about. [L 18-19]

Courageous Career Choices

Henryk Goldszmit agonized over his dream of a literary career but eventually decided to become a doctor. Realism conquered literary idealism. Henryk's friends wondered

A Hero in Training

When I was passing once over a stream's small wooden bridge I saw an insect swept away by the flow of water and trying with all its might to be saved.
Shall I save him?
But in order to save this insect I have to jump into the stream and get drenched to the bone — is it worth it?
And then I heard a voice:
"If you don't make now the small sacrifice, youngster, in order to
 save the small living thing, you won't be ready,
 when you grow up, to save a man either."
There was no limit to my satisfaction when I saw the insect afterwards on the palm of my hand as he was recovering and straightening his wings. We won't see each other again. Fly off in peace and be happy.

— JANUSZ KORCZAK, WITH THE CHILD

why he wanted to be a doctor when his literary career was going so well, but he decided: "I won't be a writer, but a doctor. Literature is just words, while medicine is deeds."

Henryk, the Assimilated Young Jew, becomes Janusz, the Aristocratic Pole

In the fall of 1898, Henryk — by then an intense young medical student of twenty with vivid blue-green eyes and reddish hair already thinning at the crown — seemed to have forgotten his determination to abandon writing. Hearing of a playwriting contest he submitted a play.

Legend has it that Henryk learned at the last moment that he needed a pen name for the contest and took it hastily from the first book he saw on his desk: *The Story of Janasz Korczak and the Swordbearer's Daughter*, by Poland's most prolific historical novelist, Josef Ignacy Kraszewski. The printer (it is said) made a mistake, and the name came out "Janusz." But in reality, pseudonyms were not a contest requirement, and Henryk's decision to take the name could not have been random chance.

Henryk might have assumed a pen name to protect the anonymity of his family — possibly even to change his luck. ("I escaped from my youth as from a lunatic asylum," he would tell an interviewer.) But it was also not chance that he chose a Polish one. In a country where one's surname reveals one's religious affiliation, Goldszmit was unmistakably a Jew, the outsider. With an old gentry name such as Janusz Korczak, Henryk could recreate himself as an insider, linked to a heroic Polish past. [L 31-32]

The children never questioned his sanity or his antics. One mother entered the sickroom to find both her child and the doctor missing; when she cried out in alarm, they both poked their heads out from under the bed. Another knew that her sick daughter would never fall asleep until Dr. Goldszmit came. Like a sorcerer he would wave everyone from the room, and then, sitting by

Korczak Understands Moses

One can understand Moses [and his parents], although they lived 4000 years ago. Moses is no different from children today, Korczak told his readers [in the 1930s]. "If we recall our own childhoods, we can become Moses and if we recall our experiences as adults, we can begin to understand how Moses' parents made the most difficult of decisions: to give up their baby."

Korczak saw Moses as a child living in terrifying times, under a death sentence. He saw him lost in the bullrushes, then found and reared in the enemy's palace. He saw him dreaming nostalgically of his lost home, having nightmares. He knew children, so he knew Moses — because Moses was a child before he was a lawgiver, and had experienced the universal emotions of childhood. [L 222]

the child's bed, he would caress her hands and tell her stories about each finger, blowing on it to make it drowsy. When he got to number ten, she was always asleep.

The Ghetto Years (1939-1942): Uncompromising Defiance to the Germans and Uncompromising Loyalty to his Orphans

After the conquest of Warsaw in November 1939, the German authorities issued a decree insisting that every Jew wear a white band with a blue Magen David.

Korczak Creates A Hero: The Little Jewish Boy and Hitler's Regrets

In the Ghetto Janusz Korczak began writing stories about heroic Jewish boys who wielded unlimited power. In one tale called "Reveries," an unnamed boy dreams of saving the Jewish people from persecution. Smuggling himself onto a plane bound for England, he manages to gain permission from the king for all the Jews to emigrate to Palestine. When the boy's discovery of a cache of buried gold makes him world-famous, Hitler regrets having expelled the Jews and invites them back. But the boy informs Hitler that the Jews have had enough of being invited and uprooted all the time, and will stay in their own homeland. The boy ignores Hitler's request for a loan, but he buys milk and butter for the starving German children. [L 232]

Korczak's Seder at the Orphanage: The Afikoman Nut

At the Holocaust Museum housed at the Ghetto Fighter's Kibbutz in Israel, the docent used to explain that Janusz Korczak created a special Pesach custom at his orphanage seder. He used to hide a nut inside a matza ball in one of the children's soup bowls, as if it were an *afikoman*.

Once when delivering the explanation, an old man visiting the museum came forward and drew an old leather pouch from his pocket. He unwrapped it carefully and produced the nut he had received in the matza ball, as an orphan before the war. He carried a piece of Korczak with him wherever he went.

Korczak was one of the few and possibly the only one who did not carry out this order. Moreover, he would not take off his Polish officer's uniform, but merely stripped it of its insignia. He refused to accept this shameful order, denying its very legality.

Reacting to the humiliating decree, Korczak decided to present the children of the Orphanage with a new green flag. The blossom of a chestnut tree was embroidered on one side and on the other, the Magen David. The green color symbolized hope, the chestnut blossom — rising youth, and the Magen David depicted the ravaged Jewish pride. Thus the flag combined elements of an ancient past with those of a noble future. This was the flag that accompanied the children throughout their days in the ghetto and they carried it on their last march to the death camp. [P 24-25]

In 1940 Korczak's Jewish orphanage was ordered to move to the newly designated area to become the overcrowded, diseased Jewish Ghetto of Warsaw. Although many of his Polish friends tried to extricate him from the ghetto, Korczak refused to leave his children and accompanied them into the ghetto.

The First Procession: From the Old Orphanage to the New One in the Warsaw Ghetto (November, 1940)

When the Jewish Orphanage was ordered closed and moved into the newly designated Jewish Ghetto of Warsaw, Korczak mused creatively about the forced movement of the children and turned it in his mind and then in reality into a theatrical performance.

The procession would be "as if it were a large theatrical troupe," a kind of parade in which the children would carry lamps, paintings, bedding, cages with pet birds and small animals."

On the day they were scheduled to depart, November 29, 1940, the children lined up in the courtyard as rehearsed, while Korczak made a final inspection of the wagons filled with coal and potatoes that he had so arduously procured on his daily rounds. The children waved goodbye sadly to the Polish janitor, who was staying behind to care for the house. His face was swollen almost beyond recognition from the beating he had received the day before when he and the laundress had applied to the Nazi police for permission to go into the ghetto with the orphans. The Germans had thrown the laundress out but detained Zalewski for questioning. Didn't he know the Aryans were no longer allowed to work for Jews? When the janitor replied that after twenty years of service he considered the orphanage his home, the Germans thrashed him with whips and with rifle butts.

The orphans tried to sing as they marched out of the courtyard and into the street, clutching their few possessions. The green flag of King Matt [with the chestnut blossom] on one side and the blue and white Star of David on the other, flew over the little parade as it made its way through the teeming streets the short distance to 33 Choldna Street. When they reached the place where the wall cut along Choldna, slicing its "Aryan" half off from the ghetto, they found German and Polish police at the gate demanding identification, as if they were crossing a foreign border.

While they were passing through, a German policeman confiscated their last wagon, which was filled with potatoes. Korczak shouted and then decided to file a protest the next day. When he arrived at Gestapo headquarters the next day, the officer on duty was at first bemused by the highly agitated man in the remnants of a Polish uniform who introduced himself in flawless German as Dr. Janusz Korczak. He offered

---

How to Love a Child

A hundred children, a hundred individuals who are people — not people-to-be, not people of tomorrow, but people now, right now — today.

— **Janusz Korczak**, How to Love a Child

A friend with whom Henryk was walking one day was amazed by an urchin who came running after them, shouting that he wanted to return the twenty kopecks he had received two years before.

"I lied when I told you my father would kill me if I didn't come home with the money I'd lost," the boy confessed. "I've been looking for you a long time so I could give your money back."

As the child counted out the kopecks with his grubby little fingers, Henryk asked how many times he'd used that trick:

"A lot."

"Did it work?"

"Most of the time."

"Have you given the money back to the others, too?"

"No."

"Then why are you giving it back to me?"

"Because you kissed me on the forehead. It made me feel sorry for what I did."

"Was it so strange to have someone kiss you?"

"Yes, my mother is dead. I don't have anyone to kiss me anymore."

"But didn't anyone tell you that it's not good to lie and beg?"

"The priest told me it's not good to lie, but he says that to everyone."

"And was there no one else who cared enough to guide you?"

"No one," says the boy, no longer able to hold back his tears. "I have no one."   [L 34]

his visitor a chair. But on hearing Korczak's tirade about potatoes being confiscated at the ghetto gate, the German began wondering why this Pole was so concerned about the Jews. Becoming suspicious, he asked, "You're not a Jew are you?" "I am," Korczak replied. "Then where is your yellow armband?" The German was angry by now, "Don't you know that you are breaking the law?" Korczak drew himself up and started to explain as he had so often: "There are human laws which are transitory, and higher laws which are eternal . . . " — but he didn't finish.

Infuriated with the impertinence of this Jew, the German officer ordered him seized by the guards. He was beaten and thrown into a cell [for several days]. [L 264-265]

The Final Play: Rabindranath Tagore's "Post Office" in the Orphanage of the Warsaw Ghetto, July 18, 1942

After two years of harsh ghetto life Korczak knew he had to offer the children something more to help them transcend their present suffering — something with which they could identify and take comfort. He found the solution in a play called *The Post Office* by the Indian poet and philosopher Rabindranath Tagore. The text about a dying child named Amal, an orphan whose nature was so pure that he enriched the lives of those who came in contact with him, could have been written by Korczak himself, so close was it to his style of fantasy and feeling for children.

> It was clear from the hushed silence at the end of the play that Korczak had succeeded in providing the adults as well as the children with a sense of liberation from their present lives.

The audience was riveted by the play. Amal, a gentle, imaginative boy who has been adopted by a poor couple, is confined to his room with a serious illness. Forbidden by the village doctor to go outside, he is shut in from the world of nature, like the orphans there on Sienna Street, awaiting an uncertain future. He longs to fly with time to that land which no one knows — a land, he is told by the watchman, to which a doctor, greater than the one he had now, will lead him by the hand.

Amal believes the Village Headman when he pretends to read the letter from the King, who promises to arrive soon with the greatest doctor in the land. No one is more surprised than the Headman and Amal's adoptive father, when the King's doctor suddenly appears in the darkened room. "What's this? How closed it is in here!" the doctor exclaims. "Open wide all the doors and windows!"

With the shutters open and the night breeze streaming in, Amal declares that all his pain has disappeared, that he can see the stars twinkling on the other side of the darkness.

Korczak's Last Hanukkah and Last Christmas

Hanukkah had a special meaning for Korczak. He admired Judah Maccabee for his toughness as well as his shrewdness.

In 1941 a few days before the holiday, the children were surprised to see a garbage truck from the Aryan side pull up to the orphanage with presents for them concealed beneath the trash. The garbagemen, contacted by the Polish underground, were delivering food and toys from Korczak's Polish friends. On their way to the ghetto, they had even cut down a small pine tree as their own personal gift.

One of the garbagemen has described that day: "Korczak asked the children to gather around the tree, which he set up on a table in the middle of the room. Our parcels were lying under it. The children stood quietly, just staring. What surprised me was that they were not like children, but like smiling old people. Their eyes were full of sorrow, even though they were happy. I started to cry as we serenaded them with a Christmas carol: *"And God please give peace to people of good will."* [L 293]

He falls asleep waiting for the arrival of the King himself, as the doctor sits by his bed in the starlight.

It was clear from the hushed silence at the end of the play that Korczak had succeeded in providing the adults as well as the children with a sense of liberation from their present lives. Whether one believed that the King whom Amal awaited was Death or the Messiah, or that Death was the Messiah, everyone felt momentarily lifted to some realm not only beyond the walls of the ghetto but beyond life itself.

A few days before *The Post Office* was performed in the orphanage that Saturday, July 18, Chairman Adam Czerniakow of the Warsaw Ghetto, wrote in his diary: "A day full of foreboding. Rumors that the deportations will start on Monday evening." [L 318-321]

Tears Beyond Consolation

Life bites like a dog.

— **JANUSZ KORCZAK,** CHILD OF THE DRAWING ROOM

Sometimes he would sit tormented, knowing there was nothing he could do to reassure a child who was mourning a dead parent or lonely for his brothers and sisters. Tears were inevitable, but he could never get used to the choked, hopeless, tragic sobs, which must have reminded him of his own at that age when he grieved over his sick father. He knew that there are as many kinds of sobs as there are children: from the "quiet and private, to the capricious and insincere, to the uncontrolled and shamelessly naked." "It is not the child, but the centuries weeping," he wrote in his notebook.

Korczak felt humble at those moments. If only he could shield his children from danger, "keep them in storage" until they became strong enough for independent flight: "An easy enough job for a hawk or hen to warm chicks with her own body. For me, a man and teacher of children not my own, there is a more complex task. I long to see my little community soar, dream of them flying high. Yearning for their perfection is my sad, secret prayer. But when I am realistic, I know that as soon as they are able they will take off — prowl, stray, or plunder — in search of nourishment and pleasure."

The Final Procession of the Orphans, August 6, 1942

Eyewitness #1 — And so a long line is formed in front of the orphanage. A long procession, children, small, tiny, weak, shriveled and shrunk. They carry shabby packages, some have schoolbooks, notebooks under their arms. No one is crying. Slowly they go down the steps, line up in rows, in perfect order and discipline, as usual. Their little eyes are turned towards the good doctor. They are strangely calm; they feel almost well. The doctor is going with them, so what do they have to be afraid of? They are not alone, they are not abandoned. Dr. Korczak busies himself with the children with a sober eagerness. He buttons the coat of one child, ties up the package of another, or straightens the cap of a third. Then he wipes off a tear, which is rolling down the thin little face of a child. Then the procession starts out. It is starting out for a trip from which everybody feels one never comes back. All these young, budding lives marching quietly and orderly to the place of their untimely doom. The children are calm, but inwardly they must feel it, they must sense it intuitively. Otherwise how could you explain the deadly seriousness on their pale little faces? But they are marching quietly in orderly rows, calm and earnest, and at the head of them is Janusz Korczak.[34]

Eyewitness #2 — A miracle occurred. 200 children did not cry out. 200 pure souls, condemned to death, did not weep. Not one of them ran away. None tried to hide. Like stricken swallows they clung to their teacher and mentor, to their father and brother, Janusz Korczak, that he might protect and preserve them. Janusz Korczak was marching, his body bent forward, holding the hand of a child, without a hat, a leather belt around his waist and wearing high boots. A few nurses marched behind

34. Hillel Seidman, *Tagbuch fun Varshever Ghetto,* 1947

him, wearing white aprons. They were followed by 200 children dressed in clean and meticulously cared for clothes, who were being carried to the altar. On all sides the children were surrounded by German, Ukrainian, and this time also Jewish policemen. They whipped and fired shots at them. The very stones of the street wept at he sight of this procession.[35]

There are those who say that at that moment a German officer made his way through the crowd and handed Korczak a piece of paper. An influential Pole had petitioned the Gestapo on his behalf that morning, and the story goes that Korczak was offered permission to return home — but not the children. Korczak is said to have shaken his head and waved the German away.

As Korczak led his children calmly toward the cattle cars, the Jewish police cordoned off a path and saluted Korczak instinctively. A wail went up from those still left on the square. Korczak walked, head held high, holding a child by each hand, his eyes staring straight ahead with his characteristic gaze, as if seeing something far away.

The Father of Orphans (1878-1942)

No one survived to tell the story of the last hours of Korczak and the children after their train left the Warsaw Ghetto on August 6, 1942. All that is known is that Treblinka, the extermination camp to which they were taken, gassed the victims immediately. [L 344-345]

At the end of Korczak's own novel *King Matt the First,* Matt is being marched down the streets of his kingdom to his supposed execution. Matt holds his head high to prove that he has more strength of character than the enemy. **"True heroes show themselves in adversity,"** he tells himself. He refuses the blindfold: to die "beautifully" is still his only wish. [L 110]

---

35. Joshua Pole

Reflections on the Angel of Death

During the last weeks of his life, Korczak reflected on death. On July 18, 1942, his orphanage put on the play, "The Post Office." July 22, 1942, Korczak's 64th birthday and the Ninth of Av, anniversary of the destruction of the Temples, was the first day of the mass deportations which would later include the orphanage.

When asked why he had chosen this particular play, Korczak replied that he wanted his children to learn how to welcome the Angel of Death calmly. This was his way of imparting to those near him, the little helpless ones, the peace of mind and serenity of those sharing the secret of death, the calm wisdom in the moment of tragedy which in his faith did not mean the end.

In Korczak's diary we find the following entry on July 18th:

"Perhaps illusions would be a good subject for the Wednesday dormitory talk. Illusions, their role in the life of mankind." [P 81]

Leo Baeck at lecture by Professor Utitz, in Terezin Ghetto, 1944

(Photos taken from the Nazi film "The Furher Presents the Jews a City," by permission of the Chronos collection, Bonn, courtesy of Beit Hatefusoth Photo Archive, Tel Aviv)

9.

LEO BAECK'S SPIRITUAL RESISTANCE AGAINST THE NAZI REGIME:

BERLIN, 1933-1943, AND THERESIENSTADT, 1943-1945

by Leonard Baker and Albert Friedlander [36]

Major Patrick Dolan of the U.S. Army spat out the words: "Who the hell," he demanded, "is Leo Baeck!" The answer came quickly. "Leo Baeck is the pope of the German Jews."

Dolan glared at the shortwave radio. After risking his life to cross Nazi lines, he had arrived safely in Prague, where his job, he thought, was working with the Czechoslovakian underground until the city had been cleared of Nazis. Now new orders were given him by an unknown voice at the other end of his radio linkup: Slip out of Prague, travel forty kilometers to Theresienstadt, a city turned to a Jewish ghetto by the Nazis, and find somebody named Leo Baeck. Damn army!

Leo Baeck had become the symbol, both of the Jews he had led in Berlin and of the Jews imprisoned at Theresienstadt. For many it was difficult to articulate whether Baeck symbolized the durability of Judaism, the courage of its leaders, or the triumph of civilized man. But they understood the excitement of his symbolism. [L.B.]

36. This section is a composite from Leonard Baker [L.B.], *Days of Sorrow and Pain: Leo Baeck and the Berlin Jews*, © 1978, reprinted by permission of Scribner/Simon and Schuster (p. 1-2, 238, 286-287, 295, 315, 338); and Albert Friedlander [A.F.], *Leo Baeck: Teacher of Theresienstadt*, © 1968, reprinted by permission of Henry Holt & Co. (p. 2-4, 45-47).

Berlin 1933-1943

Leo Baeck, after all, was not just any Jew taken by the Nazis and thrown into the blazing furnace of Hitler's "Final Solution." He was the leader of German Jewry, the last duly elected and appointed leader of a community which had come to an end after a thousand years of historic existence. He was one of the great scholars of his generation; what he had to say about Christianity and concerning mysticism or ancient philosophy was received with as much attention as his great writings on the essence of Judaism. He was Grandmaster of the German B'nai Brith

---

"I will go," said Leo Baeck, "when I am the last Jew alive in Germany."

---

fraternal organization of Jews, the leading Rabbi of the Jewish community of Berlin, professor of the last Jewish seminary in Germany still secretly ordaining young men as rabbis to a dying community, Leo Baeck had refused to leave Germany — despite the insistence of Jews all over the world and of the German leaders themselves. [A.F.]

Baeck himself had opportunities to leave,

Terezin, The "Model" Ghetto

Terezin (in Czech, Theresienstadt in German) was the "model ghetto" created in 1941 as a showplace for the world by Adolf Eichmann, the Nazi responsible for the Final Solution to the Jewish Problem. Using an ancient fortress, the Nazis created a transit camp that could be used for propaganda. When the International Red Cross paid a visit in 1944, overcrowded barracks were depleted by sending inmates to Auschwitz. Cafes, schools, and gardens were created with band music and a merry-go-round. Then a Nazi propaganda film, *The Führer Presents the Jews with a City*, was produced showing a lawn party and swim meet. Immediately after filming, the entire cast was deported to Auschwitz.

However the inmates of Terezin did create their own culture with lectures, paintings, jazz, poetry like "I never saw another butterfly," and an original opera about oppression entitled *The Emperor of Atlantis*.

but he had determined to remain in Germany to help his fellow Jews. How long would he stay? In 1939 an Englishman who had been shocked by Kristallnacht persuaded a friend to carry two passengers to safety in a private airplane. He asked Wilfred Israel, a Jew who owned a large store in Berlin, and Leo Baeck if they wanted to use the opportunity to flee from Germany.

Wilfred Israel replied, "I will go when the Rabbi goes." Then he looked at Baeck.

"I will go," said Leo Baeck, "when I am the last Jew alive in Germany." [L.B.]

Theresienstadt, Czechoslovakia, 1943-1945

The Nazis sent him to Theresienstadt. *"Das war, als ich ein Pferd war"* — "That was when I was a horse," Baeck said later of those years and of being forced to do manual labor. There was something else he recalled. "I was in Theresienstadt the number 187894," he said. "I had only this one thought: never to resign before rudeness, never to become a mere number, and always to keep my self-respect." [A.F.]

Baeck realized that the danger of the camp was not the hunger, the crowded conditions, the filth, or the vermin. Rather, he said:

Here the mass submerged the individual. He was enclosed in the mass, just as he was encircled by the crowded narrowness, by the dust and the dirt, by the teeming myriads of the insects. He was surrounded also by need and distress, by the hunger that seemed never to end — enclosed in a camp of the concentrated, never alone by himself. Each had received his transport number. That was now his characteristic feature, was the first and most important sign of his existence. It officially ousted his name and it threatened inwardly to oust his self. That was the mental fight everyone had to keep up, to see in himself and in his fellow man not only a transport number. It was the fight for the name, one's own and the other's, the fight for individuality, the secret being, one's own and the other's. Much, perhaps everything, depended on whether one stood this test, that the individual in one remained alive as an individual and continued to recognize the individual in the other. [L.B.]

"Whether one survived in a concentration camp," Leo Baeck said, "depended outwardly on circumstances: disease, torture, annihila-tion could destroy one's life." **But whether one could survive inwardly depended on two other qualities — "patience and imagination."** Baeck defined patience as "the power of resilience that did not let the will to live give way" and imagination as "the vision that ever again and in spite of everything makes him see a future." The Jews, with their tremendous optimism, their desire to fulfill God's commandment to live, lost neither their patience nor their imagination. Against all the pressures a sense of community developed at Theresienstadt. "People who had not known each other endeavored to help each other, physically and spiritually," reported Baeck. "They gave each other of whatever they had, of their belongings and of their spirit. Human beings found each other, and where the individual held on to himself, there also arose community." [L.B.]

Postscript:
Why did the Nazis allow Baeck to survive the War?

Theresienstadt, Czechoslovakia, was intended as a showplace, a "privileged" concentration camp [that the Nazis could show to the Red Cross and the world in order to counteract the anti-German propaganda and to hide the awful truth behind a facade of culture]. Lest we forget what this means, it should be pointed out that 140,000 Jews were sent there — out of which less than 9,000 survived. And it was not intended that Leo Baeck [leader of the German Jewish resistance to the Nazis] should survive the camp. [A.F. 45]

Toward the end of March, 1945, several people expressed astonishment at finding him still alive. "I just heard that you were dying," said one. He learned later that a Moravian rabbi in the camp named Beck had died. Baeck did not appreciate the significance of that death until a few weeks later, when he was in one of the offices of the Ghetto.

"The door opened and an SS officer entered. It was Eich-mann," Baeck recalled. "Eichmann was visibly taken aback at seeing me. 'Herr Baeck, are you still alive?' He looked me over carefully, as if he did not trust his eyes and added coldly, 'I thought you were dead.'" Eichmann obviously had confused the dead Rabbi Beck from Moravia with Leo Baeck from Berlin. Baeck replied: "Herr Eichmann, you are apparently announcing a future occurrence." Eichmann quickly recovered himself. "I understand now," he said. "A man who is claimed dead lives longer."

"Feeling certain that I had little time left to live," Baeck later said, "I wasted none with him. I walked to the door, he stepped aside, and I went to my quarters. I gave my wife's and my wed-ding rings to a friend and asked him to hand them onto my daughter in England. Then I wrote farewell letters and was ready for what might come." Eichmann never carried through on his implied threat [and Baeck survived the war and contin-ued to be a spiritual leader of integrity after the Shoah. [L.B.315]

Baeck was the teacher of Terezin. He was not "the saint of Theresienstadt," as some would have it. He was a man, with flaws and weaknesses. He made mistakes. What matters is that he was true to himself, to his calling as a teacher, a rabbi. And so his life and teaching shine out of those dark days, into our own existence, in a calling, commanding manner. In the darkness of Terezin, men continued to define themselves as fashioned in God's image, reaching toward the light. [A.F.]

Leo Baeck died November 1, 1956, in London, at the age of eighty-three. His gravestone carries the line in Hebrew by which he wished to be remembered — "a descendant of rabbis."

He had responded to the Holocaust in an exceptional way. "The right to be the avenger — where justice fails, where it cannot be found or where it is too weak — is denied to man. Revenge is reserved for God. Vengeance is prohibited to man. Do not have revenge in your heart, only love justice!" [L.B.]

10

CHANA SZENES: "HAPPY IS THE MATCH"

(BUDAPEST, 1944)

by Peter Hay[37]

"All the darkness cannot extinguish the light of a single candle, yet one candle can illuminate all the darkness."

— TRADITIONAL TALMUDIC PROVERB

My God, my God,
Let there be no end
To the sand and the sea,
To the rustle of the water.
To the shimmer of the sky,
To the prayer of man.

— CHANA SZENES
(HER KIBBUTZ AT CAESARA, 1942)

Happy is the match that was consumed in igniting the flame.
Happy is the flame that burned in the depths of those hearts.
Happy are the hearts that knew how to stop beating for the sake of honor.
Happy is the match that was consumed in igniting the flame.

— CHANA SZENES
(YUGOSLAVIA, MAY 13, 1944)

PREFACE: "A SINGLE CANDLE"

by Simon Wiesenthal[38]

In our times young people often find it hard to choose an example to follow. They feel that there is little opportunity nowadays to show personal courage. Amid all the evil in the world, what difference can one person make? The bravery and self-sacrifice of Chana Szenes, the sufferings of her family and other ordinary people who become heroes under extraordinary circumstances, provide inspiration that even the greatest evil can be defeated.

Chana's aspirations for a normal life as a teacher and poet were interrupted in Budapest by homegrown anti-semitism and the Nazi menace from outside. At seventeen she took her first independent step by becoming a Zionist: "This word conveys so much," she wrote in her diary in October 1938, "but to me it means this: I have developed a stronger consciousness and pride in being Jewish.

My aim is to go to Palestine and help build the country. I have become a new person and it feels right. **One must have a strong idea to feel enthusiastic about, one must feel that one's life is not superfluous or spent in vain, that one is needed — and Zionism gives me this purpose."**

---

37. Peter Hay, *Ordinary Heroes: Chana Szenes* (1986), G.P. Putnam's Sons (pp. 13-14, 18-21, 37-38, 50, 92, 94, 98-99, 124, 126, 170-171, 188-189, 195-196, 206-207, 220-221, 254-255) reprinted by the generous permission of the author. Quotations from the writings of Chana Szenes reprinted along with photographs by the kind permission of the Hannah Senesh Legacy Foundation (senesh@hever.co.il).

38. Simon Wiesenthal single-handedly led the documentation, pursuit and prosecution of thousands of Nazi war criminals who had fled from Germany and hidden all over the world.

[In 1944] Chana Szenes was working in her kibbutz in Eretz Israel at a safe distance from the Holocaust in Europe, but her conscience and her courage would not let her rest. She volunteered on a seemingly hopeless mission to organize Jewish resistance against the Nazi machinery of death. Again, nobody urged her to go; quite the contrary, all her friends and comrades tried to dissuade her.

Chana went because she believed that one woman could make a difference.

Just a few months before she made the decision that would lead to her martyrdom, Chana quoted in her diary this sentence from a Jewish writer: "All the darkness cannot extinguish the light of a single candle, yet one candle can illuminate all the darkness." The life of Chana Szenes was one such candle.

MARCH 1944 —
PARACHUTING INTO NAZI EUROPE

by Peter Hay

Chana (Aniko) Szenes and other Zionist paratroopers from the British Army's Jewish Brigade were dropped behind German lines in Yugoslavia as part of a secret mission to liberate British POW's and Jews in Hungary.

Chana had volunteered to jump first.

She groped toward the green light in the forward section of the four-engine Halifax bomber. Her movements were awkward and unsure; she felt like an adolescent again, made self-conscious by the excessive bulk of her flyer's equipment. Her suit had several zipped pockets on the hips and the legs, and each pocket was crammed with tools and essential items for survival: revolver, flashlight, compass and maps, a tiny first-aid kit. She was also carrying forged documents, money, and mail for the partisans. To be captured as British airmen who turned out to be Jews would place them in double jeopardy.

Chana had always, at every training session, volunteered to jump first. It helped to enhance her growing reputation for courage, but she knew better. She needed to prove herself, not so much to the thirty other commandos, all of whom were men, as to the *chaverim*, her friends and fellow workers left behind. Many had opposed her going. There were those who loved her and wanted to save her from danger. Others thought she was being impulsively romantic. They said she should fight the war by building peace. There was plenty of work to be done at the kibbutz, clearing centuries of dunes.

The arguments within the secretive Haganah, the Jewish self-defense organization, were more detached. Nobody doubted her talents, they said, but the chief consideration must be whether these would serve or endanger the mission. Did she fully realize what was involved? Would a twenty-two-year-old middle-class girl from Hungary withstand the Gestapo's tortures? Her stubbornness was legendary, but would she obey orders if they were contrary to what she thought best? Did she believe in the conditions of the mission, as the Haganah had thrashed them out with the British, or would her actions be guided by a more personal agenda? In the end, it was her stubbornness that had won both camps over. Month after month, without letup, she pestered them. With relentless logic she argued every objection, removing every trace of specific emotion that might be held against her candidacy. She wore them down and they yielded to her will. They were loath to let her go into certain danger; at the same time they were proud of her.

The training proved both them and her right. But Chana had hoped, desperately, that after her first few jumps the fear that dried out the throat and turned cartilage into jelly would surrender to her will. It didn't. She hated to see her comrades trying to shake their uncontrollable trembling by tensing and relaxing muscles, clamping jaws tight to prevent any tell-tale chattering of their teeth. She could not stand the idea of drawing out her agony by watching them jump. It was easier to be a hero by going first. After a dozen jumps, after two dozen, the fear never

Chana Szenes (1921-1944) at her Kibbutz Sedot Yam on the Mediterranean Sea, 1939

(Government Press Office, Jerusalem, Israel)

stopped, despite the exhilaration that followed the letting go. Each time beforehand she had to bite her tongue to prevent herself blurting out some excuse, saying that she would jump in the morning instead.

Now there was no next day. The mission, which she had joined by employing every ounce of her will and ingenuity, had begun. As the bomber droned its way from Italy

---

Chana had hoped, desperately, that after her first few jumps the fear that dried out the throat and turned cartilage into jelly would surrender to her will. It didn't.

---

toward their destination in the mountains of Yugoslavia, Chana felt the surfeit of excitement.

As Chana descended from the sky into the mountains of Yugoslavia, she tried to peer beyond the northern horizon. She wanted to glimpse the bright lights of Budapest and the little house where she had lived happily with

her family for eighteen years. But there was nothing in the distance except profound darkness. She was falling fast, watching the horizon recede until it was no more. She hit the snowy ground hard, and then came the cold reality that she was utterly alone and far from any place that could be called home.

Flashback:
Budapest, Hungary, 1939

In 1939 Chana (Anikó) Szenes, a 17 year-old poet, a Hungarian nationalist, the daughter of a well-known writer, began to become interested in Zionism as Hungarian antisemitism grew. Chana tried to learn all she could about Palestine. She read everything she could find and talked to anybody who had visited or lived there. In less than a year she was committed to the movement and could marshal eloquent arguments to propound its tenets. Describing in a speech the achievements of the Palestinian Jews — whose numbers had grown from fifty thousand at the time of Herzl's visit to half a million — she said:

> Diaspora cannot be a goal . . . We don't want handouts, but our lawful rights and our freedom, whatever we have achieved with our own hands. We must demand this as our human right, to have our homeland for the Jewish people. The solution is so clear: we need a Jewish state. If we renounce Zionism, we give up our traditions, our dignity, truth, our right to live. This small piece of land on the shores of the Mediterranean, that Jews after two thousand years once more feel is their own, has been large enough for the flowering of new Jewish life and culture, grown organically from its ancient roots. Even in its incomplete shape today, it is large enough to be an island in the sea of hopeless Jewish destinies, **where we can build a lighthouse of the Jewish spirit to shine a beacon of eternal values into the darkness, the light of faith in the one God.**

Less than six months later Chana stood on that island, learning to build that lighthouse with her bare hands.

Chana left Hungary of her own will, not as a result of direct persecution. She could easily have found better educational opportunities in France, or in England. Her family and friends would have readily supported such an idea. But she chose instead a poor, backward and remote place where she must learn to work the arid soil with her hands. She was completely unsuited for such work and knew nothing about it; it is not surprising that almost everyone she knew was baffled by her decision. The fact is that Chana would never have dreamed of going to Palestine, let alone achieved her goal, without the inspiration of a powerful ideal.

Haifa, Yom Kippur, 1939 and 1940

[On Yom Kippur, 1939, Chana's] first diary entry after arriving in Palestine reveals mixed emotions. It should have been a moment of unalloyed triumph and joy; after all, she had just achieved the greatest dream in her life against formidable odds. But her tone is subdued, poignant:

Yesterday, on the eve of Yom Kippur, I felt

Even through the tears I could feel that I had chosen well, that my life's goal lies here . . . I want my stay here to be the fulfillment of a vocation, and not a form of vegetating. I think everybody here is on a similar mission.

---

very fragile, in spirit, that is. I drew up an account of what was left behind and what awaits me here and I wasn't sure if it'll be worth it. For a moment, I couldn't see the goal. But I also let myself go deliberately; it was good to dissolve all the tension, this constant vigilance, it was good to cry for once. Even through the tears I could feel

that I had chosen well, that my life's goal lies here. I might also say, this is my vocation. I want my stay here to be the fulfillment of a vocation, and not a form of vegetating. I think everybody here is on a similar mission.

It was becoming apparent that two different personalities were developing within Chana Szenes. There was the helpful, cheerful, and outgoing Chana, who seemed totally dedicated to her ideals, her studies, and her new life. And there was another, hidden person, who was introverted, reserved, riddled with doubts, fears, and guilts that she revealed only in her diaries. As the months and years passed, filled with frantic activity, these two Chanas would grow farther and farther apart, pulling in opposite directions, until they came together again, when she chose the mission that would fulfill — and end — her life.

[A year later] it was Chana's second Yom Kippur in the land of Israel, October 11, 1940. But on this Day of Atonement her thoughts turned to the worsening international situation. The war was creeping closer to Greece and North Africa, but Eretz Yisrael was still a relatively peaceful haven. In her diary she noted the irony that while Jews were confessing their sins on this Yom Kippur, their enemies, the real sinners were busy killing, utterly unconcerned about their own guilt.

On Yom Kippur Chana wanted to confess her own sins of omission, to rid herself of the guilt that assailed her whenever she found time to reflect in her diary.

"I sinned against my mother because I did not take all her needs into consideration in deciding to leave.

"I sinned against Eretz Yisrael, by making superficial judgments and without studying in depth its problems.

"I sinned against some people by being insincere, pretending to be interested in them while I really felt indifferent.

"I sinned against myself by wasting my

Chana at one of her jobs on the kibbutz, early 1940s
(Courtesy of the Senesh family)

energies and talent, and by neglecting my own intellectual development."

But on the whole, the nineteen-year-old Chana was not displeased with her deeds of the last year: "In all my sins I was pursuing a single goal and my intentions were pure. If I did not succeed, if I lacked the strength, if I did not find the right path, the right form — I have my regrets, but little to be ashamed of." As usual, Chana felt new energy from her spiritual stocktaking and faced the new year full of resolutions and plans.

The Decision to Act, January 1943

Early in January 1943, Chana experienced what she called a shattering week. After months of worry, guilt, and helplessness, all her frustrations and doubts were suddenly merged into a single crystallized resolution: "I must go back to Hungary. I must be there

during these days and help organize the emigration of Jewish youth. I must bring my mother out from there."

[In late February 1943, Chana began a conversation with a young Hungarian Jew] that lasted far into the night. He told Chana that he was helping to organize a mission to rescue the Jews of Central Europe. The Haganah [the Jewish underground in British-controlled Eretz Yisrael] had already approved the plan.

Chana knew that she would do everything in her power to join the mission. [However, it would take a year of training and difficult negotiations between the British and the Jewish underground before Chana, as the only woman paratrooper, would be dropped behind Nazi lines in Yugoslavia in early 1944.]

Chana enters Nazi Hungary, June 7, 1944

[One day after the Allies invaded Normandy, France, on D-Day, June 6, 1944, Chana crossed into Hungary. She left a soon-to-be-famous poem for her fellow soldier, Reuven.]

Reuven walked to the end of the village with Chana and her rag-tag companions, this tiny band that was about to take on the Third Reich. He insisted that they walk in the opposite direction from her destination; it was best if the villagers did not know which way they went, in case they were questioned.

As she shook hands with Reuven, Chana, embarrassed as she usually was when her emotions took over, took out a carefully folded piece of paper and gave it to him.

"Here. Just in case . . . ."

"What is it?"

"It's a poem."

"A poem? Now . . . ?"

"I want you to have it." And she was gone, catching up with the others. Just at the end of the road she swung around and waved a final "*shalom*" to him before she turned the corner, her steps bouncy, almost dancing, and disappeared into the dusk.

Reuven stood by the road, his fist clenched with emotion. He was still angry with her. His doubts about her military competence assailed him: was this a commando who had coolly estimated the risks, or a hopeless romantic, scribbling verses in these last minutes instead of studying maps? Reuven felt so disgusted that he barely noticed crumpling the piece of paper that was still in his hand. Poetry . . . ! And he threw the ball of paper into a roadside bush.

He slept badly that night. His mind was tortured with images of Chana and apprehensions about her fate. He rose early the next morning and went for a walk. Without noticing, he stood near the spot where he had shaken Chana's hands for the last time. As he recollected the scene, he was seized by shame. Even if not all soldiers wrote poetry on a mission, this was a keepsake, something precious that a comrade had entrusted to him — and not just anybody, but this enchanting and quite extraordinary girl. And he had thrown it away! Frantically he began to search the bushes, which all looked alike now. And then he saw something like a cottonwood flower caught on a branch. Very gently Reuven untangled it, smoothed out the crumpled page, which had been torn from a notebook, and read the four lines:

> *Happy is the match that was consumed in igniting the flame.*
> *Happy is the flame that burned in the depths of those hearts.*
> *Happy are the hearts that knew how to stop beating for the sake of honor.*
> *Happy is the match that was consumed in igniting the flame.*

Heroism under Torture, Budapest, June 1944

[Immediately after crossing the border Chana (Anikó) was arrested. Refusing to reveal the secret code of the British, she was tortured. Then her mother Kato Szenes was arrested and brought to the same prison to be used in a ploy to break Chana's resistance. The Hungarian Nazi interrogator, Rozsa, interrogated Kato (Chana's mother) about Anikó (Chana).]

"Mrs. Szenes, where do you really think your daughter is at this moment?" There had been similar questions before, so Kato repeated her answer calmly.

"To the best of my knowledge, she is living and working in an agricultural settlement, somewhere near Haifa." Rozsa leaned down and peered into the face.

"Well, since you want to pretend ignorance, let me enlighten you. Your precious little Anikó is in this building, right next door, in

---

Eretz Yisrael, 1941–1942
Chana reflects on Martyrdom   BY PETER HAY

The pervasive air of pessimism around her (due to Nazi successes across Europe) inevitably led Chana to meditate on the ultimate questions. "It's noble to die like martyrs and leave the earth to the unclean," she quoted one of her favorite writers. "But if a heroic death is supposed to sanctify God's name, what about life?" Chana did not want to die. But she faced the possibility in this prophetic verse:

> So young to die . . . no, no, not I.
> But if it must be that I live today
> I love the warm and sunny skies,
> With blood and death on every hand,
> Light, songs, shining eyes.
> Praised be He for the grace, I'll say
> I want no war, no battle cry —
> To live, if I should die this day...
> No, no . . . Not I. Upon your soil, my home, my land.

(Translated by Dorothy H. Rochmis)

The closer the objective reality of mass destruction came, the more Chana rejected the idea of her own death. She believed deeply that life on earth must be meaningful; until she had achieved that meaning, or some part of it, she felt she could not die.

To Chana her mother's situation seemed much more dangerous than her own. She felt she lived in shameful luxury. "My conscience is tormented," she wrote in her diary, "that I have it too easy here. **I feel the need to do something, something difficult, which would require a great effort, so that I can justify my existence.**" "The time has come," she wrote, "to give back to society what has been lavished on me."

> His doubts about her military competence assailed him: was this a commando who had coolly estimated the risks, or a hopeless romantic, scribbling verses in these last minutes instead of studying maps?

fact. In a moment, I'm going to have her brought in here. You must convince her that it's in her best interest to tell us what she knows. If she won't, I promise you'll never see each other again."

Kato stood as she heard these portentous words, grasping the edge of the table near her for support. The floor seemed to slip from beneath her feet. Dizzy, she closed her eyes and felt in those few seconds her life drain from her, taking all meaning, all faith, and all hope with it. She heard a door open behind her and involuntarily turned around.

Four men were dragging in a young woman whom Kato could scarcely recognize. Her hair was disheveled and matted; her whole face was swollen and bruised. Her eyes, what remained visible of them, reflected an infinite well of suffering. And they were Anikó's eyes.

It took only a moment for Anikó to realize that her mother was present in the room. With the desperate strength of a wounded animal she tore herself free from the grip of the four guards and hurled herself across the room into her mother's arms.

"Forgive me, Mother!" Kato enfolded her sobbing child, feeling Anikó's racing heartbeats against her own, Anikó's tears scalding her own skin.

"Well, talk to her," said Rozsa. "She must tell us what she knows." Then he repeated his earlier threat: "If you don't convince her to talk, you won't ever see each other again."

Kato sensed only the danger; her numbed mind could hardly guess what circumstances had brought Anikó to that room. But regardless of her own pain and bewildered desire to know the truth, she was certain of this: Anikó must have good reasons for not telling these people what they wanted to know, and Kato would not try to influence her otherwise.

Anikó was equally in shock, having withstood unspeakable physical tortures. As her body was ravaged, her mind had roamed the freedom of the sea and the sand at Sedot Yam [on the beach of the Mediterranean in Eretz Yisrael]. But now her capture was inflicting enormous pain on the person she loved most. If anything could crack her will, it would be this unbearable realization. In that state, at the slightest suggestion from

Chana with her favorite cow in Nahalal farm settlement in I____, early 1940s.
(Courtesy of the Senesh family)

Kato, she might have confessed immediately everything these men wanted to hear. But her mother's unquestioning silence gave her the strength to hold out.

After a few seconds the tense silence produced another outburst from Rozsa. "Dammit, why don't you talk to her?" Kato did not recognize her own voice: "I see no point in your threats; my daughter and I heard you."

Anikó had no time to recover from the unexpected meeting with her mother. Rozsa entered the room and immediately opened

Chana and her brother Gyuri at their last reunion in Tel Aviv, the night before Chana began her mission, 1944

(Courtesy of the Senesh family)

with a new tactic — gentleness. "I'm sorry that we've had to be rough with you, miss. After all, I have always held your father [the Hungarian writer] in the highest regard. I regret about your esteemed mother, too. It's obvious how dearly you love each other."

He paused. She listened impassively. "You have committed a great crime against your country. Fortunately, it's still possible to reverse it. If you tell me where the cipher [to crack the British secret radio code] is, it's not too late to correct your error."

Anikó remained silent.

"If you don't," Rozsa's voice became ominous, "I have no choice but to execute your mother. She will be killed first, right in front of you. Then we will kill you. The decision is up to you."

"No! Don't you touch my mother! You have no right!" Anikó could not restrain herself.

Pleased with his success, Rozsa leaned over and repeated slowly: "I will have your mother killed in front of you." For the first time during her interrogations and tortures, Anikó lost control, crying hysterically.

"You can torture me to death, kill me — but don't — don't touch — my mother!"

"Where's the code?"

"Spare my mother!"

"The code!"

"My mother! Don't hurt her!"

"I'll give you three hours to think, miss," Rozsa said icily. "If you talk, you may see her again. If not, you'll be responsible for her death sentence. I'll make sure it is carried out tomorrow." Then he ordered her back to her cell.

Anikó sat in a corner of her cell, turned to stone. Her hysterics had subsided but slowly the cold reality of her dilemma awakened greater panic than she had ever known. If she betrayed the code, the Germans would use it to lure Allied aircraft into Hungary and shoot them down. She might have been able to

An Ode to a Mother's Quiet Heroism: Chana and her Mother

[Chana loved her mother Kato intensely.] If she really had great talent, Chana thought, she would be able to express all her love in a stanza, or else "not a thousand pages would suffice to create her portrait." She had written her first poem about Kato [in Hungarian] at the age of twelve:

> If the world offered a reward,
> Let there be thanks in your hearts
> A laurel for patience and love,
> And on you lips a prayer,
> One person alone would be worthy:
> Whenever you hear that loveliest word:
> Mother. Mother.

[Later in Eretz Yisrael] she made one of her first attempts in Hebrew to describe her mother's quiet heroism, expressing her marvel at all mothers. That Mrs. Szenes could not have read it without a translation was to Chana a sad symbol of the chasm between them:

> Where did you learn to wipe the tears,
> To quietly bear the pain,
> To hide in your heart the cry, the hurt,
> The suffering and the complaint? . . .
> From where is this quiet in your heart,
> Where have you learned your strength?

(Translated by Ruth Finer Mintz)

accept for herself the infamy of being a traitor. Nor was she afraid of death; if she was not executed, she would take the earliest opportunity of committing suicide. But it was only her own life and honor at stake. She felt she was a special emissary from the people of Eretz Yisrael to the Diaspora. She thought of all her *chaverim* [her kibbutz and movement comrades] and the disgrace they would feel when they heard about her betrayal. She still had a choice, if only she could hold out.

She felt calmer as her former clarity returned. But what about her mother? Suddenly all the ideals for which she was willing to lay down her own life faded into insignificance. Even if she could contemplate her own end, how could she condemn her

mother to death? Her mother had not volunteered for the mission; she did not even understand what was happening. All the love Anikó felt for this extraordinary woman, all the pain of their five years' separation, all the guilt for causing her mother this anguish now overwhelmed her. It no longer mattered what happened to herself. Her mother must come first, and then the mission, the *chaverim*, and Eretz Yisrael. She must not let her own foolish heroism destroy the person who was dearer than all the world.

The guards came to fetch her. Numb, Anikó allowed them to lead her up the stairs. She had decided to give Rozsa the title of the French book that contained the code. After all, there was a small chance that they might not find it, or know how to use it. Probably the cipher had been changed long ago. The main thing was that her mother would live, go to Palestine, where Gyuri [her brother] needed her. Anikó would end her own life soon, but her mother at least would live to explain why her daughter had turned traitor. Perhaps some might understand.

"What did you decide?" Rosza's voice came to her through a fog.

Anikó thought that her inner argument had been settled; she was ready to talk. But now an unexpected voice spoke up: Was it really true that nobody would mind if she had become a traitor? She knew suddenly with brilliant clarity that her mother would gladly die rather than see her daughter betray her cause.

Anikó looked straight into Rozsa's expectant face: "I've got nothing to say. I left the cipher book with the radio." The last thing she saw was Rozsa's head drop, like a cobra about to strike. She tried to find something to hold on to, but the world went dark as she felt her body hit the ground. [In the end the Nazis did not carry out their threat but continued to hold Chana and her mother Kato in the same prison, while they kept up the intense interrogations of Chana over the next few months].

Paper Dolls and Prison Life
(June, 1944 to November, 1944)

[Chana and her mother Kato were kept in the same prison for several months. Chana found ways to send her messages, to signal her through the window during her exercise time and to encourage all her fellow prisoners. Even the Gestapo were impressed.]

Anikó also amazed her mother with her information about outside events, despite her

---

She was full of encouragement and advice for fellow prisoners, about how to handle the interrogators and especially their own fear of the Gestapo.

---

isolation in solitary. Much of her information came from those endlessly futile Gestapo interrogation sessions. She spent a great deal of time with new prisoners in the prison van and waiting with others for her turn. She was full of encouragement and advice for fellow prisoners, about how to handle the interrogators and especially their own fear of the Gestapo. As these prisoners came back to jail they recounted stories like the following, investing Anikó with a legendary aura. A young girl overheard Anikó asking an SS soldier, who was escorting her into interrogation: "What kind of punishment would you give me, if it were up to you?" To which the SS man replied: "I wouldn't punish you at all, because I have never met a woman as brave as you."

Anikó's window became a sort of broadcast center, where other prisoners could get the latest news. A few days after her birthday Anikó climbed up at the window and ran her index finger across her upper lip and then quickly across her neck. That is how her audience learned about the attempt on Hitler's life that took place on July 20, 1944. Signaling entailed constant risk, but Anikó's daring seemed to know no limits. Although she had won the matrons over to her side, there were plenty of dangers left, especially

the prison commandant, Scharführer Lemmke.

Lemmke was a typical Nazi, a sadist who took great delight in beating his prisoners for the slightest infractions. He literally poured salt into their wounds, kicking them in the ribs when they fell to the floor. Making his rounds one day, he observed Anikó cutting out paper letters. Lemmke rushed into the cell, fist raised. He clearly expected her to cringe and beg for mercy, but Anikó looked at him calmly, without interrupting her work: "Please, take a seat," she said.

Lemmke stared at her in disbelief. "This is that British paratrooper," one of the German matrons whispered anxiously. The commandant nodded, looking around at the simple decorations that Anikó had made to create a home for herself. Lemmke's eyes paused on the bed, where a pair of paper dolls lay in a lovers' embrace.

"What's this?" he asked ominously.

"Dolls," replied Anikó matter-of-factly. The matrons waited fearfully for the explosion. A long pause ensued.

"You are forbidden to make male dolls!" Lemmke ordered at last. "If I see another male doll here, I will punish you — severely!" Then he turned and stalked out, as if he had just scored a great victory.

From then on Scharführer Lemmke visited Anikó's cell regularly. He would ask politely whether he could sit down, and listened intently to Anikó's calm explanations of why Germany had lost the war. She also told him about the retribution that would come to him and his fellow Nazis for all their crimes. After these sessions, the commandant would leave her cell lost in thought.

The Execution of an "Extraordinary Personality" (November, 7, 1944)

[In early November the Fascist Hungarian government took over the prison from the Nazis and secretly court-martialled Chana Szenes for "treason." That very day Kato,

Chana's mother, was appealing to the head of the prison for mercy for her daughter, when he interrupted her:] "These are not ordinary times. Your daughter was court-martialled. She had been found in possession of a military radio. The judges found her guilty of treason and asked for the maximum penalty. And the sentence has already been carried out."

There was a long tense silence, which forced the officer to say: "By the way, I must remark upon your daughter's courage, which she exhibited to the very last." [Although she had a chance to request clemency. She refused. She also refused to wear a black hood over her head and chose to face her executioners eye-to-eye.] Then as if he had found this incomprehensible and yet admirable, he added: "Fancy, she was actually proud of being Jewish! She really had an extraordinary personality. It's a pity that she used her talents for the wrong cause."

Chana left behind two letters. One was to Yoel Palgi, her fellow imprisoned paratrooper:

"Don't give up. Continue the struggle to the end, until the day of liberty, the day of victory for our people."

The other letter was to her mother: "My beloved mother, I don't know what to say, only this: a million thanks. Forgive me if you can. Only you can understand why words are unnecessary . . . With endless love — Your daughter."

In a package that she left behind, was found the last poem she wrote about her life in her small prison cell:

One-two-three . . . eight steps is the length,
The width is just two strides across.
Life hangs over me like a question mark.
One-two-three . . . perhaps another week,
But over my head hovers — nothing.
This July I would have been 23 . . .
In a risky gamble I stood on a number
The dice spun, I lost.[39]

---

39. The poem is quoted by Aharon Megged in the wonderful book of Israeli heroes entitled, *The Lionhearts*, edited by Michael Bar-Zohar, p. 50.

Chana Szenes' Legacy: Reburied in Israel, 1950   BY PETER HAY

[Kato Szenes ultimately survived the war and made aliyah. She watched as] Chana's fame grew daily. In December 1945, a clandestine immigration ship called the *Chana Szenes* arrived in Eretz Yisrael with its precious cargo of Holocaust survivors. Schools, settlements, a forest, cultural centers, and dozens of streets were named after her. In Budapest there was the Anna Szenes Home for Girls for the few returning orphans from Auschwitz.

By the time Israel was proclaimed a state and had won her independence, relations with Stalinist Hungary had deteriorated. Israel wanted to bring back the remains of Chana and the six other Jewish parachutists who fell in Europe. The Communist authorities acceded to the request, partly because the martyrs' section in the cemetery was attracting large numbers of people, the only place in the city where assembly was not forbidden.

In 1950 when the ship arrived in the port of Haifa, it

seemed to Kato as if the whole of Israel had turned out to welcome back her daughter. Chana's coffin lay in state in front of City Hall, flanked by a guard of honor of paratroopers from the new Israeli Defense Force.

The triumphant funeral procession continued to Tel Aviv and finally to Jerusalem, and to the Knesset, where the entire legislative body accompanied the hearse to the former Jewish Agency building that was now the seat of government. And so the solemn marchers made their ascent of Mount Herzl. There, near the tomb of Theodor Herzl, with full military honors, Chana Szenes was given a soldier's burial in the Cemetery for Heroes. Chana's heroic life was driven by an inner need, as she wrote in her diary:

"It was not by chance that my life developed the way it did. It all came from some inner need, which at the time was beyond all reason, inevitable. Any other choice would have made me miserable."

COURAGE IN THE CAUSE OF ISRAEL'S SURVIVAL:
A PHYSICAL AND AN ETHICAL STRUGGLE

The image of the hero in society fluctuates according to the needs of the times and the elite that leads the people. In the medieval period the rabbinic scholar and the religious martyr were the official role models to be emulated. In pre-state Israel the secular agricultural pioneer was praised and his life turned into poetry, song and art. After the Holocaust, Israel struggled to make the "fighter" the normative hero of society rather than the martyr or even the pre-state pioneer. That mythic soldier was one who never cries and who is a man of action, not of words. Unfortunately that image of the soldier hero is sometimes dismissed as a matter of mere animal courage or patriotic militarism. However the real soldier heroes of the Jewish people in the twentieth century are much more nuanced. They often show a sensitive as well as a contemplative side and therefore they have provided some very fine political leaders, such as Yitzchak Rabin who is described above on page 70 of the companion volume of A Different Light: The Hanukkah Book of Celebration.

We begin with Rabbi **Herbert Friedman***, an American Jewish chaplain whose gutsy heroism was not in the field of battle but in the art of smuggling arms (1945-1948) essential for the Israeli War of Independence. Then we will present the young soldier philosopher,* **Yoni Netanyahu***, who was killed tragically in the otherwise successful rescue of Jewish hostages held by terrorists in the Entebbe Airport in Uganda (July 4, 1976). His letters to his family sent between the United States and Israel reflect his intense life of soul searching. He was a sensitive young man struggling with his personal growth and his national responsibility, with a passion for life and a willingness to sacrifice his life for his people.*

Ambassador Yitzchak Rabin and Prime Minister Golda Meir consult with Rabbi Herbert Friedman in September 1970 in New York City. President Nixon had just requested Israeli military intervention to prevent a Syrian attack on Jordan after King Hussein cracked down on Palestinian terrorists.

(courtesy of
Rabbi Herbert Friedman)

11

THE RABBINIC ART OF SMUGGLING

A HEROIC LAWBREAKER

by Herbert Friedman [40]

The Reform rabbi, Herbert Friedman, learned to violate American law systematically and very creatively in the name of higher values between 1945 — 1948. Here are two delightful tales of his adventures in illegality for the sake of Israel's cultural and physical survival.

THE STOLEN BOOKS OF OFFENBACH (GERMANY, 1946)

Hitler's regime, under the direction of its philosopher, Alfred Rosenberg, planned to accumulate a vast library of Judaica. The perverted purpose: to enable Nazi "scholars" to search the literature for quotations that would serve to condemn the Jews and their religion in the eyes of the world, thus validating the charge that this whole people endangered mankind and must be exterminated. Jews, the exercise aimed to prove, worshipped money, extorted it from the Christians they despised, were sexually unclean and promiscuous, believed in communism, spat at churches, possessed a secret government that plotted to take over the whole world; and there were many other similarly poisonous accusations.

After the War, Allied inventories of Nazi government buildings turned up the [Judaica] collection. It ultimately came under the authority of the Fine Arts Section of the American military government. A professor at the Hebrew University in Jerusalem, the famed [German Jewish] scholar of mysticism, **Gershom Scholem**, applied through the Jewish Agency for permission to examine the materials. The military government granted permission on condition that he not remove a single item.

In his diligent search through the enormous pile of materials, Scholem had identified and set aside 1,100 pieces, mostly hand-written manuscripts of incalculable value, each one unique, all looted from museums, synagogues, private collections, and all absolutely irreplaceable. He was so nervous about the treasured items that, loath to see them thrown once more into the anonymous pile or stolen for sale on the black market then flourishing in Germany, he kept them segregated in five large, wooden crates. He had marked each with his name and address, but without a description of contents.

Scholem then asked the Fine Arts Section to reconsider its previous requirement and allow him to take the five crates to Jerusalem, where they would be carefully kept in the Rare Book Vault of Hebrew University Library. The American authorities refused.

[Then Scholem came to me because I was the U.S. Army chaplain in liberated Berlin.] When he finished telling me the story, he actually broke down from fatigue, strain, and worry. I came up with an instant solution: I would steal the boxes and see that they reached safekeeping in Jerusalem. I made that rash and risky declaration without consulting anyone and without having a plan in my head; my response came straight from the heart.

The following scheme soon evolved: I would tell the officer in charge of the Offenbach depot, of my intention to remove the crates of books (of whose real contents he was unaware) for distribution to the many DP camp libraries. That was permitted by Fine Arts and had already occurred many times. I would "borrow" a Joint Distribution Committee ambulance, just the right-sized windowless vehicle. On New Year's Eve, a few days hence, I would pull the ambulance up to the rear loading dock around midnight, when the personnel on duty would presum-

40. Rabbi Herbert Friedman, *Roots of the Future* (1999) (Gefen Publishing House, gefenbooks@compuserve.com) pp. 106-111, 132-136, by generous permission of the author and publisher.

ably be somewhat less than sharply alert. If not too drunk, they would see only a khaki-colored vehicle, with Army plates and an officer in uniform behind the wheel. I would ask one or two to help me load, then drive the ambulance to a locked garage, where it would sit until I could secure orders from my head-quarters for a few days leave-time in Paris. Thence the final step was to load the ambu-lance and myself into a freight car bound for Paris, and deliver the crates to Jewish Agency officials.

Everything went smoothly [and the rare books stolen by the Nazis came to the Jewish homeland via Paris to Jerusalem].

One morning, a few weeks later, I found two Criminal Investigation Department (CID) men waiting for me. They quietly and

---

They quietly and calmly charged me with grand larceny, laid out their evidence, and indicated they were submitting it to the Judge Advocate General, who would convene a general court martial.

---

calmly charged me with grand larceny, laid out their evidence, and indicated they were submitting it to the Judge Advocate General, who would convene a general court martial. They had done a very thorough job and had me dead to rights.

The best course, I decided, was to tell the whole story to the Chief Jewish Chaplain, my superior, Rabbi Bernstein. His reaction was wonderful. At first he was worried that I would have to endure some serious punishment; then he chuckled over the complexity of the adventure, and wound up praising me for the idealism of the deed. That last thought gave him a vital clue as to how to proceed.

He suggested that he would pave the way for me immediately to see General Lucius D. Clay, the new Commander of U.S. Forces in the European Theater, to throw myself on his mercy by stressing the idealistic motives that

impelled me. In other words, I should readily admit to the crime and ask for clemency. That's exactly what I did.

Clay was a quiet, firm, very intelligent man, a four-star general who was as much an administrator as a warrior. He listened, asked questions, and at the end clearly understood the circumstances and the motivation behind my action. He thought for several moments, then called the head of the CID, to inform him that charges against me were to be dropped.

My relief at the deal involving the materials proved to be short lived. The crates were stored in the library of the Hebrew Univer-sity on Mount Scopus in Jerusalem. But 18 months later, during the War of Indepen-dence in Israel, Scopus fell into Jordanian hands. What tricks fate plays!

Once again, however, patience and ingenuity solved the situation. A clause in the armistice agreement with Jordan [1949] permitted Israel to station 25 or so of her soldiers on Jordanian territory — in reality, a 100-meter trench on Mount Scopus — as a symbolic gesture of supervision over the Hadassah Hospital and the few university buildings. This group of men rotated every two weeks. The Israeli officer in charge knew that the Scholem material lay in a nearby Hebrew University building. He succeeded in bringing small numbers of manuscripts to the trench and hiding them, one at a time, under his soldiers' shirts.

When the rotating group descended from Scopus to Israeli territory in U.N. vehicles, there was no body search and the hidden cargo returned to Israeli hands. The relieving group was taken up, and two weeks later, when they came down, another batch came with them. This process was repeated — over the course of several years — until all the manuscripts had been brought down and carefully gathered by Scholem, with no loss whatsoever.

And so, in the end, the story does conclude happily. Rescued from the Nazi trap, brought to British Palestine, carried through the fire of the birth of Israel, caught in Jordan's hands, and free at last, the manuscripts seemed like living beings, their course paralleling that of the Jewish people itself.

Books! They form the soul of the Jewish people, the sustaining strength of its stubborn refusal to die out. The very core of its mysterious immortality lies in the books it has read and cherished and re-read as its essential nourishment.

Saving those books amounts to saving the People of the Book, for the intellectual and spiritual messages they contain are the best guarantee of the people's continued physical existence. These manuscripts, remnants of our people's past, at risk of destruction in the present, had been saved for the future, and I had been privileged to play a pivotal role in the adventure.

EXPORTING DYNAMITE AND PEACHES (COLORADO, 1947)

[After my discharge in 1947 and my return to the USA] I may have become a civilian in the eyes of the US Army, but not in the calculations of the Haganah, [the Israeli underground military force in British controlled Eretz Yisrael, the Hebrew name for what the British called Palestine. I had worked with the Haganah closely in arranging the illegal immigration of Jewish refugees through the American zone of liberated Germany]. Its commander in the United States was Teddy Kollek, aide to Ben-Gurion, ultimately world-famous mayor of Jerusalem (1965-1993). Teddy was headquartered in the Hotel 14, next door to the Copacabana nightclub on East 60th St. in Manhattan. Some said that the Hotel 14 served as the location where the Copa's showgirls plied a trade in addition to their dance routines on the nightclub stage. Whatever the case, there always seemed to be a steady flow of male visitors to the hotel, and all the traffic headed for Teddy's suite of rooms was buried anonymously in the general stream.

The projects involved the acquisition and then shipment of munitions to Eretz Yisrael. The acquisition part encompassed many co-conspirators, complicated logistics, the fending off of investigators — and a risk of imprisonment. The shipment involved breaking the law, which embargoed sending arms to the Middle East. Yet [when Kollek contacted me] I undertook the task without hesitation because I was convinced that it was a matter of life and death for the state-to-be.

The Jews suffered from a serious shortage of heavy artillery. In response, the Haganah's experts came up with something called a satchel charge. It consisted of assembling two stacks of dynamite bricks, three bricks to a stack, wired together, attached to a detonator cord of the desired length, and tucked inside a standard knapsack. In 1947, embargo or not, dynamite bricks and many other embargoed items had to be obtained and shipped, whatever the cost or risk.

I was to set up in Denver a mining company carefully documented with appropriate permits, quit-claim deeds, a full set of journals and ledgers, balance sheets, profit and loss statements, and tax payments on profits. Reading through all that paper work, one could well be satisfied that it described a real, operating company. The documents were executed by two skillful lawyers, selected by me for their discretion and loyalty to the cause as well as their technical expertise. The set of books was kept in a locked safe in my office at Temple Emanuel, where I served as rabbi.

My company then started ordering dynamite bricks from Dupont [in Delaware] for shipment to its office in Boulder, Colorado. A vigorous search, plus a lucky tip, had uncovered a perfect storage place a couple of miles outside Boulder; an abandoned mine shaft with tracks and ore cars still intact, running about a half-mile into a mountain. The Dupont shipments arrived by freight car. A wonderful man, Sam Sterling, with his gang of local Jewish War Veterans as stevedores, unloaded the crates in the railroad yard, trucked them to the mine shaft, and rolled them deep into the mountain on the ore cars.

During the months of the operation, there was only one mishap. Because of an error in the Dupont shipping department, several of my orders got backed up, and instead of being sent in the small quantity that each order called for, many orders were bunched together. One day the sheriff of Boulder County bellowed over my phone that 33 freight cars full of dynamite were in the railroad yard, enough to blow the city of Boulder off the map, and if I didn't get them unloaded by nightfall, he was declaring an emergency that would give him the right to

---

> After measuring various cardboard cartons, we discovered that our bricks fit exactly into Del Monte fruit cartons, with no space left over so that nothing would be loose and shifting inside. And thus it went. The dynamite came in, the "peaches" went out.

---

send them back to Delaware or turn them over to the nearby U.S. Rocky Mountain Arsenal.

Within minutes, Sam Sterling was rounding up his crew, and I was canceling my confirmation class and all other appointments. Believe it or not, working through the afternoon and all night long under lanterns, we got the stuff tucked away. At daybreak, I brought the sheriff over to the freight yards to [show him everything was gone].

[Once we had received the dynamite, we needed to disguise it and prepare it for shipment to Palestine]. We formed an export company for the selling and shipping of canned fruit to the Far East. After measuring various cardboard cartons, we discovered that our bricks fit exactly into Del Monte fruit cartons, with no space left over so that nothing would be loose and shifting inside. But how could we get thousands of cartons? Only one way suggested itself: go to California and steal them. We did exactly that. [After getting the guard drunk] a single foray yielded enough cartons.

And thus it went. The dynamite came in, the "peaches" went out. Periodically, I traveled to the Hotel 14 in New York, got a whopping amount of cash, deposited it to the special account in my Denver bank, and paid taxes on the theoretical profits of my two companies. [With these illegal arms Israel was able to defeat seven invading Arab armies and to carve out the first independent Jewish state in 2000 years, despite the American boycott on sending arms to the Middle East].

Hillel says: ■ Do not abandon the community.
■ In a place where there are no men, strive to be a man.
■ If I am not for myself, who will be for me?
And if I am only for myself, what am I?
And if not now, when?

— MISHNA, PIRKEI AVOT, CHAPTER 1-2

12

YONI NETANYAHU

THE PHILOSOPHER-SOLDIER AND THE RESCUE OF THE HOSTAGES[41] (ENTEBBE AIRPORT, UGANDA, JULY 4, 1976)

Yoni — a constant battle against sleep, fatigue, self indulgence, forgetfulness, inefficiency, helplessness, lying. Yoni turns the impossible into the possible.

— E. BAR-MEIR, A FRIEND

Because each and every minute is made up of seconds and of even briefer fragments of time, and every fragment ought not to be allowed to pass in vain... I must feel certain that not only at the moment of my death shall I be able to account for the time I have lived; I ought to be ready at every moment of my life to confront myself and say — This is what I've done.

— YONI, AGED 16 [SELF-PORTRAIT OF A HERO, P. 7]

What a mad world we live in! In the twentieth century man has reached the moon and is out for more. The twentieth century has seen Hitler and his mass murders, as well as the terrible First World War — and still all this hasn't cured us.
We watch as a whole people is being starved to death, and no one in this ugly world is moved by it sufficiently to do something. Everybody is preoccupied by his own wars (including Israel, including me), and no state goes in there with its army to put an end to the whole thing. But of course not! No one wants to get involved. Men are such strange animals. I prophesy a brilliant future for us as ugly particles floating in space after the big bomb that is bound to come.

— YONI, 1969, [SELF-PORTRAIT OF A HERO, P. 187]

Yoni Netanyahu listening to a troubling military briefing from the Commander of the Northern Front, facing Syria on the Golan Heights during the Yom Kippur War, 1973. (Courtesy of the Netanyahu Family)

---

41. The information for this section was drawn from several sources and attributed quotes derive from *Self-Portrait of a Hero*, Jonathan Netanyahu and the "Afterword" by Iddo Netanyahu [I.N.] (Warner Books, Random House, 1980 pp. ix, 6-8, 66, 125, 128, 134, 140, 163-164, 171-174, 177, 187, 258, 283-293, 298, 301-302 with corrections by Professor Benzion Netanyahu — selections are reprinted with the generous permission of the Netanyahu family); from Kent Valentine [K.V.], "Terrorists" from *Military History*; from Chaim Herzog [C.H.], *Heroes of Israel* (Little, Brown and Co, 1980, pp. 274, 276) with the permission of Wiedenfeld and Nicholson as well as one brief selection from Shimon Peres [S.P.], "The Bearer of the Sheaves," *The Lionhearts*, edited by Michael bar Zohar (p. 286), for which permission was requested.

THE BIOGRAPHY OF A YOUNG SOLDIER AND PHILOSOPHER, YONI NETANYAHU, 1946-1976

by Iddo Netanyahu and Chaim Herzog
with Letters by Yoni Netanyahu

The famous Israeli soldier who led the most daring rescue of hostages in history, at the Entebbe airport in Uganda on July 4, 1976, was born in America. His father was a professor of the history of the Jews in the Middle Ages, in particular the Jews of Spain during the Inquisition, and a committed Revisionist Zionist. The family returned to Jerusalem during the War of Independence in 1948. However, in 1963 Yoni, already an idealist leader in the Israeli scouting movement at age 16, was wrenched from Israel and taken back to the United States with his family, while his father finished his work as editor-in-chief of the Encyclopedia Hebraica.

During these high school years in Israel and in exile in America and during the next twelve years of his life in Israel, Yoni found a cause worth living and dying for. He fought for Israel in the Six Day War and the Yom Kippur War. During that whole period he would fight bravely, lead his men and then try to withdraw into urban life — studying at Harvard, getting married — but each time he would feel the call to duty and he would reenlist. Yoni lived intensely the contrasts between his American high school experience and his experience in the Israeli scout movement, between the campuses of Harvard and the Hebrew University and an elite assault unit and between urban life and killing terrorists at point blank range. These fueled his sensitive and philosophic reflections on life and death and his sophisticated commitment to the Jewish people.

These reflections teach us so much about a unique type of military heroism. They present a glimpse of a responsible citizen who loves his personal life and yet is willing to sacrifice himself for the collective life of his society. In these thoughtful letters we discover a deeply self-aware human being, aware of the deep sadness of young people like himself, who occasionally feel prematurely old when they realize they are fighting a long war possibly without end.

We begin this section with the action packed drama of the Entebbe Raid and Yoni's part in the last battle of his life. Then we will go back to the important junctures in his life bringing selections from his deeply insightful letters reprinted in Self-Portrait of a Hero.

OPERATION YONATAN NETANYAHU: ENTEBBE, JULY 4, 1976

Late in the afternoon of July 3, 1976, as the people of the United States prepared to celebrate their national bicentennial, a series of meticulously planned events were beginning to unfold halfway around the world. Four heavily laden Lockheed C-130 Hercules transports of the Israeli Air Force were skimming low over the Red Sea, hoping to avoid radar detection as they headed toward Africa.

On the flight deck of the lead "Hippo," the affectionate nickname the aircrews had for the Hercules, the pilot listened intently as a few terse code words were relayed to his headset from IDF headquarters near Tel Aviv. Moments later, the pilot turned and shouted over the din of the loud turboprops to a silent figure sitting in a jump seat in the rear of the cockpit: "Operation Thunderbolt is a go!"

Aboard the first C-130, Yoni Netanyahu, assault commander of the commandos, sat silently in the front seat of a black Mercedes-Benz sedan. Since Ugandan President Amin had made a point of visiting the hostages several times since their arrival, the planners knew that he customarily rode in a black Mercedes. They hoped that the use of a look-alike car might serve as a deception, to buy the strike force a few extra precious seconds of surprise. [K.V.]

Flashback:
The Hijacking, June 27, 1976

Six days before, on June 27, an Air France flight originating in Tel Aviv picked up passengers in Athens en route to Paris. Among the additional passengers who boarded the aircraft during its short layover in Greece were four nondescript individuals carrying a number of parcels. Unknown to the crew and passengers, two of the four were members of Germany's infamous Baader-

Meinhof left-wing revolutionary terrorist organization. They were accompanied by two Arabs, both of whom were longtime operatives in the Popular Front for the Liberation of Palestine (PFLP) — an active cell of Yasser Arafat's Palestine Liberation Organization (PLO).

Soon after takeoff, the four terrorists pulled pistols and grenades from their packages and quickly seized control of the aircraft. One of the hijackers gained entry into the cockpit and forced the Air France captain to turn the large jet toward Benghazi, Libya.

During a lengthy stop in Libya, the plane was refueled, a hostage (a pregnant woman feigning labor) was released, and three more terrorists came aboard bringing the total to seven. The terrorists ordered the pilot to take off once again, this time setting course for Entebbe, Uganda. The jet flew through the night, arriving early on the morning of June 29th. [K.V.]

In Uganda, some two hundred hostages were herded into the old terminal building. Then one of the German hijackers told them that the hall where they were being detained was overcrowded, so that some whose names would be called would be moved to an adjacent hall. All at once, the hostages

---

All at once, the hostages realized that the names being called out: Rosenberg, Aaronovich, Brodsky . . . were all Jews. The Germans were conducting a "selection," segregating those who would die from those who would live, forty years after the Holocaust.

---

realized that the names being called out: Rosenberg, Aaronovich, Brodsky . . . were all Jews. The Germans were conducting a "selection," segregating those who would die from those who would live, forty years after the Holocaust. The non-Jewish hostages were then released leaving some 103 Jewish hostages as well as the Air France crew.

That day, the President of Uganda, Idi Amin, arriving in his beloved late model black Mercedes limousine, visited the hostages in the terminal and flamboyantly assured them he was working to achieve their release and that Ugandan soldiers would remain around the terminal to ensure their safety. In fact, Idi Amin (who ironically had been trained by Israeli military advisors before his takeover of the Ugandan government) had become a vindictive enemy of Israel and was collaborating fully with the terrorists.

On June 30th at 3:30 p.m. a Palestinian terrorist nicknamed the "Peruvian" announced the terrorist demands: Release 53 convicted terrorists held in Israel (40) and in France, Germany and Kenya (13) or else the hostages would be executed one at a time beginning at 2 p.m. on July 1.

In response, the Israeli Prime Minister Yitzchak Rabin (then in his first term of office) called an emergency Cabinet meeting and reviewed the military and political options. France, whose national airline had been hijacked and who had troops stationed in nearby Djibouti, never showed any interest in mounting a rescue mission. [EDITOR]

Rabin was under tremendous pressure from the relatives of the hostages in Israel to negotiate with the terrorists. However, in Entebbe, the hostages themselves were standing up to the pressure rather better than their relatives back home. Faced with a personal demand by Idi Amin to write a letter to their government demanding the release of the terrorists in exchange for themselves, they agonized for an entire day over its composition. "It had to be acceptable to Amin," recalled Sarah Davidson, a hostage, "but we were determined to include nuances that would be understood by the government of Israel, indicating that we were not asking for surrender to the hijackers' demands." [C.H. 274]

On July 1, after the Israeli Chief of Staff Motta Gur reported that the army had no viable rescue plan, given the 2,200 miles from Israel to Uganda, Rabin agreed very reluctantly to negotiate with the terrorists. This violated a sacred principle of Israeli policy that there can be no negotiations with terrorist kidnappers. "My intention was not to use a ruse or a tactical ploy to gain time," Prime Minsiter Rabin later wrote of his government's decision, "but to enter into serious negotiations with Israel fulfilling whatever commitments it made." At that point the terrorists postponed their deadline to July 4th to give a brief chance to negotiations. [EDITOR]

Meanwhile, in Entebbe, the remaining 103 hostages were huddled in the building, as their captors awaited the expiration of their "final" deadline — Sunday, July 4. Although their considerable distance from Israel placed them outside the known combat radius of the Israel Air Force, the terrorists left nothing to chance — they posted guards around the clock, augmenting them with members of Ugandan President Idi Amin's armed forces. The terrorists were determined to ensure that this action not become a repeat of the PLO's unsuccessful attempt to capture and hold a Sabena Airlines 727 at Lod Airport in Israel on May 8, 1972. In that operation, a team of elite Israeli commandos, including Yoni's brother, future Prime Minister Benjamin Netanyahu, and Benjamin's commander, future Prime Minister Ehud Barak, had stormed the aircraft the next day, while dressed as airline mechanics, killing or capturing all four terrorists and freeing the hostages. [K.V.]

Yoni's Plan: July 1-2, 1976

In Israel the elite anti-terrorist commando unit headed by Yoni Netanyahu was called upon to prepare a rescue option to be developed while negotiations proceeded. The Defense Minister Shimon Peres explained: "Yoni had been appointed head of the unit a year earlier. This appointment requires serious deliberation, both on the part of the General Staff and of the soldiers and their officers. The commander chosen is responsible for very daring acts, which are sometimes dangerous. The morale and the skill of such are to a large extent dependent on the commander. His character, his courage, his resourcefulness, and his leadership ability are constantly being tested. Thus, before making such an appointment, the General Staff not only asks the opinion of the candidate's senior officers, but also of his future soldiers. (There are two kinds of reports given on soldiers and officers, one through the hierarchic channels of the army and one an unofficial report that circulates among the men. The official report determines the rank of the man; the unofficial one determines his status.) Yoni was a natural choice, an appointment undisputed both by those above him and by those below him. He had already proved himself in actual battles to be a man of rare courage, resourcefulness, and unusual wisdom." [S.P.]

Yoni had just finished grueling maneuvers in the desert when he was called to the Entebbe mission. He threw off his exhaustion and started analyzing intelligence reports. Many Israelis had served in Uganda years before, when it was still friendly towards Israel. Several Israeli officers had assisted in the training of Ugandan troops, and their knowledge was now utilized. Photographs of the airport were scanned and a "home movie," which showed Idi Amin arriving in a black Mercedes limousine escorted by a Land Rover, gave the planners a new idea.

At the same time Israeli agents were dispatched to Paris, where they debriefed the non-Israeli passengers [who had been released and were] now back in the French capital, and who gave full information about conditions at the airport. The interrogators were able to discover the daily routine at the airport, where the passengers were held, where the terrorists slept, the number, nature and character of the terrorists and the location of the Ugandan soldiers. More information became available from a television film of Entebbe airport by a foreign correspondent. [C.H. 276]

By Thursday night July 1 there was a basic plan of attack. The Unit's officers convened around midnight to receive an initial briefing from Yoni and instructions on preparations. "Yoni was very tired," recalls a fellow soldier. "You could see it by looking at him. Actually we were all tired from the whole week we had just finished, the officers in particular. So at a certain point I suggested that we stop and get some sleep. This was around 2 or 3 A.M. on Friday morning. Yoni agreed, and the small planning team went to sleep, but it

---

We had a problem with lack of intelligence. But Yoni said: 'Do you know of any operation that wasn't carried out half-blind? Every operation is half-blind.'

---

turned out later that Yoni remained alone at his office and continued to work on the plan. And in fact, when he presented the plan at 7 A.M. the following morning, after sleeping at most one or two hours, I saw how far he had carried the work from where we left off. There were many points in the plan that we had not considered, which Yoni had thought through to the end. That morning he presented the plan complete, perfect, down to the last detail."

The plan called for the Unit's initial force of some thirty men to be flown to Entebbe and to land at night near the new terminal. From there the men were to proceed to the old terminal, arriving in the Mercedes and two Land Rover jeeps, the kind of vehicles frequently used by the Ugandan army. It was hoped that the Ugandan guards surrounding the building would assume that this was a force of their own, perhaps the one that accompanied President Idi Amin on his occasional visit to the hostages. In this manner, it was hoped that the Unit's men would be able to approach the Ugandan guards without first being fired upon. "During the preparations for the raid Yoni foresaw where we would encounter two Ugandan guards . . . and our response in such a case was to take out the two guards with

silencers." [I.N. 284]

On Friday night, July 2, Yoni conducted a full dress rehearsal before the Chief of Staff using a pole-and-burlap mock-up of the Entebbe terminal. A Mercedes had been found in Israel and requisitioned. Since the Israeli car was a light color, it had to be painted black to match Idi Amin's limo. As Yoni once told his soldiers when he was a tank battalion commander, "I believe in getting down to the smallest details. I believe there can be no compromise with results. Never accept results that are less than the best possible, and even then look for ways to improve and perfect them. I believe that the greatest danger in the life of a unit is *not* to be a bit worried — perhaps there is something else we might have done, something we might have improved and didn't." [EDITOR]

Over and over again, the tired soldiers repeated the attack, shaving seconds off the time needed to disembark from the plane and reach the old terminal. Speed was absolutely vital if a massacre of the hostages was to be avoided. [C.H. 276]

On Shabbat morning, July 3, Yoni was called for a meeting with the Defense Minister Shimon Peres (later Prime Minister and winner with Yitzchak Rabin of the Nobel Peace Prize). [EDITOR]

"Yoni stood there (outside Peres's door) with maps in his hands, very preoccupied . . . He was pressed for time and said that he was in a terrible hurry and they should let him in already." "He presented the plan to me in detail," recalls Peres, "and I liked it very much. The two of us sat alone . . . My impression was one of exactingness and imagination . . . and complete self-confidence . . . which without a doubt influenced me. We had a problem with lack of intelligence. But Yoni said: 'Do you know of any operation that wasn't carried out half-blind? Every operation is half-blind.' Yoni told me that the operation was absolutely doable. And as to the cost, he said we had every chance of coming out of it with almost no losses."

Before the mission began, Yoni spoke to his men. He probably expressed a credo similar to what he had told his tank battalion several years earlier: "I believe that the buck should not be passed to anyone else — that it should stop here, with us. I believe with all my heart in our ability to carry out any military mission entrusted to us, and I believe in you. And I believe in Israel and in the sense of responsibility that must accompany every man who fights for the fate of his homeland." "It was a speech I'll never forget," says one of the assault soldiers. "He gave us confidence that we could do it. His leadership and his ability to affect us were simply above and beyond anything." [I.N. 283-286]

In the meantime as the Israeli planes sat in Sharm el Sheik in Sinai on Shabbat, the Israeli Cabinet debated the advisability of approving the risky rescue plan. As the hours dragged, the Chief of Staff realized time was running out for the launching of the planes. He pulled Rabin aside and got approval to send Operation Thunderbolt (later renamed Operation Yonatan) into the air with the possibility of recalling them by radio should the Cabinet relent. [EDITOR]

The lead plane was crowded. It carried Yoni's assault party with its Mercedes. They were flying over the Red Sea, just a few yards above water to avoid radar detection by Egypt and Saudi Arabia. Soon they received the go ahead from the Cabinet and they gathered their strength for their "mission impossible."

"I believe that the buck should not be passed to anyone else — that it should stop here, with us. I believe with all my heart in our ability to carry out any military mission entrusted to us, and I believe in you — the battalion. And I believe in Israel and in the sense of responsibility that must accompany every man who fights for the fate of his homeland."

The Assault on Entebbe Airport
11 P.M. July 3

At 11 P.M. on Saturday night the airport could be seen at a distance, with its runway lights fully lit. Yoni proceeded to get into the passenger seat of the Mercedes. The back ramp was being lowered as the plane was descending toward the runway, and Yoni told the driver to start the car's engine with its Ugandan flags flying and all 35 Israeli commandos dressed in Ugandan style army uniforms.

As the plane landed on the tarmac, the Ugandans in the main control tower probably did not understand what was going on. Some paratroop soldiers jumped off while the plane was taxiing, placing lighted markers on the runway, so that the other three planes would be able to land in case the runway lights were switched off by the men in the control tower. The Hercules transport came to a halt at the designated point and the vehicles got out quickly, led by Yoni's Mercedes. This runway led directly to the old terminal building, where the hostages were being held. "We were sitting in the jeep. We saw it as if in a movie. The Mercedes was advancing, and at a certain point we were approaching the terminal." However, two Ugandan guards appeared at exactly the spot that had been envisaged during the rehearsal in Israel. "When I saw those two guards waiting for us, like the guards Yoni had placed in the rehearsal, I knew that this operation would succeed," says the youngest soldier on the force.

" . . . Suddenly, the Ugandan soldier shouted and came toward us. He approached the Mercedes and made a threatening movement with his weapon . . . and cocked his rifle . . . It was obvious to me that the guard had to be taken out. He then moved into shooting position, raised the rifle to his shoulder. I was sure he was about to fire — no 'ifs' about it."

"If the guard had fired first, the whole operation might have sunk," said the man

What was Yoni reading while sitting in the Mercedes on the flight to Entebbe? We do not know but it may have been similar to his reading list described in a much earlier letter dated February 1967.

[EDITOR]

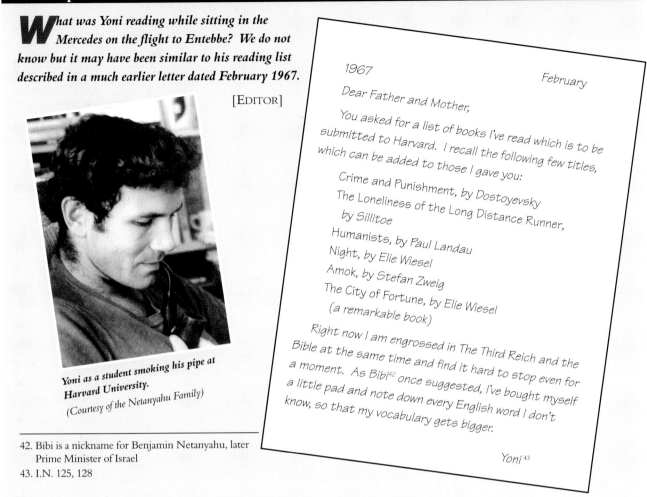

Yoni as a student smoking his pipe at Harvard University.
(Courtesy of the Netanyahu Family)

1967   February

Dear Father and Mother,

You asked for a list of books I've read which is to be submitted to Harvard. I recall the following few titles, which can be added to those I gave you:

Crime and Punishment, by Dostoyevsky
The Loneliness of the Long Distance Runner, by Sillitoe
Humanists, by Paul Landau
Night, by Elie Wiesel
Amok, by Stefan Zweig
The City of Fortune, by Elie Wiesel (a remarkable book)

Right now I am engrossed in The Third Reich and the Bible at the same time and find it hard to stop even for a moment. As Bibi[42] once suggested, I've bought myself a little pad and note down every English word I don't know, so that my vocabulary gets bigger.

Yoni [43]

42. Bibi is a nickname for Benjamin Netanyahu, later Prime Minister of Israel
43. I.N. 125, 128

who was driving the Mercedes. "Yoni told me: 'Slow down a little, we'll approach them.' He told me to slow down so that we wouldn't frighten them, as if we're about to identify ourselves . . . Yoni was quite calm." He and his fellow soldiers had silenced pistols ready in hand. When the Ugandan soldier who was aiming his rifle at them was only several yards away, they fired.

"Yoni told me now to speed up. We went at full speed for about 200 meters or so. He instructed me to stop in front of the control tower." Then the assault on the old terminal began. Any pause in the assault could have disastrous consequences had it continued longer than it did. Every second's delay increased the chances that the terrorists would begin to kill the hostages. When Yoni

saw that the lead man did not respond to his commands, he lurched ahead, thereby signaling the men to follow him.

When Yoni had led the charge up to the entrance of the terminal, he was shot by one of the terrorists. "I saw him make half a turn, with his face contorted and sink down a little bit, with his knees bent."

Someone had shouted that Yoni was hit, but the men of the force continued in their tasks, following Yoni's orders not to take care of the wounded until the hostages were freed. Each of them realized that time was of the essence, as it would have taken only seconds for the terrorists, once they realized what was going on, to have sprayed automatic fire on the huddled hostages.

"When I was about ten yards from the door, I saw the glass break and understood that someone was shooting at me," says an Israeli soldier. "Without thinking twice I shot him through the glass and saw that he was hit." An Israeli commando entered the main hall, where the hostages were being held. He discovered that he was the first soldier inside. Immediately upon his footsteps came his commander who, once he entered the room, saw two terrorists crouching, a man and a woman, aiming their Kalashnikovs at him.

The planes carrying the soldiers landed in Israel in the morning. Rabin and Peres were there to greet them. Peres turned to one of the soldiers and asked: "How was Yoni killed?"
"He went first, he fell first."

He quickly fired at them and killed them. Next, they scanned the room looking for more terrorists. "I looked to my left and saw the two terrorists who were shot. I also saw the fully lit room with all the hostages lying on the floor. After a short time, from the left, a terrorist suddenly leaped up, holding a weapon. I shot him. The first bullet hit his Kalashnikov, went through his weapon, and entered his chest. I shot three bullets that hit him and finished him off." The hostages were still in a daze, flattened out on the floor. Almost all of them were left unhurt. [I.N. 287-292]

Within three minutes of landing and fifteen seconds of opening fire, four of the seven terrorists had been killed. As Yoni's soldiers cleared the terminal, a lone terrorist ran into the building shouting. "The Ugandans have gone crazy! They are shooting at us." The element of surprise and the use of Ugandan style uniforms had worked. The soldiers shot that fifth terrorist and broke into the VIP lounge of the terminal where they found and killed the remaining two terrorists.

Within fifteen minutes of the landing, all seven terrorists were dead, the 103 hostages were freed with only three who eventually died of their wounds, and within less than one hour, at 11:52 P.M., July 3, the first Hercules transport left with the hostages and with the seriously injured Yoni Netanyahu. The rest of the soldiers took off at 12:29 A.M. after blowing up eleven Ugandan MIG fighters parked on the runway. Ninety-nine minutes after landing, the rescue mission was complete. [EDITOR]

The Return Home: Relief without Joy

"On our plane there had been endless chatter," recalls one soldier, "everyone telling everyone what happened to him. It seemed that everything was going great, that we'd succeeded. And then someone came in and said that Yoni had died, and all at once, it seemed as if someone had turned off the entire plane. Everybody was silent . . . We were hit hard, and each of us withdrew into himself."

In Jerusalem, the Chief of Staff entered Shimon Peres's office, where the defense minister had laid down to rest. Peres wrote in his diary, "At four in the morning, the Chief of Staff came into my office, and I could tell he was very upset. 'Shimon, Yoni's gone. A bullet hit him in the heart.'" "This is the first time this whole crazy week," Peres wrote, "that I cannot hold back the tears."

The planes carrying the soldiers landed in Israel in the morning. Rabin and Peres were there to greet them. Peres turned to one of the soldiers and asked: "How was Yoni killed?"
"He went first, he fell first." [I.N. 292-293]

Operation Entebbe is unique in military history. Against a peak of terror, assisted by the army and president of Uganda, at a distance of over four thousand kilometers from home, in one short hour, the posture of the entire Jewish people — in fact, the posture of free and responsible men all over the world — was straightened.

This operation necessitated the taking of an enormous risk, but a risk that seemed to be more justifiable than the other one that was involved — the risk to surrender to terrorists and blackmailers, the risk that is inherent in submission and capitulation.

The most difficult moment of this night of heroism occurred when the bitter news arrived.

A bullet had torn the young heart of one of the finest sons of Israel, one of the most courageous warriors of Israel, one of the most promising among the commanders of the Israel Defense Force — the magnificent Jonathan Netanyahu.

Jonathan was an exemplary commander. With the boldness of his spirit he overcame his enemies, with his wisdom, he won the hearts of his comrades. Danger did not deter him, and triumphs did not swell his heart. Of himself he demanded much, while to the army he gave the sharpness of his intellect, his competence of action and his skill in combat.

In university he studied philosophy. In the army he taught self-sacrifice. To his soldiers he gave human warmth, and in battle he imbued them with the coolness of judgement.

This young man was among those who commanded an operation that was flawless. But to our deep sorrow this operation entailed a sacrifice of incomparable pain — the first among the storming party, the first to fall. And by virtue of the one who fell, a stature bent under a heavy burden rose again to its full height. And of him, of them, one may say in the words of King David:

> How the mighty have fallen.
> They were swifter than eagles,
> They were stronger than lions
> O Jonathan, you were slain on your heights.
> I grieve for you, my brother Jonathan,
> You were most dear to me.
> Very pleasant have you been to me,
> Your love was wonderful to me.
> — II Samuel 1

The distance in space between Entebbe and Jerusalem has all of a sudden shortened the distance in time between Jonathan the son of Saul and Jonathan the son of Benzion.

The same heroism in the man. The same lamentation in the heart of a people.

[I.N. 301-302]

Lieutenant Colonel Yonatan Netanyahu reading the names of the fallen soldiers on Israel's Memorial Day, 1976, approximately three months before he too would be killed in action, on July 4, 1976.

(Courtesy of the Netanyahu Family)

SELF-PORTRAIT OF A HERO:

Reflections on Life and Death from the Correspondence of Yoni Netanyahu

As we follow the biography of Yoni Netanyahu in his letters, we will focus on different issues. During his adolescent period he struggled to find a purpose in life, which he could not find in an American suburban high school. Then during his army years he reflected on the ambiguity of war as an occasion for uplifting human solidarity and for deep sadness. He struggled over the question of reenlistment in the army and the priority of the army over civilian life.

His brother Iddo introduced the collection of Yoni's correspondence in this way: "He was his own biographer. The letters he wrote to the members of his family, to his friends, and to the women in his life offer a compelling record of not only the turbulent events in the life of a warrior but the passionate inner soul of a noble spirit."[44]

High School in America, 1963

In high school, Yoni was uprooted from his best friends, his ideologically motivated band of Israeli scouts, and exiled to a wealthy, suburban American high school. Confronted with personal loneliness, deprived of the collective mission that animated him in Jerusalem, he judged American middle class teenagers very harshly. At the same time however, he set himself the highest standards for judging his own life and death. His adolescent musings on death and despair propelled him as a young adult both into the study of philosophy at Harvard and into the elite commando unit in Israel. His willpower was undeniable, but he struggled to find a purpose worthy of his total devotion.

Dear Friends,   1963

I live outside Philadelphia. My school has about 1,500 students who don't know what they're doing there. It looks even more like the Tel Aviv Sheraton than a school (beautiful even by American standards, brand new, and it cost 6.5 million dollars to build). My house is "terribly" nice, surrounded by lawns and trees and empty, meaningless life.

The only thing people talk about is cars and girls. Life revolves around one subject — sex; I think Freud would have found very fertile soil here. Bit by bit I'm becoming convinced I'm living among apes and not human beings . . . .

The trouble with youth here is that their lives are meager in content, drifting as though in a dream or game . . . All this space that surrounds me leaves me without any air to breathe. I yearn for a place that's narrow, hot, rotten, filthy — a place that's more than 60 percent desert and that one can scarcely find on a map of the world; a place full of special problems, where not to be a party member is practically a crime.

That I'm alone (and believe me, in Israel too I was alone) does not detract from the fact that I, as an individual, as a single unit, constitute an entire world. My life will be complete not because of others, but because of myself. If I err and make mistakes, I'll start again and build anew. There's no reason why the tower I build around myself, around my person, whatever it may be, should not stand forever.

Death — that's the only thing that disturbs me. It doesn't frighten me; it arouses my curiosity. It is a puzzle that I, like many others, have tried to solve without success. I do not fear it because I attribute little value to a life without a purpose. And if I should have to sacrifice my life to attain its goal, I'll do so willingly.

Generally, my mood hasn't changed. I can't stand America and I'm dying to return.

Miss you,

Yoni [45]

---

44. *Self-Portrait of a Hero,* ix

Yoni marching with his soldiers in Jerusalem.
(Courtesy of the Netanyahu Family)

Dear Friend,   1963

You are almost sixteen. Do you realize you've lived nearly a quarter of your life? An insect, which lives only a few days, probably feels that its life span is enormous. Perhaps that's why we believe that we still have an eternity ahead of us. But man does not live forever, and he should put the days of his life to the best possible use. He should try to live life to its fullest. How to do this I can't tell you.

"There is no limit to human understanding." I live in this moment; I die in another. Is there any difference between the two? Are they not one and the same? There are times it's better to die than to live, and sometimes it is better not to feel than to suffer. There are times it is also good to feel that there's a purpose to your actions, that you're not helpless but strong, that you are great and mighty. Sometimes it is good to believe that man is a giant, a force before whom nothing can stand.

"Where there's a will, there's a way." Is that really so? Can man really overcome everything?

"Null and void, all is vanity" [Ecclesiastes] — concept veiled within a concept, a dense fog concealing everything, a breath on the mirror clouding the image.

I am consumed from within. I live without purpose, aching and crying out of despair.

Yoni [45]

1967

Dear Father and Mother,

For me it's enough to be alive. And I don't say that ironically. When you see death face-to-face; when you know there is every chance you too may die, when you are wounded, and alone, in the midst of a scorched field, surrounded by smoke — mushrooms of smoke exploding from shells, with your arm shattered and burning with a terrible pain, when you're bleeding and want water more than anything else — then life becomes more precious and craved for than ever. You want to embrace it and go on with it, to escape from all the blood and death, to live, live, even without hands and feet, but breathing, thinking, feeling, seeing and taking in sensation.[46]

We're young, and we were not born for wars alone. I intend to go on with my studies; I want to do so and I'm interested in doing so. But I can no longer see this as my main mission in life. Deep within my being I'm convinced of this. Hence the sadness I referred to earlier, **the sadness of young men destined for endless war**.

Yoni [47]

Reflections on the Six Day War and its Aftermath

After graduating high school in America, Yoni began a life torn between Harvard and Jerusalem, between a private life and a public one, between his family and the army. This is what made him a self-conscious philosopher of his own difficult choices. In 1964 he did his regular army service and became an outstanding officer. Discharged in early 1967, he was on his way to study at Harvard when the Six Day War broke out. In the war he fought bravely and his elbow was injured so that he lost partial use of his left arm. Though his injury should have disqualified him from further military service, Yoni hid the nature of the medical problem until he could have it partially rectified in two operations in the United States. Thus he was able to continue to serve as a combat officer.

---

45. *Self-Portrait* 6-8   46. *Self-Portrait* 140
47. *Self-Portrait* 163-164

An Enduring Sadness

Even fighting a necessary and just war of self-defense leaves a permanent deposit of sadness — "the sadness of young men destined for endless war." Later, Yoni explicated the origin of this sadness as it emerged from the act of killing another human being at point blank range.

Dear Friend,   1975

I remember a few years ago, there was a whole month of nothing but border crossings, and on three consecutive occasions I had encounters with Arabs (very deep inside their territory). On one of them I killed a man, for the first time at such close range, about two feet, and I emptied an entire clip of bullets into him till he stopped twitching and died. And each time, when I came home, I wouldn't tell my wife about it, just hold her tighter each time. It was hard then.

To kill at such very close range isn't like aiming a gun from a hundred yards away and pulling the trigger — that's something I had already done when I was young. I've learned since how to kill at close range too — to the point of pressing the muzzle against the flesh and pulling the trigger for a single bullet to be released and kill accurately, the body muffling the sound of the shot. It adds a whole dimension of sadness to a man's being. Not a momentary, transient sadness, but something that sinks in and is forgotten, yet it is there and it endures.

Yoni[48]

1969

Dear Father and Mother,

As regards the latest incidents, I really must praise the Jewish people of Israel. The cool-headedness, the lack of hysteria, and the immediate control of every situation are really surprising. You don't find here the raging mob quality that is rather typical of hard times. This is a special people, and it's good to belong to it.

In another week I'll be twenty-three. Time flies, doesn't it? My years bear down on me with all their weight. Not as a load or a burden, but as the sum of all the long and short moments that have gone into them. On me, on us, the young men of Israel, rests the duty of keeping our country safe. This is a heavy responsibility, which matures us early. It seems that the young Israeli belongs to a special breed of men. It's hard to explain this, but it can be felt. All those wonderful pilots of ours, all our paratroops and commandos, are Israelis of my age or younger, who grew up and were educated in Israel. Men of the moshav, the kibbutz and the city, united by something that is above and beyond political outlook. What unites them produces a feeling of brotherhood, of mutual responsibility, a recognition of the value of man and his life, a strong and sincere desire for peace, a readiness to stand in the breach, and much more.

In another week I'll be twenty-three, and I do not regret what I have done and what I'm about to do. **I'm convinced that what I am doing is right. I believe in myself, in my country and in my future. I also believe in my family. That's a great deal for a man of my age who has already managed to feel very young and very old.**

Yoni[49]

The Credo of a Wise Old/Young Man

Despite his realism about war, Yoni continued to respond to the idealism of duty. He re-enlisted whenever his country was endangered. His reflections reveal a "military hero" who is no simplistic militarist patriot but a moral citizen whose love of life did not lead him to avoid his duty, but to fulfill it. His pride in fellow soldiers never wavered, but he felt the burden of the premature wisdom of a fighter who knew life and death.

---

48. *Self-Portrait* 258. The letter written in 1975 recalls his military duty in 1968-1970.

49. *Self-Portrait* 179

334